AND BOOK TRAINING PACKAGE AVAILABLE

ExamSim

Experience realistic, simulated exams on your own computer with Osborne's interactive ExamSim software. This computer-based test engine offers knowledge-based and scenario-based questions like those found on the real exams, and review tools that show you where you went wrong and why. ExamSim also includes question-marking and question printing for further review, and a score report that shows your overall performance on the exam.

Knowledge and Scenario-based questions present challenging material in a multiple-choice format. Answer treatments not only explain why the correct options are right, they also tell you why the incorrect answers were wrong.

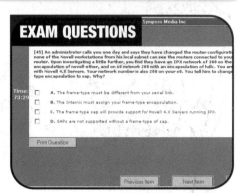

Scenario-based questions challenge your ability to analyze and address complex, real-world case studies.

Additional CD-ROM Features

• Complete hyperlinked **e-book** for easy information access and self-paced study.

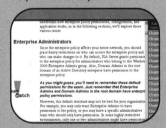

System Requirements:

A PC running Microsoft® Internet Explorer version 5 or higher

The **Score Report** provides an overall assessment of your exam performance as well as performance history.

Server+ Certification
Study Guide

Server+ Certification
Study Guide

Syngress Media, Inc.

Osborne McGraw-Hill

New York Chicago San Francisco Lisbon London Madrid
Mexico City Milan New Delhi San Juan Seoul Singapore Sydney Toronto

Osborne/**McGraw-Hill**
2600 Tenth Street
Berkeley, California 94710
U.S.A.

To arrange bulk purchase discounts for sales promotions, premiums, or fund-raisers, please contact Osborne/McGraw-Hill at the above address. For information on translations or book distributors outside the U.S.A., please see the International Contact Information page immediately following the index of this book.

Server+ Certification Study Guide

1234567890 DOC DOC 0198765432109

Book p/n 0-07-219035-3 and CD p/n 0-07-219036-1
parts of ISBN 0-07-219034-5

Publisher Brandon A. Nordin	**Editorial Management** Syngress Media, Inc.	**Copy Editor** Lynette Crane and Michael McGee
Vice President and **Associate Publisher** Scott Rogers	**VP, Worldwide Business** **Development** **Global Knowledge** Richard Kristof	**Production and Editorial** Apollo Printing and Typesetting
Editorial Director Gareth Hancock	**Technical Editor** André Paree-Huff	**Series Design** Roberta Steele
Associate Acquisitions Editor Timothy Green	**Technical Reviewer** Bradley Dunsmore	**Cover Design** Greg Scott

This book was published with Corel VENTURA™ Publisher.

From Global Knowledge

At Global Knowledge we strive to support the multiplicity of learning styles required by our students to achieve success as technical professionals. In this series of books, it is our intention to offer the reader a valuable tool for successful completion of the Server+ Certification Exam.

As the world's largest IT training company, Global Knowledge is uniquely positioned to offer these books. The expertise gained each year from providing instructor-led training to hundreds of thousands of students worldwide has been captured in book form to enhance your learning experience. We hope that the quality of these books demonstrates our commitment to your lifelong learning success. Whether you choose to learn through the written word, computer-based training, Web delivery, or instructor-led training, Global Knowledge is committed to providing you the very best in each of those categories. For those of you who know Global Knowledge, or those of you who have just found us for the first time, our goal is to be your lifelong competency partner.

Thank you for the opportunity to serve you. We look forward to serving your needs again in the future.

Warmest regards,

Duncan Anderson
President and Chief Executive Officer, Global Knowledge

The Global Knowledge Advantage

Global Knowledge has a global delivery system for its products and services. The company has 28 subsidiaries, and offers its programs through a total of 60+ locations. No other vendor can provide consistent services across a geographic area this large. Global Knowledge is the largest independent information technology education provider, offering programs on a variety of platforms. This enables our multi-platform and multi-national customers to obtain all of their programs from a single vendor. The company has developed the unique Competus™ Framework software tool and methodology which can quickly reconfigure courseware to the proficiency level of a student on an interactive basis. Combined with self-paced and on-line programs, this technology can reduce the time required for training by prescribing content in only the deficient skills areas. The company has fully automated every aspect of the education process, from registration and follow-up, to "just-in-time" production of courseware. Global Knowledge Network through its Enterprise Services Consultancy, can customize programs and products to suit the needs of an individual customer.

Global Knowledge Classroom Education Programs

The backbone of our delivery options is classroom-based education. Our modern, well-equipped facilities staffed with the finest instructors offer programs in a wide variety of information technology topics, many of which lead to professional certifications.

Custom Learning Solutions

This delivery option has been created for companies and governments that value customized learning solutions. For them, our consultancy-based approach of developing targeted education solutions is most effective at helping them meet specific objectives.

Self-Paced and Multimedia Products

This delivery option offers self-paced program titles in interactive CD-ROM, videotape and audio tape programs. In addition, we offer custom development of interactive multimedia courseware to customers and partners. Call us at 1-888-427-4228.

Electronic Delivery of Training

Our network-based training service delivers efficient competency-based, interactive training via the World Wide Web and organizational intranets. This leading-edge delivery option provides a custom learning path and "just-in-time" training for maximum convenience to students.

ARG

American Research Group (ARG), a wholly-owned subsidiary of Global Knowledge, one of the largest worldwide training partners of Cisco Systems, offers a wide range of internetworking, LAN/WAN, Bay Networks, FORE Systems, IBM, and UNIX courses. ARG offers hands on network training in both instructor-led classes and self-paced PC-based training.

Global Knowledge Courses Available

Network Fundamentals

- Understanding Computer Networks
- Telecommunications Fundamentals I
- Telecommunications Fundamentals II
- Understanding Networking Fundamentals
- Implementing Computer Telephony Integration
- Introduction to Voice Over IP
- Introduction to Wide Area Networking
- Cabling Voice and Data Networks
- Introduction to LAN/WAN protocols
- Virtual Private Networks
- ATM Essentials

Network Security & Management

- Troubleshooting TCP/IP Networks
- Network Management
- Network Troubleshooting
- IP Address Management
- Network Security Administration
- Web Security
- Implementing UNIX Security
- Managing Cisco Network Security
- Windows NT 4.0 Security

IT Professional Skills

- Project Management for IT Professionals
- Advanced Project Management for IT Professionals
- Survival Skills for the New IT Manager
- Making IT Teams Work

LAN/WAN Internetworking

- Frame Relay Internetworking
- Implementing T1/T3 Services
- Understanding Digital Subscriber Line (xDSL)
- Internetworking with Routers and Switches
- Advanced Routing and Switching
- Multi-Layer Switching and Wire-Speed Routing
- Internetworking with TCP/IP
- ATM Internetworking
- OSPF Design and Configuration
- Border Gateway Protocol (BGP) Configuration

Authorized Vendor Training

Cisco Systems

- Introduction to Cisco Router Configuration
- Advanced Cisco Router Configuration
- Installation and Maintenance of Cisco Routers
- Cisco Internetwork Troubleshooting
- Cisco Internetwork Design
- Cisco Routers and LAN Switches
- Catalyst 5000 Series Configuration
- Cisco LAN Switch Configuration
- Managing Cisco Switched Internetworks
- Configuring, Monitoring, and Troubleshooting Dial-Up Services
- Cisco AS5200 Installation and Configuration
- Cisco Campus ATM Solutions

Bay Networks

- Bay Networks Accelerated Router Configuration
- Bay Networks Advanced IP Routing
- Bay Networks Hub Connectivity
- Bay Networks Accelar 1xxx Installation and Basic Configuration
- Bay Networks Centillion Switching

FORE Systems

- FORE ATM Enterprise Core Products
- FORE ATM Enterprise Edge Products
- FORE ATM Theory
- FORE LAN Certification

Operating Systems & Programming

Microsoft

- Introduction to Windows NT
- Microsoft Networking Essentials
- Windows NT 4.0 Workstation
- Windows NT 4.0 Server
- Advanced Windows NT 4.0 Server
- Windows NT Networking with TCP/IP
- Introduction to Microsoft Web Tools
- Windows NT Troubleshooting
- Windows Registry Configuration

UNIX

- UNIX Level I
- UNIX Level II
- Essentials of UNIX and NT Integration

Programming

- Introduction to JavaScript
- Java Programming
- PERL Programming
- Advanced PERL with CGI for the Web

Web Site Management & Development

- Building a Web Site
- Web Site Management and Performance
- Web Development Fundamentals

High Speed Networking

- Essentials of Wide Area Networking
- Integrating ISDN
- Fiber Optic Network Design
- Fiber Optic Network Installation
- Migrating to High Performance Ethernet

DIGITAL UNIX

- UNIX Utilities and Commands
- DIGITAL UNIX v4.0 System Administration
- DIGITAL UNIX v4.0 (TCP/IP) Network Management
- AdvFS, LSM, and RAID Configuration and Management
- DIGITAL UNIX TruCluster Software Configuration and Management
- UNIX Shell Programming Featuring Kornshell
- DIGITAL UNIX v4.0 Security Management
- DIGITAL UNIX v4.0 Performance Management
- DIGITAL UNIX v4.0 Intervals Overview

DIGITAL OpenVMS

- OpenVMS Skills for Users
- OpenVMS System and Network Node Management I
- OpenVMS System and Network Node Management II
- OpenVMS System and Network Node Management III
- OpenVMS System and Network Node Operations
- OpenVMS for Programmers
- OpenVMS System Troubleshooting for Systems Managers
- Configuring and Managing Complex VMScluster Systems
- Utilizing OpenVMS Features from C
- OpenVMS Performance Management
- Managing DEC TCP/IP Services for OpenVMS
- Programming in C

Hardware Courses

- AlphaServer 1000/1000A Installation, Configuration and Maintenance
- AlphaServer 2100 Server Maintenance
- AlphaServer 4100, Troubleshooting Techniques and Problem Solving

About Syngress Media

Syngress Media creates books and software for Information Technology professionals seeking skill enhancement and career advancement. Its products are designed to comply with vendor and industry standard course curricula and are optimized for certification exam preparation. You can contact Syngress via the Web at www.syngress.com.

Contributors

Melissa Craft (CCNA, MCSE, Network+, CNE-5, CNE-3, CNE-4, CNE-GW, MCNE, Citrix CCA) designs business computing solutions using technology to automate processes and using business process reengineering techniques. Early on in her career, Melissa threw herself at the task of truly understanding network engineering, gaining a myriad of technology certifications and, at the same time, deploying projects for clients. Over the years, she has successfully designed, implemented, and integrated networks ranging in size from a few nodes to over 100,000 nodes. This consulting experience incorporated extensive project management, needs-analysis, LAN and WAN design, deployment, and operational turnover.

Currently, Melissa is Director of Consulting Solutions for CompuCom. CompuCom is a global systems integrator headquartered in Dallas, TX. CompuCom provides IT design, project management, and support for distributed computing systems. She is a key contributor to the business development and implementation of e-business services. As such, she develops enterprise-wide technology solutions and methodologies focused on client organizations. These technology solutions touch every part of a system's lifecycle—from network design, testing, and implementation to operational management and strategic planning. Melissa holds a bachelor's degree from the University of Michigan and is a member of the IEEE, the Society of Women Engineers and American MENSA, Ltd.

Michael Cross (MCSE, MCPS, MCP+I, CNA) is the Network Administrator, Internet Specialist, and a Programmer for the Niagara Regional Police Service. In addition to administering their network, programming and providing support to a user base of over 800 civilian and uniform users, he is Webmaster of their Web site at www.nrps.com.

Michael also owns KnightWare, a company that provides consulting, programming, networking, Web page design, computer training, and various other services. He has served as an instructor for private colleges and technical schools in London and Ontario, Canada. He has been a freelance writer for several years and has been published over two dozen times in numerous books and anthologies.

Travis Guinn (CCA, MCSE, CCSA, CCSE, A+) is a Senior Technical Officer with JPMorgan Chase & Co in Dallas, TX. Travis served four years in the U.S. Navy in Advanced Electronics and worked three years for a small computer store installing networks. After that, he started one of the first Windows NT based ISPs in Charleston, SC, where he gained extensive experience in TCP/IP and large scale dial-in solutions from US Robotics. Travis has also worked for Data Transit, a large Citrix integrator, on projects involving Citrix, 3Com Total Control, Checkpoint Firewall-1, RSA SecurID, AVT RightFax, and a Windows 2000 based Managed Service Provider initiative.

Amy Thomson (A+, MOUS Master) is an A+ Certified Technician and has been involved in several A+ and MCSE certification projects for Syngress Media. Now a Technical Writer in Halifax, Nova Scotia, Amy has previously worked as a computer technician and instructor in private colleges all over Canada.

Amy started her career in the computer industry as a Communicator in the Canadian Armed Forces, where she helped develop the military computer training curriculum for the Atlantic provinces. Amy has an Honors B.Sc. in Psychology and is a Microsoft MOUS Master.

Technical Editor

André Paree-Huff (CCNP, CCDA, MCSE+I, ASE, A+, Network+, I-Net+, Server+) has been working in the computer field for over 9 years. André currently works for Compaq Computer Corporation as a Network Support Engineer level III for the North America Customer Support Center in Colorado Springs, CO. He handles troubleshooting of network hardware, specializing in Layer 2 and 3 of the OSI model. André has co-authored 5 network-related books and has been a technical editor on more then two dozen others. He is currently working toward his CCDE and CCIE.

Technical Reviewer

Bradley Dunsmore (A+, Network+, I-Net+, MCDBA, MCSE+I, CCNA) is currently working for Cisco Systems in Raleigh, NC. He is a Technical Trainer in the Service Provider Division where he develops and issues training to the solution deployment engineers.

He has 8 years of computer experience with the last 4 in enterprise networking. Bradley has had stints with Bell Atlantic, Adtran Telecommunications, and Electronic Systems Inc., a Virginia-based systems integrator. He specializes in TCP/IP and LAN/WAN communications in both small and large business environments.

ACKNOWLEDGMENTS

We would like to thank the following people:

- Richard Kristof of Global Knowledge for championing the series and providing us access to some great people and information.
- All the incredibly hard-working folks at Osborne/McGraw-Hill: Brandon Nordin, Scott Rogers, Timothy Green, Gareth Hancock, and Jessica Wilson.

CONTENTS AT A GLANCE

CONTENTS

This book's primary objective is to help you prepare for and pass the required Server+ exam so you can begin to reap the career benefits of certification. We believe that the only way to do this is to help you increase your knowledge and build your skills. After completing this book, you should feel confident that you have thoroughly reviewed all of the objectives that CompTIA has established for the exam.

In This Book

This book is organized around the actual structure of the Server+ exam administered at Sylvan Prometric and VUE Testing Centers. CompTIA has let us know all the topics we need to cover for the exam. We've followed their list carefully, so you can be assured you're not missing anything.

In Every Chapter

We've created a set of chapter components that call your attention to important items, reinforce important points, and provide helpful exam-taking hints. Take a look at what you'll find in the chapters:

- Each chapter begins with the **Certification Objectives**—what you need to know in order to pass the section on the exam dealing with the chapter topic. The Certification Objective headings identify the objectives within the chapter, so you'll always know an objective when you see it!

EXERCISE

- **Certification Exercises** are interspersed throughout the chapters. These are step-by-step exercises. They help you master skills that are likely to be an area of focus on the exam. Don't just read through the exercises; they are hands-on procedures that you should be comfortable completing. Learning by doing is an effective way to increase your competency with the language and concepts presented.

- **From the Classroom** sidebars describe the issues that come up most often in the training classroom setting. These sidebars give you a valuable perspective into certification- and product-related topics. They point out common mistakes and address questions that have arisen from classroom discussions.

■ S & S sections lay out specific scenario questions and solutions in a quick and easy-to-read format.

SCENARIO & SOLUTION

What are the different types of level 2 cache?	Write-back and write-through.
What is the first thing you do to flash upgrade a BIOS?	Boot to a floppy disk containing the new image.
Which multiprocessing architecture is more efficient?	Symmetric Multiprocessing. It distributes the processing load more evenly across the available CPU.

■ The **Certification Summary** is a succinct review of the chapter and a re-statement of salient points regarding the exam.

 ■ The **Two-Minute Drill** at the end of every chapter is a checklist of the main points of the chapter. It can be used for last-minute review.

 ■ The **Self Test** offers questions similar to those found on the certification exam. The answers to these questions, as well as explanations of the answers, can be found at the end of the particular chapter. By taking the Self Test after completing each chapter, you'll reinforce what you've learned from that chapter, while becoming familiar with the structure of the exam questions.

Some Pointers

Once you've finished reading this book, set aside some time to do a thorough review. You might want to return to the book several times and make use of all the methods it offers for reviewing the material:

1. *Re-read all the Two-Minute Drills,* or have someone quiz you. You also can use the drills as a way to do a quick cram before the exam.

2. *Review all the S & S scenarios* for quick problem solving.

3. *Re-take the Self Tests.* Taking the tests right after you've read the chapter is a good idea, because it helps reinforce what you've just learned. However, it's

an even better idea to go back later and do all the questions in the book in one sitting. Pretend you're taking the exam. (For this reason, you should mark your answers on a separate piece of paper when you go through the questions the first time.)

4. *Complete the exercises.* Did you do the exercises when you read through each chapter? If not, do them! These exercises are designed to cover exam topics, and there's no better way to get to know this material than by practicing.

5. *Check out the Web site.* Global Knowledge invites you to become an active member of the Access Global Web site. This site is an online mall and an information repository that you'll find invaluable. You can access many types of products to assist you in your preparation for the exams, and you'll be able to participate in forums, on-line discussions, and threaded discussions. No other book brings you unlimited access to such a resource. You'll find more information about this site in Appendix B.

Server+ Certification

Although you've obviously picked up this book to study for a specific exam, we'd like to spend some time covering what you need in order to attain Server+ certification status. Because this information can be found on the CompTIA Web site, http://www.comptia.org/index.asp?ContentPage=certification/certification.htm, we've repeated only some of the more important information in the Introduction of this book, "How to Take the Server+ Certification Exam." Read ahead to the introduction.

The CD-ROM Resource

This book comes with a CD-ROM that includes test preparation software and provides you with another method for studying. You will find more information on the testing software in Appendix A.

How to Take the Server+ Certification Exam

This chapter covers the importance of your Server+ certification as well as prepares you for taking the actual examinations. It gives you a few pointers on methods of preparing for the exam; including how to study, register, what to expect, and what to do on exam day.

Importance of Server+ Certification

The Computing Technology Industry Association (CompTIA) created the Server+ certification to provide system administrators with an industry recognized and valued credential. Due to its acceptance as an industry-wide credential, it offers technicians an edge in a highly competitive computer job market. Additionally, it lets others know your achievement level and that you have the ability to do the job right. Prospective employers may use the Server+ certification as a condition of employment or as a means of a bonus or job promotion.

Earning Server+ certification means that you have the knowledge and the technical skills necessary to be a successful systems administrator. Computer experts in the industry establish the standards of certification. The test covers a broad range of advanced computer hardware issues. In fact, more than 60 organizations contributed to and budgeted the resources to develop the Server+ examination.

To become Server+ certified you must past the CompTIA exam. The exam measures your abilities on a wide range of topics. Topics include creation of RAID (Redundant Array Inexpensive Disk) arrays and backup procedures. You will be expected to know how to recover from a disaster as well as how to avoid one with the use of such things as Uninterrupted Power Supplies. You will need to know how to install items such as memory, disk drives and adapter cards. You will be tested heavily on the use of SCSI. You'll also need to be aware of the procedure for upgrading BIOS/firmware levels and the use of the POST sequence

Computerized Testing

As with Microsoft, Novell, Lotus, and various other companies, the most practical way to administer tests on a global level is through Sylvan Prometric or VUE testing centers. These sites provide proctored testing services for Microsoft, Oracle, Novell, Lotus, and the Server+ certification. In addition to administering the tests, Sylvan Prometric and VUE also score the exam and provide statistical feedback on each section of the exam to the companies and organizations that use their services.

Typically, several hundred questions are developed for a new exam. The questions are reviewed for technical accuracy by subject matter experts and are then presented in the form of a beta test. The beta test consists of many more questions than the actual test and provides for statistical feedback to CompTIA to check the performance of each question.

Based on the performance of the beta examination, questions are discarded based on how well or poorly the examinees performed on them. If a question is answered correctly by most of the test-takers, it is discarded as too easy. The same goes for questions that are too difficult. After analyzing the data from the beta test, CompTIA has a good idea of which questions to include in the question pool to be used on the actual exam.

Test Structure

Currently the Server+ exam consists of a *form* type test (also called *linear* or *conventional*). This type of test draws from a question pool of some set value and randomly selects questions to generate the exam you will take.

The exam questions for the Server+ exams are all equally weighted, no matter if they require one or several answers. This means that they all count the same when the test is scored. An interesting and useful characteristic of the form test is that questions may be marked and returned to later. This helps you manage your time while taking the test so that you don't spend too much time on any one question. Remember, unanswered questions are counted against you. Assuming you have time left when you finish the questions, you can return to the marked questions for further evaluation.

The form test also marks the questions that are incomplete with a letter "I" once you've finished all the questions. You'll see the whole list of questions after you finish the last question. The screen allows you to go back and finish incomplete items, finish unmarked items, and go to particular question numbers that you may want to look at again.

Some certifications are using *adaptive* type tests. This interactive test weights all of the questions based on their level of difficulty. For example, the questions in the form might be divided into levels one through five, with level one questions being the easiest and level five being the hardest. Each time you answer a question correctly you are asked a question of a higher level of difficulty, and vice versa when you answer incorrectly. After answering about 15 to 20 questions in this manner, the scoring algorithm is able to determine whether or not you would pass or fail the exam if all the questions were answered. The scoring method is pass or fail. At the time of this writing, Comptia has not announced plans for making the Server+ examination adaptive.

Question Types

The computerized test questions you will see on the examination can be presented in a number of ways. The Server+ exam is comprised of one-answer and multiple-answer, multiple-choice questions.

True/False

We are all familiar with True/False type questions, but due to the inherent 50 percent chance of guessing the right answer, you will not see any of these on the Server+ exam.

Multiple Choice

Server+ exam questions are of the multiple choice variety. Below each question is a list of 4 or 5 possible answers. You will need to use the available radio buttons to select one or more items from the given choices.

Graphical Questions

Some questions incorporate a graphical element to the question in the form of an exhibit either to aid the examinee in a visual representation of the problem or to present the question itself. These questions are easy to identify because they refer to the exhibit in the question and there is also an "Exhibit" button on the bottom of the question window. An example of a graphical question might be to identify a component on a drawing of a motherboard.

Test questions known as hotspots actually incorporate graphics as part of the answer. These types of questions ask the examinee to click on a location or graphical element to answer the question. As a variation of the above exhibit example, instead of selecting A, B, C, or D as your answer, you would simply click on the portion of the motherboard drawing where the component exists.

CompTIA uses this type of question for some of its certification exams but you will most likely not find any graphical questions on the Server+ exam.

Free Response Questions

Another type of question that can be presented on the form test requires a *free response* or type-in answer. This is basically a fill-in-the-blank type question where a list of possible choices is not given. You will not see this type of question on the Server+ exam.

Study Strategies

There are appropriate ways to study for the different types of questions you will see on a Server+ certification exam. The amount of study time needed to pass the exam will vary with the candidate's level of experience as a systems administrator. Someone with several years experience might only need a quick review of materials and terms when preparing for the exam.

For others, several hours may be needed to identify weaknesses in knowledge and skill level and working on those areas to bring them up to par. If you know that you are weak in an area, work on it until you feel comfortable talking about it. You don't want to be surprised with a question knowing it was your weak area.

Knowledge-Based Questions

Knowledge-based questions require that you memorize facts. The questions may not cover knowledge material that you use on a daily basis, but they do cover material that CompTIA thinks a administrator should be able to answer. Here are some keys to memorizing facts:

- ■ **Repetition** The more times you expose your brain to a fact, the more it "sinks in" and increases your ability to remember it.

- **Association**   Connecting facts within a logical framework makes them easier to remember.

- **Motor Association**   It is easier to remember something if you write it down or perform another physical act, like clicking on the practice test answer.

Performance-Based Questions

Although the majority of the questions on the Server+ exam are knowledge-based, some questions are performance-based scenario questions. In other words, the performance-based questions on the exam actually measure the candidate's ability to apply one's knowledge in a given scenario.

The first step in preparing for these performance-based scenario type questions is to absorb as many facts relating to the exam content areas as you can. Of course, actual hands-on experience will greatly help you in this area. For example, knowing how to install a video adapter is greatly enhanced by having actually done the procedure at least once. Some of the questions will place you in a scenario and ask for the best solution to the problem at hand. It is in these scenarios that having a good knowledge level and some experience will help you.

The second step is to familiarize yourself with the format of the questions you are likely to see on the exam. The questions in this study guide are a good step in that direction. The more you are familiar with the types of questions that can be asked, the better prepared you will be on the day of the test.

The Exam Makeup

To receive the Server+ certification, you must pass only the one certification exam. For up-to-date information about the number of questions on each exam and the passing scores, please check the CompTIA site at www.comptia.org.

The Server+ Exam

The Server+ exam is comprised of seven domains (categories). CompTIA lists the percentages of each as the following:

Installation	17%
Configuration	18%

Upgrading	12%
Proactive Maintenance	9%
Environment	5%
Troubleshooting and Problem Determination	27%
Disaster Recovery	12%

Signing Up

After all the hard work preparing for the exam, signing up is a very easy process. Sylvan operators in each country can schedule tests at any authorized Sylvan Prometric Test Center. There are a few things to keep in mind when you call:

1. If you call Sylvan during a busy period, you might be in for a bit of a wait. Their busiest days tend to be Mondays, so avoid scheduling a test on Monday if at all possible.

2. Make sure that you have your social security number handy. Sylvan needs this number as a unique identifier for their records.

3. Payment can be made by credit card, which is usually the easiest payment method. If your employer is a member of CompTIA you may be able to get a discount, or even obtain a voucher from your employer that will pay for the exam. Check with your employer before you dish out the money.

Taking the Test

The best method of preparing for the exam is to create a study schedule and stick to it. Although teachers have told you time and time again not to cram for tests, there just may be some information that just doesn't quite stick in your memory. It's this type of information that you want to look at right before you take the exam so that it remains fresh in your mind. Most testing centers provide you with a writing utensil and some scratch paper that you can utilize after the exam starts. You can brush up on good study techniques from any quality study book from the library, but some things to keep in mind when preparing and taking the test are:

1. Get a good night's sleep. Don't stay up all night cramming for this one. If you don't know the material by the time you go to sleep, your head won't be clear enough to remember it in the morning.

2. The test center needs two forms of identification, one of which must have your picture on it (i.e. driver's license.) Social security cards and credit cards are also acceptable forms of identification.

3. Arrive at the test center a few minutes early. There's no reason to feel rushed right before taking an exam.

4. Don't spend too much time on one question. If you think you are spending too much time on it, just mark it and go back to it later if you have time. Unanswered questions are counted wrong whether you knew the answer to them or not.

5. If you don't know the answer to a question, think about it logically. Look at the answers and eliminate the ones that you know can't possibly be the answer. This may leave you with only two possible answers. Give it your best guess if you have to, but most of the answers to the questions can be resolved by process of elimination.

6. Books, calculators, laptop computers, or any other reference materials are not allowed inside the testing center. The tests are computer based and do not require pens, pencils, or paper; although as mentioned above, some test centers provide scratch paper to aid you while taking the exam.

After the Test

As soon as you complete the test, your results will show up in the form of a bar graph on the screen. As long as your score is greater than the required score, you pass! Also a hard copy of the report is printed and embossed by the testing center to indicate that it's an official report. Don't lose this copy; it's the only hard copy of the report that is made. The results are sent electronically to CompTIA.

The printed report will also indicate how well you did in each section. You will be able to see the percentage of questions you got right in each section, but you will not be able to tell which questions you got wrong.

After you pass the exam, a Server+ certificate will be mailed to you within a few weeks. You'll also receive a credit card-sized credential that shows your new status:

Server+ Certified Professional. You are also authorized to use the Server+ logo on your business cards as long as you stay within the guidelines specified by CompTIA. If you don't pass the exam, don't fret. Take a look at the areas where you didn't do so well and work on those areas for the next time you register.

Once you pass the exam and earn the title of Server+ Certified Professional, your value and status in the IT industry increases. Server+ certification carries along an important proof of skills and knowledge level that is valued by customers, employers, and professionals in the computer industry.

Server+

COMPUTING TECHNOLOGY INDUSTRY ASSOCIATION

1

Installation

Servers do not use exactly the same hardware as desktop computers, even though they are both placed in the personal computer (PC) category of hardware. In the early years of networking, anyone could take a desktop PC with a single hard drive, add a network adapter and network operating system (NOS) software, and the result was a server. Today, such a system would perform miserably when compared to server platform hardware, even if the desktop PC had the exact same amount of memory and storage space as the server platform. Today, server platform hardware is specifically designed to offer:

- Availability
- Scalability
- Performance

To offer such value, server platforms are designed with redundant hardware components such as multiple network adapters, multiple power supplies, and Redundant Array of Inexpensive Disks (RAID) arrays. To be scalable and provide high performance with little downtime, they have multiple optional components–some that can be plugged in while the server is still running. Scalability results in some cost benefits because it is far less expensive to replace, add, or upgrade a single server component to increase the capacity of a scalable server than it is to replace an entire nonscalable server.

CERTIFICATION OBJECTIVE 1.01

Conducting Pre-Installation Planning Activities

Scalability is a highly desirable trait in a server platform. However, it affects a server installation rather significantly. When a server platform is scalable, it does not come with already installed components. Instead, each component must be selected to meet the business requirements that the server will fulfill. For example, if you need a server to perform file and print services for a 100 user workgroup, you wouldn't need to have as much storage space or processing power as you would need for a messaging server providing e-mail services to 10,000 users. As a result, when you buy server hardware, you typically end up ordering several different server parts, which then must be assembled.

Planning the Installation

Before you order parts for the server, you should carefully plan the parts that you will need, and how you intend to use them. This is essentially a capacity planning process. The various parts you should design include:

- Central processing units (CPUs)
- Random access memory (RAM)
- Storage
- Network adapters
- Power supply
- Other peripherals to set up

CPU

A CPU is a chip that has a number of transistors and is used to move and calculate data within the PC. Data is received from input devices and RAM, then it is processed and sent to output devices and back to RAM. The path it follows resembles Figure 1-1. It is considered central to the PC because when the CPU doesn't work the PC will not function.

When you select a CPU for your server, you should select the fastest available that falls within your budget. CPUs age as quickly as Intel, AMD, and other processor manufacturers can create them. Each new CPU version can support more transactions at faster speeds than the last. To get the most life out of a CPU, get the fastest you can afford.

Many server platforms support more than one processor. These are called Symmetric Multiprocessing (SMP) units. Symmetric indicates that these servers distribute a symmetrical load across the processors in the machine. You will probably run into a situation in which you want to have a single server running multiple processors (scaling up) rather than multiple servers running a single processor each (scaling out). One good reason for scaling up is that a single server is easier to manage than multiple servers, as well as cheaper.

| FIGURE 1-1 | CPU transmits data through the System Bus to RAM and devices |

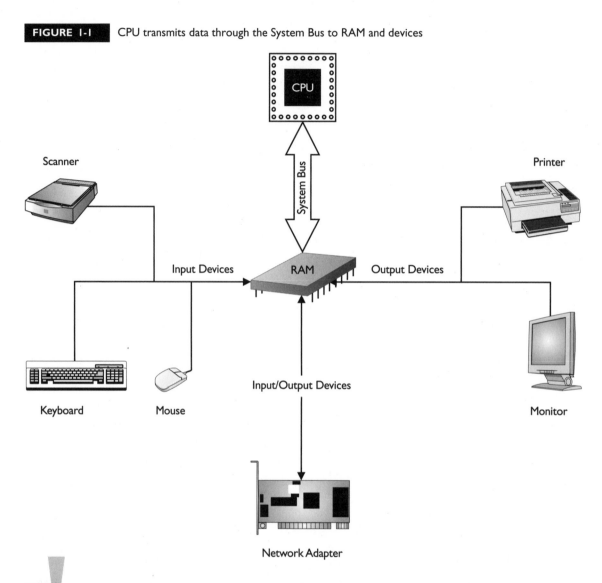

exam

  ωatch

When you upgrade a server with more hardware, such as more CPUs, more RAM, more disk space, or more network adapters, to increase capacity, you are scaling up. When you add more servers to share the workload that a single server handled in the past, you are scaling out.

Although you might think that a server with two processors can handle twice the number of transactions as a server with a single processor, that is not the way it works. There is a dependency on the rest of the server hardware that results in a bottleneck. You may be able to reach as much as 80% or more processing power with a second processor, but if you add a third and fourth processor, you will probably get about 60% of the power of each of those, as shown in Figure 1-2. Given these figures, 100% + 80% + 60% + 60% = 300%, the total processing power available on this SMP server is equivalent to three single servers.

Each vendor's SMP server platforms have different percentages of actual contributed processing power as more CPUs are added. These percentages are dependent upon the types of processor and bus speeds. Knowing that the number of CPUs is not directly proportional to the processing power will help you in planning the number of CPUs that you will need. For example, when you have a requirement to replace four servers with a single server, you cannot depend on four processors being enough processing power, and you should select a server with more CPUs.

Another factor that can impact the performance that you expect from a CPU is the bus speed. You may select a large cache Pentium III Xeon processor at 900

FIGURE 1-2

As SMP processors are added, contributed power is reduced

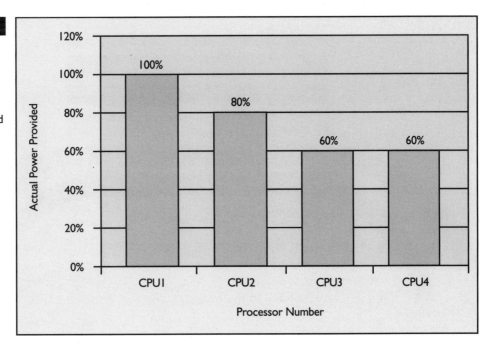

megahertz (MHz), but if you place that processor on a motherboard with a bus speed of 50MHz instead of a motherboard with a bus speed of 100MHz, you will have lower performance. The best way to imagine the bus speed of a motherboard in reference to a bus speed of a processor is to compare it to the access road to a highway. If you have a two-lane access road, you will be able to let twice as many cars onto the highway at the same time compared to a single-lane access road, as displayed in Figure 1-3.

System board bus speed affects processing power

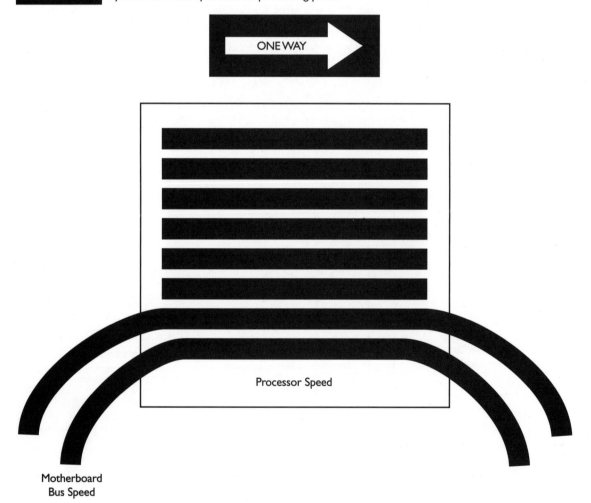

There are a number of generations of CPUs. Intel is the leading manufacturer of CPUs, but not the only one. Table 1-1 lists the various CPU generations.

RAM

One rule you'll probably encounter is that you can never have too much RAM. But that's not necessarily true. A 32-bit network operating system (NOS) can address up to 232 bytes of memory at any one time. This is equivalent to a maximum of 4 gigabytes (GB) of RAM. Some server hardware platforms allow more than 4GB of RAM to be installed. Unless there is an extension to the operating system available that you can install or you are using a 64-bit NOS, there is no reason to go beyond

TABLE 1-1

CPU Generations

Generation	Years	CPUs	Number of Transistors
1st	1978–1981	Intel 8086	29,000
1st	1978–1981	Intel 8088	29,000
2nd	1984	Intel 80286	134,000
3rd	1987–1988	Intel 80386	275,000
4th	1990–1992	Intel 80486	1,200,000
5th	1993–1997	Intel Pentium (MMX)	3,100,000–4,500,000
5th	1996–1997	Cyrix 6X86 (MX)	3,100,000–6,000,000
5th	1996	AMD K5	3,100,000
5th	1997–1998	IDT Winchip (v2 3D)	3,500,000–6,000,000
6th	1995	Intel Pentium Pro	5,500,000
6th	1997	AMD K6	8,800,000
6th	1997	Intel Pentium II	7,500,000
6th	1998	AMD K6-2	9,300,000
6th	1999	Intel Pentium II CuMine	28,000,000
6th	1999	Intel Mobile Pentium II	27,400,000
7th	1999	AMD Athlon	22,000,000
7th	2000	AMD Athlon Thunderbird	37,000,000
7th	2000	Intel Pentium IV	42,000,000

SCENARIO & SOLUTION

With all the options available for CPUs, you may run into some problems. Here are some challenges that you might run into in real life.	
Your server arrives and it has one CPU, but you asked for an SMP server. What is the problem?	Look for the remaining CPUs as parts in other boxes. Most manufacturers ship their servers with only one CPU and expect an installer to add any other CPUs in an SMP configuration.
You are upgrading a single processor server to an SMP server. The server can have up to eight CPUs installed. How many processors must you install to make this an SMP server?	You need to install only one more CPU to make the server an SMP server. If you want to add more, you can add three to make it a four-CPU server or seven to make it an eight-CPU server.
Your server platform ships with a single Pentium III Xeon CPU. Can you change this to an AMD K6?	No. The motherboard is built specifically for the CPU.

4GB of RAM. However, you should not reject using a server platform to which you can add more than 4GB of RAM, even if you only use up to 4GB of RAM to start with. There is a possibility that you will upgrade the operating system in the future to one that will support more than 4GB of RAM and then add more RAM at that time.

The lower limit for RAM should never be the minimum required to run an operating system. For example, if you are going to install Windows 2000, the recommended minimum for that operating system is 128MB RAM. However, if you install only 128MB of RAM, the server's performance will be exceedingly poor. The minimum amount of RAM will be enough to boot up the NOS, but not to run the types of services that are typically installed on a server, such as a database, e-mail, or Web services. One way to determine the amount of RAM you will need is to consult a third party or the manufacturer's benchmarks for the server platform.

Even if you are able to predict the optimal amount of RAM for the server at the outset, you may not be happy with it after a period of time. Growth in the number of users, the number of applications hosted, or the amount of data stored will alter the memory requirements for the server. To prepare for this growth, you can take your initial estimate of RAM needed and then double it.

There are various types of RAM. The motherboard of your server platform dictates the type of RAM that you can use because the motherboard will have a location for a certain size of memory module and the chipset will understand only the RAM for which it has been designed. Some motherboards have sockets for both single inline memory modules (SIMMs) and dual inline memory modules (DIMMs). In this way, you can choose whether to install Extended Data Output (EDO) RAM or Synchronous Dynamic RAM (SDRAM), although usually you can't install both.

Generally, memory falls under either dynamic RAM (DRAM) or static RAM (SRAM) categories. DRAM must be refreshed constantly—every few milliseconds. SRAM holds the data without needing to be refreshed, and can react much faster. RAM speed is measured in nanoseconds (ns). The fewer nanoseconds that it takes to access the RAM, the faster the RAM is. Table 1-2 lists the types of DRAM that you may encounter.

Storage

Small workgroup servers often use individual hard drives for storage. In addition, servers include CD-ROM and floppy drives. You may also add tape drives for backup usage. Drives are connected through a variety of interfaces:

- Hard drives up to 40GB, some tape drives, and some CD-ROMS may use Integrated Drive Electronics (IDE) or Enhanced IDE (EIDE) interfaces.

- Hard drives of all sizes, some tape drives, and some CD-ROMS may use a small computer system interface (SCSI).

TABLE 1-2   Types of RAM

Memory	Static or Dynamic	Notes
Fast Page Mode (FPM)	DRAM	Mounted in SIMMs; 60 ns or 70 ns versions.
Error Correcting Code (ECC)	DRAM	Specially developed to correct errors in memory. Preferred for use in servers.
Extended Data Output (EDO)	DRAM	60 ns or 50 ns versions.
Synchronous Dynamic RAM (SDRAM)	DRAM	Mounted in 64-bit wide 168 pin DIMMs. Access time of 8 ns to 12 ns.
Rambus Direct RAM (RDRAM)	DRAM	Future type of RAM to improve performance further, uses 16-bit wide Rambus Inline Memory Modules (RIMMs). Data is read in small packets at very high clock speeds.

■ Floppy drives and some CD-ROMs use the internal Industry Standard Architecture (ISA) interface.

Of these interfaces, SCSI is most prevalent (and preferred) in servers. An SCSI 2 interface can host seven devices using a single interrupt. By comparison, IDE and EIDE interfaces can support a maximum of two devices. (SCSI Wide, a 16-bit controller, can host 15 devices.) SCSI is superior to other interfaces because it manages its own power, freeing the CPU from that type of overhead. SCSI also has its own basic input/output system (BIOS). When the computer starts up, you will see the information on the screen as the PC communicates with the SCSI BIOS.

A single SCSI adapter can be connected to both internal and external SCSI devices. Each device is provided an identifying number. For SCSI 2, which is an 8-bit controller, the IDs are numbered 0 through 7 with the SCSI host adapter occupying ID7. Some older SCSI implementations such as the IBM PS/2 reserved SCSI ID0 for the controller. The SCSI devices are connected in a chain. Each end of the chain must be terminated in order for the devices to operate. The host adapter is automatically terminated, but the last device in the chain should be terminated through the resistors (in the form of jumpers or switches) on the device.

One of the newer interfaces for connecting to storage is Fibre Channel. Fibre Channel is faster than SCSI. A Fibre Channel interface uses a Fibre Channel arbitrated loop (FC-AL) to enable multiple devices to connect to a single server. The main benefit of Fibre Channel is its speed.

Redundant Array of Inexpensive Disks (RAID) is a form of storage that was created to provide redundancy and increased storage so that data loss was minimal in case of a hard disk failure. There were different configurations, or levels of RAID, developed, as are listed in Table 1-3. When there are multiple hard disks configured in a RAID, it is called an *array* and is often housed in an external unit called a *subsystem.*

Some network operating systems allow you to configure multiple disks as RAID arrays. When RAID is configured in the NOS, it is considered software-based RAID. From the server, you see each individual disk and manage its configuration through the operating system. Software-based RAID causes overhead on the server, so there is a slight performance hit.

exam
⊛atch

RAID 5 provides fault tolerance through disk striping with parity. If a disk fails in a RAID 5 configuration, the server can continue to function.

TABLE 1-3   RAID

RAID Level	Type	Tolerance	Minimum Number of Disks
RAID 0	Disk striping	No tolerance. Data is written to all the disks in stripes. If a disk fails, the system fails.	3
RAID 1	Disk mirroring	Good tolerance. Two disks that are identical copies of each other run from the same interface. If a disk fails, the other can be configured as the boot disk.	2
RAID 2	Disk duplexing	Good tolerance. Two disks run from separate interfaces and are identical copies of each other. If a disk fails or if a disk controller fails, the other disk can be configured as the boot disk.	2
RAID 3	Disks with parity	Some tolerance. A disk is set aside to carry error-correcting data. If a disk fails, except for the error-correcting disk, the array can be rebuilt.	3
RAID 4	Large disk striping	Some tolerance. A disk is set aside to carry error-correcting data. Data is written to disks in large stripes.	3
RAID 5	Disk striping with parity	High tolerance. Data is written to all the disks in stripes. *Parity* is provided by having a stripe of error-correcting data placed on each disk. If a disk fails, the array can be rebuilt while the server is running. Most popular RAID type for servers.	3
RAID 6	Disk striping with double parity	High tolerance. Data is written to all the disks in stripes and uses two separate parity schemes. This is not typically used today because of the expense, and few examples are available in actual use.	3

Server platforms usually come with optional hardware RAID arrays that are managed with a specific RAID array adapter interface, and use identical disks that most vendors provide as hot-plug units. Hardware-based RAID is managed from its own BIOS application. Once the network operating system is installed, the hardware-based RAID array appears to be a single disk from the perspective of the NOS. To provide the highest reliability and optimal performance, you should implement RAID 5 using a hardware-based solution.

There are two other types of storage to which you may need to connect your server:

- Network attached storage (NAS)
- Storage area network (SAN)

NAS offers a storage system that connects directly to the network, rather than directly to individual servers. These storage systems are self-contained and intelligent, enabling clients and servers to store and share data on them. An NAS device configuration is depicted in Figure 1-4. When you are planning your server, you should determine whether the server will be storing data on an NAS device.

A SAN is a group of storage systems connected through Fibre Channel interfaces directly to a storage network. The SAN uses either Fibre Channel switches or Fibre

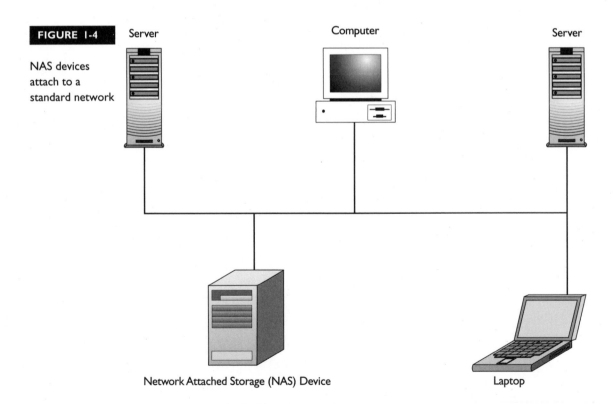

FIGURE 1-4

NAS devices attach to a standard network

Server

Computer

Server

Network Attached Storage (NAS) Device

Laptop

Channel hubs to connect multiple storage units. Servers on the regular network are configured to access the data on the storage network. A SAN is illustrated in Figure 1-5.

Because SANs can have multiple storage units connected through Fibre Channel hubs, they are scalable to terabytes (TB) of data. In addition, the local area network (LAN) bandwidth utilization is reduced because data access is conducted through the SAN. If you are connecting to a SAN, you will need to install the interfaces and configure the hardware according to the manufacturer's specifications.

FIGURE 1-5   A SAN uses its own Fibre Channel hub

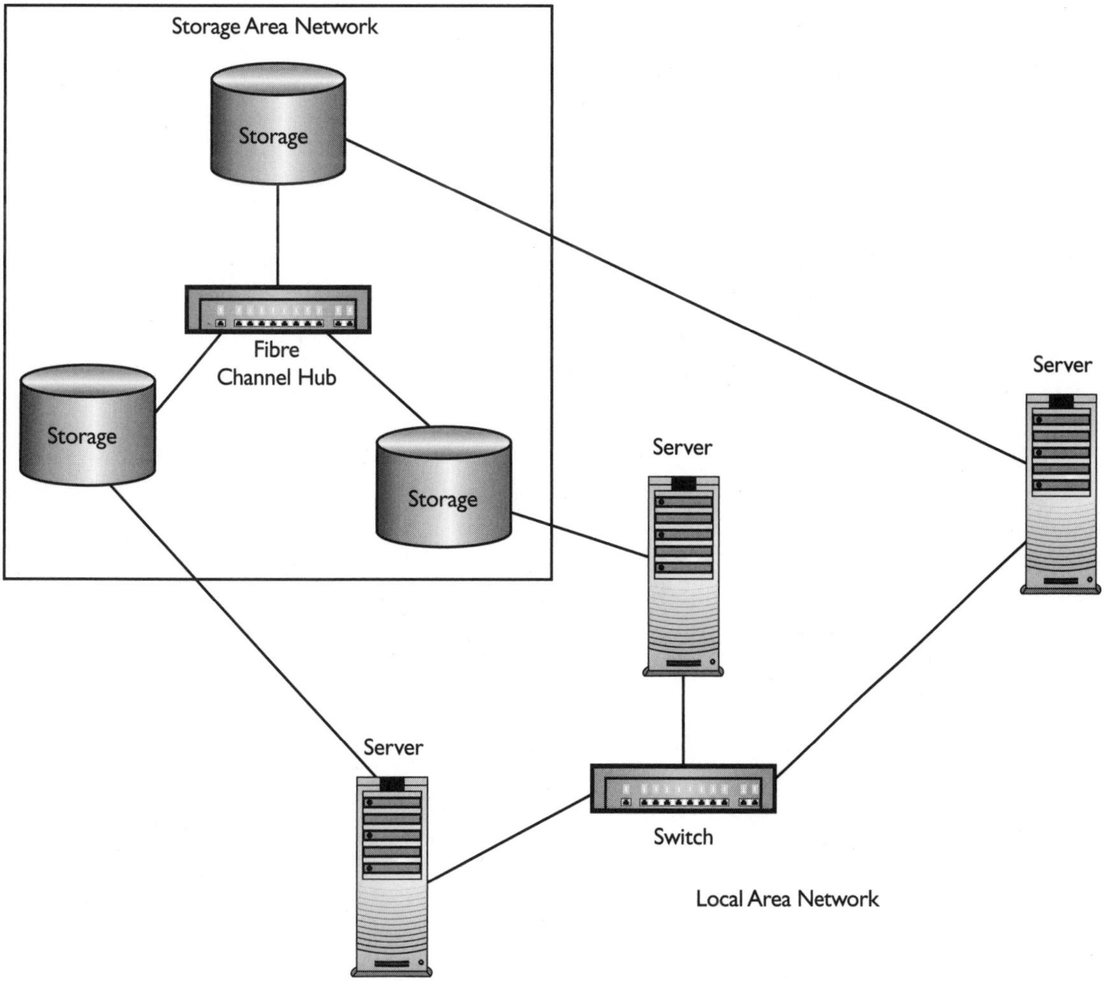

FROM THE CLASSROOM

Fiber Channel Technology

Fiber Channel technology is on the rise! Fiber Channel technology provides unsurpassed transfer speeds for demanding high-bandwidth transactions, such as High Definition TV or imaging. Because of its response and performance, businesses are snapping up Fiber Channel systems to replace older storage systems, even if they don't yet use high-bandwidth applications.

But what exactly is Fiber Channel? Fiber Channel specifies a 1 gigabit per second data transfer technology that can operate over fiber-optic cables (hence the name *fiber channel*), or even over copper wires. The fiber optic cables can be up to 10 kilometers (roughly six miles) in length, whereas copper can be up to 30 meters in length. Logically, Fiber Channel is a bi-directional point-to-point serial data channel between multiple ports. There is a hierarchical model for Fiber Channel:

- **FC 0**   Describes the physical characteristics, such as interfaces, media, and data transport speed

- **FC 1**   Describes the encoding/decoding scheme

- **FC 2**   Describes the data transfer sequence and data framing

- **FC 3**   Describes bandwidth management through a common set of services for all ports on a Fiber Channel node

- **FC 4**   Describes application and protocol management, such as how other protocols, such as SCSI, can map into the Fiber Channel system

You can find Fiber Channel physical topologies in the shape of a star, where a central Fiber Channel hub has multiple point-to-point connections with Fiber Channel devices; in a loop, where each Fiber Channel device connects to the next in a circle; or as a point-to-point connection between two Fiber Channel devices. How you configure your physical topology will depend on what media you use, and the manufacturer's specifications.

Currently, Fiber Channel is used for storage area networks. However, Fiber Channel systems are expected to completely replace SCSI systems, especially large storage subsystems holding RAID arrays, in the near future.

—Melissa Craft, MCSE, CCNA, Network+, MCNE, Citrix CCA

Network Adapters

A network adapter is also referred to as an NIC (network interface card). Some server platforms include network adapters as part of the motherboard. These are sometimes called integrated NICs. Even if the NIC is integrated, you may still need to install another adapter. Each NIC is designed for a specific network protocol and cable type. Integrated NICs are designed for the most common network protocol and cable types only—in most cases they are Ethernet or Fast Ethernet network adapters using Category 5 unshielded twisted-pair copper cabling. If you have a network that uses Token Ring over shielded twisted-pair copper cabling, then the integrated Ethernet NIC will not work.

You can configure multiple NICs in a single server to access the same local area network if the hardware and the network operating system support it. Network Fault Tolerance (NFT) occurs when you install two NICs; one of which is the active NIC and the other that only becomes active upon failure of the first NIC. Network Load Balancing (NLB) occurs when you install two or more NICs, all of which are active on the same LAN, simultaneously sharing the network traffic load.

There are a variety of network adapters that you might install. Table 1-4 lists the most common NIC types you may encounter.

Power Supply

Power problems can have disastrous effects on a server's data. Critical data can be destroyed, impacting the financial performance of the company. Preserving that data is an increasingly complex challenge. Several things should be considered when planning your server installation:

TABLE 1-4   Network Adapter Types

Type	Speed	Cabling
Ethernet	10 Mbps	Copper unshielded twisted-pair or coaxial
Fast Ethernet	100 Mbps	Copper unshielded twisted-pair
Fiber Distributed Data Interchange (FDDI)	100 Mbps	Fiber optic
Token Ring	4 or 16 Mbps	Copper unshielded twisted-pair or copper shielded twisted-pair
Asynchronous Transfer Mode (ATM)	· 155 Mbps	Fiber optic most common

- Preventing the internal power supply from causing a data loss.

- Protecting the data on a single server from an external power failure.

- Keeping the network running even in the event of an external power failure.

For servers, you can prevent an internal power supply outage by using redundant power supplies. In one type of configuration, one power supply is active, but if it fails the other power supply takes over. In another type of configuration, both power supplies are active and share the load. If one fails, the other takes over. Not all server platforms support this feature in one or both configurations.

If you want to protect the data on a single server from an external power failure, you should use an uninterruptible power supply (UPS) for that server. A UPS is a large battery. In the event of a power failure, the UPS kicks in and supplies power to the server. Instead of plugging your server into a power outlet, you plug it into the UPS, which then plugs into the power outlet. Most UPSs have a software application that runs on your server's network operating system. Because the UPS is nothing more than a big battery, it will eventually run out of power. To protect the server's data, you can configure the software application to communicate with the UPS and perform a server shutdown after a power failure event and a certain time period have passed. A regular server shutdown will close open files and disconnect users without damaging data. If you use a UPS, you need to select one that supports the wattage of your server platform. In addition, if you use an external RAID array unit, you need to support the wattage of the RAID array subsystem, the monitor, and any other external devices you want to have running in the event of a power failure.

To determine whether the UPS will support the equipment, you must determine what the VA consumption is for each piece of equipment that connects to the UPS, then add all the VA figures together. Using that figure, you should look for a UPS that will support that amount of VA, plus a little more if you expect growth. For example, if you have a server that uses 430VA, a monitor that uses 150VA, and a subsystem that uses 700VA, then you should select a UPS that provides greater than 1280VA.

If you have a business requirement to keep the network running even if there is an external power failure, you should consider a building UPS. A building UPS is intended to keep an entire building up and running if there is a power failure. This is the most expensive option, but it does not require any additional server configuration.

EXERCISE 1-1

Conducting Pre-Installation Planning Activities

1. In planning your server installation, you are preparing to select a UPS.

2. You are going to plug in five (5) servers that each consume 430VA.

3. You will install a monitor and a KVM switch each using 200VA.

4. Determine how much power your UPS needs to provide. (Multiply 5 times 430 and add it to 2 times 200 to get 2550VA.)

5. Which APC UPS provides enough power for this configuration? (Visit the APC Web page and browse to Products and then to UPS. Under the Server, Datacenter, Internetworking and Telecom, click Smart UPS. In the list of Smart UPS, you click on any one and notice that the number after the SmartUPS name is identical to the amount of the VA it provides. Therefore, you select a Smart UPS 3000.

Setup

There are typically two types of server units you can use:

- Tower
- Rack mount

Servers that come in a tower case are configured the same as desktop workstations. The only thing that you need to do is make certain not to place a server in a location where just anybody can access it. If the server is available to just anyone, it might accidentally be turned off or damaged.

A rack mountable server requires a rack and appropriate space to be mounted. Racks come in standard sizes with evenly spaced holes to mount equipment on. Although servers are built with form factors that vary, they all fit into racks perfectly. Manufacturers decided to standardize racks and rack-mountable equipment on a base unit height size and standard width. A server can be one or more multiples of the base unit size, and all you need to do is measure the number of units for each rack mounted unit—including your power strip, UPS, external storage unit, hub, switch, router, monitor, keyboard, and mouse—and make certain that they are less than or equal to the number of units that the rack can include. Racks come in sizes using base units (BU or U). A standard height rack is about 42U; half-height is about 22U. You can obtain other size racks, as well—both larger and in-between.

In most cases, you can use a standard monitor, keyboard, and mouse, but you will need to have a shelf on which to place them. Most racks can accommodate multiple servers, depending on what you put in them. But you can use up precious rack space by putting in a monitor, keyboard, and mouse for each individual server. To be able to use one monitor, keyboard, and mouse for multiple servers, you should install a keyboard, video, mouse (KVM) switch. You plug your monitor, keyboard, and mouse into the switch, and then, using the special KVM cables, you attach each server to the switch. When you place the monitor and keyboard shelves in the rack, place the keyboard shelf where it is easy to type, and the monitor just above that (preferably around eye-height for an average-sized person). The KVM switch should be placed below the keyboard.

To protect the rack-mounted equipment from dust, you should select a rack with top and side enclosures. With such protection, racks are confined spaces, and given that a confined space can heat up quickly, rack-mounted equipment can fall prey to temperature-induced failures. Some racks are equipped with fans to ventilate them, and you should select one with ventilation features. When you select your rack, you should choose one that has more than vent openings. The rack should have multiple fans to pull hot air out of the rack enclosure, and if possible, fans to pump in cool air. Some manufacturers of server platform hardware will void the warranty if the equipment is placed in an improperly ventilated, enclosed rack. Even if you have a well-ventilated rack, you should place it in a location that is air-conditioned.

Racks are filled with heavy equipment, and if they are tilted, they can fall over easily. If you have a single, free standing rack, obtain the stabilizing "feet," or *ballast*, from the rack manufacturer and attach it so that it will be difficult to push over. If you have multiple racks, you may want to connect them. This adds stabilizing force to the entire unit and you won't need to add ballast to them.

on the **job** *While installing equipment into the rack, you should install the equipment starting at the bottom and work towards the top. This method will avoid accidental tipping of the rack. The heaviest equipment should be placed at the bottom.*

When you connect racks together, you do not need the side enclosures between them—only on the ends where no racks are attached, as shown in Figure 1-6.

FIGURE 1-6

Rack configuration with sides

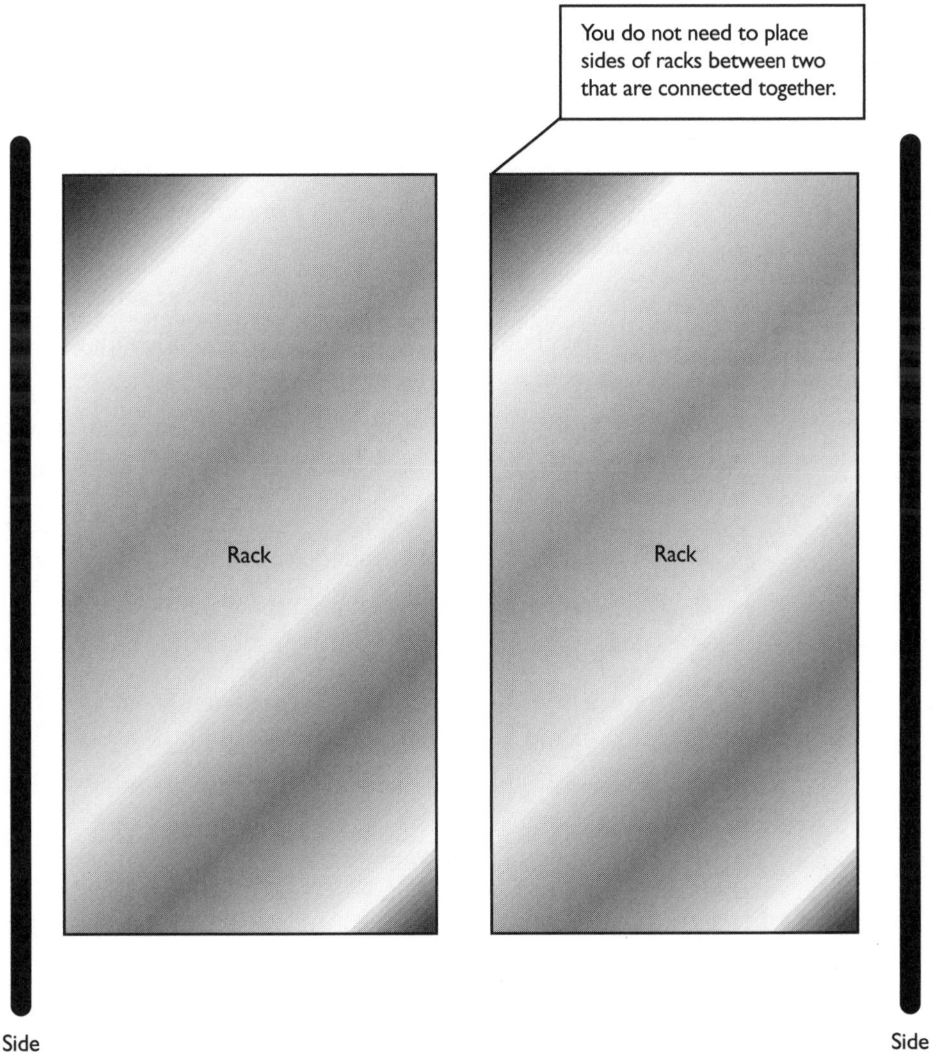

You do not need to place sides of racks between two that are connected together.

Side

Rack

Rack

Side

Verifying the Installation Plan

When you have decided on the various parts, you next need to verify that you have the correct ones to meet your business requirements. Evaluating your plan can be accomplished through answering the following questions:

- Have you selected a server platform that meets the scalability requirements of the business? In other words, is your server platform expandable so that the processor, memory, storage, adapters, and power components can be upgraded if the server usage increases?

- Have you selected one or more processors that meet your needs?

- Have you selected the correct type of memory for the server platform, and enough of it?

- Have you determined the storage needs for the server?

- Have you obtained network adapters that work with the network to which you are connecting?

- Is the location for the server well-ventilated and away from the public?

- Do you have all the rack components, including sides and stabilizing feet, if you need them?

- Do you have the correct cables to connect each component internally?

- Do you have the cables to connect the server to the network?

- Are the components compatible with the server platform?

- Do you have the drivers, BIOS, and NOS software to ensure that the hardware can be configured and accessed by the NOS?

- Do you have the tools that you will need to assemble the equipment?

- Have you received every component on the checklist?

Verifying Hardware Compatibility with the Operating System

With the exception of Apple Computers, hardware and network operating systems are rarely co-developed such that the NOS is automatically compatible with the latest hardware. New NOSs rarely support all the available hardware either. They have minimum requirements of processor, storage, and memory that prevent the installation of a new NOS on an older hardware platform. So, there are two things that you must verify:

1. That the hardware meets the minimum requirements of the NOS, and

2. That the NOS is compatible with the hardware components selected for the server.

To accomplish the first objective, you must look up the minimum requirements of the NOS manufacturer. These requirements can usually be found on the Internet at the NOS manufacturer's Web site.

To accomplish the second objective, you must look again to the NOS manufacturer for a list of approved hardware. If the manufacturer does not list the hardware on the compatibility list, you can consult each component's hardware manufacturer to determine whether the manufacturer provides drivers that enable the hardware to function with the chosen NOS.

Verifying Power Sources, Space, UPS, and Network Availability

Some buildings do not have adequate power for the load placed on it by one or more servers, monitors, external storage units, and UPSs. One thing that you must do is ensure that your hardware will be supported by the power available in the building. Another problem may arise if there are not sufficient power outlets for the equipment you intend to install. You should visit the location where you intend to place the equipment and verify that there are sufficient power outlets.

One problem can arise if you assume that there is space available for a rack or a server, then the equipment arrives and you find that there is no room. You should survey the site to ensure that there is sufficient space for the server or rack. You should also survey the server room to verify that there is a network connection available for your server, or if the server room includes the wiring terminations, that there is room on the hub or switch for another connection. You must also ensure that the drop cable is of sufficient length to reach from the server to the designated connection point. If you are installing one or more modems, you must ensure that the correct phone line connections are available in the server room.

If you already have a UPS, you may be able to use it for the new equipment you are installing. You first must verify that the UPS has sufficient power to include the additional load for your equipment. If not, you should obtain another UPS.

Verifying Delivery of Correct Components and Cables

When you receive the various components, you must validate that you have received all the components, as well as the correct components. The easiest items to forget are cables, or you might order ones with incorrect connectors. You should collect all the components as they are delivered and compare them to your invoice or a checklist. The second thing you should do is inspect the cables to ensure that they have the correct connectors for the components.

on the Job

Check, double check, and triple check your cables. You may have ordered a serial cable, and receive one with 9 pins, but when you attempt to connect that serial cable to your server you find that the server only has a 25 pin serial connection. Cables are the most easily mixed up and forgotten parts in a server installation—you wouldn't want your project delayed because of a cable mix-up!

CERTIFICATION OBJECTIVE 1.02

Installing Hardware Using ESD Best Practices

One of the most prevalent threats to a computer component is electro-static discharge (ESD), also known as *static*. Static is all around us, especially when the humidity is low. When you put on a jacket that makes the hair on your arm stand up or when you rub a balloon on your hair to make it stick it to the wall, you are encountering static electricity. When you touch a light switch and receive a jolt, you are experiencing a static discharge. ESD is caused when two objects of uneven charge come in contact with one another. Electricity has the property of traveling to areas with lower charges, and the static shock that you feel is the result of electrons jumping from your hand to the metal screw in the light switch plate. The same process can occur within the computer. If your body has a high electric potential, electrons will be transferred to the first computer component that you touch.

If an ESD charge is very low, it might not cause any damage to the computer. However, recall that most computer components are designed to receive voltages of ±12 or less. Most static electricity has a much higher voltage: up to 3000 volts if you can feel the discharge and up to 20,000 volts if you can see it! These voltages are enough to damage the circuits inside the device and render it inoperable.

exam
⚠️atch

Most static discharges are above 1000 volts, but it takes a charge of only about 30 volts to damage a computer component.

Because it takes such a small charge to damage a computer component, you might be unaware of its occurrence. This is referred to as *hidden ESD*. Hidden ESD can also come from a dust buildup inside the computer. Dust and other foreign particles can hold an electric charge that slowly bleeds into nearby components. Hidden ESD can cause more serious problems than ESD that you can feel. For example, if hidden ESD has damaged a component, you will be unaware of it until that device begins to malfunction. Because you weren't aware of the ESD damage when it occurred, it could be difficult for you to pinpoint the problem.

When ESD causes the immediate malfunction of a device, it is considered *catastrophic*. When ESD causes a gradually worsening problem in a device, it is referred to as *degradation*. As unlikely as it might seem, catastrophic damage can be less harmful to the system than degradation. When a device suffers catastrophic damage, the result is immediate and typically quite obvious, so the device will most likely be replaced right away. Degradation, on the other hand, can cause a component to malfunction sporadically. This makes it harder to pinpoint the problem, so the problem itself can persist for a longer period of time. Additionally, a total failure of one component will typically not affect the usability of other components. However, degradation can cause a component to fail in ways that also result in the failure of other components.

There are many ways to prevent ESD from damaging the computer. First, ESD is typically caused by low humidity. Always keep the room's humidity between 50 and 80 percent (but no higher than 80 percent or condensation could form).

You should also use special ESD devices, such as ESD wrist or ankle straps. ESD straps have a cuff that fits around your wrist or ankle and are designed to bleed static charges away from the computer through your body. Some ESD straps have an alligator clip that is attached to a grounded, metal object, such as a table leg. Other straps have a single prong that is plugged into the ground wire in a regular wall outlet. Make sure that you read the directions for your particular strap, and make sure that you know which part of the wall outlet contains the ground wire.

ESD mats look like vinyl placemats but have a wire lead and an alligator clip. Their function is similar to that of an ESD strap and can be used as a safe place to put expansion cards or other internal components that you have removed from the computer. Before you pick up a loose computer component, discharge any static electricity in yourself by touching something metal, such as a table leg or chair. This will prevent electrons in your body from being passed onto the device.

Another way to combat ESD is to use antistatic spray. ESD spray is commercially available and is typically used to remove static from your clothes. However, you can use it to remove static from yourself, from the carpet, and from your work area to protect computer components.

on the
job

Never spray antistatic spray directly on a computer component. If you use the spray on your work surface, make sure that it is completely dry before setting components down on it.

ESD can cause a lot of damage to your computer unless you are knowledgeable about dealing with it and take proper precautions.

SCENARIO & SOLUTION

Now that you have learned some of the best practices surrounding ESD, you can test your knowledge with these example questions.

Do you have to feel static electricity, or see a spark, in order for it to damage your computer?	No. Computer components are more sensitive to static than humans. A 30-volt discharge can damage a computer, and it takes 100 times that for you to feel the static.
What type of material should you select for a mat on which to place computer components?	You should select a nonconducting material such as vinyl.
What do you need to do before touching computer components inside a server?	You should ground yourself. One of the best ways to ground yourself is to use an ESD wristband with a clamp that you attach to a server that is already grounded.

Mounting the Rack Installation

Each vendor's rack will have a set of instructions for its installation. After you have assembled the rack, you must mount the components within the rack. It is best to place the UPS in the bottom of the rack, because it will likely be the heaviest component and can cause the rack to fall over if it is placed higher in the rack system.

Racks include rails so that you can slide components in and out of the rack to work on them. You must install half of each rail on the equipment, and the other half of the rail on the rack itself. You then slide the equipment onto the rails and attach the brackets to the equipment and affix it to the rack, so that the equipment does not accidentally slide out.

Network Cabling

Cable media use electronic signals or light conducted across copper or glass to communicate from one end to the other. There are three main types. The first is called *twisted-pair cable*, which is a series of individual copper cables encased in plastic. There is also *coaxial cable*, which is similar to what we use today for television and VCR connections. The last and the most expensive is *fiber-optic cable*, which is made up of glass or plastic fibers.

Twisted-Pair Cable

Twisted-pair cable is the most common type of cable used today in computer networking. Used heavily in LAN systems, twisted-pair cable uses a series of individually-wrapped copper wires encased in a plastic sheathing. Each cable is individually encased in plastic, and the overall outer shell is plastic as well. Each cable inside is twisted together with another. Most cable today comes with eight cables or wires, making four pairs. The cable is twisted to cut down on crosstalk. *Crosstalk* is when two wires in close proximity inadvertently share information due to interfering with each other. Figure 1-7 shows a simple example of twisted-pair cable.

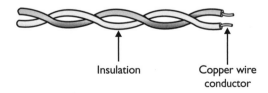

FIGURE 1-7

Twisted-pair cable

Insulation

Copper wire conductor

Twisted-pair cabling is made up of 22- or 26-gauge copper wire. There are two types of twisted-pair cable:

- Shielded twisted-pair (STP)
- Unshielded twisted-pair (UTP)

Unshielded is the more common of the two types of twisted-pair cable. Unshielded twisted pair is a series of pairs of wires twisted together with their own distinct plastic insulation, and the group of wires is encased in a plastic sheathing that holds all the other wires together as shown in Figure 1-8.

There are five types of twisted-pair cabling as ranked by the Electrical Industries Association:

- **Category 1 (CAT 1)** Low speed data and voice; less than 4 Mbps
- **Category 2 (CAT 2)** Low speed data and voice; less then 4 Mbps
- **Category 3 (CAT 3)** Data; 10-16 Mbps (100 possible)
- **Category 4 (CAT 4)** Data; less than or equal to 20 Mbps
- **Category 5 (CAT 5)** Data; high speed, 100 Mbps
- **Category 5E (CAT 5E)** Data; high speed, 100 Mbps

Typically, twisted-pair cable consists of RJ-45 or RJ-11 ends. RJ-11 ends are what you see for most telephones. RJ-45 is similar, but wider than the RJ-11 connector. RJ-45 has an 8-pin connection and RJ-11 has a 4-pin connection.

When considering the factors we described earlier in this chapter, we see the following:

- **Cost** Less expensive than other forms of transmission media.

FIGURE 1-8

Unshielded
twisted-pair

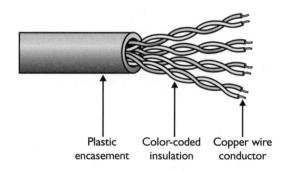

Plastic   Color-coded   Copper wire
encasement   insulation   conductor

■ **Installation** Installation is easy and necessary equipment is relatively inexpensive.

■ **Capacity** UTP can support from 1 megabit per second to 1 gigabit per second at distances of 100 meters. Most common are 10 Mbps and 100 Mbps.

■ **Attenuation** UTP attenuates more quickly than other types due to the copper conductor. For this reason, distance is limited.

■ **Interference** The copper conductor is very susceptible to interference from outside signals.

Shielded twisted-pair is similar in features to UTP. The main difference is the extra shielding that STP has. Figure 1-9 illustrates this difference.

Shielded twisted-pair has enhanced protection with a foil wrap and extra shielding outside the individual twists inside the cable. The considerations for STP are as follows:

■ **Cost** More expensive than UTP but less expensive than other forms of transmission media such as coax and fiber.

■ **Installation** Similar to UTP but there are a few other considerations. Certain STP implementations will use special connectors. STP also requires an electrical ground like that of coax.

■ **Capacity** STP can support from 500 Mbps at distances of 100 meters. The most common is 16 Mbps. This is not widely implemented at over 155 Mbps.

■ **Attenuation** STP attenuates more quickly than other types due to the copper conductor. For this reason, distance is limited.

FIGURE 1-9

Shielded
twisted-pair

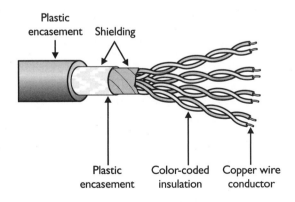

■ **Interference**   The copper conductor is very susceptible to interference from outside signals. STP is better than UTP due to the protection given by the extra shielding.

Coaxial Cable

Coaxial cable is made up of two conductors that share a common axis. This is where the name comes from. Figure 1-10 shows an example of a coaxial cable.

The inside of the cable is made up of a solid or stranded copper wire typically surrounded by foam. Next is an outer wire mesh tube that further protects the signal travelling along the inner wire. The outside is a tougher plastic encasement that protects all the inner components.

There are different types of coaxial cable that are used in computer networking. The main difference is the ohm rating and size standard:

■ 50 OHM RG-8/RG-11 (Thick Ethernet)

■ 50 OHM RG-58 (Thin Ethernet)

■ 75 OHM RG-59 (Cable television)

■ 93 OHM RG-62 (ARCNet)

When connecting coaxial cables, the most common type of connection is a T-connector. Another type of connection that is used is the "vampire" tap. T-connectors are more generally used, because thick coax is no longer common. Remember, in either case, the cable has to be grounded on one end only and terminated on both ends. If the cable isn't grounded and terminated, you will not be

FIGURE 1-10

Coaxial cable

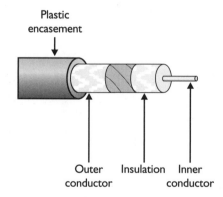

Plastic encasement

Outer conductor   Insulation   Inner conductor

able to successfully communicate across the medium. Coax has the following considerations:

- **Cost**   Increases as the cables get bigger in diameter and depends on the construction of the internal conductor. Thin coax is relatively inexpensive (less than STP and CAT 5 UTP). Thick coax can be more expensive than STP or UTP.

- **Installation**   The initial installation of coax is easy. Most of the coax cabling situations use one long cable (referred to as a drop) that connects each computer to the network.

- **Capacity**   Current limitations allow for transmission speeds somewhere between twisted-pair and fiber-optic cables. The most common speed is 10 Mbps.

- **Attenuation**   The attenuation of coax is less than either form of twisted-pair. Maximum distance of 10Base2 is 185m, whereas 10Base5 is 500m.

- **Interference**   The inner copper is limited in resistance but the shielding makes the resistance better or equal to STP.

Fiber-Optic Cable

Distinctly different from both twisted-pair and coax, fiber-optic cable is made up of a light-conducting glass or plastic core. More reflective material, called cladding, surrounds the core, and the outer plastic sheath protects the inside. Figure 1-11 shows different configurations of fiber-optic cable.

Common types of fiber-optic cable include the following:

- 8.3 micron core/125 micron cladding single-mode

- 62.5 micron core/125 micron cladding multimode

- 50 micron core/125 micron cladding multimode

- 100 micron core/140 micron cladding multimode

When deciding on a transmission medium, consider the following:

- **Cost**   Fiber cable used to be much more expensive than coax or twisted-pair but the costs are coming down. The major cost is doing the installation.

FIGURE 1-11

Fiber-optic cable

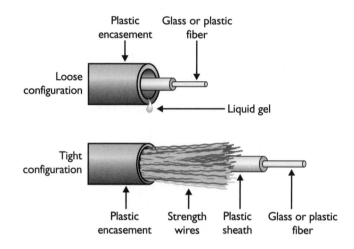

- **Installation** Installation is much more challenging than with coax or twisted-pair.

- **Capacity** The optical nature of fiber allows for high bandwidth over great distances. The current capacity is 100 Mbps to 2 Gbps at distances of 2 to 25 kilometers.

- **Attenuation** Attenuation is much less in fiber-optic cables versus any copper conductor cables. Attenuation for fiber-optic cable is measured in kilometers.

- **Interference** Due to the fact that the signal is a light transmission, there is no chance for interference as along as the surrounding covering and cladding are not harmed in any way.

Installing UPS

An uninterruptible power supply (UPS) can be used to prevent or remedy some of the power issues mentioned earlier. A typical UPS has a battery that provides temporary backup power in the case of a blackout. This backup gives users enough time to properly save their work and safely shut their computers down in the event of a power loss. One type of UPS is a *standby power system (SPS)*, which is attached to the computer. The UPS enables its battery power when it detects a loss of electricity. Unfortunately, there can be a brief lapse in power during the time it takes for the UPS to detect a power problem and switch to battery power.

A more expensive but more efficient type of UPS is an *online UPS*, which is located between the computer and the power supply. Incoming power keeps the UPS battery charged, and all power to the computer comes from the battery. When the power goes out, the UPS simply continues to provide the computer with power from the battery's reserve. This means there is no "break" in the power, as there is in an SPS.

To prevent problems resulting from power surges and power spikes, you can use a *suppressor*. Suppressors are designed to "smooth out" the flow of electricity by removing excess voltage caused by power surges and spikes. Suppressors are available as individual devices or integrated with a UPS.

To combat noisy or dirty current, you should use a *noise filter*. Noise filters are designed to condition the flow of electricity by removing EMI. Like suppressors, noise filters can be used as individual devices or as part of a UPS.

Verifying SCSI ID Configuration and Termination

SCSI hard drives have a few more configurable settings, but in most cases, only the SCSI ID and the termination need to be set. Like the IDE drives discussed earlier, SCSI drives are configured with jumpers that shunt pins together. On a SCSI disk, it is the ID of the drive that distinguishes it from any other devices that may also be on the bus. On an 8-bit SCSI controller, there are eight IDs available but only seven can be used for devices. One address, typically ID 7, is used for the

SCENARIO & SOLUTION

Power problems plague only the unprotected. These questions and answers describe situations that you might encounter.

Every desktop workstation is protected from power problems using suppressors. The network administrator wants to use the same suppressor for a new server. What should you tell her?	A surge suppressor will be helpful in making certain that a power surge doesn't disable the server; however, if the power completely fails the suppressor cannot save data from damage. To best protect the server, use a UPS.
Matt is installing a server in a warehouse that exists in a rural area. While he is there, he notices that lights flicker. What should Matt do to protect his server?	The power in the warehouse is apparently noisy and/or surging, thus causing the lights to flicker. Matt should select a UPS that includes a suppressor and noise filter function.

controller card itself. On a 16-bit SCSI controller, up to 15 devices can be connected to the bus. The 16-bit SCSI controller also requires an address for itself. Figure 1-12 shows the jumper location and a chart showing the various settings for the SCSI ID.

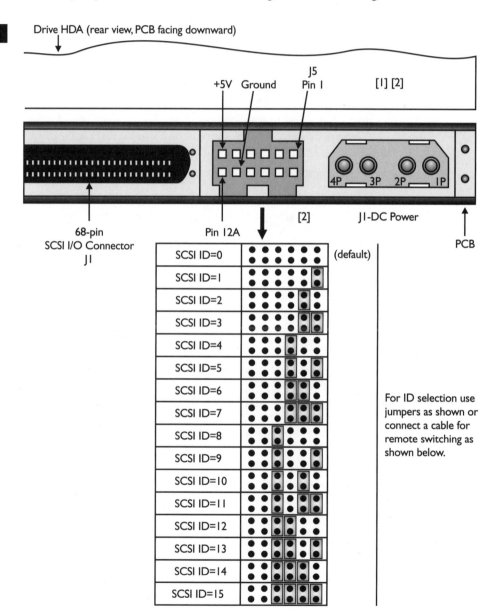

FIGURE 1-12

Wide SCSI jumper block

Drive HDA (rear view, PCB facing downward)

+5V Ground J5 Pin 1 [1] [2]

68-pin SCSI I/O Connector J1

Pin 12A

[2]

J1-DC Power

PCB

For ID selection use jumpers as shown or connect a cable for remote switching as shown below.

SCSI ID=0	(default)
SCSI ID=1	
SCSI ID=2	
SCSI ID=3	
SCSI ID=4	
SCSI ID=5	
SCSI ID=6	
SCSI ID=7	
SCSI ID=8	
SCSI ID=9	
SCSI ID=10	
SCSI ID=11	
SCSI ID=12	
SCSI ID=13	
SCSI ID=14	
SCSI ID=15	

SCSI devices must have proper termination, through the jumpers or switches on the device, to work. Only the last device in a SCSI chain should have termination turned on. The SCSI adapter provides the other end of the chain and should already be terminated.

Unlike the IDE drive, the SCSI drive must be terminated if it is the last device on the bus. Over the years, manufacturers have devised a few ways to terminate the SCSI bus. One of the more modern ways is to include a built-in terminating resistor in the hard drive, which can be turned on or off with a jumper. Figure 1-13 shows a

FIGURE 1-13

SCSI terminator
jumper positions

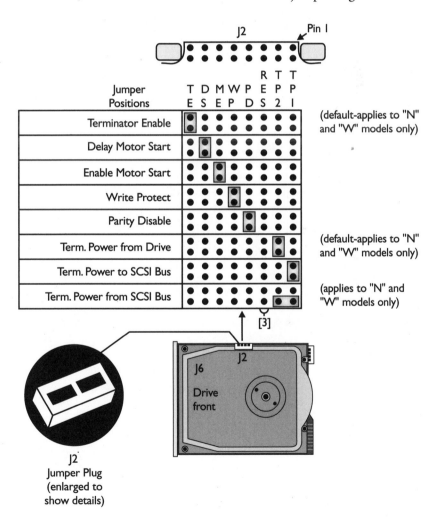

Jumper Positions	TE	DS	ME	WP	PD	RE2	TP2	TP1	
Terminator Enable	■								(default-applies to "N" and "W" models only)
Delay Motor Start		■							
Enable Motor Start			■						
Write Protect				■					
Parity Disable					■				
Term. Power from Drive							■		(default-applies to "N" and "W" models only)
Term. Power to SCSI Bus								■	
Term. Power from SCSI Bus							■		(applies to "N" and "W" models only)

J2
Jumper Plug
(enlarged to
show details)

J6
Drive
front

J2

[3]

drive with a built-in terminating resister. If this were the last physical device on the bus, you would place a jumper on Pins 15 and 16 (farthest left pair on the jumper block) to enable the terminator.

Built-in termination facilities are convenient, especially compared to older SCSI drives which required a separate resistor in a socket on the PCB board of the drive or plugged into the last connector on the SCSI cable. These older-style SCSI drives requiring a physically separate termination resistor are slowly being replaced by the drives with built-in termination.

Another often overlooked feature of the SCSI bus is that the devices are assigned priority based on their SCSI ID number. For example, if you had a tape drive and a hard drive on the SCSI bus, you could place the hard drive at SCSI ID 0 and the tape device at ID 6. This would help prevent tape drive requests from slowing down requests to the hard drive. This will not speed up the tape drive, or for that matter, the hard drive, but will give priority to requests for the hard drive over the tape drive when they arrive in the SCSI controller command queue at the same time.

Installing External Devices

After assembling the internal components of the server and installing it into the rack, you must attach the external components. Each component connects using its own cable to ports on the server itself or a special adapter. For keyboards, monitors, and mouse devices, you can use a KVM switch to connect a single keyboard, a single monitor, and a single mouse to multiple servers.

Keyboards

A *keyboard* connects to the serial port of your computer and enables you to type data. Because the keyboard is the primary input device, you rely on the keyboard more than you think. The keyboard contains certain standard function keys, such as the ESC key, TAB key, cursor movement keys, SHIFT keys, and CTRL keys, and sometimes other manufacturer-customized keys, such as the Windows key.

Monitors

The function of a *monitor* is to produce visual responses to user requests. Most desktop computers use cathode ray tube (CRT) monitors. CRTs use an electron gun to activate phosphors behind the screen. Each dot on the monitor, called a *pixel,* has the ability to generate red, green, or blue, depending on the signals it receives. This combination of colors results in the total display you see on the monitor.

Monitors are available in a wide array of colors and resolutions. The word *resolution* refers to the size and number of pixels that a monitor can display. Higher resolutions display more pixels and have better visual output. Lower resolutions result in grainy displays.

Color graphics adapter (CGA) monitors are an older type and can display combinations of red, green, and blue at different intensities, resulting in 16 different colors. The maximum resolution of a CGA monitor is 640 x 200 pixels in monochrome mode and 160 x 100 pixels in 16-color mode.

Enhanced graphics adapter (EGA) monitors are capable of generating up to 64 colors, of which 16 can be displayed at any one time. EGA monitors have a maximum resolution of 720 x 350 when displaying text only and 640 x 350 in graphics mode.

Virtual graphics array (VGA) monitors were the first to use analog rather than digital output. Instead of creating displays based on the absence or presence of a color (as in digital CGA and EGA monitors), VGA monitors can display a wide range of colors and intensities. They can produce around 16 million different colors but can display only up to 256 different colors at a time. This color setting is often called *16-bit high color*. VGA monitors have a maximum resolution of 720 x 400 in text mode and 640 x 480 in graphics mode.

Super VGA (SVGA) monitors introduce yet another improvement: They also use analog input and can provide resolutions as high as 1280 x 1024. Some SVGA monitors can provide even higher resolutions. SVGA monitors can display up to 16 million colors at once, referred to as *32-bit true color*. Because the human eye can distinguish only approximately 10 million different colors, it is likely that monitor technology will focus on improving resolution only.

All monitors receive their signals from video cards attached to the motherboard. The monitor technology must match the technology of the video card to which it is attached. That is, an EGA monitor will work only with an EGA video card, and an SVGA monitor must be attached to an SVGA video card. Table 1-5 presents a summary of monitor types and characteristics.

Subsystems

Subsystems hold multiple disks, which you can configure as separate disk drives, or as a single RAID array, or some combination of these. A storage subsystem will occupy its own space in the rack. You should place the subsystem next to—either immediately below or immediately above—the server to which it will provide

TABLE 1-5   Monitor Types and Their Characteristics

Monitor	Total Number of Colors	Number of Colors That Can Be Simultaneously Displayed	Maximum Resolution	Input
GA	16	16	Monochrome: 640 x 200 Color: 160 x 100	Digital
EGA	64	16	Text mode: 720 x 350 Graphics mode: 640 x 350	Digital
VGA	More than 16 million	256	Text mode: 720 x 400 Graphics mode: 640x480	Analog
SVGA	More than 16 million	More than 16 million	1280 x 1024	Analog

storage. After mounting the subsystem, you will attach it to the adapter card in the server with an appropriate cable. Next you install each disk into the subsystem. To configure the subsystem, you need to run the BIOS for the subsystem and follow the prompts to insure that each disk is recognized and then configured according to your plan.

Modem Racks

Some servers are used for remote access into the network. This means that multiple people will be connecting to a single server. Because a server usually can accommodate between two and four communication ports, you must add a special adapter to expand the number of COM ports available, such as a Digiboard. Adapters are limited to the size of the slot in which they are placed, so the modems are actually housed in a separate rack and attached to the adapter with a single cable. You connect each port in the modem rack to a phone line. When you install the NOS, you will likely need to configure the NOS as a remote access server so that it will either accept incoming calls, place outgoing calls, or do both.

Verifying Power-on Using the Power-on Sequence

Server platforms are shipped with a BIOS already installed. The BIOS version may not be the latest, so you should make certain to have the latest version available to update the hardware. Hardware components, such as SCSI interfaces and a subsystem, will have their own BIOSs. When you first turn on the server, the monitor will display the memory installed, then you should see the BIOS communicate with SCSI or subsystem adapters. Note that under some NOSs, the SCSI may need to be disabled.

exam

Ⓦatch

When you first boot up a server after assembling its hardware, you should watch to make sure that the memory counts up to the amount that you installed. You then should verify that the other components you installed were recognized by the server.

To absolutely verify that the server recognizes all the components and to ensure that you do not have any conflicts in the server resources (such as two adapters set to use the same IRQ), you should access the BIOS. The power-on sequence will show the function keys that you need to press to access the BIOS; each manufacturer specifies their own, so they will not be the same from one server platform to another.

EXERCISE 1-2

Verifying Hardware Configuration

1. Your server is now assembled.

2. Double-check that the power cables are plugged in.

3. Double-check that the monitor is plugged in, and if you are using a KVM switch box, that the cables are all connected properly.

4. Turn on the server.

5. Watch the monitor for information to scroll across the screen. (If no information appears, repeat Step 2 and Step 3.)

6. Document the amount of RAM that was recognized, whether the SCSI controller BIOS is displayed, and the version of the BIOS.

7. Press the function keys that will access the BIOS.

8. Once the BIOS screens are displayed, browse through the memory, CPU, storage, and other options to verify that the equipment you installed is recognized. Document the IRQ, DMA, and other information about the components.

CERTIFICATION SUMMARY

Planning the server installation will reduce the possibility of problems during the server installation. When you plan, you should consider the capacity that you will need for processors, memory, storage, network access, and power protection. In addition, you should plan for redundancy in these components to provide availability and high performance. The server platform you select should be expandable so that you can scale the server up in size as the needs of the network grow.

You should verify that you have all the components before beginning the server installation. In addition, you should survey the location where the server will be placed to ascertain whether it has sufficient power, power outlets, network terminations, phone lines, and cabling.

When you begin installing the server, you should observe ESD precautions. The sensitive components of a server can be damaged by static electricity—even by discharges that are too slight for a human to feel. The installation will likely require a rack installation and mounting of rack components, unless you are installing a tower server unit. Following the rack installation, the server components must be mounted and the cables connected to all the external devices and to the network. Once the server is fully assembled and all parts connected, you can power on the server the first time and verify that the BIOS will power on and recognize the new components correctly.

✓ TWO-MINUTE DRILL

Here are some of the key points from each certification objective in Chapter 1.

Conducting Pre-Installation Planning Activities

❑ Server platform hardware differs from workstation hardware because it is designed for availability, scalability, and performance using redundant components.

❑ Symmetric Multiprocessing (SMP) processors are two or more CPUs that share the load of the processing on a server.

❑ Dynamic random access memory (DRAM) is the most commonly produced and used type of memory.

❑ Network Attached Storage (NAS) is a single storage system that participates directly on the network.

❑ Storage area networks (SANs) are groups of storage systems that participate with each other through Fibre Channel connections to Fibre Channel hubs or switches.

❑ Redundant Array of Inexpensive Disks (RAID) version 5 offers high tolerance through disk striping with parity.

❑ Multiple network adapters can share the load of network traffic through Network Load Balancing (NLB).

❑ You should survey the location where you will place the server to ensure it has sufficient space, power, network connections, phone lines for modems, and ventilation.

Installing Hardware Using ESD Best Practices

❑ A computer component can withstand 12 volts of static or less.

❑ Static can damage a computer component with a static discharge that a human may not be able to see or feel.

❑ Copper unshielded twisted pair is the most common type of cabling used today.

❑ Thin coax uses T connectors and is more common than thick coax which uses vampire clamps.

❑ SCSI 2, an 8-bit controller, can host seven devices, and SCSI Wide, a 16-bit controller, can host 15 devices.

❑ Each end of a SCSI chain must be terminated.

❑ The server ships with a BIOS that, after powering on, can show whether the installed components are recognized on the server.

SELF TEST

The following questions will help you measure your understanding of the material presented in this chapter. Read all of the choices carefully, as there may be more than one correct answer. Choose all correct answers for each question.

Conducting Pre-Installation Planning Activities

1. How many processors might you find in a server using SMP?

   A. 1

   B. 3

   C. 4

   D. 5

2. You are given the task of planning a server installation for a Web server that will provide its services to thousands of people. The minimum amount of RAM for the operating system is 128MB of RAM. The server will max out at 4GB of RAM and supports ECC RAM. You expect that you will need 1GB of RAM to run the server at first. How much RAM should you plan to install if you are given the following options?

   A. 128MB

   B. 64MB

   C. 1GB

   D. 2GB

3. You are planning to install a server that will have five hard drives and one tape drive. What type of interface should you plan to include in your server configuration?

   A. SCSI

   B. IDE

   C. EIDE

   D. ISA

4. Your server plan calls for 100GB of storage space. Your boss tells you that he wants to make certain that a single disk failure will not render the server inoperable. The disk drives that you must use have 20GB of space each. You decide to implement which of the following:

   A. RAID 0

   B. RAID 1

   C. RAID 5

   D. RAID 6

5. When planning your server configuration, you discover that the switch you will connect the server to has a Fast Ethernet port as well as a standard Ethernet port available. The server has an integrated 10/100 Ethernet NIC. You want to give the server the fastest access possible to the network, and spend as little money as possible. Which of the following will you do?

    A. Connect the integrated 10/100 Ethernet NIC to the standard Ethernet port because that is what the workstations connect to.

    B. Purchase another Ethernet adapter and connect the new adapter to the standard Ethernet port because the 10/100 integrated Ethernet NIC will not work.

    C. Connect the integrated 10/100 Ethernet NIC to the Fast Ethernet port.

    D. Purchase another Ethernet adapter and connect it to the Fast Ethernet port and make it the active NIC, then connect the integrated NIC to the standard Ethernet port, configuring it as a failover NIC in the case of a NIC failure.

6. When planning your server installation, you find out that there is an existing UPS available that is supporting another server. You investigate the situation and find that the UPS will support a capacity of 1500VA, the existing server uses 700VA, and a monitor is also attached that uses 100VA. Can you use this UPS?

    A. No; it does not have enough capacity.

    B. Yes; if you are only attaching a single server that uses 700VA or less.

    C. No; it is maxed out.

    D. Yes, but you must attach more than one component to it and use more than 700VA.

7. You have a project to install a server to provide file and print services on a Fast Ethernet network to a group of 125 users. The workgroup is being moved to a new building directly following your installation. What should you do to prepare for the installation?

    A. Purchase a color scanner.

    B. Install RG 59 coaxial cabling throughout the new building.

    C. Inspect the location to see if there is enough space, power outlets, and network terminations.

    D. Review several different Web server applications.

8. You are installing a server that will run Novell NetWare v5. One of the components of the hardware is a new type of Fibre Channel controller that was developed after NetWare 5 was released. How do you verify that the hardware is compliant with the network operating system? (Choose all that apply.)

    A. You browse through the NetWare 5 installation guide.

    B. You ask your brother-in-law because he installed a similar controller on a Windows 2000 Server.

C. You look up the compatibility on Novell's Web site.

D. You check online at the Fibre Channel controller's manufacturer's Web site for compatibility.

9. You are planning a rack installation with a server, a UPS, a power strip, a subsystem, a KVM switch, a keyboard, a monitor, and a rack-mount hub. Working from the bottom up, which of the following is the best order to install the hardware?

A. UPS, subsystem, server, hub, power strip, KVM switch, keyboard, monitor.

B. Keyboard, monitor, KVM switch, power strip, subsystem, UPS, server, hub.

C. Power strip, keyboard, subsystem, UPS, hub, server, KVM switch, monitor.

D. Monitor, KVM switch, hub, subsystem, keyboard, power strip, UPS, server.

10. You have just been notified that the equipment you ordered for your server has arrived. What do you need to do next?

A. Install the cabling.

B. Test the UPS.

C. Survey the location where you will place the server.

D. Verify that all the components were delivered.

Installing Hardware Using ESD Best Practices

11. Why should you select a rack that is surrounded by sides and a top?

A. To keep the server away from the light.

B. To decrease ventilation.

C. To keep out the dust.

D. To match the other racks in the room.

12. Which of the following types of cable consists of two conductors sharing a common axis?

A. Unshielded twisted pair

B. Thin Ethernet

C. Fiber optic

D. Shielded twisted pair

13. Of the following types of equipment, which will provide time for a proper shutdown of your server in the event of a power failure?

A. Uninterruptible power supply

B. Suppressor

C. Subsystem

D. Noise filter

14. You have just installed a SCSI controller and four external tape drives. When you test the server, you find that it doesn't recognize the SCSI equipment. What could be the problem?

    A. The motherboard has a bad slot that now holds the SCSI controller.

    B. The cables are wrong.

    C. The last tape drive wasn't terminated.

    D. Two of the tape drives have conflicting IRQs.

15. You are planning a three-server installation in a rack. What piece of equipment can you use to share the keyboard between the three servers?

    A. UPS

    B. Noise filter

    C. Ballast

    D. KVM switch

16. You are setting up a server in a rack that will have a network operating system requiring more than 16 million colors and 1280 by 1024 resolution. What type of monitor should you select?

    A. 15-inch SVGA

    B. 14-inch EGA

    C. 15-inch VGA

    D. 30-inch SVGA

17. What might you find in a subsystem?

    A. A set of modems

    B. A set of NICs

    C. A set of tape drives

    D. A set of disk drives

18. You are installing a remote access server for a Fast Ethernet network. You will have 32 phone lines. Which of the following should you install?

    A. Subsystem

    B. UPS

C. Modem rack

D. Fiber-optic cable

19. What should you do after you completely assemble the server?

A. Power it on and verify that components are recognized.

B. Survey the site.

C. Verify that all components were delivered.

D. Install the rack components from the bottom up.

20. Which of the following controllers will allow up to 15 devices to be connected?

A. ISA

B. EIDE

C. SCSI 2

D. SCSI Wide

LAB QUESTION

You have determined that you need the following equipment for your server installation:

■ Two Compaq 8500 rack-mounts with four processors, 1GB RAM.

■ One Compaq StorageWorks Enclosure 4200 (rack mount) with 10 1-inch hard drives in RAID 5 array.

■ One Compaq R3000 rack mount UPS.

■ One power strip in your possession that is 1U in height.

■ A keyboard and shelf in your possession using 1U in height.

■ A KVM switch in your possession using 2U.

■ A monitor and monitor shelf in your possession using 10U.

You must select a rack that is either 22U or 42U in height. You do not have the specifications for the Compaq equipment to see what size it will take in the rack. How do you find out these heights if the equipment is not available for you to look over? What size rack will you select: 22U or 42U?

SELF TEST ANSWERS

Conducting Pre-Installation Planning Activities

1. ☑ **C.** You might find 4 processors in an SMP server. SMP refers to the fact that the number of processors is symmetrical, so the number must be even. Usually, SMP servers have 2, 4, 8, 16, or 32 processors.
    ☒ **A, B,** and **D** are all incorrect because they are odd numbers and not symmetrical.

2. ☑ **D.** You can never have enough RAM, especially if you are building a server that will have hundreds of thousands of users. Because you expect that 1GB of RAM will be enough to start, you should add more RAM to handle growth in server usage. Because 2GB is the only option that is more than 1GB, that is the option you should select.
    ☒ **A** is incorrect because 128MB will not support any services above the operating system. **B** is incorrect because it will not even support the operating system. **C** is incorrect because although it is enough to support your server's initial usage, it will not be enough to handle growth.

3. ☑ **A.** You should plan for a SCSI controller interface. You will have six total devices to connect to the interface, and SCSI will accept up to seven devices.
    ☒ **B** and **C** are incorrect because neither will not support more than two devices. **D** is incorrect because it does not support hard drives or tape drives.

4. ☑ **C.** You will implement RAID 5 using 6 20GB drives for an aggregate of 100GB usable disk space. Under RAID 5, a single disk drive can fail and the server will continue to operate.
    ☒ **A** is incorrect because there is no fault tolerance under RAID 0. **B** is incorrect because a mirrored 20GB disk drive will not supply the required 100GB of space. **D** is incorrect because, although it will meet the objectives, RAID 6 is not widely available to implement.

5. ☑ **C.** To gain the fastest network access and spend the least amount of money, you will connect the integrated 10/100 Ethernet NIC to the Fast Ethernet port on the switch. Some NICs will automatically detect what type of network they are connected to and switch to that version of Ethernet. They are called 10/100 NICs.
    ☒ **A** is incorrect because the standard Ethernet port on the switch provides only 10 Mbps access whereas the Fast Ethernet port provides 100 Mbps access to the network. **B** is incorrect because the 10/100 Ethernet NIC will work, and using the standard Ethernet port will give only 10 Mbps access instead of the 100 Mbps access available on the Fast Ethernet port. **D** is incorrect because you will be spending more money to purchase the other NIC, even though the Network Fault Tolerance is provided this way.

6. ☑ **B.** You can use the UPS if you are attaching only the server and it uses 700VA or less. Because the original server uses 700VA, it is likely that you will be able to use the UPS. ☒ **A** is incorrect because you do not know whether the UPS has enough capacity without knowing the wattage of the components you are adding. **C** is incorrect because only 800VA of the 1500 available have been consumed. **D** is incorrect because you do not want to exceed the 1500VA limit by attaching anything with more than 700VA.

7. ☑ **C.** You need to make certain that the location where the server will be placed has enough power and network terminations so that it can be plugged in, and enough space so that you won't have problems during your installation.
☒ **A, B,** and **D** are incorrect because the project description does not require scanners, coax cables, or Web server applications.

8. ☑ **C** and **D.** To verify that the Fibre Channel controller is compatible with NetWare 5, you would look on Novell's Web site for the latest compatibility information, and you would check the controller manufacturer's Web site to see if the manufacturer has compatibility information. ☒ **A** is incorrect because the NetWare 5 installation guide will not have information about a controller that was released after NetWare 5 was released. **B** is incorrect because a controller can be compatible with one NOS, such as Windows 2000, and not with another, such as NetWare, and the brother-in-law won't be able to give you good information.

9. ☑ **A** is correct because the heaviest piece of equipment, the UPS, is placed on the bottom and the monitor is at the top which is likely to be about eye-height.
☒ **B, C,** and **D** are all incorrect because the monitor is near the bottom for two of them, and the UPS is never on the bottom for any of them.

10. ☑ **D.** Once the server equipment has been delivered, you should verify that all of the components have arrived. In addition, you should check to make sure you have all the cables and that they have the appropriate connectors.
☒ **A** is incorrect because cabling should be installed before the server equipment arrives. **B** is incorrect because you would not need to test the UPS until you are in the process of installing the server. **C** is incorrect because you should have surveyed the site for the server's location before ordering the equipment. You would want to survey the location first to see if there are any special needs for the server to be placed in that location.

Installing Hardware Using ESD Best Practices

11. ☑ **C.** You should select a rack that has sides and a top to protect the equipment from dust. Dust buildup inside a server can cause an electro-static discharge which can damage the server components. Protecting the server reduces the likelihood of failure.

☒ **A** is incorrect because light is not a factor that would affect the server seriously. **B** is incorrect because decreasing ventilation causes more problems. **D** is incorrect because, even though you might want matching racks, that is not the only reason to obtain a rack with sides and top.

12. ☑ **B.** Thin Ethernet is a name given to one of the types of coaxial cables. Coax is a type of copper wiring where two conductors share a common axis.
☒ **A, C,** and **D** are incorrect because none of these types are coaxial cabling. Unshielded twisted pair is a series of pairs of wires twisted together with their own distinct plastic insulation, and encased in a plastic sheathing. Fiber optic is either glass or plastic light-conducting strands. Shielded twisted pair is similar to unshielded except that it is further encased in heavy nonconductive material, thus preventing electro-magnetic interference.

13. ☑ **A.** An online uninterruptible power supply (UPS) sits between a computer and the power. It acts as a battery in the event of a power failure and lets the server shut down properly.
☒ **B** is incorrect because a suppressor evens out the power that is received, but doesn't work during a power outage. **C** is incorrect because a subsystem holds disk drives for storage, not power equipment. **D** is incorrect because a noise filter will correct a noisy power line but will not function when the power has failed.

14. ☑ **C.** If the SCSI equipment does not function the way that you expect it to, you should check to make certain that the last SCSI device is terminated. Termination of the last device is required for SCSI equipment to work.
☒ **A** and **B** are incorrect because, although it is remotely possible that these are the problems, it is not as likely that the motherboard has a bad slot or that you didn't realize that the cables were wrong after connecting them. It is more likely that there is a problem with improper termination of the SCSI equipment. **C** is incorrect because the tape drives automatically share an IRQ under the SCSI controller—there is no possibility of an IRQ conflict.

15. ☑ **D.** A KVM switch will share a single keyboard, monitor, and mouse between multiple servers.
☒ **A, B,** and **C** are incorrect because none of these items will connect to a keyboard or share it out. A UPS will provide battery-operated power for backup in case of a power failure. A noise filter will combat dirty current by filtering that out. Ballast is used to provide heaviness to the bottom of a rack to prevent it from tumbling over.

16. ☑ **A.** A super video graphics adapter (SVGA) monitor is required to display more than 16 million colors and a 1280 by 1024 resolution. A 15-inch monitor will also fit into the rack.
☒ **B** is incorrect because an EGA monitor will not display 16 million colors, nor will it provide 1280 by 1024 resolution. **C** is incorrect because VGA monitors cannot provide a 1280 by 1024 resolution. **D** is incorrect because a 30-inch monitor will not fit into a rack.

17. ☑ **D.** A subsystem is an external housing that contains multiple disk drives. It is typically used for RAID arrays.

☒ **A, B,** and **C** are incorrect because a subsystem does not hold modems, network adapters, or tape drives.

18. ☑ **C.** A remote access server will require multiple modems, which can be housed in a modem rack.

☒ **A, B,** and **D** are incorrect because none of them are absolutely required for a functioning remote access server on a Fast Ethernet network.

19. ☑ **A.** Once you have completely assembled the server, you should power it on and verify that the components you just installed, such as the RAM, are recognized by the BIOS. This may involve accessing the BIOS directly or looking for the SCSI BIOS to recognize all the SCSI devices.

☒ **B, C,** and **D** are all incorrect because you should have completed each of these steps earlier in the process, before the server was completely assembled.

20. ☑ **D.** SCSI Wide allows up to 15 devices to be connected to a server.

☒ **A, B,** and **C** are incorrect because none of these will allow 15 devices to be connected.

LAB ANSWER

You can do all your research on the Internet. Most vendors have their equipment specifications posted online.

You will find that each Compaq 8500 will take up 7U of space by visiting http://www.compaq.com/products/servers/platforms/.

You will discover that the StorageWorks Enclosure takes up 3U of space by looking at this Web page: http://www.compaq.com/products/storageworks/enclosure4200/enc4200index.html.

You will find that the UPS takes up 3U of space by visiting this Web page: http://www.compaq.com/products/quickspecs/10255_na/10255_na.HTML.

To determine how much space you will need, add the following:

```
  2 * Compaq 8500 @ 7U = 14U
+ 1 Compaq Storageworks @3U = 3U
+ 1 Compaq 3000 UPS @3U = 3U
+ 1 power strip @1U = 1U
+ 1 keyboard shelf @1U = 1U
+ 1 KVM switch @2U = 2U
```

+ 1 monitor & shelf @10U = 10U
= total space needed = 34U.

Because the total space required is 34U, you cannot use a 22U height rack and must select the 42U rack.

Server+
COMPUTING TECHNOLOGY INDUSTRY ASSOCIATION

2

Configuration

Once your hardware has been assembled, your next step towards installing a server is to work on the firmware and the network operating system. This is the configuration stage. Firmware refers to the operating systems that are installed on chips in a system or component. The network operating system is the software that is loaded into memory from the storage system after the server boots up to share out network services and resources. Both of these systems need to be configured to function as you *intend* the server to function.

When you configure a server, you should follow the plan that you developed previously. This will ensure that the server has the correct size storage areas, boot partitions, and memory usage. It will ensure that the redundant features in your server hardware will perform correctly—either through balancing the load or by taking over upon failure of a primary device.

Installing and configuring the firmware and network operating system are highly sought after skills. You will find that your ability to perform these functions will give you an edge on the job.

CERTIFICATION OBJECTIVE 2.01

Checking and Upgrading BIOS/Firmware Levels

Firmware levels on the basic input/output system (BIOS) and other hardware within the computer must be maintained at the highest available revision. These revisions are created to correct bugs from previous versions and add new features. Often, an incompatibility with an operating system is quickly fixed by checking to ensure that the hardware is at its most current revision. Microsoft is very good about issuing a Hardware Compatibility List (HCL) that states what hardware at what firmware revision is compatible with the operating system (OS).

Recall that the BIOS is used to translate communications between devices in the computer. The BIOS is able to do this because it contains the basic instruction set for those devices. However, if you install a device with which the computer seems unable to communicate, you might need to upgrade or replace the existing BIOS.

One way to inform the BIOS of a new device is to access the computer's complementary metal oxide semiconductor (CMOS) settings and select the new device in the BIOS options. For example, if you upgrade the hard disk, you might need to inform the BIOS of its new type and capacity.

It is possible that the device is too new and therefore cannot be selected from the CMOS settings. For example, if you are using an old BIOS, you can't inform it of a new 10 gigabyte (GB) hard disk, because the BIOS simply won't allow you to enter or select that size. When this is the case, the BIOS itself (not just its options) must be upgraded.

When a BIOS cannot be flash upgraded, you can remove the BIOS chip and replace it with a new BIOS chip. If the BIOS chip cannot be upgraded, then you must consider replacing either the motherboard or the entire server. Usually this won't be an issue with a new server installation. You may run across it if you are installing a server on older hardware or if you have selected a server platform that is not a name brand.

Methods for Upgrading the BIOS

Flash BIOS chips can be electronically upgraded using a disk from the BIOS manufacturer. Turn the computer off, insert the manufacturer's floppy disk, and restart the computer. The disk contains a program that automatically "flashes" (updates) the BIOS so that it can recognize different hardware types or perform different functions than it could before. The BIOS retains the new information, so it has to be flashed only once.

Another way to upgrade the BIOS is to physically replace it with another. You will need to do this if the BIOS's manufacturer has stopped supporting that particular BIOS model or when it hasn't released a flash program with the options you need your BIOS to support. To physically replace the BIOS, locate the old BIOS chip and remove it with a chip puller. Orient the new BIOS in the same position that the old one used, then push it gently into the socket.

exam
ⓦatch

When you install a server, it nearly always needs a BIOS update before you install the network operating system. This is mainly because the original equipment manufacturer (OEM) has continued to develop new BIOS updates since the equipment was installed and shipped out. In addition, a network operating system may require the BIOS to communicate certain information to it and a manufacturer may create a second BIOS simply for that network operating system.

System Board

The BIOS on the system board is the first information that you will see flashing across the screen as the server boots up. It recognizes all the components in the server and loads their BIOSs, if there are any to load. To update the BIOS:

1. Document the version and date of the BIOS that is installed. If the BIOS version is not readily available while the server is booting up, access the BIOS using the keystrokes that it indicates (usually a function key, such as F2 or F9, or a set of keystrokes such as CTRL-ALT-INS) and view the BIOS version there. You should check the manufacturer's documentation for the correct key sequence if it is not displayed on the screen.

2. Visit the server OEM's Web site and find information about BIOS updates for the server.

3. Compare the version number and date of your server's BIOS to the latest BIOS version number and date available.

4. If there is a newer BIOS available, download it.

5. Follow the manufacturer's directions to install the new BIOS. Usually, there are steps to create a diskette, which you then use to boot up the server. After the BIOS has been updated, the directions usually direct you to remove the diskette and perform a hard reboot by turning the power switch off and back on again.

on the job

It can be fatal to the server if you interrupt a BIOS update in progress. Make certain that a power failure cannot cause any problems by using an uninterruptible power supply (UPS) and ensuring that all power plugs are securely placed in power outlets.

RAID

Possibly the biggest concern of any company today is ensuring that its data stays intact. Companies can lose millions of dollars if the data that drives their business is corrupted.

A technology called Redundant Array of Inexpensive Disks (RAID) minimizes the loss of data when problems occur with accessing data on a hard disk. RAID is a fault-tolerant disk configuration in which part of the physical storage contains redundant information about data stored on the disks. Standardized strategies of fault tolerance are categorized in RAID levels 0–5. Each level offers various mixes of performance, reliability, and cost. The redundant information enables regeneration of data if a disk or sector on a disk fails, or if access to a disk fails. RAID 0 has no redundant information and therefore provides no fault tolerance. Table 2-1 shows the common RAID levels.

TABLE 2-1	RAID Level	Description
	RAID 0	Disk striping
RAID Levels	RAID 1	Disk mirroring
	RAID 2	Disk striping across disks. Also maintains error correction codes across the disks.
	RAID 3	Same as level 2, except the error correction information is stored as parity information on one disk.
	RAID 4	Employs striping data in much larger blocks than in levels 2 and 3. Parity information is kept on a single disk.
	RAID 5	Disk striping with parity across multiple drives.

RAID array firmware updates are tricky. If the network operating system is installed on the RAID array already, the manufacturer will most likely require you to power down the server and run the firmware update through terminal emulation. Otherwise, you will probably update it using a bootable floppy disk. Either way, the process is dependent upon the manufacturer's requirements. As always, follow the manufacturer's directions carefully.

EXERCISE 2-1

Updating RAID Firmware through Terminal Emulation

1. Power down the server.

2. Connect a serial cable between the serial port on the RAID controller and a serial port on another computer, which you will use to run a VT100 session.

3. Boot up the other computer.

4. If you are using a Windows 9x, Windows NT 4.0, or Windows 2000 system, you should start HyperTerminal.

5. In the first dialog box in HyperTerminal, type a name for the terminal session and click OK.

6. In the second dialog box, click the Connect Using arrow and select the COM port for the serial port that the cable is connected to, as shown in Figure 2-1, and click OK.

FIGURE 2-1

Selecting a COM
port in
HyperTerminal

7. You are prompted for the port settings. Follow the manufacturer's directions for these settings. For example: 9600 baud, 8 bits, No Parity, 1 stop bit, XON/XOFF.

8. When you click OK to these settings, the session automatically opens the serial port and your next step is to activate the controller. There are one or more keystrokes required to do this, such as pressing the ESC key.

9. When activated, you should be able to compare the controller's firmware version to the one that you are planning to use in the upgrade process. Compare versions before beginning the update process to make certain you don't downgrade the controller's firmware!

10. Run the firmware flash utility program, and follow the manufacturer's directions to complete the RAID firmware upgrade. Because you are using a serial connection, the firmware update can take a long time to complete—sometimes over an hour. After completion, verify that the firmware version has changed, and then boot the server.

Controller

Most controllers are either fibre channel arbitrated loop (FC-AL) interfaces or small computer system interfaces (SCSIs). In either case, you may need to upgrade the controller's firmware. In most cases, you can update the SCSI BIOS using the same method that you use when updating the standard BIOS. Depending on the vendor, you may find that a particular vendor's updating process differs from other methods. Obtain the vendor's directions and follow them precisely.

FROM THE CLASSROOM

Troubleshooting a SCSI Controller

When you install hardware you are more likely to encounter technical problems than at any other time during the hardware's lifetime. If you do find a problem with your SCSI devices—for example, none of them work—you can follow some of these best practices.

The first thing that you need to do is check the termination. Devices at both ends of the SCSI cable need to be terminated. The device at one end happens to be the SCSI controller. If you have a SCSI controller that supports both internal and external devices, then termination could be active for the internal devices and not for the external devices. You may need to change jumpers or switches, or you may be required to change the termination through the SCSI firmware menus.

If your SCSI controller is connected to a RAID array, you can prevent future problems by using an external terminator at the end of the bus and disabling termination on the drives themselves. The reason for this is that if the terminated drive fails, then the SCSI bus will lose termination and the entire set of SCSI devices will fail. This may not be an issue for subsystems, however, because many of them automatically use external termination.

While you are looking over the physical termination of the SCSI devices, you should also check the SCSI cables. Not only should you inspect the pins, you should make certain each cable is firmly connected and that the cable is the correct type. SCSI cables should be less than 4.5 feet in length. If the cables are longer than that, you may have errors.

Next, you should determine whether you are using the latest version of the SCSI firmware. If you are not, you should load the latest version.

Finally, SCSI IDs may be in conflict. You should check to make certain that all SCSI devices have been assigned a unique ID. You should also check for loose jumpers or switches, because they can cause the ID to change and be in conflict.

—*Melissa Craft, MCSE, CCNA, Network+, MCNE, Citrix CCA*

Hard Disk

It is possible, that you may need to upgrade the firmware on the hard disks you install. Most server platforms support hot-pluggable drives that interface directly with a backplane of a storage system. The backplane then connects to a controller which will enable the hard disks to either be recognized as individual storage systems or configured into a RAID array.

Hard disk technology is constantly being updated. Not only is the storage capacity of the hard disks being increased, but the form factor of the disks is decreasing as well. Smaller hard disks take less space and allow for more storage space in a single server. Smaller servers allow you to fit more equipment in each rack. Therefore, the form factor of hard disks are becoming more compact, yet, curiously, have more available space.

Updating firmware is always performed according to the manufacturer's directions; if it is to be done successfully. Even so, there are some common themes in how the firmware updates are performed. The following Scenario & Solution questions will help guide you in making firmware update decisions.

SCENARIO & SOLUTION

What is the best way to update a Flash BIOS?	Boot the server with the manufacturer's Flash update utility on a bootable floppy diskette.
When should you downlevel a BIOS?	You should never take a BIOS to an older revision.
What should I do if I'm updating the disk subsystem's firmware and the manufacturer says to use a VT100 session?	VT100 refers to a common type of terminal emulation. You will need to connect a computer to the port on the subsystem, most likely a serial port, and then run a terminal emulation program, such as HyperTerminal.

CERTIFICATION OBJECTIVE 2.02

Configuring RAID

When you configure RAID, you are organizing multiple disks so that they can work together to reduce read-write time (disk I/O), increase performance, provide redundancy, and provide fault tolerance. A disk array is a collection of disks that appear to work as a single storage unit, or a set of storage units, called volumes. These volumes look and act exactly like a hard disk to the network operating system (NOS). When the NOS writes data to the array, that data is spread across several of the disks. The I/O is shared among the disks, improving performance. A sample RAID array configuration is shown in Figure 2-2.

FIGURE 2-2   RAID configuration sample

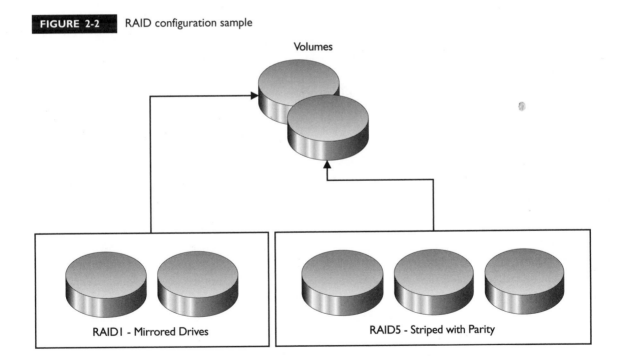

Volumes

RAID1 - Mirrored Drives

RAID5 - Striped with Parity

Once you have established your RAID configuration plan, the process of configuring the RAID array is dependent upon the vendor's configuration utility. You first need to boot up the configuration utility. Some vendors will let you install the configuration utility on a partition of a hard disk. Others can only be run from a diskette or bootable CD-ROM. Next, you should verify that each hard disk is identified by the utility, because most configuration utilities include some troubleshooting information. If there is a faulty hard disk, you should remove the hard disk physically from the casing, examine the pins to determine if there is any apparent physical problem, and if not, re-insert it to see if the hard disk simply was not placed in the casing securely in the first place. If the hard disk is still not recognized, you should replace it with a working hard disk before going further.

Your next task is to use the RAID configuration utility to select the hard disks that will be placed in your selected RAID configuration. You will also use the utility to configure a spare hard disk, if you have determined that a hot spare is needed. After selecting and configuring your RAID array, you next need to save the configuration. At this point, the configuration utility will write your configuration changes to the hard disks. This can take a couple minutes to complete. After this is done, you may reboot the server and begin installing the network operating system of your choice.

exam
Ⓦatch

You use a RAID array configuration utility to create a RAID array before you begin installing the network operating system.

Mirroring

One of the more common ways to back up your data is to create a mirrored copy of the data on another disk. The mirroring system utilizes a code that duplicates everything written on one hard disk to another hard disk, making them identical. Figure 2-3 shows an example of two disks mirrored.

The best way to incorporate disk mirroring is at the hardware level with what is known as an array controller. An array controller is an interface card that connects to both hard disks using a SCSI cable and has the configuration information on the logical disk that is created. Today's network operating systems also allow for software-level mirroring of two hard disks. Windows NT and Novell both offer a software-level mirroring configuration.

Of all the types of RAID, you will find that RAID 1, or mirroring, and RAID 5 are the most often implemented. When you configure RAID 1, you install two disks and either one or two controllers. When you use two controllers, it is called *duplexing*.

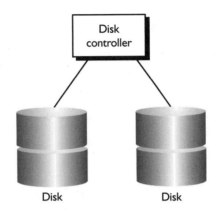

Most network operating systems allow you to configure the operating system to
write data to both disks simultaneously. This is done at a software level. You can
also configure a RAID array controller to configure a mirrored set of disks as well.

Duplexing

Duplexing ensures fault tolerance not just with your data, but also with your disk
controller. With traditional mirroring there is one disk controller. If the controller
fails then the server is down until that component is replaced. Duplexing gives you a
second controller. There can be a mirror with this type of configuration, but each
drive is connected to its own controller. If a controller fails, you still have an intact
configuration. This can also speed up response time when writing to disk. Figure 2-4
shows an example of disk duplexing with the multiple controllers.

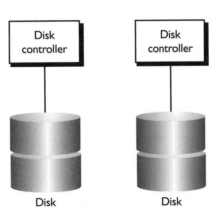

Striping (with and without Parity)

Striping is becoming more and more popular. The striping of data is a way to spread the data out across the disks. This can improve performance. To do striping properly you need a minimum of three hard disks. Three or more different hard disks all acting to get a piece of the data will make the I/O (input/output) faster. Striping also gives you the option of adding parity to the drive set.

RAID 5, also known as disk striping with parity, provides the performance of RAID 0 but with fault tolerance. Disk striping consists of data being written in stripes across a volume that has been created from areas of free space. These areas are all the same size and spread over an array of 3 to 32 disks. The primary benefit of striping is that disk I/O is split between disks, improving performance, although improvements do not exceed the I/O capabilities of the disk controllers. Fault tolerance functionality is added to disk striping with the addition of parity information in one of the stripes. The parity stripe is the exclusive OR (XOR) of all the data values for the data stripes in the stripe. If no disks in the stripe set with parity have failed, the new parity for a write can be calculated without having to read the corresponding stripes from the other data disks.

With stripe set with parity, disk utilization increases as the number of disks increases, thus providing a lower cost per megabyte. Disk read operations can occur simultaneously, resulting in better disk performance. But the system or boot partition cannot be on a stripe set with parity. Also, if a disk that is part of the stripe set fails, read operations for data are substantially slower than that of a single disk. Because a stripe set with parity works with the operating system, it requires more memory than a mirror set.

Again, some vendors sell disk subsystems that implement RAID technology completely within the hardware. Some of these hardware implementations support hot swapping of disks, which enables you to replace a failed disk while the computer is still running.

Windows NT and Windows 2000 provide software support for two fault-tolerant disk configurations: mirroring and stripe sets with parity. The Disk Administrator utility configures mirror sets and stripe sets with parity and regenerates the volume when a disk fails. Here are some points to consider:

- Hardware fault tolerance is faster.

- Software fault tolerance is less expensive.

- The capability to swap a failed disk while the system is still running is only available with hardware fault-tolerant equipment.

When you configure RAID 5, you install at least three disks and connect them to a SCSI array controller. Then you run the RAID array controller configuration utility to select the drives and establish the array. Figure 2-5 displays how data is striped across three disks in a RAID 5 configuration.

EXERCISE 2-2

Configuring RAID 5

This exercise assumes that you are using a subsystem to house a RAID array.

1. Install the SCSI RAID array controller in the server.

2. Install the drives in the subsystem.

3. Attach the cables between the array controller and the subsystem.

4. Obtain the RAID configuration application and run it on the server. In most cases, you can boot the utility from a bootable floppy disk on the server.

5. Verify that all the drives can be seen in the configuration utility. Most configuration utilities have a graphical user interface. You should be able to point and click the drives to select them, and then add them to one or more RAID volumes. For RAID 5, you must select at least three of the drives in your subsystem and add them to a single RAID 5 volume.

6. When complete, save the configuration and exit the utility.

7. To test the RAID volume, boot the server with a DOS floppy disk and run FDISK. You should see the volume recognized as a single hard disk, but not yet formatted.

FIGURE 2-5

RAID 5 data and parity striping

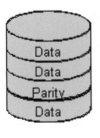
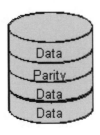
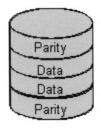

Stripe 1
Stripe 2
Stripe 3
Stripe 4

CERTIFICATION OBJECTIVE 2.03

Installing the Network Operating System

Every network operating system has its own unique installation process. Performing a NetWare installation is different from Windows 2000, whereas performing a UNIX installation is different from either of the first two. Even though each NOS has its own installation process, they each require similar actions from the installer.

Before You Begin

Preparation is key to a successful installation. You should know what kind of information you may encounter while performing the installation, and be prepared with the answers. The information that you should have includes the following:

- **Names**   Computer NetBIOS name, server Internetwork Packet Exchange (IPX) name, Domain Name System (DNS) host name, domain name, directory service name, workgroup name, administrative account name, Simple Network Management Protocol (SNMP) community name.

- **Passwords**   Power on password, administrative account password, guest account password, anonymous password, directory service restore password.

- **Network information**   IPX network address, Internet Protocol (IP) address, DNS server names and addresses, SNMP server addresses, Dynamic Host Configuration Protocol (DHCP) server addresses, default gateway addresses, Windows Internet Name Service (WINS) addresses, whether to use NetBIOS over TCP/IP, IP Security information.

- **Hardware information**   Interrupt requests (IRQs), Direct Memory Access (DMA), component configuration.

- **Services**   What services to install on the server, file and printer sharing configuration.

- **Verification process**   A method of verifying that the server is functioning online.

You will also need to collect the items you need to install. These include the NOS installation software (either the CD-ROM or a network location that includes the installation files), license files, drivers, updates, and service packs.

Installation Process

Installation follows a general progression of phases. Depending on the NOS you are installing, you may have to enter more information in some phases than for a different NOS. These phases are:

- **Disk Preparation** The RAID array, or hard disk, is configured—the disk is partitioned and a file system applied. In some NOSs, like NetWare, you can configure software-based mirroring. In other NOSs, such as Windows 2000, you must wait until after the NOS is fully installed before you configure software-based disk configuration options. Disk preparation is sometimes incorporated into the NOS's Setup program; otherwise, you must prepare the disk separately using FDISK and FORMAT commands.

- **File Copying** The network operating system files are copied to the disk.

- **Hardware Configuration** The installer is asked for information that configures the network operating system to work with the hardware.

- **Network Configuration** The installer is asked for information that configures the network operating system to function on the network.

- **Administrative Configuration** The installer configures file sharing, printer sharing, and other services.

exam
ⓦatch

Before files are copied to the disk, the disk must be partitioned and formatted with a file system. This may be part of the NOS Setup program, or it must be performed separately prior to running Setup.

EXERCISE 2-3

Installing NetWare 5.1

NetWare is unique in that it does not load directly upon server boot up. Instead, NetWare loads after a version of DOS. This means that with NetWare, you must configure a partition (no more than 1GB is necessary, and usually less than 100MB is required) that boots DOS. Then you can install NetWare on the remaining free space on the hard disk. This exercise assumes that you have already installed DOS. You will need to have the NetWare 5.1 installation CD-ROM and a NetWare 5.1 licensing disk.

1. Insert the CD-ROM.

2. Type **D:\Install.bat** where D: is the drive letter of your CD-ROM, or allow your server to boot from the CD-ROM.

3. Select a language. This language will be used for your installation.

4. Accept the license agreement. If you do not accept the license agreement, the installation will end.

5. Start disk partitioning. If there are existing NetWare partitions, they should be recognized and you will be asked if you want to use them for the installation. If there are no NetWare partitions, you will be prompted to configure one or more of them.

6. Create NetWare volumes. You must have at least one SYS: volume. However, it is recommended that you create two or more volumes. The SYS volume contains system files. You should create a second volume to contain data.

7. Files copy to disk. If you press ALT-ESC, you can watch the NetWare Loadable Modules (NLMs) as they are being loaded.

8. Provide the server name and address. Type a *file server name* and either accept the suggested internal IPX address number, or provide a new one.

9. Select DOS directory. This directory on the DOS partition holds the NetWare kernel, SERVER.EXE, and memory managers and disk drivers.

10. Select server settings. You may select either Novell Directory Services (NDS) version 7 or NDS version 8. Use NDS7 if the NDS tree consists of both NetWare 4.*x* and 5.*x* servers. Otherwise, you may use NDS8.

11. Load server at reboot. If you want the server to automatically reboot itself, you should select Yes to this question.

12. Configure Server SET parameters. You are able to configure the SET parameters that optimize how the server functions.

13. Select regional settings. Select the language and keyboard that the server will use after it is installed.

14. Files are copied to SYS:SYSTEM. The server now creates the SYS volume and various required subdirectories, then files are copied from the CD-ROM to the SYS volume, with most being placed in SYS:SYSTEM.

15. Configure device drivers. You will now review the device drivers that the installation process has detected. If there are changes required, or new drivers required, you can select them here.

16. Configure network boards. This option displays the detected network adapters and allows you to configure the hardware settings for them.

17. Java Virtual Machine (JVM) loads. Files for the graphical user interface run by Java are copied and loaded into memory. The GUI will begin.

18. Mount all volumes. You can now mount any volumes other than SYS, which is already mounted.

19. Specify protocol information. Select and configure the protocols, whether IP or IPX or both.

20. Specify Domain Name System (DNS) parameters. Type the DNS server information where this server will look to for host-to-IP address mapping information.

21. Install NetWare Directory Service (NDS). Select a tree, or create a new one. Type the names of the organization and organizational units that lead to where the server should exist in the tree.

22. Select the Admin password. Type the password for Admin.

23. Provide server licensing. Place the licensing disk in the drive, or point to a path that has licensing information in .NLF files.

24. Select components. Of the optional services available for NetWare, you can select and install them now.

25. Finish. You will be prompted to finish, there will be more file copying, and the server will need to be rebooted.

Configuring the Network

There are two parts to configuring the network. The first part is to configure the network adapter to be able to access the network media. This means that you should have the correct driver for the network adapter, and that you have configured the correct parameters for it.

The second part is to configure the protocols so that the server can communicate with other hosts on the internetwork. Although there are a lot of protocols available, there is only one that is used universally: TCP/IP. TCP/IP is prevalent in most networks because of its use on the Internet. You will need to know what protocols are used on your network, and which ones are required for the server you are installing. You can determine this by finding out what systems must access your server, and vice versa, and which protocols those systems are using.

TCP/IP is a protocol stack that can be routed around an internetwork, as is NetWare's IPX/SPX. NetBEUI, on the other hand, cannot be routed. Because NetBEUI is unroutable, you are faced with limitations if you select it. IPX/SPX is a protocol stack that was originally proprietary to Novell, although some other network operating systems can interoperate with it. TCP/IP requires an individual IP address for each host on the network. The IP address can be delivered to a computer by a DHCP server, or it can be permanently assigned to the server. In addition, you must configure the network adapter to look for a DNS server and define policies for IPSec, if you are using IPSec. Most servers should be setup with a static IP address. You want to make sure that your server resources are always in the same place.

Verifying Network Connectivity

You can verify network connectivity by communicating with another host on the network. This process can be done in different ways on different network operating systems. For example, you could simply open the My Network Places on a Windows 2000 Server and begin browsing through the network, or you could run Internet Explorer and connect to a Web site somewhere. Either of these actions will verify that the network is connected.

If you are using TCP/IP, one of the utilities that you can use when verifying network connectivity is PING. PING stands for Packet Internet Groper. All network operating systems that use TCP/IP have some form of PING available to them. PING is a TCP/IP utility. To test whether you can contact other network hosts, type PING *ip_address* where ip_address is the IP address of another host on the internetwork. You can also type PING *dns_hostname*. The screen will show a result similar to Figure 2-6. If the network cannot be reached, the response will show a timeout. PING sends out an Internet Control Message Protocol (ICMP) echo to the IP address. The destination host responds, unless the echo message does not reach it.

exam
⚙️atch
PING is a utility that is included with the TCP/IP protocol stack. It can verify network connectivity by communicating with another network host and receiving a response.

CERTIFICATION OBJECTIVE 2.04

Configuring External Peripherals

As the days of serial and parallel go to the wayside, the future is Universal Serial Bus (USB) technology. This USB technology allows the user to add multiple external peripherals, ranging from printers, hard disks, modems, scanners, to just about anything, to a single port without the conflicts associated with serial and parallel connections of the past. When configuring a legacy serial peripheral you must

FIGURE 2-6	
PING response	

```
C:\WINNT\System32\cmd.exe                                          _ □ ×
Microsoft Windows 2000 [Version 5.00.2195]
(C) Copyright 1985-2000 Microsoft Corp.

C:\>ping www.novell.com

Pinging www.novell.com [64.209.188.136] with 32 bytes of data:

Reply from 64.209.188.136: bytes=32 time=140ms TTL=53
Reply from 64.209.188.136: bytes=32 time=120ms TTL=53
Reply from 64.209.188.136: bytes=32 time=120ms TTL=53
Reply from 64.209.188.136: bytes=32 time=121ms TTL=53

Ping statistics for 64.209.188.136:
    Packets: Sent = 4, Received = 4, Lost = 0 (0% loss),
Approximate round trip times in milli-seconds:
    Minimum = 120ms, Maximum =  140ms, Average =  125ms

C:\>
```

configure it to either be on COM port 1, 2, 3, or 4. The COM ports are addressed so that COM1 and COM3 share IRQ4, and COM2 and COM4 share IRQ3. This means that if you have a modem plugged into and configured on COM1 you will have problems if you have a mouse configured on COM3.

Parallel peripherals have their own configuration problems. Many of them are not happy unless they are the only item connected to the parallel port. This means that on most systems that come with only one parallel port you can have only one parallel peripheral connected at one time.

The configuration of the external peripherals consists of a software driver that resides on the system and possibly some additional configuration of the peripheral through the item itself. Once the peripheral is configured it will rarely need to be reconfigured.

Uninterruptible Power Supply

An Uninterruptible Power Supply (UPS) is one form of power protection that you can install for your server. You should know the differences between the functions of these devices: UPSs provide backup power, suppressors smooth out surges and spikes, and noise filters remove electromagnetic interference (EMI). A UPS can also come with an integrated suppressor or noise filter.

Refer to the following Scenario & Solution to test your knowledge of power protection devices before continuing in the chapter.

SCENARIO & SOLUTION

Which device can absorb excess power?	A suppressor.
What can I use to remove EMI from the power source?	A noise filter.
What should I use to provide backup battery power?	A UPS.
How can I prevent problems from blackouts, surges, and EMI, all at the same time?	Get a UPS that has an integrated suppressor and noise filter.

Some operating systems come equipped with applications that can manage a UPS. Even so, the manufacturer usually provides its own utility to manage the UPS. To use all the features of the UPS, you should use the manufacturer's utility. To use the manufacturer's utility, you should obtain the software from the manufacturer then install it on the server. Once the software is installed, it will either detect the type of UPS, or you will configure the type of UPS that you are using. Then, you may browse through the various options—such as triggering alerts, length of time to remain on battery backup, and shutdown alternatives—and select the ones that make sense for your installation.

EXERCISE 2-4

Configuring a UPS on a Windows 2000 Server

1. On the Windows 2000 Server, click Start | Settings | Control Panel | Power Options.

2. Click the UPS tab.

3. Click the Select button to select the manufacturer and model of your UPS and the port to which it is connected.

4. Click Finish to close the selection dialog box.

5. Click the Configure button to enable notifications, set the number of minutes before alarms are triggered, and specify the actions that the server will take in the event of a power failure.

6. Click OK.

External Drive Subsystems

External drive subsystems can be managed from the network operating system by using the manufacturer's utility. Even though the subsystem's initial configuration is completed before the server's operating system installation, you may need to make further changes. The utility is provided for managing the subsystem, performing configuration changes on the drives within the subsystem, and for alerting the administrator in the case of an error.

The manufacturer's software may include both a monitoring agent and a notification utility. The agent will monitor the subsystem and trigger alerts if there are problems detected with it. The notification utility will send pager alerts, local alerts, or e-mail alerts in the event of a problem. After installing the manufacturer's utility, you should configure it to alert you in case of the error conditions that make the most sense for your environment.

CERTIFICATION OBJECTIVE 2.05

Installing Network Operating System Updates to Design Specification

Network operating systems are complex. They consist of millions of lines of code and are expected to support both native and third-party applications on a variety of hardware. As you can probably guess, between millions of lines of software code, and a nearly infinite variety of hardware and application combinations, there are a multitude of opportunities for the network operating system to produce an error.

Given the impossibility of being able to find and fix every problem, manufacturers depend upon service packs and hotfixes to repair operating system faults. Both service packs and hotfixes are created by teams of people who are tasked with repairing problems with the network operating systems. Service packs generally include generic code changes, bug fixes, driver updates, and additional utilities. Hotfixes are intended to fix a single, specific error for a single, specific combination of NOS, hardware, or applications. Hotfixes are usually created when there is a major problem for a very specific configuration.

on the **Job**

When you install a new server, you should almost always update the system to the latest service pack before placing it into production. Service packs provide fixes that will affect almost all server configurations. Before installing the service pack, check online to verify that there are no major issues with it (some service packs have been known to cause more problems than they resolve). You should also check for available hotfixes and determine if any hotfixes are applicable to your server configuration. If so, apply the hotfix. Otherwise, you shouldn't apply the hotfix because it will probably be a waste of time.

EXERCISE 2-5

Installing a Service Pack on Windows 2000

You must be connected to the Internet to perform this exercise.

1. Log on the Windows 2000 server as an administrator.

2. Double-click Internet Explorer.

3. Type **windowsupdate.Microsoft.com** in the browser window.

4. Click the Product Updates option.

5. Select the check box for Windows 2000 Service Pack. You may receive a notice that you will not be able to install other product updates if you install the service pack. Click OK to this message.

6. Click Download.

7. Click Start Download.

8. The installation portion of the Service Pack will download and let you select options, such as whether to allow the service pack to be uninstalled.

9. After the options are selected, files will copy from the Internet to the server, and then you will be prompted to reboot.

10. Reboot the server, log on as an administrator and verify that the server is functioning properly.

Updating Manufacturer-Specific Drivers

One of the things you need to do after installing your server is to update the drivers to the latest ones available from the manufacturer. By doing this, you will be able to use all the features of the hardware components in your server. For example, if you have a new video card and the network operating system doesn't include the driver for that video card, you can still run the server in VGA compatible mode. But this only gives you 16 colors and 640 x 480 resolution, which is not optimal. What you can do is update the video driver with the manufacturer's latest and receive full color and resolution options. The devices you should consider updating are:

- Video
- Modem
- Network interface card
- Printer

New versions of the preceding devices are being developed all the time. You should also consider updating device drivers for any other adapters that you have placed in the server. Additionally, you can check the server OEM's Web site for updated device drivers for the integrated components in the server. You may have a device for which the network operating system does not include drivers. Or, the manufacturer may have created a driver that functions better than the one that is included in the network operating system, or on the diskettes accompanying the component.

After you update the device driver for any internal component, you should verify that the driver update was successful. You can do this by:

- Rebooting the server and verifying that the operating system boots correctly. Perform a hard boot, if possible.

- View the hardware information for the device driver to ensure that the driver was installed.

■ Verify network connectivity for network adapter updates. Verify modem connectivity for modem driver updates. Verify that you can print to the printer for printer driver updates. Verify video capabilities for video driver updates.

exam
ⓦatch
Video drivers commonly need updating after the server's network operating system is installed so that you can gain full functionality of the video adapter. This holds true for network adapters, modems, and printers.

EXERCISE 2-6

Updating the Video Driver on Windows 2000

1. Download the new video adapter driver from the manufacturer's Web site.

2. Right-click My Computer and select Properties from the pop-up menu.

3. Click the Hardware tab.

4. Click the Hardware Wizard button.

5. The Add/Remove Hardware Wizard begins. Click Next.

6. Select Add/Troubleshoot a device and click Next.

7. Windows 2000 will scan for new hardware. It may suggest a new driver for the device, but if not, you should select Add a New Device and click Next.

8. The hardware wizard will offer to scan for new hardware again. Click No, I Want to Select the Hardware from a List and click Next.

9. Select Display adapters from the list and click Next.

10. Because you are using a manufacturer's driver, click the Have Disk button and point to the location where the video driver exists. When the driver appears in the window, click Next.

11. After the driver has installed, reboot the server and verify that the driver functions correctly.

Installing Service Tools

When you have one server, there is not much you need to do to manage the server. You check on the server regularly to make certain it is performing well. If the server goes down, then you can go straight to it and start working on the problem. Life is not so simple when you have many servers.

Multiple servers need to have as much active monitoring as a single server, but it isn't cost effective to have a server administrator for every server, or even every ten servers. To monitor a lot of servers, you need to install and configure an automated system for network management.

SNMP

Network management has become a crucial aspect of the network administrator's job. The need to monitor, view, and configure devices on the network has led to the introduction of many management systems that make an administrator's day-to-day work much easier to manage. At the same time, administrators get better control of their environments and provide better uptime of network services.

When looking at the framework of any good management system, we will see a system built on five components:

- Platform
- Application
- Agent
- Element
- Protocol

Although we will focus primarily on the protocol portion of this architecture, we need to define each of these components individually.

At the highest level, we have the management platform. This can be defined as the system on which the management application and agent will function.

The next two components are the agent and the application. A management application is a program that provides us with the interface to communicate with an agent. Compaq Insight Manager is a perfect example of a management application. A management agent is a software application that resides on the managed device. This component defines the information made available to the management application.

Compaq Insight Agent is an example of a management agent. Understanding the difference between these two components is a very important aspect of the SNMP architecture. It is important to note that the management agent is not always installed on a computer. Many network devices, such as routers and switches, run a form of an SNMP-configurable agent.

The objects that a management application makes available are called elements. The most common elements on a network are servers, workstations, printers, and network devices such as routers, bridges, and switches. Vendors can also define elements that are subsystems of these devices. For example, not only can a server be defined as an element, but devices such as the processor, hard disks, network adapters, and drive controllers can also be defined as elements.

The protocol provides the means for the agent and the application to communicate with one another. As its name implies, SNMP is an example of a management protocol. SNMP has emerged as the industry standard and is used as the protocol of most standards-based management platforms.

SNMP defines a set of commands that a management application uses to retrieve or change the values made available by a management agent. In simpler terms, it provides a means of communication between a device that we want to manage and the system we want to use to manage it.

To perform its function as defined earlier, SNMP uses a set of commands (called SET and GET) to communicate with information made available to it by the management agent. The management agent contains all of the parameters that are available to the SNMP client. The information made available can consist of performance thresholds, error conditions, or even device configurations. It is limited only by what information has been defined in the management agent. Another way SNMP communicates is by using a trap. A trap is SNMP's means of notifying or alerting us of a specific condition.

SNMP communicates over the TCP/IP network protocol. This allows for SNMP's use across many network systems and devices. SNMP is used in the industry for everything from configuring and monitoring routers to the performance of a hard disk array on a Windows NT server. Because of its simplicity and capabilities, SNMP has also been selected as the protocol on which many vendors have based their management solutions.

The ability to take a proactive approach to managing your network is vital to your success on the job. The use of a management application allows you to monitor your network, even a very large network, with great ease and flexibility. In many cases, it even allows you to become aware of a problem before it becomes a big problem. For example, finding out that your processor is consistently exceeding a threshold, your hard disk is about to fail, or your network switch is encountering a significant number of dropped packets is especially useful to providing a reliable network to your end users. Implementing a network management solution is well worth the cost, if only because of the improved confidence it will bring to the staff supporting it.

SET

The SET command is the first of two commands used by the management application. This command is used to perform the write function of the SNMP protocol. It is used to change, or set, the parameters available in the management agent.

As shown in Figure 2-7, the SET is actually a two-way communication. The first is the actual SET command itself. This portion contains the information to be set on the management agent. The second portion is in the form of a response trap. This trap provides the management application with an acknowledgment that the SET was completed successfully.

Let's say we wanted to define a threshold on our processor utilization. From our management application, we could define a processor utilization of 80 percent. The management application would then send a SET to the management agent configuring the threshold on the managed device.

FIGURE 2-7

Two-way
communication of
a SET command

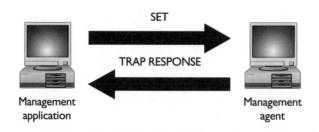

Management
application

Management
agent

We will use this processor utilization example throughout this chapter. This will provide us with a common example for many of the different features and functions of SNMP.

GET

The GET command should be considered the read function of SNMP. When a management application needs to retrieve information from the agent, it uses the GET command to do so.

As with the SET command, the GET is obviously a two-way process, as shown in Figure 2-8. This time, instead of simply an acknowledgment, the response trap contains the information requested by the GET.

Keeping with our earlier example, let's say we want to retrieve a managed device's current processor utilization. From our management application, we could query the current processor utilization on the managed device. The application would then send a GET to the managed device. The managed device's agent would process this command and return the information to your application interface, where you would then see the results.

Traps

You have already seen two situations that rely on the use of a trap. Both the SET and GET use traps to function. There is one more use of the trap that we have not yet discussed. SNMP agents also have the capability to send an unsolicited trap to a management application based on defined, event-driven criteria.

To understand this aspect of SNMP, let's first discuss the concept of event-driven criteria. A simple way of looking at it is that when a specific event occurs, a specific action should take place. On the job as a Compaq-certified professional, this event could be anything from a software application error to the failure of a managed

FIGURE 2-8

Two-way communication of the GET command

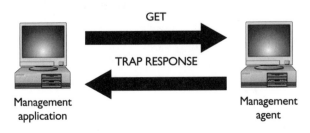

hardware device, such as a hard disk. In the world of SNMP, the course of action taken is usually to send a message, or trap.

Let's take another look at our CPU utilization threshold, which we discussed earlier. We have seen how we can set this threshold using our management application and the SET command. We have also seen how using the GET command allows us to retrieve the managed object's current CPU utilization. Both of these are nice features to have, but they require us to take action to use any of the information available. We are made aware of a potential problem only if we happen to check the status at the exact moment the problem exists. The trap provides us with a means of being alerted at the moment our threshold is exceeded. When the CPU utilization exceeds 80 percent, the threshold is crossed. The management agent sends the trap to the predetermined locations. Most management applications are capable of making us aware of the trap by a variety of methods. They support methods as basic as logging the trap, to more complex e-mail notifications.

Unlike the SET/GET commands, a trap is a one-way communication process, as shown in Figure 2-9. This means that when the agent sends the trap, it has no way of knowing whether it was received. Providing that the trap destinations are defined correctly and the network is correctly configured and operating, this should not pose too many problems for you.

The destination to which the trap is sent is determined by the SNMP configuration. In Windows NT, the trap destinations are configured within the SNMP Service configuration under Network Properties. Trap destinations are the IP address or network name of the machine to receive the traps. Management agents, such as Compaq Insight Agents, will then use this configuration to determine the trap recipients. Most often, the traps will be sent to the management application. From here, the traps will be recorded and processed accordingly.

FIGURE 2-9

One-way communication of a trap

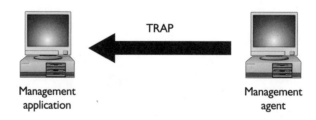

TRAP

Management application

Management agent

on the job

The use of SNMP traps is perhaps one of the most important aspects of an SNMP-based management platform. Often a trap will alert you to a problem and allow you to fix it before you get that panicked call, or that line of angry end users begins to form outside your office. Many management platforms allow you to configure trap forwarding. This allows you to configure your management application to notify you of a potential problem through e-mail or a page.

Community Names

By now, you are starting to see some of the power that SNMP brings to you for managing resources on your network. However, you are also probably starting to see that you don't want just anybody to have access to the managed objects that you use SNMP to control. Community names are SNMP's security solution.

A good way to look at a community name is as a password. When configuring SNMP, you provide a list of community names that will have access to the managed objects on the system. Then, the same community name must be supplied in the management application. If the community names match, the application will be permitted to communicate with the management agent. If the names do not match, then access will be denied and no exchange of information will take place. An important detail to note here is that community names are case-sensitive. This is often the cause of many communication problems between the management agent and the management application, for those new to the process.

By default, many applications and systems use the community name of *public*. It is recommended that you not only use a different name for your systems, but also remove the *public* community name from the configuration. Because the community name is like a password, the community name you select should be something that would be difficult for outsiders to guess. If users were able to determine your community name, they would have access to whatever capabilities that the management agent provided. The rebooting of a remote computer is an example of a feature available to a server running Compaq Insight Agents that you would probably not want to make available to your general user base. (Note: The Remote Reboot option is not enabled by default, but provides an example of a feature available to SNMP that would require some security measure to be in place.)

Care should be given when choosing the community name. Because there are many different types of devices that can utilize SNMP, each with its own set of management capabilities, you may want to use more than one community name. For example, you probably don't want to use the same community name for your network switches or routers as you do for your Windows NT servers. This will provide an additional layer of security between the different devices in your enterprise, while also allowing more separation in the management tools that you use.

The SNMP configuration offers one additional layer of security. For each community name provided, two potential security settings exist. The first option is READ and the second is READ/CREATE (read/write). This configuration option allows you to use separate levels of security for your environment. For example, if you wanted a group of individuals only to be able to view the elements in your network, you could create one community string that was set up with READ permission only. You would then want to configure the management application to use this restricted community name. Then you could use a second community string for those users whom you want to allow to modify the elements provided by the management agent.

on the job

In many larger network enterprises, the roles and responsibilities of support are spread across many different groups. These groups are often of varying experience and expertise and their responsibilities are often different. For example, many organizations use a tiered-support approach, with responsibility and expertise increasing with each tier. Because of this, it is often necessary to provide one group a more restricted level of control than the one above it. Using two community names gives you the flexibility you need to accomplish this. For example, if your organization has a network operations group responsible for frontline support, you may need them to have read control to your network management solution, but you don't want them to be able to change a configuration. You also may have a network administration group that needs to have the ability to configure the management platform. With the use of two community names, along with the appropriate security settings, you can be sure that everyone has the resources they need to perform their jobs, without the fear that someone has too much control.

Requirements for SNMP Usage

SNMP requirements are rather simple. To function, it needs only a network to communicate across, an application that utilizes SNMP, and an agent that defines the objects (elements) to be managed.

With Windows NT, the SNMP service can be installed through the Network Properties interface on the Services tab. Once installed, there are only a few configuration requirements you have to meet before SNMP will be ready for use.

First, upon installing the service, you will be asked to provide the community names that you want to use. Because you may be using multiple applications, each with its own community string, you are able to enter more than one. As noted, community names are case-sensitive, so be sure to enter each one correctly. An incorrectly entered community name will result in the failure of SNMP application communication.

The second configuration option you will need to enter is the SNMP trap destination. This option tells the SNMP service where to send traps that the management agent wants to send. This way, when the CPU threshold that we have configured is crossed, the trap will know where to go so that we are made aware of the situation and can look into the problem.

It is important to note that both the SNMP service and the TCP/IP protocol must be installed for Compaq Insight Manager to function. In fact, besides the hardware requirements required by Compaq Insight Manager, these are the only two common requirements that need to be present for this management platform to function.

Management Agents

So far, we have referred to an agent primarily as a software application that has been installed on a managed device. However, because these devices are not always capable of running applications (such as in the case of a network bridge), agents can also reside in the device's firmware. Any device that is going to be managed must be defined as an element within the management agent.

The agent code defines all of the parameters available to the management system. They can either be written into a device's software driver or incorporated as a separate application. This separate application will communicate with the device either through its driver or firmware to provide these parameters to the management system. Compaq has chosen to use the separate-application approach in their management agent software.

The easiest way to look at the role the management agent plays in your management system is as a middleman. Basically, the agent provides the interface between your management application and the element you are managing.

MIB

So far in this chapter, we have examined the role the management agent plays. We have discussed the fact that the agent provides the definition of a managed element to the application. What we haven't discussed is how these definitions are formatted. Before we do, let's spell out exactly what information these definitions contain. The definition contains the properties of the object defined, the functions that are supported against the object, and the information that can be retrieved on the object. We refer to these definitions as Management Information Base (MIB).

Now let's take this information and look at it in a way we can understand. To do this, we will return to our CPU utilization example. In this example, the CPU represents our element. The CPU's utilization represents an example of a property, as would the CPU utilization threshold that we have been working with. Using the SET to define the threshold is an example of a function that can be performed against the object. The CPU's utilization or trap are examples of information that can be obtained or retrieved from the object.

The CPU utilization model is an easy way to look at a MIB, but it is very simple in its structure. Many managed elements actually contain hundreds or even thousands of pieces of information. To handle this amount of information, a structured format is needed to make the MIB manageable. It is equally important to ensure that the definitions used by one organization will never interfere or conflict with those of another. To accomplish this, the collection of information is organized in a hierarchical structure, where it is made available to the network management protocol (SNMP). This structure is in a complex, tree format that is a based on an equally complex numbering system. Each MIB is represented by a numeric object identifier. This tree is actually a global entity with each vendor (or on a larger scale, each organization) being given its own branch and numbering range to use. This is done very much the same way IP addressing is structured.

Backup Software

Most network operating systems will include a backup application. However, this backup application nearly always lacks the options that an enterprise server needs to have for backup. Therefore, most organizations install a third-party backup application on the server. There are generally two methods of doing this:

- Install a backup software application for use only on one server
- Install a backup agent to be used

When you run a backup on a single server, you have the backup application and the tape backup device running on the same server. When you backup multiple servers, you can save costs by pooling resources on one server. The server would run a backup application, be attached to a backup storage system, and be able to connect to all the other servers running the backup agents and back up their data systematically over the network. Third-party backup software usually is available in an "enterprise" version with backup agents.

exam
ⓦatch

Backup software can be installed as a full software application, or as an agent. You install the full software application on a server that is directly attached to a backup device. This is the source server. You install agents on servers that do not have backup devices. These are target servers. The source server can then back up the target servers over the network, according to your backup software configuration and scheduling.

EXERCISE 2-7

Configuring Windows 2000 Backup

1. Click Start | Programs | Accessories | System Tools | Backup.

2. Click Backup Wizard.

3. Click Next at the Welcome screen.

4. Select Back up Everything on My Computer, as shown in Figure 2-10 and click Next.

5. The following screen lets you select where to place the backup file. If your tape drive is not recognized, you will not be given any options in this dialog box. Otherwise, click the arrow on the Backup Media Type drop-down box and select Tape.

6. If you want, provide a new name for the backup file and then click Next.

7. You will be shown a summary screen. Click the Advanced button.

8. In the advanced features, select Copy from the Select the Type of Backup Operation to Perform drop-down list. This will not mark the files as backed up so it won't interrupt any existing backup schedule for your server. Click Next.

9. You can select data verification and hardware compression in the next dialog box. A best practice is to verify all backups, so select that check box, and click Next.

10. The following dialog box will let you overwrite the data on the backup media, or to append the data to it. Select the option to Replace the Data on the Media with This Backup and click Next.

11. Type a label for the backup and the media, then click Next.

12. Because we are running this backup a single time, you should select Now in the When to Back Up dialog box. In production, you should schedule your backups. If you were scheduling the backup, you would select Later in this dialog box, and specify the dates and times to run the backup job. Click Next and then click Finish.

System Monitoring Agents

Network management systems are gaining importance due to the growing sizes of networks. In a distributed internetwork, a central network management system can monitor servers in multiple locations if those servers have been installed with system monitoring agents.

FIGURE 2-10

Backup Wizard
data selection in
Windows 2000

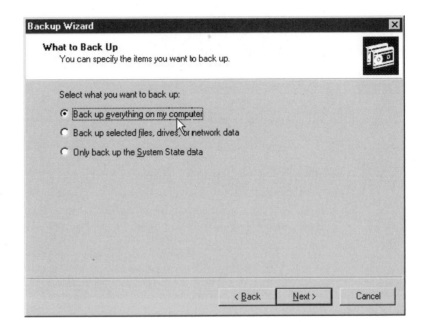

When you install your server, you should also install the agents for the network management system in use on your internetwork. Once the installation is complete, you can test the installation from the network management station. You should be able to locate the new server and verify its information from that station. If the internetwork is large, you may find yourself depending on another person to verify the new server for you.

Event Logs

During any point in time after the server installation, you can check the event logs to verify event messages. Most event logs are simply files of text written to the hard disk. Almost always, an event log is saved in the partition that is most easily available if the network operating system didn't boot. This is usually the system partition for the server. In the case of NetWare, you can find log information stored on the DOS partition.

CERTIFICATION OBJECTIVE 2.08

Performing Server Baselines

One of the best practices for server management is performing server baselines. A server baseline documents the status of the server's performance as a snapshot. You can document these snapshots on a periodic basis to keep track of the way the server is functioning. Server baselines can reveal problems before a failure takes the server down. For example, if you documented a server's baseline and found that the server's CPU performance had suddenly spiked from a steady 30 percent utilization to a 90 percent utilization, you can then discover what was causing the CPU spike and prevent a possible server failure.

 on the *Job*

Server baselines should be performed periodically. You can compare the baselines to previous baselines to determine whether performance has degenerated.

It is challenging to decide what aspects of the server's performance you want to include in your baseline. You should include information about the following components' performance:

- Processor
- Memory
- Disk
- Network

EXERCISE 2-8

Using Windows 2000 Performance Monitor to Create a Graphic Baseline

1. Click Start | Settings | Control Panel | Administrative Tools | Performance.

2. Right-click the graph (right-side pane) and select Add counters from the pop-up menu.

3. Select Processor from the Performance Object drop-down box.

4. Select %Processor time from the Select Counters list, then click Add. Repeat this process for %Privileged time and % User time. The %Privileged time displays the amount of time used for the operating system and drivers, whereas the %User time displays the amount of processor utilized for applications.

5. Allow the graph to fill up, then right-click the graph and select Save As. Type a name for the graph and click Save.

6. When you look at the graph later, you will see something similar to Figure 2-11.

 **FIGURE 2-11** Processor snapshot baseline

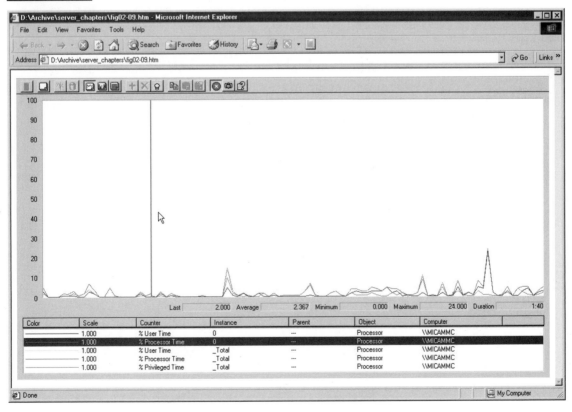

7. If you want to expand the baseline, you can also add the following counters:

- **System: % Total Processor Time**   To show the averaged value that the processors are being used to execute non-idle threads. This will provide a solid utilization value for the CPU.

- **Memory: Pages/sec**   To view how memory is being used overall. If this is higher than 75 percent, then you may not have enough RAM.

- **Logical Disk: %Free Space**   To see if free space on critical partitions, especially that of the system partition, is dwindling. If so, you should move files to other partitions.

- **Logical Disk: %Disk Time**   To see if the disk is running excessive I/O operations. Excessive would be 80 percent or more for long periods of time. When the disk I/O becomes excessive, you may look at the memory to see if there are too many pages swapped to disk, which in turn means that you need more RAM. Or you can look at upgrading the controller and disks themselves because they are too slow to keep up with demand.

- **Physical Disk: Average Disk Queue Length**   To measure the actual performance of the disk. A disk should average three or less. If it averages four or more for a long period of time, you should consider upgrading the disk.

- **Network Interface: Output Queue Length**   To measure the actual transmission performance of the adapter. If the output queue averages three or higher over a long period of time, there may be a problem with the network or the adapter itself.

Performing a server baseline is a tedious process. Refer to the following Scenario & Solution for some guidelines that can assist you.

SCENARIO & SOLUTION

I'm installing a Novell NetWare server and I don't know where to find information.	NetWare includes a utility called MONITOR.NLM. If you run Monitor, you should see parameters for all aspects of the memory, disk, network, and processor
Can I perform the server baseline before I run the service pack update?	You should not perform a server baseline until after the server has been updated with the service pack. Service packs include a number of fixes that can affect the server's performance.
Should I store my server baseline electronically on the server?	You should keep a server baseline that is stored in a location other than the server. That way, should the server fail, you can access the information about it.

CERTIFICATION OBJECTIVE 2.09

Documenting the Configuration

If you keep records of every server within your network, you will find that managing those servers is much easier. The time to start is at the time of server installation. To document your configuration, you should include all aspects of the server:

- Processor
- Motherboard
- System BIOS
- Cabinet
- Asset Tag
- Cooling
- Components and parameters

■ Peripherals and parameters

■ Applications installed

■ Admin/Recovery Passwords

EXERCISE 2-9

Documenting Your Configuration

1. Write down the information about your server that is presented in Table 2-2.

2. Start the server, access the BIOS, and write down the information in Table 2-3.

TABLE 2-2	Component	Example	Your Server
Server Information for Exercise 2-9	Hardware	Compaq Proliant 8500R	
	Cabinet	Rack mount, 4 external bays, 8 expansion ports	
	Cooling	4 internal fans	
	Location	Building 1, room 2, rack #8	
	Floppy	3.5 floppy diskette drive	
	CD-ROM	24x CD-ROM drive using IDE	
	Monitor	15" SVGA NEC monitor	
	Hard disks	4 8GB Hot swap 1" drives	
	Keyboard	US Standard PS/2 keyboard	
	Mouse	PS/2 mouse	
	Ports	1 enhanced parallel port 2 serial 16550 UART 2 USB ports	
	UPS	None	
	Asset Tag #	123456789-UP	

TABLE 2-3	Component	Example	Your Server
BIOS Information for Exercise 2-9	Processor	Intel Pentium III 500 MHz 512K Cache	
	BIOS	AMI	
	Motherboard	133 MHz Bus	
	Memory	128MB PC100 SDRAM	
	Video	Generic SVGA	
	NIC	3Com 10/100 Mbps Fast Ethernet, uses IRQ3	
	NOS	Windows 2000	
	Service packs	Service Pack 1	
	BIOS password	None	

3. Exit the BIOS and boot the operating system, then write down the information in Table 2-4.

TABLE 2-4	Component	Example	Your Server
Information after Existing BIOS for Exercise 2-9	Administrator's password	Dezsoe!883A	
	SNMP	Community—NotPublic	
	DNS	Primary 123.34.45.56 Secondary 133.34.45.56	
	WINS	Not configured	
	Server Name	NoApples.mydomain.local	
	Applications	SQL Server 2000 IIS Application Center 2000	

CERTIFICATION SUMMARY

Installing a network operating system requires you to have a viable and preconfigured server hardware. To get to that point, you must check the BIOS and upgrade it to the latest level. Additionally, you should upgrade all the firmware in the server, including that of the SCSI controllers and RAID subsystems.

After firmware is completed, your next step is to perform the network operating system installation. This process differs from one network operating system to another. After the network operating system is installed, you can update drivers to the latest from the manufacturer and begin installing service management tools.

The final steps in the installation process are based on documentation. You should perform a server baseline for component performance and then fully document the configuration. This process completes the main steps for installing a network server.

TWO-MINUTE DRILL

Here are some of the key points from each certification objective in Chapter 2.

Checking and Upgrading BIOS/Firmware Levels

❏ Microsoft's Hardware Compatibility List (HCL) lists the minimum firmware level that the hardware should be at for compatibility with their network operating systems.

❏ System BIOSs are typically updated using a bootable floppy diskette.

Configuring RAID

❏ RAID 5, striping with parity, and RAID 1, mirroring, are two of the most common RAID configurations.

❏ The RAID array controller's configuration utility is used to create a RAID array.

Installing the Network Operating System

❏ Before you begin the installation, you should have configuration information available for the server components.

❏ During the server installation, you need to configure the network adapter to be able to access the media and communicate with other hosts on the internetwork.

Configuring External Peripherals

❏ Some network operating systems include support for UPSs, but to access all the peripheral's capabilities, you should install the manufacturer's utility.

❏ Subsystem management utilities can monitor the subsystem for error conditions and trigger an alert.

Installing Network Operating System Updates to Design Specifications

❏ You should update a newly installed network server to the latest service pack before placing it into production.

❏ Service packs contain generic code fixes, operating system enhancements, and new drivers.

Updating Manufacturer Specific Drivers

❏ You should update the drivers for the video adapter, network adapter, printers, and modems.

❏ Manufacturers are constantly updating drivers for hardware components.

Installing Service Tools

❏ A management agent is a software application that resides on the managed device.

❏ SNMP defines a set of commands that a management application uses to retrieve or change the values made available by a management agent.

Performing Server Baselines

❏ A server baseline documents the status of the server's performance as a snapshot.

❏ You should include processor, memory, disk, and network performance in your baseline.

Documenting the Configuration

❏ You should document the components of your server, as well as the parameters.

❏ The server documentation should contain all aspects of the server, from the cabinet type to the administrative passwords.

SELF TEST

The following questions will help you measure your understanding of the material presented in this chapter. Read all of the choices carefully, as there may be more than one correct answer. Choose all correct answers for each question.

Checking and Upgrading BIOS/Firmware Levels

1. What is used to translate communications between devices in the server?

    A. MIB

    B. SNMP

    C. RAID

    D. BIOS

2. How must you upgrade a Flash BIOS?

    A. Boot the computer with a floppy disk that includes the manufacturer's update utility.

    B. Run a configuration utility to select drives and add them to a volume.

    C. From the network operating system, access the BIOS and run FLASH.EXE.

    D. Open the computer, remove the chips, and replace them with new ones.

3. You are getting ready to upgrade the Flash BIOS on your server. Your computer's BIOS is version F188823xEE dated 4/11/2001. Which of the following BIOSs should you download from the manufacturer?

    A. version F188823xEE dated 4/11/2001

    B. version F188823xEF dated 5/28/2001

    C. version H18LLLxJJ dated 4/12/2001

    D. version F188823xED dated 2/22/2001

Configuring RAID

4. Which of the following will not be provided by RAID?

    A. reduce read-write time (disk I/O)

    B. reduce performance

    C. provide redundancy

    D. provide fault tolerance

5. Which are the most common forms of RAID configurations? (Choose all that apply.)

   A. RAID 1

   B. RAID 6

   C. RAID 4

   D. RAID 5

6. You are configuring a RAID 5 array. Of the seven disks you have installed in your subsystem, how many can you include in your RAID 5 array? (Choose all that apply.)

   A. 8

   B. 2

   C. 3

   D. 7

Installing the Network Operating System

7. You have just completed the server hardware assembly, the firmware updates, and the hardware RAID configuration for your server. What is the next step towards installation of the network operating system?

   A. Run setup from the NOS CD-ROM.

   B. Configure the network adapter.

   C. Set up a UPS box.

   D. Gather information that you will need during installation.

8. You are installing a network operating system. Before files copy to the server's storage system, what must occur?

   A. Administrative configuration of the operating system

   B. Network adapter configuration

   C. Disk preparation

   D. Application installation

9. You have just installed and configured a Linux server that is intended to be used on the Internet as a Web host. The IP address of your server is 123.45.67.89. Your favorite Web site uses an IP address of 207.16.88.21 You want to verify that the network is connected. What do you do?

   A. Type PING 123.45.67.89 at a command prompt.

B. Open My Network Places and browse the network.

C. Type SERVERS at a command prompt.

D. Type PING 207.16.88.21 at a command prompt.

Configuring External Peripherals

10. Which device will enable its battery when it detects a lapse in electrical power?

    A. Suppressor

    B. Standby Power System

    C. Noise filter

    D. Disk subsystem

11. You have installed a Windows 2000 server that is attached to a UPS. You want to configure triggers for the UPS but you cannot find any software from the UPS's manufacturer, not in with the equipment box nor online. What do you do?

    A. Leave the system as is.

    B. Call the manufacturer.

    C. Configure the UPS.NLM on the server.

    D. Configure the UPS tab in the Control Panel | Power utility.

Installing Network Operating System Updates to Design Specifications

12. Which of the following is a piece of code that is developed to fix a specific problem for a specific hardware and software configuration?

    A. Hotfix

    B. MIB

    C. Service pack

    D. Setup

13. You have just completed installing a server. It is a Compaq 8500R with Windows 2000 and an APC UPS. You have located the following hotfixes and service packs. Which should you install? (Choose all that apply.)

    A. Service Pack 1

    B. Hotfix for Dell servers using APC UPS and Windows 2000

C. Hotfix for Compaq 8500R attached to a Compaq UPS and using Windows 2000

D. Hotfix for all APC UPS attached to Windows 2000 Servers

Updating Manufacturer-Specific Drivers

14. You've installed your server, updated the service pack, and have logged on for the first time. The screen shown is 640 x 480 and the colors are odd. You try to change the video configuration and find that the server has defaulted to VGA compatible mode. What do you do?

    A. Nothing, this is how the server should be.

    B. Reinstall the network operating system.

    C. Install the latest service pack.

    D. Download and install the latest video drivers from the manufacturer.

15. During the server installation, you find that the network adapter was not detected and that the drivers for it were not included in the network operating system. This was not unexpected because you have one of the latest Gigabyte Ethernet adapters made. What should you do?

    A. Download the latest driver from the manufacturer and install it.

    B. Change out the network adapter for a different one.

    C. Install two separate adapters.

    D. Configure the Infrared device on the server.

Installing Service Tools

16. Which two commands does simple network management protocol use? (Choose all that apply.)

    A. SET

    B. GET

    C. MIB

    D. SNMP

17. You have a tape backup device attached to your server's SCSI controller. Which of the following should you do to begin running backups from this server and three others that do not have tape backup devices?

    A. Configure the server's minimal backup software.

    B. Install a third-party backup agent on your server.

C. Download a driver from the backup device manufacturer's Web site.

D. Install a third-party backup software application on your server.

Performing Server Baselines

18. Your server has been running for two months. All of the sudden, users are complaining of poor performance. What can you look at to determine what's wrong?

A. Tape backups

B. RAID configuration

C. Server baseline

D. Device drivers

19. Which of the following items in your server baseline comparison can help you find out whether you need more RAM?

A. Pages per second

B. Free space

C. Network output queue

D. Disk queue

Documenting the Configuration

20. Which of the following items should you include in the server documentation? (Choose all that apply.)

A. Processor

B. Location of the server

C. Names of the users

D. BIOS revision

LAB QUESTION

This exercise requires you to have a Windows 2000 Server. You have just completed a Windows 2000 server installation, including installing service packs and critical update packages. Your next task is to perform a server baseline on the processor, the disk, the network, and the memory. How do you proceed?

SELF TEST ANSWERS

Checking and Upgrading BIOS/Firmware Levels

1. ☑ **D.** The BIOS, or basic input/output system, translates communications between devices in the server.

   ☒ **A**, MIB, is incorrect because Management Information Bases define the elements that are managed on a computer at a software level. **B**, SNMP, is incorrect because Simple Network Management Protocol is a protocol that communicates management information across a network. **C**, RAID, is incorrect because Redundant Array of Inexpensive Disks is a set of disks that are configured to work together as a single storage unit.

2. ☑ **A.** To upgrade a Flash BIOS, you should boot the computer with a floppy disk that contains the manufacturer's BIOS update utility.

   ☒ **B** is incorrect because that is the process for configuring a RAID array. **C** is incorrect because there is no such process for BIOS upgrades. **D** is incorrect because it is a process that was used before Flash BIOSs were developed.

3. ☑ **B.** You should download version F188823xEF dated 5/28/2001. This is the latest version, and it postdates the version already installed on your server.

   ☒ **A** is incorrect because that is the version already installed on your server. **C** is incorrect because the version number is very different and the date is not as late as the correct option. **D** is incorrect because this version predates the one already installed on your server.

Configuring RAID

4. ☑ **B.** RAID will not reduce the performance of your system.

   ☒ **A, C,** and **D** are incorrect because RAID does reduce the disk I/O, it does provide redundancy, and it does provide fault tolerance.

5. ☑ **A** and **D.** RAID 1, mirroring, and RAID 5, disk striping with parity, are the two most common configurations for RAID.

   ☒ **B** and **C** are incorrect because RAID 6 and RAID 4 are rarely implemented.

6. ☑ **C** and **D.** You can include anywhere between 3 and 32 disks in a RAID 5 array.

   ☒ **A** is incorrect because you do not have 8 disks. **B** is incorrect because you must have a minimum of 3 disks for a RAID 5 array.

Installing the Network Operating System

7. ☑ **D.** Your next step is to gather the information that you will need during the operating system installation.

☒ **A** is incorrect because you should gather the information before you run setup. **B** is incorrect because you should configure the network adapter after running setup. **C** is incorrect because you should already have a UPS ready.

8. ☑ **C.** Disk preparation must occur before files copy to the disk. During disk preparation, the disk is partitioned and a file system is applied.

☒ **A, B,** and **D** are incorrect because all of these actions occur after files are copied to the disk during the network operating system installation.

9. ☑ **D.** You will type PING 207.16.88.21 at a command prompt. This will echo a response from your favorite Web site if both hosts are online on the network.

☒ **A** is incorrect because you would be pinging your own server, and not testing connectivity across the network. **B** is incorrect because My Network Places is a Windows 2000 icon. **C** is incorrect because SERVERS is a NetWare command.

Configuring External Peripherals

10. ☑ **B.** A standby power system (SPS) is a type of battery backup that enables its battery after a lapse of electrical power is detected. This may cause a short length of time where power is not available, however, and a UPS is a better selection.

☒ **A,** a suppressor, is incorrect because it absorbs power surges. **C** is incorrect because a noise filter filters out the electromagnetic interference in the power cable. **D** is incorrect because a disk subsystem does not provide a standby battery backup for a server.

11. ☑ **D.** You can configure the UPS tab in Control Panel. This is located in the Power icon and will allow you to configure alerts and actions to take upon loss of power.

☒ **A** is incorrect because that would not enable the UPS to function correctly. **B** is incorrect because, although you may call the manufacturer to update the server later, you do have the options available in the operating system. **C** is incorrect because UPS.NLM is not a Windows 2000 Server program, it works on NetWare.

Installing Network Operating System Updates to Design Specifications

12. ☑ **A.** A hotfix is a piece of code that is generated to fix a specific problem for a specific hardware and software configuration.

☒ **B** is incorrect because a MIB defines elements of a managed object. **C** is incorrect because a service pack contains many bug fixes, new options, and new device drivers that apply to a wide variety of configurations. **D** is incorrect because setup is usually an installation program.

13. ☑ **A** and **D**. You would install the latest service pack, which is Service Pack 1. And you would install the hotfix for all APC UPSs that are attached to Windows 2000 Servers.
☒ **B** and **C** are incorrect because you are not using a Dell server nor are you using a Compaq UPS.

Updating Manufacturer-Specific Drivers

14. ☑ **D**. You should download and install the latest video drivers from the manufacturer.
☒ **A** is incorrect because your video adapter should support SVGA. **B** is incorrect because the drivers should have been installed upon the video adapter detection. **C** is incorrect because you already completed the service pack update.

15. ☑ **A**. You should download the latest driver from the manufacturer's Web site and install it and configure it. Then you should verify network connectivity.
☒ **B**, **C**, and **D** are incorrect because none of these actions will enable the Gigabyte Ethernet adapter to function.

Installing Service Tools

16. ☑ **A** and **B**. Simple Network Management Protocol (SNMP) uses SET and GET to perform write and read functions.
☒ **C** is incorrect because MIB contains information and is not a command. **D** is incorrect because SNMP is a management protocol.

17. ☑ **D**. You should install a third-party backup software application on your server. Then you should install backup agents on the other servers to back up all four servers.
☒ **A** is incorrect because minimal backup software included in a network operating system will not be able to back up more than the local server. **B** is incorrect because the backup agent should not be installed on the server that has a tape backup device attached to it. **C** is incorrect because a driver will not be able to perform backups.

Performing Server Baselines

18. ☑ **C**. You can refer to the original server baseline and compare it to the current server baseline performance. From there, you can determine what component is performing poorly and take steps towards optimizing the server.

☒ **A, B,** and **D** are incorrect because none of these items will provide information that will help you determine the cause of performance problems.

19. ☑ **A.** Pages per second measures RAM performance. When this item increases, there may be a need for more RAM.
☒ **B** is incorrect. Free space is used to determine whether there is sufficient space on the disk. **C** is incorrect because network output queue is used to determine the network adapter's performance. **D** is incorrect because the disk queue is used to determine how well the disk is performing.

Documenting the Configuration

20. ☑ **A, B,** and **D.** You will want to document all aspects of the server installation that may affect its performance, including the processor, the location of the server, and its BIOS revision.
☒ **C** is incorrect because you do not need to document the names of the users (unless you really want to) because the names of the users do not affect the usage of the server at present or in the future. The number of users may make a difference to server performance, as well as their usage patterns.

LAB ANSWER

1. First, click Start | Programs | Administrative Tools | Performance.

2. Right-click the graph and select Add Counters from the pop-up menu.

3. Processor is the default object, so you may add those first. In the Select Counters from list, click %Processor Time and make certain to select the All instances radio button to capture all the processors, then click Add. Repeat this process for %Privileged Time and %User Time and add those to the graph.

4. Click the Performance Object arrow and select PhysicalDisk. Select the %DiskTime counter for all instances and click Add. Repeat this for %Read Time and %Write Time and Average Disk Queue Length.

5. Click the Performance Object arrow and select IP. From the Select Counters from list, add Datagrams/sec, Fragment Re-assembly failures, and Fragmentation failures. Click the Performance Object arrow and select Network Interface. From the Select Counters from list, add Bytes total/sec for each interface, Output Queue Length, Packets Outbound Errors, and Packets Received Errors.

6. Click the Performance Object arrow and select Memory. From the Select Counters from list, add Available Bytes, Cache Bytes, and Page Faults/sec.

7. Click the Close button to display the graph. Allow the graph to complete for each item. Right-click the graph and select Save As. You may save the data as a Web page or as a report.

Server+

COMPUTING TECHNOLOGY INDUSTRY ASSOCIATION

3

Increasing Productivity

W ith today's server hardware, taking advantage of a machine's upgrade potential is critical to maximizing the Return on Investment (ROI). With the price of memory, CPUs, and hard disks plummeting, upgrading servers is a very cost-effective way to maintain a server's performance level without doing a "forklift upgrade." The myriad of options available in the different types of memory, CPUs, and hard drives can present problems when upgrade time arrives. Each server has a Hardware Compatibility List (HCL) that lists the specific types of components with which the server is compatible.

This chapter will cover the processes needed to decide when, how, and with what to upgrade servers. It will cover memory questions such as the differences between Extended Data Out (EDO), Error-Correcting Code (ECC), Memory Interleaving, Buffered, Unbuffered, and Registered architectures. It will also cover hard drive types such as Integrated Drive Electronics (IDE), Advanced Technology Attachment (ATA), AT Attachment Packet Interface (ATAPI), and small computer system interface (SCSI), as well as hard drive configurations such as Master/Slave and Redundant Array of Inexpensive Disks (RAID). It will also discuss the different types of CPUs and their configurations such as single CPU and Symmetric Multiprocessing (SMP).

CERTIFICATION OBJECTIVE 3.01

Adding Processors

Adding or changing processors can be a very effective way to extend the life cycle of existing servers. Most servers have the capability to support faster single processors or multiple processors. Most servers support one, two, or four processors, whereas some support up to 16. Those supporting more than four CPUs usually require custom drivers or even specialized versions of the operating system to function.

Verifying Compatibility on a Single Processor Upgrade

Processor architectures include many different speeds per design. Upgrading a CPU can be very easy if you are upgrading within the same processor family. These types of upgrades usually involve no more than a physical replacement. Depending upon the motherboard, the new CPU could be recognized automatically or the motherboard may require jumpers to be changed to accommodate the new speed by utilizing a frequency selection and a multiplier. See Table 3-1 for a list of possible frequencies and multipliers.

If changing from one processor architecture to another, verify that the new processor will be compatible with the motherboard by visiting the motherboard manufacturer's Web site and consulting the processor compatibility matrix. The motherboard may have a Slot1 CPU connector, which will support designs from at least two different architectures, but not necessarily all speeds from both architectures. The voltage requirements must also be taken into consideration, as different CPUs use varying voltages, and some CPUs require specific voltage regulator modules be installed along with the new CPU.

Verifying Speed and Cache Matching

When installing additional CPUs for SMP, all the CPUs must match each other both in speed and installed on-board cache to achieve optimal performance.

TABLE 3-1	Frequency	Multiplier
Common Frequencies and multipliers. Combine these in a pair that will equal your CPU's desired frequency.	66.8	1.5
	68.5	2
	83.3	2.5
	100	3
	103	3.5
	112	4
	117	4.5
	124	5
	129	5.5
	133.3	6
	138	6.5
	143	7
	148	8
	153	

Multiprocessor servers require that all installed CPUs be the same speed and be clocked with the same parameters. Also, to achieve the best performance, all CPUs must have the same amount of on-board cache. Cache memory comes in four sizes: 256KB, 512KB, 1024KB and 2048KB.

on the
job

Ensure when adding additional CPUs that the new CPU comes with a voltage regulator that it is the same revision as the regulator for the other CPU. Some motherboards require that all regulators be the same revision level.

Cache memory is a small amount of very fast static random access memory (SRAM) that resides between the CPU and the main memory. There are two kinds of cache memory: Primary and Secondary.

- **Primary**   L1 or Level 1 cache is very small (4KB to 16KB) and built directly in the CPU.

- **Secondary**   L2 or Level 2 is external to the CPU but sometimes on the same chip. It is very fast, operating from 12ns to 25ns and ranges in size from 256KB to 2048KB.

Sometimes Level 2 cache is on the motherboard and may be upgradeable. If it uses parity it requires a chip called TAG RAM. The TAG RAM helps to locate the data inside the cache and is also responsible for delaying data transfer from cache to main memory.

Within cache, there are two architectures for writing data: Write-Back and Write-Through.

- **Write-Back**   Changes are not copied into main memory until necessary.

- **Write-Through**   Data writes occur simultaneously to the cache and the main memory. Write-through cache is faster than write-back but may cause data loss if power fails.

There are two methods of reading data:

- **Look-Aside**   Look-aside caches mean that the cache sits on the same bus as the main memory and is accessed at the same time. Because the cache sits on the same bus, it is limited to the speed of memory. It has faster response times to cache miss cycles, a lower cost, and is fast for standalone applications.

■ **Look-Through**   In this architecture the cache sits in serial with the system memory and the CPU, requiring the CPU to look-through to the RAM. It reduces the system bus utilization, allows system concurrence, completes write operations in zero wait-states, and has higher performance in systems with multiple bus masters. A request to main memory will only be made if there is a cache miss.

Performing BIOS Upgrade

The basic input/output system (BIOS) is used to translate communications between devices in the computer. The BIOS is able to do this because it contains the basic instruction set for those devices. However, if you install a device with which the computer seems unable to communicate, you might need to upgrade or replace the existing BIOS.

When to Upgrade the BIOS

One way to inform the BIOS of a new device is to access the computer's complementary metal oxide semiconductor (CMOS) settings and select the new device in the BIOS options. For example, if you upgrade the hard drive, you might need to inform the BIOS of its new type and capacity.

In some cases, however, the device might be so much newer than the BIOS that it cannot be selected from the CMOS settings. For example, if you are using an old BIOS, you can't inform it of a new 10GB hard drive, because the BIOS simply won't allow you to enter or select that size. When this is the case, the BIOS itself (not just its options) must be upgraded.

Methods for Upgrading the BIOS

Flash BIOS chips can be electronically upgraded using a disk from the BIOS manufacturer. Turn the computer off, insert the manufacturer's floppy disk, and restart the computer. The disk contains a program that automatically "flashes" (updates) the BIOS so that it can recognize different hardware types or perform different functions than it could before. The BIOS retains the new information, so it has to be flashed only once.

Another way to upgrade the BIOS is to physically replace it with another. You will need to do this if the BIOS's manufacturer has stopped supporting that particular BIOS model or when it simply hasn't released a flash program with the options you need your BIOS to support. To physically replace the BIOS, locate the old BIOS chip and remove it with a chip puller. Orient the new BIOS in the same position that the old one used, then push it gently into the socket.

exam
ⓦatch

Be very familiar with the steps to upgrade a BIOS.

Performing an OS Upgrade to Support Multiprocessors

There are two types of multiprocessing: Symmetric and Asymmetric. Asymmetric processing reserves one CPU for system tasks and one for application execution. This results in lost performance when there are many system processes but few application processes and vice versa. Symmetric Multiprocessing (SMP) is the more common type used today. SMP allows any free processor to execute requested instructions; thus there is no lost performance. SMP works best when the operating system (OS) and applications are coded to take advantage of SMP by using multithreaded processes. If the application does not take advantage of SMP directly, a performance increase can still be achieved by running multiple instances of one application, or multiple applications, as each application will be assigned to a new CPU.

Most operating systems will recognize multiple CPUs if they are present during the installation, but may not recognize additional processors if they are installed after the OS. Some OSs have license requirements when upgrading to additional processors. Consult the OS documentation and license agreements to verify the requirements and costs of adding processors. Some OS versions also have limits to the number of CPUs they can support, so ensure that the correct version of the OS is installed.

SCENARIO & SOLUTION

Read through the following Scenario & Solution and see if you can answer some basic questions.	
What are the different types of level 2 cache?	Write-back and write-through.
What is the first thing you do to flash upgrade a BIOS?	Boot to a floppy disk containing the new image.
Which multiprocessing architecture is more efficient?	Symmetric Multiprocessing. It distributes the processing load more evenly across the available CPU.

EXERCISE 3-1

Upgrading Windows NT to Multiprocessing

1. Right-click My Computer and select Properties.

2. Choose the Hardware tab and click the Device Manager button.

3. Expand the Computer branch and record the CPU type listed.

4. Right-click the computer type listed and choose Properties.

5. Select the Drivers tab, select the Update Driver button, and click Next to continue.

6. Select Display a List of Known Drivers for This Device, and then click the Show All Hardware radio button.

7. Choose the correct computer type or click Have Disk if the server has a driver disk for multiprocessor support. Click Next, Finish, and then reboot your server. Note: Perform a full backup of the server before performing this or any change to your system.

Using an Upgrade Checklist

Before upgrading, follow a checklist to ensure all steps are considered and all resources are available to make the upgrade go smoothly. This is especially critical when working with production equipment to ensure the upgrade is completed on time and is successful so the device may be placed back into production with no loss of uptime. The following are some of the items that should be on your upgrade checklist:

■ Locate and obtain the latest drivers, OS service packs, and patches.

■ Review FAQs and instructions.

■ Test and conduct a Pilot.

■ Schedule downtime if needed.

■ Use ESD (electrostatic discharge) best practices by using an ESD wrist strap.

- Confirm the OS recognizes the upgrade.
- Review the settings and baseline the new system.
- Document all procedures.

CERTIFICATION OBJECTIVE 3.02

Adding Hard Drives

Most computers use Integrated Drive Electronics (IDE) or AT Attachment (ATA) hard and CD-ROM drive systems. The relationship between IDE and ATA is that IDE drives are built using the ATA body of standards. The terms are therefore used interchangeably. The IDE family includes IDE and Enhanced IDE (EIDE) drives. Other drives based on the ATA standards include ATAPI (typically associated with CD-ROM drives), Fast-ATA, and Ultra-ATA. Because IDE drives are built on ATA technology, the term *IDE* is often used to refer to any non-SCSI drive type (SCSI systems are discussed later in the chapter).

Because IDE drives are standardized, they can usually be recognized by the computer's BIOS. In the simplest cases, all that is needed to make a hard drive or a CD-ROM drive functional is to physically install it in the computer. However, some configurations are more complex. The following sections describe alternative drive installations, including how to configure and install multiple drives in a single system.

Master/Slave Configurations

The hard drive or CD-ROM drive controller's function is to receive commands to the drive and control the action of the drive itself. The technology incorporated in IDE and ATA devices allows one controller to take over the function of more than one drive. This means that you can install up to two drives on a single ribbon cable. This setup is called a *master/slave configuration* because one drive's controller directs the activities of both drives. It is important to note here that most computer systems can support a mixture of IDE and ATA drives.

on the **Job**

After adding hard drives ensure that adequate airflow is present. High-speed hard drives can create great amounts of heat and the Mean Time Between Failure (MTBF) will be greatly reduced.

To create a master/slave configuration, follow the steps in Exercise 3-2.

EXERCISE 3-2

Installing Master and Slave Hard Drives

1. Determine which drive will be the master.

2. Locate the master/slave jumpers, which can be found on the bottom of the drive or, more commonly, on the end by the power and ribbon cable connectors. In Figure 3-1, the jumpers are located to the left of the power connector and the jumper settings are indicated by the "Standard Settings" information on the label.

3. Use the drive label information to determine which jumper settings to use for a master or a slave configuration.

4. Set this drive as a master using the jumpers.

5. Using the procedure explained in Chapter 1, physically install this drive on the end of the ribbon cable and secure it to an available drive bay.

FIGURE 3-1	

The master/slave jumper set on a typical hard drive

6. Using the proper jumper setting, configure the second drive as a slave.

7. Install the second drive in the middle of the ribbon cable. Your hard drive setup should look similar to the one shown in Figure 3-2. Note the position of the hard drives on the ribbon cable.

The specification of the IDE cable is a maximum of 46cm (18 inches). Make sure your cable does not exceed this length.

Another method of cabling IDE drives is the Cable Select Method (CSEL). CSEL has been a part of the ATA specification for quite some time but has never been fully implemented. CSEL is implemented using a special cable that has one connector with pin 28 not connected. This disconnected pin indicates to the drive that it is the slave. To implement CSEL, both drives must support it and be jumpered accordingly, a CSEL cable must be used, and the host adapter must support CSEL. An adapter that supports CSEL will have pin 28 grounded. Although most hard drives support this configuration, it is rare to find the cable or a BIOS that supports it. CSEL may become more prevalent as the Plug and Play (PnP) initiative becomes more prevalent.

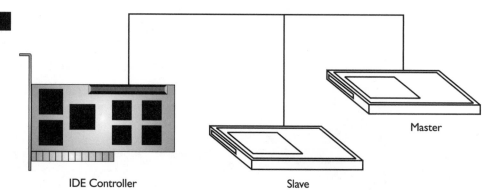

FIGURE 3-2

The finished product of a master/slave configuration

IDE Controller   Slave

Master

It is not recommended that you use the "cable select" option on drive configuration. This option is used only on systems that support this, such as Compaq's and some other IBM clones. It tends to cause problems. You must have a special cable that has a hole in the middle of it or a twist in the middle. The problem with these is if someone decides to change a drive and doesn't know you are using cable select, it can cause problems that are sometimes hard to troubleshoot. If the second drive on a cable select system is marked as slave or the primary drive is marked as master, the system will not boot. I've seen technicians spend a long time trying to figure out this problem. It is generally suggested to just use Master/Slave because you can have only two drives on a cable.

Verifying the Drive Type

When upgrading or adding a hard drive to the system, the drive type must be verified to be the right interface. The two main types of interfaces are IDE and SCSI, with both having many subtypes. Table 3-2 lists the different subtypes of IDE drives.

TABLE 3-2   IDE/ATA Subtypes

Standard	Facts
ATA	Advanced Technology Attachment is also known as IDE. This architecture integrates the disk controller onto the drive itself. IDE supports up to two drives on a 16-bit interface and PIO modes 0, 1, and 2.
ATA 2	Created by the Small Form Factor Committee to increase the capacity of the ATA interface. Also known as Enhanced IDE (EIDE) and Fast ATA, ATA 2 supports PIO modes 3 and 4, DMA modes 1 and 2, block transfers, and LBA (Logical Block Transfers).
ATA 3	ATA 3 includes Self Monitoring Analysis and Reporting Technology (SMART), which improves the reliability of the ATA 2 standard and allows the drive to warn you about certain types of impending failure.
ATA 33	ATA 33, or Ultra-DMA runs at 33 Mbps by utilizing mode 3 multiword DMA.
ATA 66	One of the recent advances in ATA technology supports transfer rates up to 66 Mbps.
ATA 100	The newest ATA specifications increases the throughput to 100 Mbps.

Make sure to check the compatibility of ATA drives from different manufacturers. Some ATA drives do not work well if cabled to ATA drives from other manufacturers. Test the implementation before placing it into production, and back up all important data prior to the test.

SCSI drives also come in many "flavors." Table 3-3 outlines some of the different subtypes of SCSI drives and their physical characteristics as defined by the STA (SCSI Trade Association).

Confirming Termination and Cabling

SCSI drives require a defined bus using specific cables and connectors with each end being terminated to eliminate noise and standing waves. Table 3-4 lists the different SCSI types and the connectors and cable lengths for each design.

TABLE 3-3	STA Term	Information
SCSI Subtypes	SCSI-1	The original standard is 8 bit, 5 Mbps at 5 MHz, maximum cable length of 6 meters, and a maximum of 8 devices(including the controller). Devices are numbered 0-7.
	SCSI-2	This is the ANSI standard (X3.131-1994) which was an update to the SCSI-1 standard. Changes included faster data rates and mandated message and command structure to improve compatibility.
	Fast SCSI-2	Doubles the clock speed from 5 MHz to 10 MHz, thus doubling the transfer rate to 10 Mbps
	Wide SCSI-2	Doubles the 8-bit bus to 16 bits.
	Ultra SCSI	20 MHz bus speed with 20 Mbps transfer rates.
	Ultra Wide SCSI	20 MHz bus speed with 16-bit bus and 40 Mbps transfer rates.
	Ultra-2 SCSI	LVD drivers bring this up to 40 MHz and 40 Mbps transfer rates.
	Wide Ultra-2 SCSI	This doubles the bus on the Ultra-2 SCSI thus increasing the transfer rates to 80 Mbps.
	SCSI-3 or Ultra-3 SCSI	16-bit bus with an 80 MHz clock gives this type 160 Mbps transfer rates.

FROM THE CLASSROOM

Primary Responsibilities of a Server Administrator

The Server + exam concentrates on the primary things a server administrator might do in the course of his or her job. The questions I've seen most and heard students talk about are the SCSI specifications and Disaster Recovery. You especially need to know the SCSI cable lengths, bus speeds, and architectures. Some versions of the test seem to have a very high percentage of SCSI specification questions. Write out the chart several times and make sure you know the differences in the bus speeds and widths, and in the cable lengths.

—Travis Guinn, CCA, MCSE, CCSA, CCSE, A+

The SCSI specification also defines four types of connectors as listed in Table 3-4. Table 3-5 and Figure 3-3 illustrate these connectors.

TABLE 3-4   SCSI Specifications

	Connector	Bus Frequency	Bus Width	Transfer Rate	Maximum Devices	Cable Length
SCSI-1	C50	5 MHz	8	5 Mbps	8	6 m
SCSI-2 Fast	MD50	10 MHz	8	10 Mbps	8	6 m
SCSI-3 Ultra	MD50	20 MHz	8	20 Mbps	16	1.5, 3 m
Ultra2	MD68	40 MHz	8	40 Mbps	8	25 m
Fast Wide	MD68	20 MHz	16	20 Mbps	16	6 m
Ultra Wide	MD68	20 MHz	16	40 Mbps	16	1.5, 3 m
Ultra2 Wide	MD68	40 MHz	16	80 Mbps	16	25 m
Ultra160	MD68	80 MHz	16	160 Mbps	16	25 m

TABLE 3-5	SCSI Connector Types
Connector	**Details**
50 Pin External	Shielded and nonshielded varieties; resembles a large Centronics printer cable or a smaller D-shaped connector with clips on the side to secure it to the device.
50 Pin Internal	There are two types: the 50 pin resembles a typical IDE connector, and the 50 pin connector is narrower with a D-shaped housing to protect the pins.
68 Pin Internal	Wide SCSI with shielded and nonshielded variations.
80 Pin SCA (Single Connector Attachment)	This connector is used for drives that can be hot swapped. It provides both data and power on one connector.

SCSI buses must be terminated at each end. There is both internal and external termination; internal is a chip on the device, external is a either a chip or a snap on a connector. The external terminator must be the same type as the cable being terminated. There are three types of terminators:

■ **Active**   Uses a voltage regulator to normalize the termination voltage.

■ **Passive**   Uses an array of resistors but does not work for some higher performance drives.

FIGURE 3-3

Internal SCSI connectors

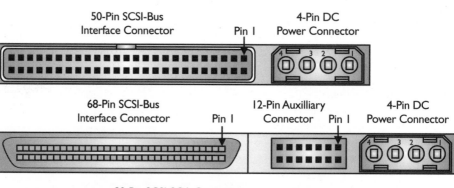
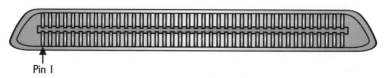

■ **Forced Perfect Termination (FPT)**   FPT uses diode switching and biasing to force the impedance of the cable to match each device. Forced perfect termination actively monitors the bus to ensure that no signal reflection occurs.

It is possible to mix termination types on one SCSI chain, but at least one device on the SCSI chain must supply termination power. Most new devices have built-in termination that is enabled using a jumper; others require an external termination piece. Wide SCSI is 16 bits and has twice the throughput of 8-bit Narrow SCSI at the same clock speeds. When mixing Narrow and Wide SCSI, be sure to place the wide devices closest to the SCSI host bus adapter and use the proper adapters to go from wide to narrow.

SCSI utilizes SCSI IDs to distinguish devices. SCSI-1 and SCSI-2 support IDs from 0–7, SCSI-3 single channel supports 0–15, and SCSI-3 dual channel supports 0–31. All the devices on the chain must have a unique ID which is usually set on the device by a jumper or a switch. Most adapters will boot to a SCSI hard drive set at ID 0 by default. SCSI IDs are prioritized from highest to lowest where 7 is highest priority and 0 is the lowest. SCSI interface cards, also known as Host Bus Adapters (HBA), are usually set at ID 7.

exam
ⓌatcH

Understand where different devices should fall in the SCSI ID chain. Hard drives should get lower IDs than tape drives or scanners. It sounds backward but remember, a hard drive's default ID is 0.

SCENARIO & SOLUTION

Now that you have seen the different types of SCSI buses and connectors, refer to the following Scenario & Solution as a quick reference for possible scenario questions and the appropriate answers.

Maximum number of drives for Ultra Wide SCSI-3?	16
Maximum cable length for Wide SCSI-2	3 m
What is also known as Ultra 160?	Ultra SCSI-3
How many pins does the SCA connector have?	80
What is the bus frequency for Fast Wide SCSI?	20 MHz.

exam
ⓦatch ***Know the SCSI cable lengths, connector specifics, bus speeds, and transfer rates by heart.***

SCSI uses three different signaling systems to define cable types, voltage requirements, and SCSI bus control. The three systems are Single Ended (SE), Low Voltage Differential (LVD), and Differential. Be sure to know which signaling system the drives are using and do not mix SE and Differential as it may cause damage to the drives and HBA.

- **LVD**   All Ultra-2 SCSI devices use LVD to provide up to 80 Mbps with 16 bit and 40 Mbps with 8-bit buses. LVD is backward compatible with SE and can co-exist on a SE bus by switching to SE mode. LVD and Ultra SCSI are used interchangeably. LVD signaling provides:
  - Greater cable lengths
  - Low power requirements
  - Increased reliability
  - Common mode noise immunity
  - Improved device connectivity
  - Reduced EMI'

- **Single Ended**   SE devices are the most common signaling method used. They are unbalanced electrically, using a common return line for all the outgoing signals. This "unbalanced" technique makes SE more susceptible to interference so the cable length is limited to 6 meters, and there should be 12 inches of cable between devices.

- **Differential (HVD: High Voltage Differential)**   "Balanced" SCSI bus. Uses one return line for every outgoing line, thus doubling the amount of wires from an SE method. HVD is more expensive than SE but is less likely to accept interference and extends the cable length to 25 meters.

exam
ⓦatch ***If it is Ultra it is LVD.***

Upgrading Mass Storage

Upgrading mass storage devices can present unique challenges. This is especially true if the device contains the operating system. If replacing a hard drive that contains the system files for the OS, it may be necessary to transfer the existing data from the old device to the new one. There are basically two ways this can be accomplished, depending on the devices and the OS.

One method is to back up all data from the drive, replace the drive, and restore the data. This can be done manually or using a third-party software program. Some third-party programs provide Disaster Recovery procedures that may be used to accomplish this goal. Or the data can be backed up, the OS re-installed, and then the backup restored over the new install. Returning an OS to a new hard drive is usually simple if the controller does not change. If a new controller is installed, then special procedures may be required to allow the OS to use the new controller after the upgrade is complete.

The other method is to use a third-party imaging product to make an exact copy of the drive to the new one. This method is usually faster, but can be more sensitive with some operating systems. Imaging still suffers from the same controller driver issues as the previous method.

Regardless of the method used, always back up all critical data and have a documented back out plan in the event the upgrade fails.

Adding Drives to an Array

Hard drives, being the mechanical devices they are, can and *will* fail. Hard drives are also limited by several physical factors concerning performance. To prevent loss of data due to failure and increase performance, Redundant Array of Inexpensive Disks (RAID) was developed. RAID distributes the performance factors and failure risks across several disks by interleaving the data, thus enabling the OS to read and write data to multiple drives at once to increase performance and reduce the risk of data loss by using different methods of data integrity. Table 3-6 details the different RAID levels and the minimum number of drives needed to achieve the level. There are other RAID levels, but they are not common or practical in most corporate environments.

exam
ⓦatch

Know how many drives are required for each RAID level and what the definition of each RAID level is...there will be questions on RAID.

There are two methods to implement RAID: software and hardware.

■ **Hardware**   Hardware RAIDs are the most flexible and usually have higher performance. They also allow for more levels of RAID and have the least overhead on the OS.

■ **Software**   Software RAIDs are implemented in the OS and take a larger toll on OS performance. They usually do not allow for hot swap functionality, so if a drive fails, the server must be taken offline to replace it.

TABLE 3-6   RAID Levels

RAID Level	Minimum Number of Drives	Details
RAID 0	2	Striped Disk Array without Fault Tolerance. Stripes data across multiple drives. High performance, but no fault tolerance.
RAID 1	2	Mirroring and Duplexing. One write or two reads possible per mirrored pair. 100% redundancy of data. Highest disk overhead of all RAID types (100%)—inefficient.
RAID 0+1	4	High Data Transfer Performance. Mirrors two RAID 0 arrays. High I/O performance. High overhead. Very expensive.
RAID 3	3	Parallel transfer with parity. Very high read data transfer rate. Very high write data transfer rate. Disk failure has an insignificant impact on throughput.
RAID 4	3	Independent Data disks with shared Parity disk. Very high read data transaction rate. Worst write transaction rate and write aggregate transfer rate. Difficult and inefficient data rebuild in the event of disk failure.
RAID 5	3	Independent Data disks with distributed parity blocks. Highest read rate. Medium write rate. Disk failure has a medium impact on throughput. Most common.
RAID 6	4	Independent Data disks with two independent distributed parity schemes. Uses two-dimensional parity. Can sustain multiple drive failures. Great for mission critical applications. Very poor write performance. Requires N+2 drives.

Adding drives to an array depends upon the RAID level and the method. Hardware RAIDs usually have a BIOS utility or an OS utility to facilitate organizing drives. Software RAIDs use OS admin tools to create RAID sets.

In addition to RAID levels, many hardware RAID controllers allow for a hot spare. A *hot spare* is an additional hard disk that is plugged into the array controller that can assume the role of any drive that fails. This is a very effective solution, but it requires an investment in hardware that will not be used until a failure occurs.

Replacing Existing Drives

When drives fail they may be replaced in different ways. The server hardware configuration will determine to a great extent how the drive is replaced and reintegrated into the storage solution. High-end servers provide a "hot swap" method that usually employs the 80 Pin SCA connector. These drives usually can be replaced while the server is running with no effect on the OS. Simply remove the malfunctioning drive and replace it with a new one. Depending on the RAID controller, the array may automatically rebuild itself or it may require user intervention to initiate the rebuilding. If a software RAID is being used, hot swap is normally not an option, and the server must be brought down to replace the drive. RAID 5 and RAID 0 will continue to function with one drive offline with most controllers and will automatically begin rebuilding when the drive is replaced, eliminating the need to restore from backup.

Integrating into a Storage Solution and Making it Available to the OS

After the drives have been added to the array and configured to the desired RAID level, they can be made available to the OS. Some RAID arrays can be shared among multiple hosts and each host can use a portion of the available space. The RAID array could be part of a storage area network (SAN) and provide individual hosts access to pieces of the RAID array using Logical Unit Numbers (LUNs). LUNs are actually subunits of SCSI devices. Each SCSI device can have up to 8 LUNs, and LUNs can also have subunits called LSUNs (Logical Sub Unit Number) up to 255 devices per LUN. SANs use LUNs to tell the Fibre Channel HBA which partition on the SAN to attach to and use.

Fibre Channel was developed by a consortium of computer and mass storage manufacturers for new mass storage technologies that have higher bandwidth requirements than standard SCSI. Fibre Channel is a serial data transfer architecture that uses three standards: Arbitrated Loop, Fibre Switched, and Point to Point. The Arbitrated Loop is the most widely used and supports full-duplex data transfers up to 100 Mbps and is compatible with SCSI. Fibre Channel uses optical fiber to connect devices up to six miles (6 km) apart. Fibre Channel technology will eventually replace standard SCSI on high-performance systems.

CERTIFICATION OBJECTIVE 3.03

Increasing Memory

Adding more memory to a server is probably the most cost-effective way to get more performance from existing servers. More RAM will allow the server to use less virtual memory on the hard drives, thus speeding up operations because RAM is much faster than any disk subsystem. This will also alleviate traffic on the mass storage bus and allow more of the I/O operations to real disk-based activity and give the system a true performance boost all around.

Verifying Hardware and OS Support for Capacity Increase

Before adding RAM to any server, consult both the server's vendor's Web site to check the compatibility matrix and then check the operating system's memory requirements and limitations. Table 3-7 lists some common operating systems and the maximum amount of RAM they support. Consult the documentation for the OS in question to ascertain its particular memory specifications.

Table 3-8 outlines some of the different memory types and specifications.

exam
⍟atch   *Be prepared to differentiate between memory types and what they do.*

Checking the Hardware Compatibility List

Prevent incompatibility before upgrading by visiting the vendor's Web site and consulting the Hardware Compatibility List (HCL). The HCL will also list what types of RAM are compatible.

TABLE 3-7	OS	Memory Limitations
Maximum Memory Supported by Common Operating Systems	Windows NT 4.0	2GB
	Windows 2000 Server	4GB
	Windows 2000 Advanced Server	8GB
	Windows 2000 Data Center Server	64GB
	Netware 3.12	4GB
	Netware 4.x	4GB
	Netware 5.x	8GB
	SCO Unix 3.2v5.0.4	4GB
	AIX Unix	16GB

TABLE 3-8	Memory Types

Type	Specification
ECC	Error-Correcting Code. Differs from parity in that errors are not only detected but are corrected before being transmitted.
EDO	Extended Data Out dynamic RAM. Capable of speeds of about 50 MHz. It holds its last requested data in a cache after releasing it.
BEDO	Burst EDO DRAM is combined with pipelining technology and special latches to allow for much faster access time than regular EDO.
Unbuffered	The chipset controller directly interfaces with the DRAM memory.
Buffered	Some memory module designs (usually those involving large numbers of chips) require a device to re-drive or amplify the signals. On EDO modules this device is called a buffer; on synchronous modules this device is called a register.
Registered	Delays the release of memory one clock cycle. Used on heavily loaded systems.
FPM	Fast page mode DRAM works by sending the row address just once for many accesses to memory in locations near each other, improving access time.
Memory Interleaving	Process of dividing system memory into multiple sections so the CPU can access several sections at once.
SRAM	Static RAM. SRAM is very fast and does not require the refresh technology of DRAM. However, it is very expensive and takes about four times the silicon area to create. It uses a serial presence detect chip to inform the motherboard of its characteristics.
Direct Rambus DRAM	DRDRAM works on a narrower 16-bit bus than the 64-bit DRAM bus, but it operates at much higher speeds to achieve very high performance. Like SDRAM, it uses a serial presence detect chip to inform the motherboard of its characteristics.

EXERCISE 3-3

Upgrading Server RAM

1. Consult your server's documentation or the vendor's Web site and determine what type of RAM is compatible with the server and OS you are using.

2. Order as much of that RAM as the server/OS will support.

3. Once the RAM arrives, schedule downtime with the users if necessary.

4. Shut down the operating system and power off the server.

5. Open the case and remove any components blocking access to the RAM slots on the motherboard. Remember to observe ESD precautions.

6. Take note of the position of the notches on the RAM modules and match them to the spaces in the socket.

7. Fold the clamps back and slide the RAM into the slot carefully so that the clamps automatically move into position.

8. Firmly close the clamps and reassemble the server.

9. Apply power and verify that the BIOS recognizes the new memory.

Verifying Memory Compatibility

As an HCL can be a static document and not keep up with advancements in technology, it is up to the server administrator to verify that the memory is compatible with the operating system, the hardware, and the existing RAM. Make sure to match the speed, the brand if possible, and any capacity requirements. Some motherboards require specific sized memory modules in specific slots to achieve different total memory amounts.

Some motherboards require that memory modules be added in pairs or even four at a time. Check the motherboard documentation to determine if the pairs need to the be the same speed (they almost always do) and capacity. Occasionally, it is allowable to mix and match RAM speeds between banks but all transactions will occur at the speed of the slowest installed module.

Although adding memory of a different speed may still function, the system will function only as fast as the slowest memory installed. Some systems will not even produce video unless all RAM is exactly matched.

EDO

Extended Data Output (EDO) RAM is a type of random access memory chip that improves the time to read from memory on faster microprocessors such as the Intel Pentium. EDO RAM was initially optimized for the 66 MHz Pentium. For faster computers, different types of synchronous dynamic RAM are recommended.

ECC/Non-ECC

ECC allows data that is being read or transmitted to be checked for errors and, when necessary, corrected "real-time." ECC differs from parity-checking in that errors are not only detected but also corrected. ECC is increasingly being designed into data storage and transmission hardware as data rates increase.

Here's how it works for data storage:

1. When a data word is stored in RAM or peripheral storage, a code that describes the bits in the word is calculated and stored along with the data word. For each 64-bit word, an extra 7 bits are needed to store this code.

2. When the unit of data is requested for reading, a code for the stored and newly read word is again calculated using the original algorithm. The newly generated code is compared with the code generated when the word was stored. If the codes match, the data is free of errors and is sent.

3. If the codes don't match, errors are determined through the code comparison and the bits are corrected.

4. The stored data is not corrected because it will soon be overwritten with new data.

5. If an error occurs after the system power is cycled, a message with the error location is sent to a log for the system administrator to evaluate.

SDRAM/RDRAM

Synchronous DRAM is a generic name for various kinds of dynamic random access memory. SDRAM is synchronized with the CPU speed and thus provides better performance. SDRAM is rated in MHz rather than nanoseconds to more easily compare the CPU speed to the RAM speed.

Rambus dynamic random access memory (RDRAM) promises to transfer up to 1.6 billion bytes per second. Rambus DRAM consists of three parts:

- The RAM
- A RAM controller
- The bus connecting the RAM to the CPU

Rambus provides this speed by using a 16-bit bus rather than the 8-bit bus used by DRAM. Rambus RAM running at 800 MHz can produce data transfer rates up to 1.6 billion bytes per second. These speeds are needed to enhance the performance of 3-D games and streaming multimedia.

SCENARIO & SOLUTION

You have seen the differences in the types of memory, now test your knowledge with the following Scenario & Solution.

I am running Data Center server and want to max out my RAM…	64GB, one gigabyte for each processor it will support.
I have a dual Pentium 4 server with 256MB of EDO…	Upgrade! EDO was designed for the Pentium 66.
I need memory transfer rates more than 1 billion bytes per second…	Rambus is the memory for you.

Using an Upgrade Checklist

The following is a an upgrade checklist:

- Locate and obtain the latest drivers, OS service packs, and patches.
- Review FAQs and instructions.
- Test and conduct a Pilot.
- Schedule downtime if needed.
- Use ESD (electrostatic discharge) best practices.
- Confirm the OS recognizes the upgrade.
- Review the settings and baseline the new system.
- Document all procedures.

Verifying that the Server and OS Recognize Additional Memory

After adding memory to a server it must be powered on and checked to see if the BIOS recognizes the additional RAM. Some servers do a visual count of the installed memory during power on self test (POST). Others require you to enter the complementary metal oxide semiconductor (CMOS) to view what the machine sees as installed RAM.

When it is confirmed that the computer sees the new RAM, the operating system must be examined to ensure that it sees the new memory. Some operating systems do not recognize newly installed RAM without startup commands, patches, or Registry entries. Consult your operating system's manuals on how to enable usage of additional RAM.

Performing Server Optimization for Full Use of Additional RAM

After everything is confirmed to recognize the new memory, the operating system or environment may have to be modified to make optimal use of the new resources. Resizing swap partitions, virtual memory files, and so on, are all things that may need to be adjusted to match the new configuration.

CERTIFICATION SUMMARY

Server+ should bring an added measure of confidence to those who achieve it, and of course, the added ammunition in an acronym war. This chapter covered the three most important things in a server: its memory, the hard drive, and the CPU, and these items constitute a major part of the exam. We covered the types of CPUs and how to determine compatibility with existing memory, as well as the different types of cache CPUs take advantage of. We covered upgrading the BIOS and the reasons, advantages, and procedures of doing so. The BIOS upgrades are important to keep the hardware communicating efficiently with new hardware features and they enable your server to perform at the height of its potential.

Upgrading and adding hard drives is one of the most common tasks a server administrator will perform. Know thoroughly the SCSI specifications such as cable lengths and bus transfer rates. We covered in depth the SCSI interfaces, termination requirements, and architecture. RAID levels provide us with fault tolerance and performance increases by spreading the risk and transfer capabilities across multiple spindles. Each RAID level has specific advantages and weakness which are critical when choosing the appropriate level for an implementation.

As mentioned before, an upgrade to a server's memory is the most cost-efficient method to get more performance out of servers running short on resources. Memory is a critical element to a server's stability and must be matched to the Hardware Compatibility List to ensure it will operate reliably. Wearing an ESD wrist strap during the install and running diagnostics after the install will help to ensure a dependable platform.

Plan for your upgrades and follow the plan during the implementation. Your success will be determined by the reliability and performance of the servers you manage. Listen to your users and make improvements or corrections where necessary to achieve a rock-solid platform for doing business.

✓ TWO-MINUTE DRILL

Here are some of the key points from each certification objective in Chapter 3.

Adding Processors

❑ Write-through cache is the fastest.

❑ BIOSs can be upgraded by flash or chip replacement.

❑ A failed BIOS upgrade can render the system unusable.

❑ Proper airflow is required to prevent thermal errors that could lock up your server at regular intervals.

❑ High speed CPUs need heatsink and/or fans. Ensure that the fan/heatsink is dissipating heat adequately.

❑ Symmetric Multiprocessing allows any free CPU to handle a request.

❑ Asymmetric Multiprocessing assigns specific tasks to specific processors.

Adding Hard Drives

❑ IDE/ATA supports two hard drives per channel.

❑ ATA drives are configured to master or slave, with the master getting the first available drive letter.

❑ ATA 33 is also known as Ultra ATA.

❑ Wide SCSI is 16 bits wide and supports 16 devices.

❑ Ultra SCSI is LVD.

❑ Single Ended and Differential are not compatible.

Increasing Memory

❑ ECC is capable of detecting and correcting single bit errors.

❑ EDO is optimized for older computers (Pentium 66).

❑ Registered memory delays the release of data for one clock cycle.

❑ Memory Interleaving is the process of dividing memory into sections for simultaneous access to increase performance.

❑ Rambus memory provides transfer rates of 1.6 billion bytes per second.

SELF TEST

The following questions will help you measure your understanding of the material presented in this chapter. Read all of the choices carefully, as there may be more than one correct answer. Choose all correct answers for each question.

Adding Processors

1. You have just added a new processor to your server. What is the first thing you need to do to verify the processor will function correctly?

    A. Upgrade the display drivers.

    B. Check the system BIOS and make sure the processor registers.

    C. Apply the latest service pack.

    D. Boot to a DOS floppy disk.

2. What multiprocessing architecture allows requests to be completed by any available CPU?

    A. Asymmetric

    B. Pre-Emptive

    C. Symmetric

    D. Co-operative

3. After adding a second processor to your system and the BIOS reporting it correctly, the users are now complaining of decreased performance. What could be the problem?

    A. The power supply is too small.

    B. The CPUs are incompatible.

    C. The BIOS needs upgrading.

    D. The CPU is inserted into the wrong socket.

4. What cache memory is external to the CPU but is very fast and ranges from 256KB to 2048KB?

    A. TAG RAM

    B. Level 2

    C. Write-through

    D. Look-aside

5. You need to upgrade the BIOS in a server. What is the first step you need to perform?

    A. Reboot.

    B. Apply the upgrade.

    C. Boot to a DOS diskette.

    D. Verify the new version.

6. What is a multiprocessor system in which no processor is special with respect to its access to memory, interrupts, or I/O?

    A. Multithreaded

    B. Asymmetric

    C. Symmetric

    D. Co-operative

Adding Hard Drives

7. What is the maximum transfer rate available with Ultra-2 SCSI?

    A. 10 Mbps

    B. 20 Mbps

    C. 40 Mbps

    D. 160 Mbps

8. You have 12 9GB SCSI hard drives to install into a server. Which SCSI architecture will *not* support 12 devices on one channel?

    A. WIDE SCSI-2

    B. Ultra SCSI-3 16bit

    C. Fast SCSI-2

    D. Wide Ultra-2 SCSI

9. Your boss wants you to add another ATA hard drive to his computer. He has one hard drive and one ATAPI CD-ROM, each on separate channels. What would be the best configuration in this situation?

    A. Configured as a Master on the primary channel.

    B. Configured as a Slave on the secondary channel.

C. Configured as a Master on the secondary channel.

D. Configured as a Slave on the primary channel.

10. Which bus type transfers data at up to 33 Mbps?

A. ATA

B. Ultra-DMA

C. ATA 66

D. ATA 3

11. What interface supports 16-bit SCSI and power as well as Hot Swap?

A. 50 Pin internal

B. 80 Pin SCA

C. 68 Pin

D. 50 Pin external

12. What two signaling systems can be used on the same bus?

A. Active and Differential

B. Active and Forced Perfect

C. Single Ended and Differential

D. LVD and Single Ended

13. You need to implement a fault-tolerant solution that will provide efficient use of drive space, a high read rate, a medium write rate, and will sustain a single drive failure. What RAID level would you choose?

A. RAID 0+1

B. RAID 0

C. RAID 5

D. RAID 4

Increasing Memory

14. Buffered and Unbuffered memory can be mixed in one system.

A. True

B. False

15. ECC memory uses how much extra data to store the calculated code?

    A. 16 bytes

    B. 7 bits

    C. 64 bits

    D. 8 bytes

16. Registered memory is used on heavily loaded systems to do which of the following?

    A. Increase data throughput to the network card.

    B. Delay the release of memory one clock cycle.

    C. Control the level 2 cache.

    D. Hold the last requested data in its cache after releasing it.

17. In a buffered memory system, the memory and the controller are:

    A. One integrated unit

    B. Hardwired together for greater throughput

    C. Separated

    D. Delayed from releasing memory for one clock cycle

18. _____ memory holds its last requested data in cache after the memory is released.

    A. Registered

    B. Unbuffered

    C. Extended Data Out

    D. Buffered

19. Which is not a common type of DRAM?

    A. FPM

    B. EDO

    C. Registered

    D. SRAM

20. You want to implement Windows 2000 Data Center server. What is the maximum amount of RAM Data Center will support?

    A. 256MB

    B. 8MB

C. 4GB

D. 64GB

LAB QUESTION

You have a server that has been upgraded and does not recognize the new hard drives. The vendor has informed you that you need to upgrade the BIOS to correct the problem. Identify the correct steps to upgrade the BIOS and allow the server to see the newly installed hard drives. Some steps may not be valid.

___ Reboot the system.

___ Copy the motherboard BIOS download file onto a clean bootable floppy disk.

___ Prepare a bootable floppy disk.

___ Verify the system now sees the new hard drives.

___ Reboot the system with the diskette.

___ To flash your BIOS you'll need flash utility and a BIOS file.

___ Go to the vendor Web site to download the motherboard BIOS for your model number.

___ At the DOS prompt, type the name of the flash utility and any parameters needed.

___ Copy the downloaded BIOS file that matches your motherboard and flash utility to the diskette.

___ Copy the flash to the same clean bootable floppy disk.

SELF TEST ANSWERS

Adding Processors

1. ☑ **B.** First check to see if the BIOS recognizes the new CPU. If it is not registered here, the OS will never see it.
   ☒ **A** is incorrect because the video drivers have no effect on the CPU. **C** is incorrect because the service pack won't help if the BIOS does not pick up the new CPU. **D**, booting to DOS, is for upgrading the BIOS, which may be necessary after determining the BIOS does not see the new CPU.

2. ☑ **C.** Symmetric Multiprocessing allows any available CPU to process an instruction.
   ☒ **B** and **D** are incorrect because they are types of multitasking. **A**, Asymmetric, assigns system processes to one CPU and application processes to the other.

3. ☑ **B.** When adding an additional CPU, you must ensure the CPUs are the same speed and have the same cache sizes or it could actually decrease your performance.
   ☒ **A** is incorrect because if the power supply was too small, there would be random reboots. **C** and **D** are incorrect because the BIOS does recognize it.

4. ☑ **B.** Level 2 cache is very fast RAM that the CPU can use as temporary storage for data and instructions.
   ☒ **A** is incorrect because TAG RAM is a controller chip for some implementations of Level 2 cache. **C** and **D** are incorrect because they are both reading/writing architectures.

5. ☑ **C.** The first thing is to boot to a DOS diskette containing the flash image.
   ☒ **B** is incorrect because it is the second step, which would be to apply the upgrade. **A**, reboot, is the next step, and then **D**, verify the new version, is next.

6. ☑ **C.** Symmetric Multiprocessing is a system in which all CPUs are equal and can service any request.
   ☒ **B**, Asymmetric, is incorrect because it is a system in which each CPU services only one type of request such as system or application. **A** and **D** are incorrect because they are both multitasking methods.

Adding Hard Drives

7. ☑ **C.** Ultra-2 SCSI has a bus clock of 40 Mbps with an 8-bit bus.
    ☒ **A, B,** and **D** are incorrect because they are the transfer rates of SCSI-2, Wide SCSI-2, and Ultra-3 SCSI respectively.

8. ☑ **C.** Fast SCSI-2 supports only eight devices due to the bus width of 8 bits.
    ☒ **A, B,** and **D** are incorrect because they all have 16-bit buses, thus supporting 16 devices per channel.

9. ☑ **D.** This the best answer because it will add the drive with the least amount of changes to the system.
    ☒ **A** is incorrect because it would replace the drive the operating system is on and require you to transfer that information or reinstall the operating system. **B** is incorrect because it would probably not work with the CD-ROM as master. **C** would work but would require reconfiguring the CD-ROM drive.

10. ☑ **B.** Ultra DMA is also known as ATA 33 which provides for data transfers up to 33 Mbps.
    ☒ **A** is the original ATA specification. **D,** ATA 3, implemented the SMART architecture. **C,** ATA 66, transfers data at up to 66 Mbps.

11. ☑ **B.** The 80 pin SCA provides both data and power over one cable. It also provides a Hot Swap connector.
    ☒ **A** and **D** are incorrect because the 50 pin internal and external both only provide 8 bit data. **C** is incorrect because the 68 pin cable provides 16 bit data only.

12. ☑ **D.** LVD is backward compatible with Single Ended.
    ☒ **C** is incorrect because Single Ended and Differential are not compatible; Differential will damage Single Ended devices on the same bus. **A** is incorrect because Active and Differential are not both system buses. **B** is incorrect because Active and Forced Perfect are both termination methods.

13. ☑ **C.** RAID 5 is independent disks with a distributed parity block. No single drive failure will result in data loss.
    ☒ **A** is incorrect because RAID 0+1 is Disk Mirroring of Striped arrays. **B** is incorrect because RAID 0 is a striped array that has good performance but no fault tolerance. **D** is incorrect because RAID 4 provides very high read rates but poor write performance. Fault tolerance is difficult to manage.

Increasing Memory

14. ☑ **B.** False. Buffered and Unbuffered memory cannot be mixed in one system.
    ☒ **A** is incorrect because Buffered and Unbuffered memory cannot be mixed in one system.

15. ☑ **B.** ECC memory uses 7 extra bits to store the calculated data description of the 64-bit word.
    ☒ **C** is incorrect because it is the size of the data word. **A** and **D** are incorrect because, as byte values, they are larger than the data itself.

16. ☑ **B.** Registered memory delays the release of memory one clock cycle. It is used on heavily loaded systems to better control the accuracy of error correcting.
    ☒ **A** is incorrect because the memory speed will not affect the network performance because the network is much slower than memory transfers. **C** is incorrect because the chipset controls the level 2 cache. **D** is incorrect because it is EDO RAM that holds its last requested data in cache after releasing it.

17. ☑ **C.** In a buffered memory system, the memory and the chipset controller are separated by a buffer.
    ☒ **A** and **B** are incorrect because the memory is an add-in module, and the chipset controller is part of the motherboard. **D** is true of registered memory.

18. ☑ **C.** Extended Data Out (EDO) holds the last requested data in cache after it is released.
    ☒ **A** is incorrect because registered memory delays the release of data one clock cycle. **B** is incorrect because in unbuffered memory the chipset controller directly interfaces with the memory. **D** is incorrect because in buffered memory the chipset controller is separated from the memory by a buffer.

19. ☑ **D.** SRAM is Static RAM not Dynamic RAM. SRAM does not require refreshes to hold its data.
    ☒ **A**, **B**, and **C** are incorrect because they are all types of DRAM.

20. ☑ **D.** Windows 2000 Data Center server will support 64GB of RAM and 32 CPUs.
    ☒ **A** is incorrect because it is the minimum amount of RAM needed. **B** is incorrect because 8MB is below the minimum requirement of Professional. **C** is incorrect because it is the maximum amount for Windows 2000 Server.

LAB ANSWER

Upgrading the BIOS on a server is very easy if you remember to do things in order and remember some points. Make a plain boot disk with no CONFIG.SYS or AUTOEXEC.BAT and use DOS,

Windows 95, or Windows 98. Do not use Windows ME, Windows NT, or Windows 2000 to make a boot disk. Each system may have a different method of upgrading the BIOS such as Compaq's ROMPaqs. Be sure to consult the documentation for your particular hardware and have a back-out plan in the event something goes awry.

9. Reboot the system.
4. Copy the motherboard BIOS download file onto a clean bootable floppy disk.
1. Prepare a bootable floppy disk.
10. Verify the system now sees the new hard drives.
7. Reboot the system with the diskette.
2. To flash your BIOS you'll need flash utility and a BIOS file.
3. Go to the vendor Web site to download the motherboard BIOS for your model number.
8. At the DOS prompt, type the name of the flash utility and any parameters needed.
6. Copy the downloaded BIOS file that match your motherboard and flash utility to the diskette.
5. Copy the flash to the same clean bootable floppy disk.

4

Upgrading

CERTIFICATION OBJECTIVES

4.01	Upgrading BIOS/Firmware
4.02	Upgrading Adapters
4.03	Upgrading Internal and External Peripheral Devices
✓	Two-Minute Drill
Q&A	Self Test

T his chapter continues with server upgrade procedures; specifically, with upgrading the system's basic input/output system (BIOS), adapters, and peripheral devices. Before performing any upgrade, make sure you are familiar with the upgrade checklist described in Chapter 3. That is, review all FAQs and instructions for the hardware or software that you plan to upgrade and check to ensure you have the latest drivers from the manufacturer. Schedule and prepare for server downtime and always follow the electrostatic discharge (ESD) procedures described in Chapter 1. When the upgrade is complete, test your solution and document the upgrade using the procedures described in Chapter 2.

CERTIFICATION OBJECTIVE 4.01

Upgrading BIOS/Firmware

The BIOS is a small chip inside the computer that is responsible for informing the processors about which devices are present in the system and how to communicate with those devices. Whenever the processor makes a request from a component, the BIOS steps in and translates the request into instructions that the required component can understand. All communication to the computer's components must go through the BIOS. If the BIOS cannot communicate with a component, the computer, in effect, cannot make use of that component.

The BIOS is also responsible for maintaining some of the system's basic configuration settings. For example, the computer's boot sequence, use of RAM parity checking, use of hard disk Logical Block Addressing and some power options (sleep, wake on LAN), to name a few, are configured in the BIOS.

Determining When to Upgrade

Upgrading a BIOS is not as common a procedure as upgrading memory, processors, expansion cards, or the motherboard. However, there are some cases in which the BIOS chip itself can be upgraded to improve or enable system performance.

Recall that the BIOS is required in communications between the processor and the system's components. If a device cannot be recognized, the computer cannot use it. For example, if a DVD drive is physically installed in a machine whose BIOS cannot recognize DVD technology, the drive will be inaccessible. Likewise, a

Universal Serial Bus (USB) port cannot be installed and used unless the BIOS can recognize and communicate with USB devices. In these cases, you may be able to upgrade the BIOS to make use of a technology that is newer than the system's BIOS.

You may also be required to upgrade the BIOS if it does not support the appropriate configuration options for installed devices. For example, you cannot take full advantage of a 2GB hard disk if the BIOS is designed to recognize only 500MB. In this case, the BIOS can recognize and make use of the hard disk, but will not be able to use the disk's full capacity. Additionally, suppose the BIOS setup program does not allow you to configure the system to boot from the CD-ROM drive. In these cases, you will need to upgrade the BIOS to support the desired configuration options.

Typically, you will become aware that a BIOS upgrade is required only when you try (and fail) to access a newly installed device, application, or feature. If the device simply cannot be recognized, or if the new feature cannot be accessed in the BIOS setup program, consider upgrading the BIOS. You may also become aware of the need to upgrade the BIOS by the manufacturer. Some hardware and software manufacturers routinely release upgraded products to address bug fixes or enhancements for the product. Look for BIOS upgrade information on the manufacturer's Web site.

Flash BIOS

BIOS chips are referred to as read-only memory (ROM) chips because they have traditionally been readable only, meaning that their instructions were hard-coded on the chip and could not be changed. However, newer types of BIOS chips have since been introduced in which the chip's instructions can be overwritten. These chips are Electronically Erasable Programmable Read Only Memory (EEPROM) chips, commonly referred to as Flash BIOS chips.

Flash BIOS chips can be electronically upgraded using a floppy disk supplied by the chip's manufacturer. The disk contains a program that automatically "flashes" (updates) the BIOS so that it can recognize new hardware types or support different configuration options. The BIOS then retains the new settings, so it has to be flashed only once. Manufacturers typically provide flash upgrades on a floppy disk, or as Internet downloads that are saved by the user to floppy disk. In most cases, you flash the BIOS simply by shutting the computer off, inserting the disk, and rebooting the computer from the floppy disk. The upgrade program will launch automatically.

Replacing the BIOS

In some cases, the BIOS cannot be sufficiently upgraded using a flash application. This is typically the case when the BIOS's manufacturer has stopped supporting that particular BIOS model or when it simply hasn't released a flash program with the options you need your BIOS to support. In these cases, the BIOS can only be upgraded through a physical replacement. That is, the old BIOS is physically removed from the computer and an upgraded BIOS is installed. Follow the steps in Exercise 4-1 to replace an old BIOS chip with a new one.

EXERCISE 4-1

Replacing the BIOS

1. Turn the computer off and carry out standard ESD procedures. Remove the computer case.

2. Locate the old BIOS chip on the motherboard and note its orientation in the socket. The BIOS can typically be identified by the manufacturer's name printed on the top.

3. Remove the BIOS chip with a multi-pronged chip puller (not a 2-pronged chip puller).

4. Orient the new BIOS in the proper position over the socket and gently push it into place.

on the **job**

Refer to the BIOS and motherboard documentation to ensure the BIOS is compatible for your system.

<table>
<tr><td colspan="2" align="center">**SCENARIO & SOLUTION**</td></tr>
<tr><td colspan="2">Test your knowledge of the information presented in this section by answering the following Scenario & Solution questions.</td></tr>
<tr><td>How do I "flash" the BIOS?</td><td>Turn the computer off, insert the manufacturer's floppy disk containing the flash application, and restart the computer.</td></tr>
<tr><td>The manufacturer of my computer's BIOS no longer supports electronic upgrades for that model. Can I upgrade the BIOS?</td><td>Yes, if the motherboard is compatible, you can physically replace the BIOS with one that supports the desired features.</td></tr>
<tr><td>When should I upgrade my system's BIOS?</td><td>When the existing BIOS does not support a feature, device, or application that you would like to install.</td></tr>
</table>

CERTIFICATION OBJECTIVE 4.02

Upgrading Adapters

This section discusses upgrade procedures for hardware adapters, with a focus on network, small computer system interface (SCSI), and Redundant Array of Inexpensive Disks (RAID) adapters. Recall from previous chapters that these devices require configuration beyond simple allocation of hardware resources, such as drivers and interrupt requests (IRQs). For example, it is not enough to configure a network interface card (NIC) with the proper hardware settings; it must also be configured to communicate on the intended network. Likewise, when upgrading a SCSI adapter, you must configure the adapter to work with the computer, and you must also configure it with the appropriate SCSI resources so that it will work properly within the SCSI subsystem.

When upgrading any adapter, you must first identify the need to upgrade. In most cases, a slow subsystem will be your first indication that an upgrade is required. When performing an upgrade, first check with the manufacturer to determine if the device can be upgraded electronically, through a patch or a newer configuration utility. If the device must be physically replaced, start by removing the old adapter. Next, install the new adapter in the computer and configure it with the appropriate hardware resources. Next, configure it for the subsystem on which it will operate. For example, configure the RAID adapter with the desired RAID type or configure the SCSI adapter with the appropriate SCSI address. In some cases, when you upgrade a subsystem's adapter, you will also be required to update all components of that subsystem. The following subsections assume you will upgrade the adapter only.

Network Adapters

One of the server's most valuable components is its NIC. Without the network interface, the server cannot communicate with the network. As the (potentially) busiest system on the network, it is critical that the server's NIC be able to keep up with network requests for data.

When to Upgrade

In most cases, the server's NIC will require upgrading only if the entire network is upgraded from a slower speed to a faster speed, or from one type of cabling to another. However, if the server's NIC acts as a constant network bottleneck, consider adding another NIC or upgrading the existing NIC to one that supports different features or has better caching abilities.

exam
ⓌatcH

All NICs in a network must support the same network type, such as Ethernet or Token passing. If the network type or speed is upgraded, all NICs must be upgraded. For example, if the NIC is upgraded from 10Mbps to 100Mbps on a single computer only, the network will continue to run at 10Mbps.

Installing and Configuring the New NIC

Once you have performed proper shutdown and ESD procedures, remove the NIC from the server's motherboard. To do this, remove the retaining screw and gently pull the NIC from its expansion slot. Install the new NIC in the server using the procedure described in Exercise 4-2. This exercise assumes you have already carried out proper shutdown and ESD procedures.

EXERCISE 4-2

Installing a NIC

1. Position the NIC over the appropriate expansion slot on the motherboard.

2. Place your thumbs along the top edge of the adapter and push straight down. If necessary, gently rock the adapter along its length (never side to side).

3. Secure the adapter to the computer chassis using the existing screw holes.

4. Once the NIC has been physically installed in the computer, turn the server on and configure it to use the NIC. If the NIC and operating system both support Plug and Play, there is no further configuration. Otherwise, ensure the NIC has been assigned the appropriate IRQ (according to the manufacturer's specifications) and load the appropriate device driver (supplied by the manufacturer).

5. Once the NIC has been configured to function within the server, it must be configured to communicate on the network. This process varies, depending on the server's operating system and the network protocol to be used. Refer to the Network Configuration information presented in Chapter 2.

SCSI Adapter Cards

Because servers typically require fast hard disk access, it is common for the server to include a SCSI system. To make use of SCSI technology, a SCSI controller, or adapter, must be installed and configured to manage the SCSI components.

on the
job

Computers communicate with SCSI devices through the SCSI adapter. The adapter is the only device in the SCSI system that requires hardware resources, such as IRQs and Direct Memory Access (DMA). SCSI is therefore a great way to add more devices to a computer with limited hardware resources.

When to Upgrade

Like NICs, SCSI adapters are system-specific. For example, just as you cannot use a token ring NIC to access an Ethernet network, you cannot use a Fast SCSI-2 adapter to control SCSI Ultra-3 devices. Therefore, the SCSI adapter is likely to require an upgrade only if you decide to upgrade the entire SCSI system. However, if the adapter cannot keep up with requests and creates a bottleneck within the server, or if it will not recognize a required type of SCSI device, you will need to perform a SCSI adapter upgrade.

Installing and Configuring the New SCSI Adapter

The SCSI adapter is installed in the server using the same procedure as other expansion cards. If the SCSI device is addressed and terminated using jumpers, make the appropriate settings according to the manufacturer's instructions. Once the adapter is physically installed on the motherboard, start the computer and configure it to communicate with the adapter. If the operating system and adapter do not support Plug and Play, this will entail assigning the appropriate hardware resources, such as an IRQ. Finish by loading the adapter's device driver. If the SCSI adapter can be electronically addressed and terminated, use the manufacturer's configuration program to make the appropriate settings. Refer to Chapter 1 for SCSI addressing and termination guidelines.

RAID

Fault tolerance, load balancing, and redundancy are important features of most servers. It is therefore very important for the RAID adapter to function properly in the server and not create system bottlenecks.

When to Upgrade

Like NICs and SCSI adapters, RAID adapters are simply one component of another subsystem. Therefore, you are unlikely to have to upgrade the RAID adapter unless you are upgrading the entire RAID system. However, if the RAID adapter will not support a RAID type that you want to implement, or if it creates a bottleneck, replace it with a more appropriate RAID adapter.

Installing and Configuring the RAID Adapter

Install the RAID adapter as you would any expansion card, and configure it to work within the server. This means assigning the appropriate resources and loading a device driver. If the RAID adapter is part of a SCSI system, configure it using the SCSI addressing and termination guidelines discussed in Chapter 1. The RAID adapter must then be configured to manage the attached disks in the desired RAID arrangement (for example, disk mirroring or striping with parity). Use the manufacturer-provided RAID configuration utility to create the appropriate RAID configuration, as described in Chapter 2.

exam
ⓦatch
When upgrading a SCSI RAID controller, you must configure the device to communicate with the computer, configure it to work properly in the SCSI system, and configure it to manage the disks in the RAID array.

SCENARIO & SOLUTION

Before continuing in the chapter, test your knowledge of the adapter upgrade procedures described here by answering the following Scenario & Solution questions.

What do I need to configure after I install a NIC?	You must configure the NIC to communicate with the hardware and to communicate with the network.
How do I upgrade a SCSI adapter?	Install the new adapter, configure it with the appropriate system resources, terminate it, and assign it a SCSI ID.
How do I upgrade a RAID adapter?	Install the new adapter on the motherboard, configure it with the appropriate system resources, and use the RAID configuration utility to configure the disks in the appropriate RAID array.
When should I upgrade the NIC?	Upgrade it if the entire network is being upgraded from one type to another, or if the existing NIC is creating a bottleneck.

CERTIFICATION OBJECTIVE 4.03

Upgrading Internal and External Peripheral Devices

Peripheral devices, with the exception of the video system, are typically considered nonessential devices, meaning that the computer will function without them. This does not mean, however, that they are not essential to the desired functions of the server. For example, a computer will function normally without a modem, but if dial-up remote management is an essential function of the server, then the modem is a required component of the management procedure.

Because peripheral devices are not the real workhorses of the system, they do not often require upgrading. When they do require upgrading, the procedures typically are fairly simple. Most peripheral devices require only physical installation and configuration with the appropriate hardware resources (IRQ, driver, and so on). Other components, such as the video system and USB, may require unique procedures, and are described in the following subsections.

Display Systems

The server's display system relies on the proper function of both the monitor and the internal video card. The video card's function is to create the images that will result in the picture you see. The monitor simply displays the images sent to it by the video card. When you upgrade the video system, you must make sure that the monitor and the video card are compatible. That is, you must use a VGA monitor with a VGA video card, or an SVGA monitor with an SVGA video card.

exam
⚠ atch

The video card and monitor technology must be compatible for the video system to function.

The video system will not create a system bottleneck, and is not responsible for supporting other devices (as a SCSI adapter is responsible for supporting other SCSI devices). Therefore, you typically will need to perform a video system upgrade only when the current system doesn't support a particular desired video technology, such as DirectX, or a particular resolution. In most cases, video system upgrades are performed for aesthetic purposes.

If the video card must be upgraded, follow the steps in Exercise 4-3.

EXERCISE 4-3

Installing a Video System

1. Position the video adapter card over the appropriate expansion slot on the system board.

2. Place your thumbs along the top edge of the card and push straight down. If necessary, rock the card along its length (never side to side) while you apply downward pressure.

3. When the card is fully seated in the expansion slot, secure it to the computer chassis using the existing screw holes.

4. Plug the monitor into the port at the back of the video adapter card and turn it on.

5. Turn the computer on. If the video card is Plug and Play, it will automatically be detected and assigned resources, and the proper device driver will be loaded. If this is the case, skip the next step.

6. If the computer is not Plug and Play, insert the floppy disk or CD that came with the video adapter and run the Setup or Install program to load the proper device drivers and assign the appropriate system resources.

7. In Windows, right-click the desktop and select Properties. Set the desired resolution, number of colors, color scheme, and screen saver.

Modems

Because modems are responsible for transmitting data to and from the computer, they can be the cause of a server bottleneck. When this is the case, you will need to upgrade the modem to support the demands of remote users. You may upgrade using a similar modem type, for example, from a slower analog to a faster analog modem, or you may upgrade from one modem type to another, for example from an analog modem to a cable modem.

Analog Modems

To upgrade to a faster analog modem, remove the slower modem and replace it with the faster one. If it is an external analog modem, simply plug it into a COM port at the back of the computer. If the modem is Plug and Play, it will be automatically detected and configured when you turn the computer on. If it is not Plug and Play, you will have to run its Setup or Install program to load its device driver. Because the modem is attached to a COM port, it will use that port's system resources (IRQ and I/O).

The upgrade procedure for an internal modem is a bit more work. Remove the modem from the motherboard slot. Next, install the modem as you would any other expansion card. Again, if the modem is Plug and Play, the OS will automatically configure it. However, if the modem does not support Plug and Play, you will have to configure it manually.

To configure an internal modem, assign the modem to an available COM port, even though it is not actually physically attached to that port. Depending on the modem itself, this may be done using a jumper setting or, more commonly, electronically using a Setup program or the server's operating system. Take care not to choose a COM port whose resources are already being used by another device. For example, if COM1 is already in use, you cannot assign COM3 to the modem (COM1 and COM3 share IRQ4, and COM2 and COM4 share IRQ3).

exam
ⓦatch

Internal analog modems must be configured to use a COM port even though they do not actually attach to the port. The modem will use the COM port's resources.

Before the new modem can communicate with another modem, it must be configured within the operating system to establish a dial-up connection. The dial-up settings include the phone number to dial and other dialing properties, such as how to get an external line or disable call waiting. These procedures vary, depending on the modem and the operating system used.

Cable Modems

There is no need to upgrade from a slower cable modem to a faster cable modem, as all cable modems support the same speed. However, you may want to upgrade from an analog modem to a cable modem. To do so, first uninstall the analog modem. Cable modems are external devices that communicate with the computer using an

Ethernet NIC and network cable. Therefore, you must begin the cable modem installation by installing an Ethernet card. Refer to the Network Adapters section earlier in the chapter for the proper installation and configuration procedure. Finish the installation by plugging the cable modem into the Ethernet card and plugging the modem into a cable outlet using coaxial cable. Cable modems do not require dial-up properties; rather, they have a direct connection to the ISP.

USB Peripherals

USB devices are Plug and Play and hot swappable. This means that a USB device can be attached to the computer while the computer is in operation, and requires very little configuration. The device will be immediately and automatically recognized and configured by the system. The USB system will even provide power to most devices. Some USB devices that you may need to upgrade include the mouse, keyboards, scanners, and printers. To upgrade a USB device, simply detach the old one from the USB port and attach the new device in its place. See the From the Classroom sidebar for guidelines about installing USB devices.

FROM THE CLASSROOM

Using USB Hubs

Most USB-compliant computers include two ports at the back of the computer. This means that you can attach two USB devices. How, then, can USB claim to support up to 127 devices? To create more USB ports, you can use an external *USB hub*. An external USB hub contains one cable and several (up to seven) additional ports and serves to increase the number of ports available for other devices. To attach a USB hub, connect its cable to an available USB port at the back of the computer (called the *root hub*). No additional configuration is required (see Figure 4-1).

To add more USB devices, simply attach them to the USB hub. If you require even more ports, add another tier by attaching another hub to the existing one. However, you should avoid connecting more than five hubs together, because to do so could affect device performance.

—Amy Thomson, A+ Certified Technician, MOUS Master

FIGURE 4-1

USB Hub

IEEE 1394

Like USB, IEEE 1394 systems support Plug and Play and hot swapping. However, IEEE 1394 is more expensive than USB and much faster (up to 400Mbps). IEEE 1394 is typically used for devices that require fast transmission of large amounts of data, such as video cameras and digital versatile disk (DVD) players. IEEE 1394 is often referred to as *FireWire*, the trademarked name given to Apple Computer's IEEE 1394 systems. IEEE 1394 is also referred to by other manufacturer-specific names, such as *i.link* or *Lynx*

Like SCSI, FireWire devices are attached in a daisy-chain (peer-to-peer) topology. No single cable in the system can exceed four meters. To upgrade an IEEE 1394 device, unplug the device to be replaced and plug the new device into its place in the chain. The FireWire system will provide the device with power and will automatically detect and configure it.

on the
job

FireWire systems can support up to 63 external devices from a single port. To use FireWire, the computer must be running a compatible operating system, such as Windows 98 or Windows 2000, and you must have an IEEE 1394 controller.

Verifying Appropriate System Resources

Any time you install or upgrade an adapter or peripheral, you must ensure that there are appropriate system resources available for it. System resources that the device may require include expansion slots, IRQs, input/output (I/O) addresses, and DMA channels.

Expansion Slots

Expansion slots are the means through which adapters and expansion cards communicate with the rest of the computer—they are the slots used to attach cards to the motherboard. Before installing an adapter or an expansion card, ensure the motherboard supports that type of card and that there is a slot available for it. There are several types of expansion slots, and the slot type must match the card type. One of the most common card/slot types is Industry Standard Architecture (ISA). ISA devices are 16 bit. Extended ISA (EISA) devices are 32 bit, and the slots are backward compatible with ISA devices. That is, you may install an ISA card into either an ISA or an EISA slot. EISA cards, however, cannot be installed into an ISA slot.

Another common slot/card type is Peripheral Component Interconnect (PCI). PCI architecture is 64 bit and is faster and newer than ISA and EISA architecture. PCI slots are smaller than ISA and are white (where ISA slots are black). PCI slots can be used by PCI cards only.

When upgrading devices, ensure that the motherboard supports the architecture of the device you want to install. That is, if there are no PCI slots on the motherboard, you cannot upgrade from an ISA to a PCI sound card. Furthermore, ensure there are slots available. You cannot upgrade from an EISA video card to a PCI video card if all of the system's existing PCI slots are in use by other devices.

IRQs, I/O Addresses, and DMAs

One type of computer resource is an *input/output (I/O) address*. When the computer is started, the BIOS loads into RAM device-specific information about the existing devices, including their drivers and other rules of communication. Whenever the processor needs to communicate with a device in the computer, it first checks RAM for the entries pertaining to that device. Without an I/O address, components would appear nonexistent to the processor.

Once the processor has finished communicating with or requesting a task from a device, it continues on with other functions, rather than waiting for the device to finish its task. When the device has a result to report to the processor, it places the result in RAM. Next, the device "interrupts" the processor's function to indicate that the task is completed. Devices accomplish this through *interrupt request (IRQ) lines.* When the processor receives an interrupt, it can identify the initiating device by its IRQ and then turns to that device's I/O (RAM) address to retrieve the information.

In some cases, devices require data from other components in order to complete their tasks. In these cases, it is more efficient to allow the two devices to communicate directly with each other than it is for them to communicate through the processor. Devices communicate with one another using *Direct Memory Access (DMA)* channels. DMA channels allow devices to write data directly into memory without first being asked by the processor. Other devices can read this data directly from memory without asking the processor for it.

In some cases, IRQs, DMAs, and I/O addresses are automatically assigned to devices by the BIOS. Plug and Play operating systems, such as Microsoft Windows 9*x* and Windows 2000, can also automatically assign resources. However, in older machines, or in other operating systems, you might need to allocate resources manually. Furthermore, in some operating systems, such as Microsoft Windows and OS/2, you can view the system's allocated and available resources. In other systems, however, you will need to rely on documentation about the system's configuration to determine which resources are assigned and which are available.

Before upgrading or installing a device, you must also ensure there are sufficient system resources for it. Devices cannot share these resources, and some devices are configured to use one of only two or three possible settings. This can make for a bit of juggling on your part. For example, suppose you want to upgrade to a SCSI adapter that can only make use of IRQ 5 or IRQ 10. What if IRQ 5 and IRQ 10 are already assigned to other devices? Which device do you reassign? And what if that device's possible resources are already in use by other devices? Planning ahead and becoming familiar with the standard resource assignments can help you work around these issues and properly configure devices on the first try.

Table 4-1 includes standard IRQ addresses and their assignments. Keep in mind that these settings may vary from one machine to another. Furthermore, if a listed device is not present, that IRQ is considered available (for example, if there is no LPT2 in the computer, its IRQ (5) is available for use by another device.

exam
Ⓦatch   *Make sure you are familiar with the standard IRQ assignments, as they will likely be part of several upgrade planning questions on the Server+ exam.*

TABLE 4-1	IRQ	Device
	0	System timer
Standard IRQ	1	Keyboard
Assignments	2	Cascade, redirect to IRQ 9
	3	Serial ports (COM2 and COM4)
	4	Serial ports (COM1 and COM3)
	5	Parallel port (LPT2)
	6	Floppy drive controller
	7	Parallel port (LPT1)
	8	Real-time clock
	9	Redirected from IRQ 2
	10	Available
	11	Available
	12	PS/2 mouse
	13	Math coprocessor
	14	Hard disk controller
	15	Secondary hard disk controller

SCENARIO & SOLUTION

Use the following Scenario & Solution questions to reinforce your knowledge about IRQ addresses.	
Which device typically uses IRQ 6?	Floppy controller
Which IRQ is typically used by the primary hard disk controller?	IRQ 14
I'm attaching a device that can use either IRQ 11 or IRQ 15. Which should I use?	If the computer uses the secondary hard disk controller, you must use IRQ 11 for the new device. If there is no secondary hard disk, you can use either IRQ 11 or IRQ 15, with no noticeable performance difference.

CERTIFICATION SUMMARY

When a server component cannot support desired features or creates a bottleneck in the system, you should consider an upgrade. Fortunately, this does not always require an entire system upgrade, as many of the system's components can be upgraded individually. For example, if the system BIOS cannot support a desired feature, such as the ability to boot from the CD-ROM drive, you can often flash or replace the BIOS to support that feature.

When upgrading an adapter, such as a NIC, SCSI, or RAID adapter, consider that the new component must be configured to communicate with the hardware, through the allocation of system resources and the installation of a device driver. The adapter must then be configured to work within its subsystem. NICs must be configured to communicate with the network, SCSI adapters must be configured to communicate with the SCSI system, and RAID adapters must be configured to manage the disks in the RAID array.

Most peripheral upgrades are straightforward; simply replace the component and ensure it is configured to communicate with the hardware (through system resource allocation and device drivers). Some peripherals, however, such as modems and the video system, require special consideration, as discussed in the chapter. Whenever you perform a component upgrade, ensure the proper system resources are available, such as expansion slots, IRQs, I/O addresses, and DMA channels.

TWO-MINUTE DRILL

Here are some of the key points from each certification objective in Chapter 4.

Upgrading BIOS/Firmware

❑ The system BIOS translates communications between the processor and the system's components, and stores basic system configurations.

❑ The BIOS should be upgraded when it cannot recognize a new component, or does not support a desired system feature.

❑ The BIOS can be upgraded electronically (flashed) or can be replaced with another BIOS chip.

❑ Flash the BIOS using the manufacturer-provided floppy disk.

❑ Before replacing the BIOS chip, ensure the new one is supported by the motherboard.

Upgrading Adapters

❑ Upgrade the NIC when the entire network is upgraded to a different type or a faster speed, or when you require a NIC feature that is currently unsupported.

❑ Upgrade the SCSI adapter when it creates a bottleneck or will not recognize a new SCSI device.

❑ After configuring the SCSI adapter with the proper system resources, terminate it and configure it with a SCSI ID.

❑ Upgrade the RAID adapter when it creates a bottleneck or doesn't support a desired RAID configuration.

❑ Configure the RAID adapter with the appropriate system resources, then configure it to manage the disks in the desired RAID arrangement.

Upgrading Internal and External Peripheral Devices

❑ When upgrading the video system, ensure the video adapter and monitor are compatible.

❑ When upgrading from one analog modem to another, simply replace the modem and configure it with the proper system resources and dial-up settings.

❑ When upgrading from an analog modem to a cable modem, install and configure an Ethernet card and plug the external modem into it.

❑ When upgrading a USB or IEEE 1394 device, simply unplug the old device and plug the new device in its place.

❑ Before upgrading any adapter or peripheral, ensure there are available resources, such as expansion slots, IRQs, I/O addresses ,and DMAs, if required.

SELF TEST

The following questions will help you measure your understanding of the material presented in this chapter. Read all of the choices carefully, as there may be more than one correct answer. Choose all correct answers for each question.

Upgrading BIOS/Firmware

1. Which type of ROM chip does a flash BIOS use?

    A. FROM

    B. PROM

    C. EEPROM

    D. EPROM

2. Under which circumstance would you recommend that a customer "flash" the BIOS?

    A. When the customer wants to erase the contents of the BIOS.

    B. When the customer wants to upgrade the BIOS.

    C. When the customer wants to remove a virus from the BIOS.

    D. You should never recommend flashing the BIOS.

3. Your current system BIOS requires an upgrade. Assuming the system uses a flash BIOS, which upgrade methods may be available?

    A. The BIOS must be physically replaced.

    B. The BIOS must be electronically upgraded.

    C. The BIOS may be upgraded either physically or electronically.

    D. Flash BIOS chips cannot be upgraded, as they are incorporated into the motherboard.

4. You wish to have the server boot from a setup program on the CD-ROM, but the option to boot from CD does not appear in the BIOS settings program. What should you do first?

    A. Upgrade the BIOS.

    B. Upgrade the CD-ROM drive.

    C. Upgrade the server.

    D. Copy the setup program from the CD to a floppy disk and boot from the floppy disk.

5. You have just installed a new 2GB hard disk on the server and configured it as a secondary master. However, the system will recognize only 500MB, and the system's setup program will not allow you to enter the full capacity of the hard disk. Which of the following is true?

    A. You may be able to use the full capacity of the hard disk by upgrading the BIOS.

    B. You may be able to use more than 500MB of hard disk space by upgrading to a different type of hard disk.

    C. You may be able to use the full hard disk capacity by reconfiguring the new hard disk as a primary master.

    D. There is nothing you can do to make the computer use the full capacity of the hard disk.

6. Which of the following accurately describes the procedure for flashing the BIOS?

    A. Expose the BIOS chip to ultraviolet light and reprogram it.

    B. Remove the BIOS chip from its motherboard socket and install another BIOS chip in its place.

    C. Remove the CMOS battery from the motherboard, then reinstall it and reconfigure the BIOS settings.

    D. Insert the manufacturer's flash application floppy disk and start the computer.

Upgrading Adapters

7. Under which circumstance will you upgrade the NIC on the server only (and not on the network's workstations)?

    A. When you want to change the network from token ring to Ethernet.

    B. When you want to speed up the network by upgrading the server's speed from 10Mbps to 100Mbps.

    C. When you want to improve the server's ability to cache incoming network requests.

    D. Any time you upgrade the server's NIC, you must also upgrade the NIC on each workstation.

8. You want to use the server's NIC to monitor network signal strength. However, this feature is not supported by the existing NIC, and there are no manufacturer upgrades to support this feature. Which of the following procedures do not need to be performed to make use of the desired monitoring feature?

    A. Replace the NIC and ensure the new NIC is configured with the appropriate system resources, such as an IRQ.

B.   Replace the NIC and ensure the new NIC is configured with the proper network settings.

C.   Upgrade the configuration application for the existing NIC and ensure the monitoring feature is enabled.

D.   You will need to perform all of the above procedures.

9. A server-based network currently runs at 10Mbps. Which of the following can you do to upgrade the network to 100Mbps?

A.   Upgrade the NIC on the server only.

B.   Upgrade the NIC on the workstations only.

C.   Upgrade the NIC on the server and at least one workstation.

D.   Upgrade the NIC on the server and all of the workstations.

10. Under which circumstance will you upgrade the SCSI adapter, but not the other SCSI devices?

A.   When you want to install a SCSI device that the adapter does not recognize.

B.   When you want to speed up the SCSI system (for example, from 20MBps to 80MBps).

C.   When you want to upgrade the SCSI system from Fast SCSI-2 to Ultra SCSI-3.

D.   Any time you upgrade the SCSI adapter, you must also upgrade all attached SCSI devices.

11. A client wants to implement parity in the server's existing RAID array, but the RAID adapter does not support this option. Which of the following should you recommend?

A.   Upgrade the hard disk that will contain the parity information.

B.   Upgrade the RAID adapter.

C.   Upgrade each disk in the existing system to support parity.

D.   Upgrade the entire RAID system.

12. Your server currently uses a SCSI RAID adapter to manage disk mirroring. After upgrading the hard disks, you notice that the system is not recognizing the full capacity of the hard disks. Which of the following will most likely resolve the problem?

A.   Upgrade the RAID adapter.

B.   Upgrade the SCSI adapter.

C.   Upgrade the hard disks.

D.   Upgrade the system BIOS.

13. Your server contains a SCSI system that includes a SCSI printer, a SCSI scanner, and a SCSI raid subsystem. Which of the following steps must you perform to properly upgrade the SCSI adapter? Assume the SCSI devices themselves do not need to be upgraded.

    A. Install a new SCSI adapter and assign it the appropriate system resources.

    B. Install a new SCSI adapter, assign it the appropriate system resources, and assign it the appropriate SCSI ID.

    C. Install a new SCSI adapter, assign it the appropriate system resources, ensure it is properly terminated, and assign it the appropriate SCSI ID.

    D. Install a new SCSI adapter, ensure it is properly terminated, assign it the appropriate SCSI ID, and configure it to manage the disks in the RAID array.

Upgrading Internal and External Peripheral Devices

14. Your server's video system currently makes use of SVGA ISA technology, and you are planning to upgrade it so that it makes use of SVGA PCI technology. Which components will you need to replace to perform the upgrade?

    A. The video adapter's BIOS

    B. The video adapter only

    C. The monitor only

    D. The video adapter and monitor

15. You are planning to upgrade your server's external 14.4Kbps analog modem to an internal 28.8Kbps analog modem. Which of the following steps must you perform?

    A. Install the new modem and assign it an available IRQ.

    B. Install the new modem, assign it an available IRQ, and configure its dial-up properties.

    C. Install the modem and assign it to an available COM port.

    D. Install the modem, assign it to an available COM port, and configure its dial-up properties.

16. You are planning to upgrade your analog modem to a cable modem. Which of the following steps is not required?

    A. Install and configure the NIC in an available expansion slot.

    B. Ensure the modem is assigned the appropriate system resources.

    C. Plug the modem into a cable outlet using coaxial cable.

    D. All of the above are required steps.

17. A server is currently using the following IRQ assignments:

3 analog modem

4 serial mouse

5 parallel scanner

7 parallel printer

You are planning to upgrade the modem with a cable modem, but the NIC is designed to make use of IRQ 4 or IRQ 5 only. After working out a solution that will accommodate all of the listed devices, which IRQ assignment will the NIC have?

A. 3

B. 4

C. 5

D. You cannot accommodate all of the devices.

18. A server currently uses an IDE RAID array and a SCSI printer. You are planning to upgrade from an IDE RAID subsystem to a SCSI RAID system, and you are also planning to install a sound card. However, the only available IRQ in the system is IRQ 10. Assume that the devices are Plug and Play and that the server uses standard IRQ settings. Which devices can the system support?

A. The SCSI RAID adapter only

B. The sound card only

C. The SCSI RAID adapter and the sound card

D. Neither the SCSI RAID adapter nor the sound card

19. You are planning to upgrade your USB black-ink printer to a USB color printer. Which of the following steps must you perform?

A. Remove the old printer and attach the new printer in its place.

B. Remove the old printer, attach the new printer in its place, and assign the new printer the appropriate IRQ.

C. Remove the old printer, attach the new printer in its place, and assign the new printer the appropriate SCSI ID.

D. Add a USB hub to the last device in the system and attach the new printer to it.

20. A customer is complaining that the server's cable modem is too slow, and wants to upgrade to a faster cable modem. Which of the following steps should you recommend that the customer perform?

   A. Install a NIC in an available expansion slot.

   B. Ensure the NIC is assigned the appropriate system resources.

   C. Plug the modem into a cable outlet using coaxial cable.

   D. None of the above.

LAB QUESTION

Throughout this chapter, you have been presented with the procedures for upgrading a number of computer devices. For each of the procedures listed in Table 4-2, enter the letter denoting each devices to which that procedure applies. Note that some procedures apply to more than one type of device and some procedures do not apply to any of the listed devices. Refer to Table 4-3 for the answers to this Lab Question.

TABLE 4-2 Lab Question Table

A. Flash BIOS	____ Assign the device an available IRQ
B. NIC	____ Install the device in an available expansion slot
C. External Analog Modem	____ Configure the device with a SCSI ID
D. IDE RAID adapter	____ Configure the device to manage the hard disks in the appropriate array
E. SCSI RAID adapter	____ Configure the device with the appropriate dial-up settings
F. SCSI adapter	____ Terminate the device
	____ Reboot the computer using a manufacturer-provided floppy disk
	____ Unless the device supports Plug and Play, load a device driver
	____ Attach the device to an available USB port
	____ Attach the device to an available COM port

SELF TEST ANSWERS

1. ☑ **C. Flash BIOS chips are EEPROM chips.** EEPROM (Electronically Erasable Programmable ROM) chips can be electronically upgraded, using a "flash" application supplied by the manufacturer.
   ☒ **A**, FROM, is incorrect, as this is not a valid ROM chip type. **B**, PROM, is incorrect, as this type of chip can be programmed once by the user, but cannot be electronically upgraded. **D**, EPROM, is incorrect because this type of chip can be erased (using ultraviolet light) and reprogrammed, but cannot be electronically "flashed."

2. ☑ **B. You should recommend flashing the BIOS when the customer wants to upgrade the BIOS.** By using a manufacturer-provided flash application, the customer may be able to electronically upgrade the BIOS to support a new feature or recognize a new device.
   ☒ **A** is incorrect because it suggests flashing the BIOS to erase its contents. The flash application will upgrade the BIOS, but will not erase its contents. **C** is incorrect because it suggests flashing the BIOS in an attempt to remove a BIOS virus. The BIOS itself cannot get computer viruses, as the BIOS can only be written to by a flash application. **D**, you should never recommend flashing the BIOS, is also incorrect. When the BIOS has to be upgraded, flashing is often a simpler and less expensive method than physical chip replacement.

3. ☑ **C. The BIOS may be upgraded either physically or electronically.** One feature of a flash BIOS is that it can be electronically flashed, or upgraded, using a manufacturer-provided flash application. If the appropriate electronic upgrade is not available from the manufacturer, you may physically replace the BIOS on the motherboard.
   ☒ **A** and **B** are incorrect because they suggest physical *or* electronic upgrading only, respectively. Again, one feature of a flash BIOS is that it supports both physical *and* electronic upgrading. For this reason, **D**, which states that the BIOS chip cannot be upgraded, is also incorrect.

4. ☑ **A. You should upgrade the BIOS.** Most of the newer BIOS chips can be electronically upgraded using a flash application, provided by the BIOS manufacturer. If the BIOS cannot be flashed, physically replace the BIOS chip with one that supports the option to boot from the CD.
   ☒ **B**, upgrade the CD-ROM drive, is incorrect because the option to boot from CD is a function of the BIOS, not of the CD-ROM drive itself. **C**, upgrade the server is also incorrect. Before replacing the entire server, you should attempt to upgrade the BIOS, as this is a cheaper and often easier procedure than replacing the server. **D** is incorrect because it suggests copying the desired application to floppy disk and booting from the floppy drive. However, the capacity of a floppy drive is limited to 1.44MB, which is typically not enough to store an entire

setup program. Furthermore, many setup programs rely on the existence of required setup files on the same media as the setup application itself. If the setup program is run from a floppy disk, it may not be able to find the required files if they reside on the CD.

5.   ☑ **A.** You may be able to use the full capacity of the hard disk by upgrading the BIOS. If the system's BIOS was manufactured before the release of hard disks with a capacity over 500MB, the BIOS may simply not be programmed to recognize larger capacities. Try flashing or replacing the BIOS to support the new capacity.

☒ **B** and **C** are incorrect because they suggest upgrading or reconfiguring the hard disk to resolve the capacity recognition problem. However, the ability of the system to recognize a hard disk's capacity lies with the BIOS, not with the hard disk itself. **D** is incorrect because it suggests you can do nothing to make the computer recognize the full capacity of the hard disk. Again, you may be able to support the new capacity by upgrading the BIOS. As an aside, you may also use the full capacity by partitioning the hard disk into four 500MB disks.

6.   ☑ **D.** To flash a BIOS, insert the manufacturer's flash application floppy disk and start the computer. The flash application program will launch, allowing you to select the appropriate features and upgrade the BIOS.

☒ **A**, expose the BIOS chip to ultraviolet light and reprogram it, is incorrect. This is the procedure for upgrading an EPROM BIOS chip. However, the term *flash* is specific to electronic upgrades, and is unique to EEPROM chips. **B** is incorrect because it suggests physically replacing the BIOS chip. Although this is one method for upgrading the BIOS, the term *flash* is used specifically to refer to upgrading the BIOS electronically. **C** is incorrect because it suggests temporarily removing the CMOS battery and reconfiguring the BIOS. This procedure will erase the current BIOS settings (or set them back to their defaults), but it will not upgrade the BIOS so that the BIOS will support a new feature. Erasure of the BIOS settings is not the same thing as flashing the BIOS.

Upgrading Adapters

7.   ☑ **C.** You may upgrade the NIC on the server only (but not on the network's workstations) when you want to improve the server's ability to cache incoming network requests. The NIC itself is able to cache a certain amount of incoming data, and if the server is acting as a bottleneck, you may want to replace the NIC with one that has improved caching ability. This will lead to fewer retransmissions and result in less overall network traffic.

☒ **A**, when you want to change the network from token ring to Ethernet, is incorrect. Every NIC on the network must support the same network type. By changing the NIC on a single computer only, you will render that computer unable to communicate with the rest of the network. **B** is incorrect because it suggests that you can increase the network speed from 10Mbps to 100Mbps by upgrading the NIC on the server only. However, all NICs on the network must support the same speed in order for the communications to run at that speed. If the server NIC runs at 100Mbps and each workstation continues to run at 10Mbps, the server will continue to run at 10Mbps. **D** is incorrect because it suggests that there are no circumstances in which you would upgrade the server NIC only. However, as explained earlier, you may want to upgrade the NIC to support a currently unsupported feature, such as greater caching ability. In this case, there is no need to upgrade all NICs on the network.

8. ☑ **C.** When upgrading the NIC to support the desired feature, you will not be required to upgrade the configuration application for the existing NIC. Recall that the manufacturer of the current NIC does not support the monitoring feature. Therefore, the only option is to physically replace the NIC with one that supports this feature.
☒ **A** and **B** are incorrect. In this scenario, the existing NIC cannot be made to support the new feature. Therefore, the NIC will have to be physically replaced and the new one will have to be configured with the appropriate system resources and the proper network settings. **D** is incorrect because it suggests that you will be required to perform all of the listed procedures. Again, because the manufacturer does not support the desired feature, you cannot resolve the problem by upgrading the existing NIC's configuration application.

9. ☑ **D.** To upgrade the network to 100Mbps, you must upgrade the NIC on the server and all of the workstations. Network communications are transmitted at the speed of the slowest device. Therefore, if a computer configured for 100Mbps is communicating with a computer configured for 10Mbps, data will be passed at 10Mbps. To upgrade the entire network, all computers must be upgraded to support the new speed.
☒ **A, B,** and **C** are incorrect because upgrading the server or workstations only will not affect the speed of the entire network.

10. ☑ **A.** You may upgrade the SCSI adapter without upgrading the SCSI devices when you want to install a SCSI device that the adapter does not recognize. For example, if the SCSI adapter cannot recognize a new CD-ROM drive, you will need to upgrade the SCSI adapter to make use of the new drive.
☒ **B** and **C** are incorrect because they suggest upgrading the SCSI adapter to support a different SCSI type or speed. However, all SCSI devices must support the new speed or type for the new system to be upgraded. That is, you cannot improve the speed or type of the entire system simply by upgrading the adapter. **D** is incorrect because it suggests that there are no circumstances in which you would upgrade the SCSI adapter only. Again, if you want to install

a new device that the current adapter does not recognize, you may be able to upgrade the adapter only (and not the entire SCSI system).

11. ☑ **B.** You should recommend that the client upgrade the RAID adapter. If the current adapter will not support a desired option, check with the manufacturer for a software patch or upgrade. If one does not exist, upgrade the adapter itself.

☒ **A, C,** and **D** are incorrect because they suggest upgrading hard disks to support parity. Parity information is simply a type of data that is stored on the hard disk, just as files are stored on the hard disk. It is the RAID adapter, not the disk, that is responsible for configuring the RAID system to generate and store parity information.

12. ☑ **B.** You may be able to resolve the problem by upgrading the SCSI adapter. Recall that all communications between the computer and SCSI devices goes through the SCSI adapter. The adapter is responsible for recognizing and managing those devices, and is also responsible for detecting SCSI hard disk capacities.

☒ **A,** upgrade the RAID adapter, is incorrect because the RAID adapter is responsible for managing available disk space in the appropriate RAID array. The RAID adapter is not responsible for recognizing the hard disks and their capacity. **C,** upgrade the hard disks, is also incorrect. The ability to make use of a hard disk's full capacity is the function of the system BIOS, or in this case the SCSI adapter's BIOS, not the hard disk itself. **D,** upgrade the system BIOS, is incorrect because although the system BIOS is responsible for recognizing and communicating with IDE drives, it is not responsible for recognizing and communicating with SCSI devices, including SCSI drives.

13. ☑ **C.** To properly upgrade the SCSI adapter, you should install a new SCSI adapter, assign it the appropriate system resources, ensure it is properly terminated, and assign it the appropriate SCSI ID. After physically installing the new adapter, you must ensure it is recognized by the computer. Do this by assigning it the appropriate system resources, such as an IRQ and I/O address. Next, to ensure the adapter will work within the SCSI system, terminate it and configure it with a SCSI ID.

☒ **A** and **B** are incorrect because they do not include all of the steps required to properly configure the adapter to work in the SCSI system (terminating and assigning a SCSI ID). **D** is incorrect because it suggests configuring the SCSI adapter to manage the RAID array. However, although the SCSI adapter itself is responsible for recognizing and communicating the SCSI devices, it cannot configure and manage a RAID array. This is the responsibility of a separate SCSI RAID controller.

Upgrading Internal and External Peripheral Devices

14. ☑ **B.** You will need to replace the video adapter only. ISA and PCI are two different bus architectures, each supporting a different type of expansion card. To perform the upgrade, remove the ISA video adapter and install the PCI video adapter in an available PCI slot. Next, ensure the adapter is configured with the appropriate system resources and device driver.
☒ **A,** the video adapter's BIOS, is incorrect because ISA and PCI support different card types. The video adapter itself must be replaced to take advantage of PCI architecture. **C** and **D** are incorrect because they suggest replacing the monitor. However, PCI denotes an internal card type, not a monitor type. Furthermore, in this case, the video technology (SVGA) is not being changed, so as long as the new PCI adapter matches the monitor type (SVGA), there is no need to replace the monitor.

15. ☑ **D.** To properly upgrade the modem, you must install the modem, assign it to an available COM port, and configure its dial-up properties. Start by physically installing the modem in an available expansion slot. The modem is then configured to make use of an available COM port, even though it is an internal device and is not actually plugged into the COM port. The modem will make use of that COM port's system resources. Finish by configuring the modem with the proper dial-up properties (typically supplied to you by the ISP).
☒ **A** and **B** are incorrect because they suggest assigning an available IRQ to the modem. However, as discussed in the preceding explanation, internal modems do not receive separate IRQs, rather, they are assigned to COM ports and they make use of that port's existing resources. **C** is incorrect because it does not include the configuration of the modem's dial-up properties. Without this step, the computer can communicate with the modem, but the modem itself cannot do its job, as it cannot communicate with other modems.

16. ☑ **B.** When upgrading from an analog to a cable modem, you will not be required to assign the modem with appropriate system resources. Cable modems are external devices that communicate with the computer through an internal Ethernet NIC. The modem itself is not recognized by the computer, and behaves as any other external networked device (such as a workstation on the network).
☒ **A** is incorrect because it suggests that you will not need to install and configure a NIC. Again, cable modems are external devices that rely on the installation of an internal Ethernet NIC to communicate with the computer. **C** is incorrect because it suggests that you are not required to plug the modem into a cable outlet using coaxial cable. Without this step, however, the modem has no means to communicate with other modems. **D** is incorrect because it suggests that all steps listed are required.

17. ☑ **B.** The NIC will be assigned IRQ 4. The solution requires a bit of juggling and IRQ reassignment. The serial mouse must make use of a COM port, so it can use either IRQ 3 (COM2 and COM4) or IRQ 4 (COM1 and COM3). When you remove the analog modem, IRQ 3 will become available. Reassign the serial mouse from IRQ 4 to IRQ 3 and assign IRQ 4 to the NIC.

☒ **A,** 3, is incorrect because although this IRQ will be available after removing the analog modem, the NIC cannot make use of it (recall that the NIC must use IRQ 4 or IRQ 5). **C,** 5, is incorrect because this IRQ is currently in use by the parallel scanner. Standard IRQ assignments allow for 2 parallel ports only, at IRQ 5 and IRQ 7. Therefore, you cannot assign an alternate IRQ to the parallel scanner. **D** is incorrect because it suggests that there is no way to accommodate all of the devices.

18. ☑ **C.** The system can support both the SCSI RAID adapter and the sound card. Because the system already contains a SCSI system (recall the system uses a SCSI printer), the SCSI adapter can be installed as any other SCSI device would. Therefore, it will be assigned a SCSI ID rather than an IRQ. This leaves IRQ 10 available for the sound card. As an aside, because the RAID system is being upgraded from IDE to SCSI, the hard disks will have to be replaced, thereby freeing up the IRQs formerly in use by the IDE drives (IRQs 14 and 15).

☒ **A, B,** and **D** are incorrect because they suggest that the system will not be able to support both of the new devices. However, as explained earlier, because the RAID adapter will be part of the SCSI system, it does not require an IRQ.

19. ☑ **A.** To upgrade the printer, remove the old printer and attach the new printer in its place. USB devices are Plug and Play, meaning that the USB controller will automatically recognize and configure the new printer with the appropriate resources.

☒ **B** and **C** are incorrect because they suggest configuring the new printer with an IRQ or SCSI ID, respectively. Because the printer is part of the USB system, it will be assigned a USB ID by the USB controller. Therefore, the printer does not require a system IRQ or SCSI ID. **D** is incorrect because it suggests adding a USB hub to attach the new printer. However, because you are upgrading from one printer to another, you can remove the old printer and attach the new printer in its place.

20. ☑ **D.** None of the above. Cable modems are all capable of supporting the same speed. Therefore, there is no such thing as a "faster" cable modem. In this case, you should suggest that the customer look elsewhere for the source of the problem, such as the speed limitations set by the ISP.

☒ **A, B,** and **C** are all incorrect. They all describe appropriate procedures for installing a cable modem, but in this case, you should not recommend upgrading the modem.

LAB ANSWER

TABLE 4-3	Lab Answer Table	
A. Flash BIOS	<u>B, D, F</u>	Assign the device an available IRQ
B. NIC	<u>B, D, E, F</u>	Install the device in an available expansion slot
C. External Analog Modem	<u>E, F</u>	Configure the device with a SCSI ID
D. IDE RAID adapter	<u>D, E</u>	Configure the device to manage the hard drives in the appropriate array
E. SCSI RAID adapter	<u>C</u>	Configure the device with the appropriate dial-up settings
F. SCSI adapter	<u>E, F</u>	Terminate the device
	<u>A</u>	Reboot the computer using a manufacturer-provided floppy disk
	<u>B, C, D, E, F</u>	Unless the device supports Plug and Play, load a device driver
	<u> </u>	Attach the device to an available USB port
	<u>C</u>	Attach the device to an available COM port

Server+

COMPUTING TECHNOLOGY INDUSTRY ASSOCIATION

5

System Health

Nothing lasts forever. It's a fact that you can't escape when dealing with computers, and it should come as no surprise that you will need to upgrade various elements every so often. To ensure you have the latest upgrades for software, you will need to regularly check with manufacturers. In addition, hardware will break down or become obsolete after awhile, requiring you to install and configure new components.

In this chapter we will discuss a number of areas requiring upgrades. We will discuss system monitoring agents, which are programs that monitor a computer for specific activities or errors. We will also look at upgrading service tools that come with your system, including diagnostic tools, EISA configuration, diagnostic partitions, and system setup utilities. Finally, we will discuss upgrading uninterruptible power supplies (UPSs). A UPS will ensure that good electrical currents are passed to your computer and that backup battery power is provided during power failures.

CERTIFICATION OBJECTIVE 5.01

Upgrading System Monitoring Agents

Agents are programs that monitor, gather information, or process a specific task in the background. In terms of system monitoring agents, these are programs that monitor your system for changes that indicate possible problems. Agents are generally part of a larger software package, where these small programs have a specific task of gathering information and passing it back to a larger management system. There are a variety of reasons why agents may be used, and subsequently, different methods in which they can be upgraded.

SNMP

One of the most common places you'll find agents is in Simple Network Management Protocol (SNMP). SNMP is part of the TCP/IP suite. This protocol uses agents that monitor network hardware and drivers. The information gathered by the agent is then reported to an SNMP manager (or management system), which is a program that receives information from the agents and then acts on it.

Remember that SNMP agents work with a management system. The agent works as a middleman between the management system and the device. The management system allows you to work with the agent.

Through SNMP, you can monitor network devices and their functions, and then manage the hardware from a remote computer. The SNMP agent acts as a middleman between the management system and your device, allowing you to connect to it. This means that you won't need to visit each piece of equipment that has an agent, as the agent provides a method of accessing the device remotely. SNMP agents allow you to access settings on a device, so that you can send commands to it and configure it remotely. You can also view statistics (such as throughput and collisions) based on information that's passed to the SNMP manager from the agents.

Agents may be installed as software that is loaded on a managed device or they may be part of a device's firmware. It will often be installed as software when you are managing something such as a server or some other piece of equipment that uses software. The agent may also reside in the firmware of a device, as is the case with network bridges and other devices that don't support software being loaded into them. As you can see by this, agents may need to be upgraded in different ways, depending on the device using the agent.

Upgrading SNMP Agents

Upgrading SNMP agents may be a matter of upgrading software or it may require upgrading the firmware of a network component. Updating the SNMP agents can be done in a variety of ways, depending on what the SNMP agent is running on. These methods include:

- Applying the latest service pack or patch to the operating system or software.
- Upgrading the operating system to a later version.
- Upgrading the firmware on a network device.

Windows 2000 includes SNMP agent and management support, allowing you to monitor your server or workstation for problems. Because these are part of the operating system, applying the latest service pack or upgrading the operating system to a later version (when one becomes available) performs an upgrade of the agent. Fortunately, you can obtain service packs easily using the Windows Update Web site at http://upgrade.microsoft.com. Visiting this site with Internet Explorer will cause your system to be analyzed, and software updates will be suggested that are applicable to your computer and haven't been installed yet.

Other operating systems and software that use agents can also benefit from upgrades, patches, and service packs. Similar to Microsoft, the Web sites of these operating systems and programs will offer files that can be downloaded and run to perform the upgrade. Because these will modify your system's software, you should perform a backup of your system before the software is updated. If a problem occurs, you could lose more than the ability to benefit from SNMP agents.

To upgrade agents that are part of your network equipment's firmware, you will need to upgrade the firmware. This changes the programs that are stored in the memory of the hardware, and it also changes the software for the agent. The memory the agents are stored in is read-only memory (ROM), which can be upgraded using Flash ROM software. This is a program that updates the code in the memory, with what is contained in a file that you download from the equipment's manufacturer.

Steps involved in updating the firmware may vary depending on the equipment being upgraded. As such, you will need to review the documentation for the upgrade. Because the firmware acts as the brain for the equipment, a problem with the upgrade could conceivably lobotomize it.

Network Management

Agents may be used with network management software, which can be used to gather information on hardware on your network. This is seen with tools like System Management Server (SMS), where various agents and polling processes evaluate devices on a network. This allows you to view components making up your network, which can then be used to automatically create an accurate inventory of equipment.

Agents for these agents can be upgraded through service packs or by upgrading the actual software to a later version. For example, if you wanted to upgrade SMS to a later version, you would go to Microsoft's Web site, download the latest service pack for this program, and then apply it. This would fix any problems identified with the agents and add any additional features that have been added since the original release.

SCENARIO & SOLUTION

Now that we've discussed agents in such detail, refer to the following Scenario & Solution for some scenario questions or situations that you may encounter.

Are agents always software that runs on a machine?	No. Agents may be software that runs on equipment that can load software, but agents may also reside in the firmware of devices that can't load software.
What types of equipment on a network can use agents?	A variety of network components can use agents. These include routers, network bridges, and so forth. Even servers may use agents. Windows 2000 includes its own SNMP agent and management system.

CERTIFICATION OBJECTIVE 5.02

Upgrading Service Tools

Service tools are programs that allow you to configure and monitor your system, thereby allowing you to detect and fix possible problems. These include the setup programs and diagnostic tools that are available at bootup and control how your system functions. Unlike other programs discussed in this chapter, many of the service tools discussed here are available from the computer manufacturer itself, and may be stored in special areas of the hard disk. In some cases, special versions of diagnostic and setup software are also available for different operating systems, or may be provided by the manufacturer of the operating system. Without these tools, you would be unable to run your computer or detect problems when the operating system fails to load.

To give you an example of a service tool, think about the last time you pressed DELETE or F10 at bootup and accessed the setup utility for your computer. Here, you accessed settings that controlled access to the hard disk, the type of floppy disk used on the machine, and so forth. Because of the importance of these settings, it is important that you don't upgrade such programs without documenting their settings first. If a problem occurs during an upgrade, or settings are restored to their defaults, you will want to change the configuration to the correct settings.

You should also consider some downtime with such upgrades, as they will generally require you to reboot the machine to complete and test the upgrade. If the upgrade is being performed on a server, then users may be unable to authenticate or access their files.

Diagnostic Tools

Diagnostic tools are used to troubleshoot your computer. Such tools may be included with the computer itself, available through the operating system installed on it, or added separately as utilities and software packages. Due to the various ways diagnostic tools are available to you, the methods in which they are used and upgraded vary.

Computers commonly include some diagnostic tool as part of the system. As we'll see later in this chapter, some of these tools may be installed on a separate partition of the hard disk (called a diagnostic partition). When the setup program for the computer is accessed (by pressing the DELETE or F10 keys at bootup), you will be able to access these tools. Using them, you can view information about your computer, and the components installed on it, and run tests to ensure they are functioning correctly.

In some circumstances, the manufacturer of your computer will also include versions of the diagnostic software that will run on various operating systems. An example of this is seen with Compaq computers, where diagnostics are provided when accessing the F10 System Setup and Diagnostics, which is also available through Windows Control Panel. As shown in Figure 5-1, this tool will analyze your system and determine whether any components are experiencing problems.

Although upgrading the diagnostics available at system startup is discussed in a later section, the Windows version of this tool can be upgraded through software available on Compaq's Web site. It is common for such upgrades to be available on the computer manufacturer's site. By downloading and running the installation files for the new version of the software, or by downloading and running patches for such programs, you will be able to upgrade these diagnostic tools to newer versions. Because they are designed for specific operating systems, it is important that you get the version for the operating system that's run on your computer.

Your operating system should also include diagnostic tools that allow you to detect problems, and these will also need upgrading from time to time. One of the most popular diagnostic tools for Microsoft operating systems is Microsoft Diagnostics (MSD). MSD is a DOS-based program named MSD.EXE that can be

FIGURE 5-1   Compaq Diagnostics

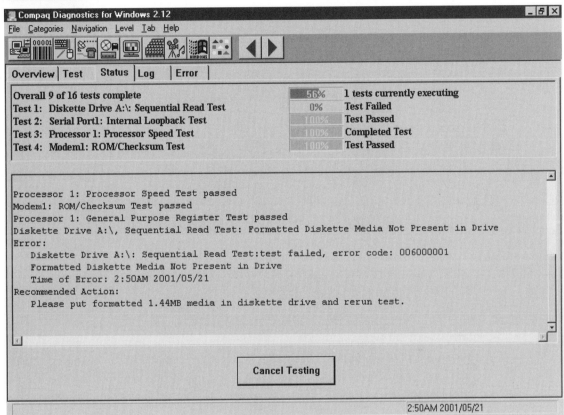

run from the command prompt. It allows you to view information about your system, even when you're having to boot it from a floppy disk. In recent versions of Windows, MSD moved away from being a DOS-based program and became a graphical Windows tool, as shown in Figure 5-2. Like its predecessor, the diagnostics tool for Windows NT provides information about your system and its resources.

So how does one upgrade such tools that come with the operating system? Generally, it's by upgrading the operating system itself. Although some tools may have upgrades or patches that specifically deal with them, most of the diagnostic tools that come with your operating system are upgraded when you apply service packs, patches, or upgrade the OS to a later version. When this happens, any changes to the diagnostic tools that are included in these upgrades are also applied.

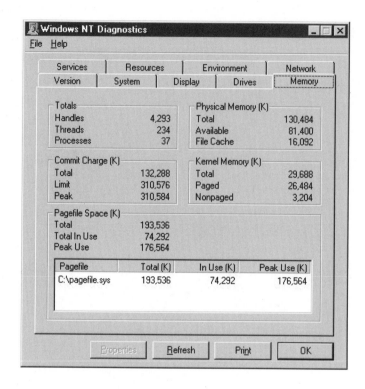

Because you are applying service packs, patches, or upgrades to the operating system itself, you should back up all data on that computer so that it can be restored if a problem occurs.

on the **Job**

Backing up the system is an important part of upgrades, as upgrades may cause more headaches than expected. To give a real-life example, in some cases when a service pack was applied to a Novell NetWare server, it fixed the problems that the service pack was supposed to address, but potentially caused new problems. You may have also experienced this if you applied Service Pack 6 for Windows NT. This was available on the Internet for about a day before problems began to be reported by users of the pack. Whereas Service Pack 6a was reliable, the previous version of it was not. If a patch, service pack, or upgrade is applied and you wanted to remove it from your system, the backup of your system becomes vital.

You may also use various types of diagnostic tools that aren't provided through the operating system or by the computer manufacturer. Such diagnostic tools are purchased or acquired through a third party. An example of such a diagnostic tool is Norton Utilities. This suite of programs includes analysis and diagnostic utilities that can help to identify problems with your computer. Being a third-party product, Norton Utilities is upgraded by purchasing an upgraded version of the software and then installing it on your machine. This is a similar process to installing the program for the first time, and you should consider backing up your system before adding the new version of the software in case problems arise.

In any of the upgrades, it is important to document the changes to your system. At the very least, you should keep a list of what computers have which versions of programs, so that a fellow member of your IT staff doesn't attempt to install the same upgrade on a machine that already has it. By keeping changes documented, you can look back at your information when problems arise and determine what has changed on the system. For example, if you upgraded software on July 1, and problems began to appear on July 2, then you could consider the upgraded software as a reason for the problem.

EISA Configuration

The Enhanced Industry Standard Architecture (EISA) is an extension of the ISA specification. It provides additional functionality, such as 32-bit memory addressing and 33-Mbps bus bandwidth, while maintaining ISA compatibility. EISA was developed primarily by Compaq as a way of competing with IBM's MCA bus, so that other companies wouldn't have to pay IBM royalties for using the MCA bus. By the time it appeared on the market however, very few EISA adapters were used in PCs; they were mainly used in file servers.

EISA uses bus mastering, which is a technology that allows a controller connected to the bus to communicate directly with other devices on the bus without going through the CPU, thus increasing performance. To further increase speeds, devices that use EISA can use burst mode to transfer data at a faster rate than normal. Burst mode is implemented by allowing a device to seize control of the bus while not allowing other devices to interrupt. This gives EISA its 33 Mbps data transfer rate.

A new configuration process was introduced with EISA that required the use of a configuration utility. The EISA Configuration utility (ECU) is a utility that reads a card's configuration file, which describes the card's characteristics and system resource requirements. It is used each time an EISA or ISA expansion card is added, removed, or repositioned on a system. Because the utility assigns resources for the system and adapters (a precursor to Plug-and-Play), the administrator is spared from having to keep a list of all of the resources that have already been assigned.

The configuration information on the card is stored in a .CFG file and is used by the utility when reconfiguring the system. If a .CFG file does not exist, the utility can be used to create one. When the EISA Configuration Utility is run, it will list all available expansion slots on your computer and use information in the .CFG file to show where that card resides on your system. In the utility, you can then change the configuration for the card.

Systems that use EISA generally provide an automated setup, which automatically recognizes potential conflicts and configures the system to deal with interrupt and addressing issues. If you find these automated settings incorrect, you can modify them using the EISA Configuration Utility, or configure the boards through jumpers and switches.

Diagnostic Partition

A diagnostic partition is a specially protected section of the hard disk used to store setup and diagnostic utilities that are used by your computer. The setup software is used to configure your system, change security settings, and configure power management. The diagnostic software is used to test and analyze the computer to determine whether problems exist. Not all computers use diagnostic partitions, as many will use a complementary metal oxide semiconductor (CMOS) setup routine. However, many computers—such as those manufactured by Compaq—use a hidden drive on the hard disk. When the manufacturer initially configures the computer, images of the setup diskette and diagnostic diskettes are loaded onto a non-DOS partition. You can access these utilities by pressing F10 during bootup.

The diagnostic partition contains software used for setting up and detecting problems with the computer. Being software, new versions will be released. In some cases, the new versions will deal with problems that appeared in earlier versions. For example, it may be unable to restore defaults or you may find that you can't change the PCI IRQ configuration. The newer version fixes such problems and may address other issues that have been recognized since it was originally released with the computer.

exam
⚙atch

Diagnostic partitions are not used on all computers. When they are used, they contain the setup and diagnostic software that configures the system and allows you to identify components and detect problems.

Another reason to upgrade the diagnostic partition occurs when the hard disk is upgraded. Because this software is stored on the hard disk, the new hard disk won't have a diagnostic partition on it. The loss of the diagnostic partition may also occur when you remove and create new partitions on the hard disk. In either of these situations, you will need to reload the setup and diagnostic software onto the hard disk.

You can determine whether a problem exists with the diagnostic partition by attempting to access the setup program during bootup. When a Compaq machine boots up, you would press the F10 key to initialize the setup routine. If this cannot be started, then you may need to reinstall the setup and diagnostic software.

When you purchase a computer that uses a diagnostic partition, floppy disks should be included with your computer for when you need to restore this partition. If you don't have these diskettes, you can create disk images from the boot utility that appears when F10 is pressed. However, if you have lost the floppy disks and your setup utility has been either corrupted or is nonexistent on a new hard disk, then up-to-date copies of the setup and diagnostic software can be obtained from the computer manufacturer's Web site. You should visit the manufacturer's site periodically to determine whether updates for this software are available. Whether you are installing or upgrading existing software, you will find the procedures almost identical.

on the job *Compaq is one of the most common computers that uses a diagnostic partition. You can obtain updated setup and diagnostic software for a Compaq server or workstation from the URL http://www.compaq.com/support/files.*

Generally, when you download the file used to create the setup and diagnostic software, you will need to expand it. In the case of Compaq computers, the file will automatically expand when you double-click it, and it will ask you to insert floppy disks, where the files will be copied. When these disks are created, you should label them so that you can use them in the proper order.

The first disk created will be made into a bootable floppy. When you start your computer with this disk in the floppy drive, you will be launched into a program that allows you to define whether you are creating a diagnostic partition or installing a new one. If there is no diagnostic partition on your disk, you will be prompted to create one. Once you've specified whether you are creating or upgrading the diagnostic partition, you will be prompted to install the other disks in a specific order. When the files from each of these floppy disks have been copied to the diagnostic partition, the system can be restarted. You should then be able to access the updated setup and diagnostic software by pressing F10.

EXERCISE 5-1

Updating the Diagnostic Partition on a Compaq Computer

1. Visit the Compaq Web site and find the updated F10 Setup and Diagnostic Software for your particular model of computer. Download the updated software.

2. When it has finished downloading, double-click the file. You will be prompted to place formatted 1.44 floppy disks into the floppy disk drive. You will need to label them accordingly, as they need to be used later in a specific order.

3. Insert the first floppy disk into the floppy disk drive, and reboot your computer.

4. When the Compaq Utilities menu appears after booting from the floppy disk, select Manage Diagnostics. From this menu, you can select to either Create or Upgrade the diagnostics partition. As you are upgrading in this exercise, select Upgrade.

5. Insert the floppy disks in the requested order.

SSU

As we saw in the previous section, the System Setup Utility (SSU) allows you to perform configurations to your system. On some machines, such as many Compaq machines, the SSU is located on the diagnostics partition. On many other machines, it is located in the ROM basic input/output system (BIOS). When your system boots up, you can access the information in the SSU by pressing DELETE or F10.

exam
Watch

The System Setup Utility is used to configure the computer. It provides information to the operating system and allows you to modify computer settings (such as the IRQ of various devices) and set security options (such as power-on passwords).

The BIOS is a collection of programs that is stored in an Erasable Programmable ROM (EPROM) chip. These programs are small in size, and are the first programs loaded when the computer is booted. During startup, the BIOS will run the power on self test (POST) that checks memory, motherboard, and other components installed on the computer. It will then boot the operating system using a boot strap loader routine. Once the operating system has loaded, the BIOS will provide access to video cards, hard disks, and other components. The BIOS does this based on settings that you or the computer's manufacturer configures through the System Setup Utility.

Whereas we discussed how to upgrade the SSU on a diagnostic partition in the previous section, this section will focus on upgrading the SSU on a machine that stores it in the ROM BIOS. Although the BIOS is stored in a chip, the chip itself generally doesn't need to be replaced during an upgrade. What does need to be upgraded are the programs contained in the BIOS. These programs can be upgraded using software available through the BIOS or computer manufacturer.

on the
Job

Many computer manufacturers will customize a BIOS to their machines. Although a company such as Phoenix Technologies may have originally created the BIOS, a computer manufacturer may have changed the code. As such, you will need to determine whether your BIOS can use a BIOS upgrade from the manufacturer of the BIOS, or whether it will need an upgrade available through a third party.

Most modern computers use a Flash BIOS that allows you to upgrade the BIOS using a special program. The upgrade utility is small and will fit on a floppy disk. In using such an upgrade program, you will generally have the options to verify whether an upgrade is needed, or if this particular upgrade will work with your existing BIOS. Such programs also commonly give you the ability to save your current BIOS to a disk, which can then be restored if a problem occurs.

Some planning is required before you begin the process of upgrading your BIOS. First, you will need to decide whether you want to upgrade it. It is common to upgrade a BIOS to take advantage of new features or support for new technologies. The biggest reason people upgraded their BIOS in recent years was due to Y2K, so that their computers would roll over properly to the year 2000 and be Y2K compliant. If you are upgrading for the sake of change, or to simply have the latest version of the SSU, then these may not be sufficient reasons. Remember that if a problem occurs, and the BIOS is erased or corrupt, then you won't be able to use the computer.

Once you've made your decision, you must determine the BIOS upgrade needed. To determine this, you should gather the following information about your computer:

- Make and model number, which is the manufacturer, type, and model number of the machine. The model number is usually imprinted on the case of the computer.

- BIOS revision, which is usually displayed in the corner of your screen when you boot up the computer. You can also determine the revision number by looking at the motherboard. However, this BIOS number on the motherboard will be out of date if you have previously upgraded the BIOS.

After you've determined this information, visit the Web site of the BIOS's or computer's manufacturer and find the upgrade file corresponding to the information you've gathered.

After downloading the update file and saving it to your hard disk, you would double-click it to expand it. Some of these upgrades will run directly from the hard disk, whereas others will require the files to be copied to a floppy disk. If they are extracted to a diskette, then the floppy disk will be made bootable and you will need to boot from this disk to perform the upgrade. In either case, directions will appear on the screen informing you of what to do to upgrade the BIOS from the program. In many cases, this consists of confirming that you want to perform the upgrade.

Once the BIOS is upgraded, the System Startup Utility will also be upgraded. When you access it by pressing the DELETE or F10 key at system startup, the SSU may appear different than before, offering different options for configuring your system.

SCENARIO & SOLUTION

Now that we've discussed upgrading service tools in such detail, refer to the following Scenario & Solution for some common situations that you may encounter.

How do I know whether my computer uses a diagnostic partition to store the System Setup Utility, or if it is stored in the ROM?	Check the documentation for the computer. If you installed the motherboard and processor yourself, then you should check the documentation for the motherboard.
I ran FDISK on my computer's hard disk and removed the diagnostic partition by accident. How can I replace it?	Obtain the disks that came with your computer, or download an upgrade for your diagnostic partition from the computer manufacturer's Web site. An option on the upgrade program will allow you to recreate the diagnostic partition.

CERTIFICATION OBJECTIVE 5.03

Upgrading the UPS

The uninterruptible power supply (UPS) is a power supply that includes a battery that takes over when a power outage occurs. When there is power, the UPS serves a similar purpose to a power bar. It is plugged into an outlet and passes the electricity on to components plugged into it. It may provide surge protection and will filter noise, so that components using the UPS don't suffer from power spikes or electromagnetic interference. However, the primary benefit of the UPS is seen when there is a power outage. When power fails to be passed to the UPS, sensors in the UPS will detect the change in voltage and the battery in the UPS will take over. The battery will continue passing electricity to the server or other network components attached to it until the battery is discharged of power or normal power is restored.

exam
Watch

The UPS is a vital part of protecting yourself against disaster. If the power is lost, the UPS can safely shutdown your computer, protecting data from being corrupted due to losing power. It also protects against various fluctuations in power from external sources.

By using a UPS, your data is protected from unexpected power failures. The battery on the UPS will continue providing power to components plugged into it for a limited amount of time. Typically, this is 5-15 minutes on most UPSs. During this time, the main power may return or you will be able to do a controlled shutdown of the server and other systems attached to it.

Software included with many UPSs and operating systems allows you to automate shutdown procedures. Even if you're unavailable to shut down the server, this software will close any open applications and gracefully shut down the operating system. A serial cable connection between the UPS and the server allows the UPS to tell the server to shutdown.

Because you may be dealing with a combination of software and hardware, the areas in which upgrades must occur are twofold. You will need to be aware of issues concerning the UPS hardware itself, but also remember that device drivers and other software that interact with the UPS will also need to be upgraded. In the sections that follow, we will discuss procedures for each.

Upgrading UPS Hardware

The UPS can be broken into two main hardware components: the UPS device and the battery contained within it. The UPS device is plugged into a wall outlet and monitors the voltage coming into it. It powers up the battery, and when the voltage changes (such as during a brownout or blackout), it will notify you with audible

FROM THE CLASSROOM

Check Your UPS Regularly

It is important to check your UPS regularly so that you don't find out a battery has gone bad when a power outage occurs. Batteries may need to be replaced every few years, so you should document when the battery for different UPSs has been replaced. It is also wise to mark the UPS with a piece of masking tape as a backup method of documentation that shows when the UPS had its battery replaced last.

—*Michael Cross, MCSE, MCP+I, MCPS, CNA*

beeps or messages. Power will then be supplied to the components plugged into the UPS from the battery. The UPS device has an average lifespan of about 10 years, but the battery has a shorter lifespan, ranging from 3-5 years. This lifespan will vary depending on the number of components plugged into the UPS and how often the battery is used. In any case, the UPS is not immortal and will need to be upgraded at one point in your career as an IT professional.

In addition to the UPS getting old and beginning to fail, there are other reasons why you may consider upgrading a UPS. One of the most common reasons is growth. Your system will grow and thereby require more power than the current UPS can supply. Because UPSs can supply different amounts of power to a system, you will need to upgrade so that the UPS can support the power requirements of your system. Another common reason for upgrading is that features are available with new UPSs that aren't available through the UPS currently being used. As we'll see later in this chapter, there are a number of features available in different UPSs that may be useful to your organization. Finally, you may find that the cost of replacing a UPS's batteries has become too high, and it is cheaper in the long run to replace the UPS system itself.

Upgrading a UPS takes more than simply unplugging the old one and plugging in the new. There are several steps that should be followed for an upgrade. These are:

- Planning
- Installation
- Configuration
- Testing

In the sections that follow, we will discuss these steps in greater detail. Because configuration and testing are issues that also deal with software, we will discuss those in the section on UPS software.

Planning

As with any kind of hardware upgrade, some planning must be involved. This is similar to the planning that was done when you originally installed your UPS. A major difference is that you won't need to decide what components will require a UPS, as this was decided during the initial installation of UPSs on your network. However, by not planning during upgrades, you may wind up with a UPS that doesn't have the features you need, or one that can't supply the power necessary for the attached equipment to function. As you can tell by this, you will need to do some investigation and then document your findings for future reference.

Because you are dealing with hardware, you should check the Hardware Compatibility List (HCL) for the operating system used on the machine that will be attached to the UPS. The HCL is a listing of hardware that has been tested with the operating system and found to work correctly with it. As we'll see later in this chapter, UPSs can communicate with a server or workstations attached to it, and tell the computer to shut down gracefully during a power outage. If the UPS isn't on the operating system's HCL, then it is possible that it won't be able to perform this function or use features available through the UPS software running on this computer. If the UPS isn't on the HCL, then you can also check documentation that comes with the UPS, or the Web site of the manufacturer to determine if it is compatible with the operating system being used.

exam
ⓦatch
The Hardware Compatibility List is a listing of hardware that's compatible with a particular operating system. An HCL may be included on the installation CD for the operating system, but may not be up-to-date. As such, you should visit the Web site of the company that makes your OS, and see if a more recent HCL is available. If your UPS isn't on the HCL, then you should check with the manufacturer to determine if it will work correctly with the operating system being used.

The primary feature of a UPS is its ability to provide battery backup power when a power failure occurs. However, power problems may occur in a variety of forms, including:

■ **Brownouts or sags** These are temporary reductions in power, which may occur when large machinery starts up or when the electric company drops the electricity to an area (such as when a transformer blows out or there is a high demand for power in a particular area). Brownouts are a problem because if a computer loses power for longer than 50 milliseconds, it will generally reboot itself.

■ **Blackouts** This is a total loss of power that may be caused by anything from a blown circuit breaker to a loss of power from the electric company.

■ **Spikes** A spike is a sudden increase in voltage, such as when lightning strikes a power line.

■ **Surges**   A power surge is also an increase in voltage, but it is one that lasts more than 1/20th of a second. This commonly occurs when large machinery is shut down, causing excess voltage to be spread across a circuit.

■ **Noise**   Noise occurs when outside interference affects the flow of electricity. There are two kinds of noise that can affect the alternating current of an electrical line: electromagnetic interference (EMI) and radio frequency interference (RFI). EMI is caused by other electrical components, such as lighting, generators, and so forth. RFI is caused by radio transmissions, which are picked up by the cables as antennas would.

To deal with the various power problems, some UPSs include an AC Line Status feature that allows you to view the quality of input power. This will show you whether your UPS is experiencing sags, spikes, and surges in power. Whereas some UPSs will use an LED display or lights to indicate problems, others will allow you to view this information through software that's included with the UPS.

In addition to dealing with power problems, there are a number of other features included with many UPSs on the market today. In some cases, the UPS will have features that notify you of different events through lights, LED displays, or audible noises, whereas other options will allow you to interact with the UPS through software (discussed later in this chapter). In deciding which UPS to use, you will need to determine which features are valuable to you.

Because battery backup power is the main reason you use a UPS, there are a number of features that deal specifically with the battery. Many UPSs include a method of showing the status of the battery, allowing you to see if the battery is in need of replacement. In some cases, the UPS will have an LED display that shows the percentage of battery charge in relation to its total capacity. In other cases, a single light or audible beep will indicate that the battery needs replacement. When replacement is needed, some UPSs support hot-swappable batteries, which can be changed without having to bring down the system. In addition, a UPS may support battery modules, which are batteries that are added to the existing UPS device. This saves you from having to purchase additional UPSs or replace the UPS system with another one.

Battery life can be impacted by the temperatures the UPS is exposed to. For this reason, some UPSs will include a temperature sensor that allows you to determine whether temperatures are too high or too low. This may be especially important if your server and other equipment are stored in a closet, instead of an air-conditioned room where you can easily monitor temperatures.

UPSs provide a number of features that determine how you'll be notified when a problem occurs. There are a number of options for alarms available with UPSs, including:

- **Audible alarms** Notify you by sounds. This is one of the most common methods of informing administrators of a problem. However, it requires someone to be within listening range to detect the alarm.

- **Lighted displays** Use lights or LED displays to indicate a problem. Although this is also one of the most common methods of alerting administrators, it also requires someone nearby to see the flashing lights or LED display on the UPS.

- **Messages** Send a message to all computers or specific computers on a network. In some cases, an e-mail message will be sent to a specific user, whereas other UPSs may have a message box pop-up on a user's screen.

- **Pagers** The UPSs software is configured to send a message to a pager number. This allows you to be paged, regardless of where you are.

Once you've decided on the features that you want included with your UPS, you will need to determine the load that will be placed on it. This is the voltage requirement of all equipment plugged into the UPS and the amount of power that the UPS can provide. Although this may have been initially calculated when the original UPS was put in place, additional hardware may have been purchased since then that also needs to be plugged into the UPS.

In determining the requirements of the UPS, you will need to investigate the power rating of your new UPS to ensure that it can handle the load presented by hardware plugged into it. To do this, you will begin by adding up the amps required by each component that will be attached to the UPS. This is available through the hardware's documentation. Once you've determined the total amount of power required by the collective equipment, then you will need to match these requirements to what the UPS can provide. In looking at the UPS ratings, you will be comparing the volt-amps of one UPS over another. The higher the VA rating, the more powerful the UPS.

You may also need to decide whether one UPS will be needed, or multiple UPSs. If you will be using a single UPS for more than one server, then you will need to add up the total requirements of each of these servers. For example, if you had two servers with 400VA requirements each, you would need a UPS that could support 800VA or more. In calculating this, however, you will also need to be aware that as the VA rating of the UPS increases, the cost of the UPS also increases.

Installation

When properly planned, the installation of the UPS is a simple process. It can take less than a half-hour to install the hardware and configure it properly. However, as mentioned earlier, it takes a little more than plugging in your equipment and flipping a switch.

Installation begins with deciding where you will place the unit. It should be placed in an area that is secure. You should remember that you can shut off a UPS by pushing a button, so you don't want it accessible to the general public. This generally isn't an issue, as the UPS will be stored in the same secure location as equipment being attached to the UPS, such as a server room. In this location, you should keep the UPS elevated so that it is protected from any disasters or accidents. By keeping it on a table, you will avoid someone accidentally kicking a plug loose or a flood damaging the UPS.

The UPS should be accessible and placed in a well-ventilated area. All too often, administrators will put their UPS in a corner, behind other equipment, or on the floor covered with cables and wires. In doing so, the UPS isn't properly ventilated and may heat up beyond recommended levels. Being hardware, the UPS will generate heat, and will need air to remain cool. This is particularly important when it is running off its battery, as the UPS may put out as much as ten times its normal heat. By not making the UPS accessible, it will also make it difficult to maintain. When batteries need to be replaced or you need to check displays on the UPS, you will want the unit to be easy to reach.

Once you've decided where you will place it, you must then shut down the server and other equipment that will be plugged into the UPS. Some downtime will be involved in this installation, so you should perform your upgrade when network usage is low, and inform users that the server or network will be unavailable for a specified amount of time. Remember that problems may happen, so schedule this into your downtime. Once the system is shutdown, you are ready to install the hardware.

Hooking up the equipment to the UPS is easy, as it consists of unplugging the power cables from the old UPS and plugging them into the new one. You should evaluate whether there are some items that shouldn't be plugged into the new one. For example, someone may have used an open socket on the old UPS for a nonessential device, such as an unused power bar, radio, or other hardware. Once you've plugged the equipment into the new UPS, you should plug the UPS into a wall socket and unplug the old one.

You will need to hook up the serial cable that attaches the UPS to a server. This is the server monitoring cable, which allows the UPS and server to communicate with one another. Without this, any software used to monitor the UPS will be unable to see the device. Also, if a power failure occurs, the UPS will be unable to send a signal to the server telling it to shut down gracefully.

After everything is plugged in and the serial cable is connecting the UPS and the server, you are ready to install any software that comes with the UPS. This may include drivers that allow UPS software included with your operating system to work with the UPS. If your network operating system is UPS-aware, you won't have to do much of anything to configure your system to work with the UPS. In many cases, you may use the vendor's software that allows you to benefit from features available through your UPS.

UPS Software

Originally, UPSs were little more than oversized power bars with battery backups. Over the last few years, the features available from an uninterruptible power supply have increased dramatically. Many of these features are available through the software that comes with the UPS or through the operating system of the computer that is attached to the UPS.

Because the latest version of software may not be included on the installation CD that comes with your UPS, you should visit the Web site of the manufacturer. Here, you may find updated drivers or software for your UPS. This can be downloaded from the site and installed on a server or workstation attached to the UPS, ensuring that they will be able to interact with one another correctly. To properly configure software for individual UPSs, you will need to refer to the documentation for that particular UPS.

Configuration

As mentioned, a number of operating systems provide services that allow you to configure your UPS. If configuration isn't done, then your UPS will generally be limited to supplying power from the external power source or the battery. One such OS that provides this ability is Windows 2000 Server. It allows you to use a graphical user interface (GUI) to configure various types of UPSs so that Windows 2000 can work with them.

The applet used to configure the UPS is called Power Options, and is found in Windows Control Panel. Once you've opened Power Options, you will see a dialog box similar to the one shown in Figure 5-3. By clicking the UPS tab, you will be able to access the settings that allow you to configure your UPS.

As you can see by the information in this figure, if no UPS has been configured at this point, then the information on this tab will be unavailable. To install or upgrade to a new UPS, you begin by clicking the Select button on this tab. This will display the UPS Selection dialog box, shown in Figure 5-4.

The UPS dialog has a drop-down list that allows you to select the manufacturer, and a listing below which allows you to select the model of the UPS being used. The

FIGURE 5-3

UPS tab of Power Options in Windows 2000 Server

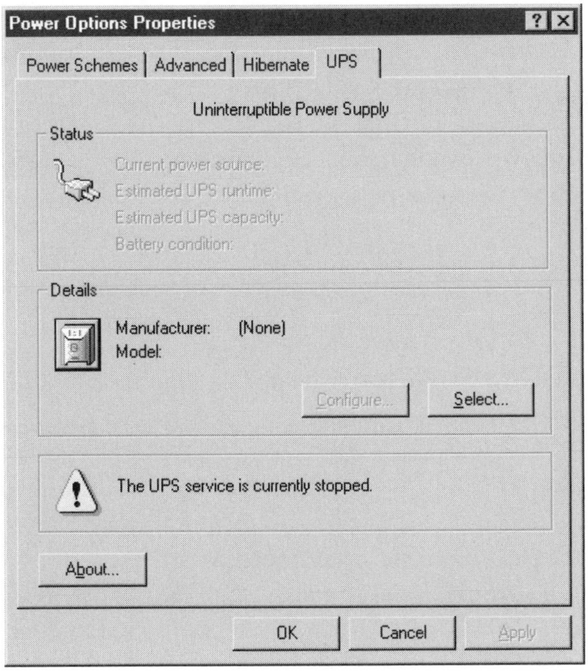

Selecting the
manufacturer
from the UPS
Selection dialog
box

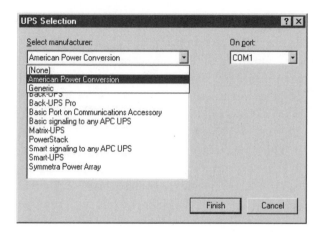

Select Manufacturer drop-down list contains two options: American Power
Conversion, and Generic. American Power Conversion (APC) is the largest
manufacturer of UPSs. If this is selected, then you can select the model of your UPS
in the listing below, select the COM port it's attached to, and then click Finish. If
your UPS is manufactured by another company, then you would select Generic, and
then set the COM port it is attached to. An entry will appear in the listing called
Custom. By selecting Custom, the Finish button will change to a Next button,
allowing you to use a UPS setup wizard.

The wizard takes you step-by-step through the process of configuring your UPS
interface configuration. After clicking Next, you will see a dialog box that allows you
to set the signal polarity of the UPS. The dialog box has three check boxes:

- **Power Fail/On Battery**   Allows your UPS to send a signal indicating
  whether power has failed and the UPS is providing power from the battery.

- **Low Battery**   Allows your UPS to send a signal indicating that its battery
  power is low.

- **UPS Shutdown**   Allows your UPS to send a signal indicating that the server
  should shut down properly.

There are two options for each of these check boxes: positive and negative.
Depending on the option chosen here, the server will expect either a positive or
negative signal polarity to indicate each of the events. To determine which you
should choose for each event, you will need to refer to your UPS's documentation.

Once you've completed these settings, you can then click Finish to return to the UPS tab in Power Options.

After making these settings, you will notice that the Configure button on the UPS tab is now enabled. By clicking this button, you will open the UPS Configuration dialog box, shown in Figure 5-5.

At the top of this dialog box is the Enable All Notifications check box. When selected, Windows 2000 will display warning messages when the UPS switches to battery power. This allows you to know that a problem has occurred with the main power source. Below this check box, you are given the ability to specify the number of seconds Windows 2000 Server should wait before displaying the messages. Here you can specify how long Windows 2000 will wait before the first warning is displayed and how long before subsequent messages are displayed.

The section below this is for setting critical alarms. A critical alarm occurs when the battery is almost out of power. The Minutes on Battery before Critical Alarm option allows you to set how many minutes the UPS will supply battery power before the critical alarm occurs. The value set here will be based on the number of

---

FIGURE 5-5

UPS
Configuration
dialog box

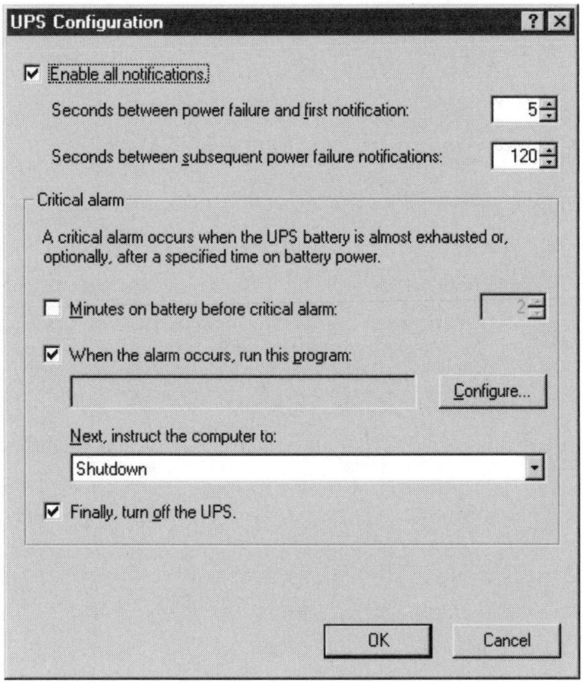

minutes your UPS can run before it runs out of battery power. The check box below allows you to specify a program or task that will run when the critical alarm is activated. By clicking the Configure button beside the When Alarm Occurs, Run This Program check box, you can enter a program or browse your hard disk for the program to run.

Below these check boxes are two settings that will allow you to shut down the computer and UPS. The Next, Instruct the Computer to drop-down list will allow you to specify the system state your computer should enter when the critical power alarm occurs. This will allow you to specify that your server should automatically shutdown after previous actions have completed. The Finally, Turn Off the UPS check box allows you to specify whether the UPS should also shutdown after the computer has shutdown.

EXERCISE 5-2

Configuring a UPS in Windows 2000

1. On the Start menu, select Settings | Control Panel, and double-click Power Options to open it.

2. When the Power Options dialog box opens, click the UPS tab.

3. Click the Select button.

4. When the UPS Selection dialog box appears, select the COM port your UPS is attached to from the drop-down list.

5. Click the Select Manufacturer drop-down list. If your UPS is manufactured by American Power Conversion, then select this entry, and then select the model from the Select Model listing. Click Finish, and proceed to Step 7 of this exercise. If your UPS is made by another company, then select Generic from the drop-down list, and select Custom from the Select Model listing. Click the Next button to continue.

6. The dialog box that appears is the UPS Interface Configuration, where you set the signal polarity. You will need to refer to the recommended settings in

your UPS documentation to configure this. Set whether your UPS uses negative or positive signals to indicate Power Fail/On Battery, Low Battery, and UPS Shutdown. Click Finish.

7. Click the Configure button to open the UPS Configuration.

8. Ensure that the Enable All Notifications check box is selected. Set the time before the first message is displayed to 10 seconds.

9. Select the Minutes on Battery before Critical Alarm check box, and enter 5 minutes. Please note that the value should be based on how long your UPS can run on battery backup before running out of power.

10. Clear the When the Alarm Occurs, Run This Program check box.

11. From the Next, Instruct the Computer to drop-down list, select Shutdown.

12. Ensure that the Finally, Turn Off the UPS check box is checked.

13. Click OK to confirm your settings, and exit the Power Options dialog box.

Testing

You don't want to wait for a problem to find out whether your UPS will work properly. If the UPS doesn't function as expected during a power outage, then you might as well have never installed the UPS to begin with. Once you've installed and configured the UPS, you will need to test your work to see if it functions properly.

To test an uninterruptible power supply, you will need to interrupt its power. The test is to disconnect the power to the UPS and then see if the equipment plugged into it continues to run. Because there will be some downtime, you will need to do this when there is a minimal number of users on the network, and inform users that the server will be going down at a specific time for testing purposes.

Once disconnected, the server and peripherals connected to it should continue running normally. Aside from this, you may notice that other events occur, depending on configuration settings and the UPS being used. You will notice that warnings of some kind will be provided. The UPS may make a sound that warns that power to it has stopped, and a message may appear on the server's screen or may sent to specific computers. Once the battery on the UPS runs low, the server should shut down properly.

After the UPS has shut down the server, you will need to restore power to the UPS and ensure that everything shut down properly. Log files should be checked. For example, if a Windows NT or Windows 2000 server is being used, then you could check the system log to ensure that no errors occurred. At this time, you should also document how long the UPS supplied power to the equipment attached to it, and any issues you noticed (such as services that did not shut down properly).

Most UPSs also provide a self-test switch, which allows it to run a test that simulates how it will functions during a loss of power. It will allow you to see whether a problem exists with the UPS and whether it will need to be replaced. During the test, the UPS won't actually stop providing power to components attached to it. For this reason, the self test can be run at anytime.

SCENARIO & SOLUTION

Now that we've examined issues concerning UPS upgrades in such detail, refer to the following Scenario & Solution for some scenario questions and answers on this topic.

The UPS I was planning to buy isn't on the Hardware Compatibility List for Linux. It is, however, on the HCL for Windows 2000. Do I have to switch operating systems if I want to use this UPS?	There is a possibility that the UPS will be compatible with Linux. Check with the UPS manufacturer to find out for sure before purchasing the UPS. If it isn't compatible, then you can still keep your operating system, but may have to use a different UPS.
I have just plugged my computer and peripherals into a new UPS, which is plugged into the wall. When I unplug the UPS from the wall socket, it supplies power from the battery to the computer. I have not done any configuration on the computer, but it seems to run fine. Why?	The configuration allows you to use various features available with the UPS. When configured on the computer, the UPS may be able to have the computer automatically shut down safely, display messages, and so forth.

CERTIFICATION SUMMARY

Agents are small programs that provide a specific function, such as gathering information from various devices on a network. The purpose and functionality of the agent will vary. Some will allow you to connect to a device remotely and pass commands through the agent to make modifications.

Service tools are programs that allow you to configure your system or diagnose problems. These tools can be accessed at system startup, by pressing F10 or the DELETE key to access diagnostic tools or a System Setup Utility. Other diagnostic tools may be available through the operating system being used or through third parties. In addition, there are tools such as the EISA Configuration Tool that is used to configure EISA systems. These tools may be upgraded through software available from various manufacturers.

A UPS is an uninterruptible power supply, and is used to supply power to computers and other devices plugged into it when a power failure occurs. When upgrading a UPS, planning, installation, configuration, and testing are required. You should find out whether it is on the Hardware Compatibility List for the operating system of the computer attached to it. This will ensure that any features and configurations will work properly, and that the computer and the UPS will be able to communicate. You will also need to refer to the UPS's documentation to ensure that any specific settings are configured properly. Once you've finished installing and configuring the UPS, you should test it to ensure that it functions as expected.

✓ TWO-MINUTE DRILL

Here are some of the key points from each certification objective in Chapter 5.

Upgrading System Monitoring Agents

❏ Agents are programs that monitor, gather information, or process a specific task in the background. System monitoring agents are used to monitor your system.

❏ The information gathered by an agent is reported to an SNMP management system.

❏ SNMP is the Simple Network Management Protocol. It uses agents to monitor network hardware and drivers.

❏ An agent may be installed as software or it may reside in the firmware of a device.

❏ In addition to upgrading the agent, you will need to remember that the management system may also have to be upgraded, as they work together.

❏ SNMP agents may be upgraded in a variety of ways, including: applying the latest service pack or patch to the operating system or software, upgrading the operating system to a later version, or upgrading the firmware on a network device.

Upgrading Service Tools

❏ Service tools are programs that allow you to configure and monitor your system, thereby allowing you to detect and fix possible problems.

❏ Diagnostic tools are used to troubleshoot your computer.

❏ EISA is the Extended Industry Standard Architecture. Each time an EISA or ISA expansion card is added, removed, or repositioned on a system, the EISA Configuration utility (ECU) is used. This utility reads a card's configuration file, which describes the card's characteristics and system resource requirements.

❏ A diagnostic partition is a specially protected section of the hard disk that is used to store setup and diagnostic utilities that are used by your computer.

❑ System Setup Utilities are used to configure your system, change security settings, and configure power management.

❑ The diagnostic partition containing the diagnostic tools and SSU can be upgraded. This may need to occur if the diagnostic partition is removed, corrupted, or the hard disk is replaced.

Upgrading the UPS

❑ A UPS is an uninterruptible power supply.

❑ Equipment plugged into a UPS can receive battery backup power in the event of a total power failure. It can also be protected from brownouts, spikes, and surges in power.

❑ When planning which UPS to upgrade to, you should consult the Hardware Compatibility List. The HCL is a listing of hardware compatible with your computer's operating system, and will allow you to determine if the computer and UPS will be able to function together.

❑ To configure the signal polarity settings of a UPS, you will need to refer to the documentation included with the UPS.

❑ A UPS can be configured to work with a server or workstation using software included with the UPS or configuration options available through the operating system of the computer attached to the UPS.

❑ To test a UPS, you can either use the self test on the UPS itself or remove external power from the UPS.

SELF TEST

The following questions will help you measure your understanding of the material presented in this chapter. Read all of the choices carefully, as there may be more than one correct answer. Choose all correct answers for each question.

Upgrading System Monitoring Agents

1. Which of the following best describes a system monitoring agent?

   A. It is a program that receives information from other programs that interact with devices on your system.

   B. It is a program that is used to configure EISA devices.

   C. It is a small program that gathers and processes information about your system.

   D. It is another term for a device driver on your system.

2. Which of the following best describes an SNMP management system?

   A. It is a type of agent.

   B. It is a small program that gathers and processes information about your system.

   C. It is a program that receives information from other programs that interact with devices on your system.

   D. It is a program that upgrades SNMP agents.

3. You are upgrading all agents that are currently running on your network. In which of the following ways may you need to upgrade the agents? (Choose all that apply.)

   A. Upgrade the firmware of a device.

   B. Upgrade the cabling.

   C. Upgrade agent software on a device that can load software.

   D. Upgrade the equipment itself.

4. You are planning to use SNMP agents on your system. Which of the following protocols will you need to install to use SNMP?

   A. TCP/IP

   B. NetBEUI

   C. FTP

   D. AppleTalk

5. Which of the following will you use to upgrade an agent that is stored in the firmware of a network bridge? Choose the best and least expensive solution.

  A. Upgrade the operating system of servers on the network.

  B. Use a Flash ROM upgrade.

  C. Replace the network bridge.

  D. Install the upgrade disk into the network bridge, and load the software.

6. Which of the following programs uses agents to obtain information about devices located on your network?

  A. Internet Explorer

  B. System Management Server

  C. System Monitor

  D. Performance Monitor

Upgrading Service Tools

7. You have decided to upgrade the diagnostic program that is available for your model of Compaq computer. This program runs on Windows NT Server 4.0, which uses Service Pack 4. How will you acquire and install the upgrade?

  A. Upgrade the operating system to Windows 2000.

  B. Install the Windows NT Server 4.0 Service Pack 6a.

  C. Download the upgrade from the computer manufacturer and install it on the computer.

  D. Upgrade the diagnostic program from the installation CD that came with the computer.

8. You want to upgrade a Performance Monitor tool that comes with your operating system. On checking the Web site of the operating system's manufacturer, you find that there are no upgrades for this particular program available. There is, however, a more recent service pack than is currently being used, and a new version of the operating system has been released. You also check the Web site of your computer's manufacturer and find that a BIOS upgrade is available. What options could possibly upgrade the diagnostic software? (Choose all that apply.)

  A. Upgrade the operating system to a later version.

  B. Install a more recent service pack.

  C. Download a BIOS upgrade from your computer's manufacturer and install it on your computer.

  D. Upgrade the diagnostic program from the installation CD for your operating system.

9. You are preparing to upgrade the diagnostic tools that came with your computer. Before doing so, which of the following should you do? (Choose all that apply.)

    A. Remove the existing diagnostic tools from your computer.

    B. Document the upgrade.

    C. Back up your computer's data and system.

    D. Gather information on your computer.

10. You have repositioned an EISA adapter on your system. What tool, if any, do you need to use to reconfigure it?

    A. System Monitor

    B. MSD

    C. EISA

    D. EISA Configuration Tool

11. What is a diagnostic partition?

    A. It is the partition on your hard disk that stores diagnostic tools used by the operating system. Generally, it is the C:\.

    B. It is a specially protected section of the hard disk that is used to store setup and diagnostic utilities that are used by your computer.

    C. It is a section of memory used by the computer to store setup and diagnostic utilities.

    D. When repartitioning your hard disk, a diagnostic partition is a test partition created before it is actually created.

12. You install a new hard disk on your Compaq computer to replace an old one that is corrupt. There is only one hard disk on this computer. When you attempt to restart the computer, you try and access the System Setup Utility, but find you cannot. Why?

    A. The diagnostic partition has been corrupted.

    B. The diagnostic partition doesn't exist.

    C. The hard disk hasn't been formatted.

    D. The System Setup Utility hasn't been installed onto the operating system yet.

13. Your computer stores the System Setup Utility in the BIOS, and you have decided that you would like to upgrade the BIOS to benefit from new features available. Which of the following information will you need to gather before upgrading? (Choose all that apply.)

    A. Make and model of the computer.

B. Operating system running on the computer.

C. BIOS revision number.

D. Information on adapters installed on the computer.

Upgrading the UPS

14. You are trying to decide which UPS to buy as a replacement for an existing UPS. You aren't pleased with the existing UPS and have decided to go with a different make and model. You want the UPS to work with the operating system running on a server, which will be attached to the new UPS. Which of the following should you use during the planning phase to determine which UPS to use? (Choose all that apply.)

A. Documentation that comes with the existing UPS being used.

B. Documentation that comes with the new UPS that will replace the existing UPS.

C. Hardware Compatibility List.

D. Information available on the UPS manufacturer's Web site.

15. You have just taken over as administrator for a network with four servers running Windows 2000 Server. One of these servers is located at a remote site and has been rebooting itself on a weekly basis. A UPS was installed at this site several years ago, and the server is attached to it. The previous administrator installed software that allows you to detect power problems. The software indicates temporary reductions in power to one of the servers. Which of the following should you do? (Choose all that apply.)

A. Upgrade service tools on the server.

B. Upgrade system monitoring agents for the server.

C. Upgrade the UPS.

D. Check the outlet providing power to determine the quality of electricity.

16. You are the network administrator of a large corporation, where construction is being done in the building where your server room is located. Due to this construction, you are concerned about the server losing power, and see a need to be alerted at night when you are away from the office. There is a night shift working in the building, but none of these employees have access to the server room. Which of the following alert options supported by the UPS will you use to notify you of problems? (Choose all that apply.)

A. LED display

B. Audible alarms

C. Paging

D. Broadcast messages

17. You have four servers with a maximum amp draw of 500VA each. You want the UPS to maintain power to these for at least 15 minutes, and want to use only a single UPS for all of these. Due to cost restrictions, you want to use the minimum VA rating available to support these servers. What is the VA requirement of the UPS?

    A. 500VA

    B. 1000VA

    C. 3000VA

    D. 4000VA

18. You are setting up a UPS. Space is limited, so you place the UPS in a corner of the room that is poorly ventilated. You shut down the server and peripherals and then unplug them from the old UPS. You then plug these into the new UPS. You unplug the old UPS from the wall socket and then plug the new UPS into it. Once this is done, you restart the server and install the software that comes with the UPS. When you test the UPS software, you find that it cannot find or communicate with the UPS. Why?

    A. The location of the UPS.

    B. There is no power to the UPS.

    C. The server isn't plugged into the UPS.

    D. The serial cable hasn't been hooked up to the server.

19. You are setting up a new UPS, which will be attached to a Windows 2000 Server. Which of the following applets in Windows Control Panel will you use to configure the UPS?

    A. Power Options

    B. Advanced Power Management

    C. UPS

    D. There is no way to configure a UPS through the native programs in Windows 2000.

20. Which of the following methods can be used to test a UPS after you have installed and configured it? (Choose all that apply.)

    A. Press the self-test button on the UPS.

    B. Remove external power from the UPS.

C. Shut off the UPS.

D. Shut off the computer.

LAB QUESTION

You are the administrator of a network running a Windows 2000 Server and 50 workstations running Windows NT Workstation 4.0 and Linux. The server hasn't been updated in any way and is running with the original software that came on the installation disk. To protect data on the server, you have installed and configured a UPS, so that power is provided to it from a battery when power failures occur.

One of the Linux machines uses EISA cards, and one of these has failed to continue working. As such, you decide to replace it with another EISA card. To do this, you use the proper configuration program, but notice that the card doesn't have a configuration file.

1. You have decided to upgrade the SNMP agent running on the Windows 2000 Server. How will you do this?

2. What will you do to have a configuration file for the EISA card?

3. How can you test the UPS so that users aren't disrupted?

4. In performing the test from the preceding question, what information won't you be able to acquire from the test?

SELF TEST ANSWERS

Upgrading System Monitoring Agents

1. ☑ **C.** It is a small program that gathers and processes information about your system. Agents are programs that monitor, gather information, or process a specific task in the background. In terms of system monitoring agents, these are programs that monitor your system for changes that indicate possible problems.

    ☒ **A** is incorrect because this describes the management system that an agent works with. **B** is incorrect because system management agents do not configure EISA adapters. **D** is incorrect because a system management agent isn't a device driver.

2. ☑ **C.** It is a program that receives information from other programs that interact with devices on your system. The information gathered by the agent is then reported to an SNMP manager (or management system), which is a program that receives information from the agents and then acts on it.

    ☒ **A** is incorrect because the management system isn't a type of agent. It does however work with SNMP agents. **B** is incorrect because this describes the agent, and not the management system. **D** is incorrect because the management system isn't merely a program that upgrades an agent.

3. ☑ **A and C.** Upgrade the firmware of a device and upgrade agent software on a device that can load software. Agents may be installed as software that is loaded on a managed device, or it may be part of a device's firmware. It will often be installed as software when you are managing something such as a server or some other piece of equipment that uses software. The agent may also reside in the firmware of a device, as is the case with network bridges and other devices that don't support software being loaded into them.

    ☒ **B** is incorrect because the cabling doesn't need to be upgraded to support the upgrading of agents. **D** is incorrect because you are only upgrading agents that are currently running on your network. As such, the equipment would already support agents and wouldn't need to be replaced simply to upgrade the agent.

4. ☑ **A.** TCP/IP. SNMP is part of the TCP/IP protocol suite; thereby, TCP/IP will need to be installed on the network.

    ☒ **B, C, and D** are incorrect because none of these are necessary to run SNMP agents.

5. ☑ **B.** Use a Flash ROM upgrade. To upgrade agents that are part of your network equipment's firmware, you will need to upgrade the firmware. In doing so, you change the programs stored

in the memory of the hardware and also change the software for the agent. The memory the agents are stored in are read-only memory (ROM), which can be upgraded using Flash ROM software.

☒ **A** is incorrect because upgrading the servers will have no effect on the upgrade of an agent on a network bridge. These are different components of your network. **C** is incorrect because replacing the network bridge is not the least expensive solution. **D** is incorrect because agents are stored in the firmware on components such as network bridges because they cannot load software.

6. ☑ **B.** System Management Server. This is software that uses agents to obtain information about your network.

☒ **A, C,** and **D** are incorrect because Internet Explorer, System Monitor, and Performance monitor do not use agents to obtain information about devices located on a network.

Upgrading Service Tools

7. ☑ **C.** Download the upgrade from the computer manufacturer and install it on the computer. Such tools may have upgraded versions available on the manufacturer's Web site. By downloading and running the installation files for the new version of the software, or downloading and running patches for such programs, you will be able to upgrade these diagnostic tools to newer versions. Because they are designed for specific operating systems, it is important that you get the version for the operating system that's run on your computer.

☒ **A** and **B** are incorrect because service packs and upgrades to the operating system will only upgrade programs that were provided by the operating system manufacturer. They will not upgrade software made available from the computer manufacturer. **D** is incorrect because upgrading the diagnostic program using the installation CD that came with the computer will install the same version of the software, or a previous version.

8. ☑ **A** and **B.** Upgrade the operating system to a later version or install a more recent service pack. Although some tools may have upgrades or patches specifically for them, most of the diagnostic tools that come with your operating system are upgraded when you apply service packs, patches, or upgrade the OS to a later version.

☒ **C** is incorrect because the diagnostic software is from the operating system's manufacturer and not the computer manufacturer. **D** is incorrect because using the installation CD for the operating system will install the same version of the software or a previous version.

9. ☑ **B, C,** and **D.** Document the upgrade, back up the computer's data and system, and gather information on the computer. Documenting the upgrade will allow you to chronicle what changes have been made and refer to them later. Backing up the computer's data and system will allow you to restore it if a problem occurs. Gathering information on your computer will allow you to obtain the diagnostic tools that are designed for your particular computer and restore settings if a problem occurs.

☒ **A** is incorrect because the upgrade will replace any of the existing files or code used to run the diagnostic tools.

10. ☑ **D. EISA Configuration Tool.** The EISA Configuration utility (ECU) is a utility that reads a card's configuration file, which describes the card's characteristics and system resource requirements. It is used each time an EISA or ISA expansion card is added, removed, or repositioned on a system.

☒ **A** is incorrect because System Monitor is a Windows tool that monitors your system. **B** is incorrect because MSD is Microsoft Diagnostics, which is used to monitor your system for problems. **C** is incorrect because EISA is Extended Industry Standard Architecture. None of these are used to reconfigure EISA cards.

11. ☑ **B.** It is a specially protected section of the hard disk that is used to store setup and diagnostic utilities that are used by your computer. The setup software is used to configure your system, change security settings, and configure power management. The diagnostic software is used to test and analyze the computer to determine if problems exist.

☒ **A, C,** and **D** are incorrect because a diagnostic partition is a specially protected section of the hard disk that is used to store setup and diagnostic utilities that are used by your computer.

12. ☑ **B.** The diagnostic partition doesn't exist. The loss of the diagnostic partition may also occur when you install a new hard disk. This requires you to reload the setup and diagnostic software onto the hard disk. When you purchase a computer that uses a diagnostic partition, floppy disks should be included with your computer for when you need to restore the diagnostic partition. Up-to-date copies of the setup and diagnostic software can also be obtained from the computer manufacturer's Web site.

☒ **A** is incorrect because when the original hard disk was removed, the partition was removed with the physical disk. **C** is incorrect because the diagnostic partition is hidden on the hard disk, and is a non-DOS partition. Therefore, it doesn't matter that it hasn't been formatted. **D** is incorrect because the SSU would be located on the diagnostic partition of this computer and wouldn't be loaded after the operating system. In fact, it would be loaded before the OS.

13. ☑ **A** and **C.** Make and model of the computer and the BIOS revision number. The make and model number is the manufacturer, type, and model number of the machine. The BIOS revision number is the version of the BIOS on your computer. This is usually displayed in the corner of your screen when you boot up the computer. You can also determine the revision

number by looking at the motherboard. This information is used to acquire the correct BIOS for your machine.

☒ **B** is incorrect because the operating system has nothing to do with the BIOS. The BIOS is loaded before the operating system. **D** is incorrect because the adapters on your computer don't affect the upgrading of the System Setup Utility in the BIOS.

Upgrading the UPS

14. ☑ **C** and **D**. Hardware Compatibility List, and information available on the UPS manufacturer's Web site. The Hardware Compatibility List is a listing of hardware that's compatible with a particular operating system. If your UPS isn't on the HCL, then you may find information as to whether the UPS is compatible with your OS on the manufacturer's Web site.

☒ **A** is incorrect because the existing UPS will be different from the new one. The question states that you will be choosing a different make and model than the one currently being used, so the new one may not be compatible like the existing one. **B** is incorrect because using documentation that comes with the new UPS requires you to buy the UPS before you can read the documentation. This means if the UPS isn't compatible, you're stuck with it anyway.

15. ☑ **C** and **D**. Upgrade the UPS and check the outlet providing power to determine the quality of electricity. Temporary reductions in power are called brownouts or sags in power. If a computer loses power for longer than 50 milliseconds, it will generally reboot itself, which is why the server has probably been rebooting itself on a weekly basis. If there is a problem with the UPS, then it may not be providing power during these brownouts and may need to be upgraded. If there is a problem with the outlet or quality of electricity it provides, then it may shorten the life of any UPS plugged into it.

☒ **A** and **B** are incorrect because none of these deal with the problem of why the server is rebooting itself on a weekly basis, or deal with the problem of temporary reductions in power.

16. ☑ **C** and **D**. Paging and broadcast messages. Paging has a message sent to a pager number and allows your pager to be beeped when a problem occurs. Broadcast messages allow the UPS software to send a message to all computers on the network.

☒ **A** is incorrect because LED displays require someone nearby to see the LED display on the UPS. **B** is incorrect because audible alarms notify problems by sounds, which also require someone to be within listening range to detect the alarm.

17. ☑ **C**. 3000VA. Each of the four servers have a maximum amp draw of 500VA each, so you will need to combine these to determine the minimum VA rating of the UPS needed to support

them. As 500 multiplied by 4 is 2000, this would mean the minimum VA rating would be 2000VA. Because 2000VA isn't offered as a choice, you would select the next highest in the choices offered, which would be 3000VA.

☒ **A** and **B** are incorrect because the VA rating is too low. **D** is incorrect because the cost of a UPS is partially based on its VA rating. Because cost is an issue, 4000VA would be too costly in this situation.

18. ☑ **D.** The serial cable hasn't been hooked up to the server. You will need to hook up the serial cable that attaches the UPS to a server, so that the UPS and server can communicate with one another. Without this, any software used to monitor the UPS will be unable to see the device.

☒ **A, B,** and **C** are incorrect because none would explain why the server and UPS couldn't communicate. **A** is incorrect because although the poor ventilation could overheat the UPS, it wouldn't immediately keep the UPS from performing. **B** is incorrect because if there was no power, then the server attached to the UPS couldn't have rebooted and allowed you to install the software. **C** is incorrect for this same reason.

19. ☑ **A.** Power Options. The applet used to configure the UPS in Windows 2000 Server is called Power Options, and is found in Control Panel. The UPS tab in Power Options is used to configure your UPS.

☒ **B** is incorrect because there is no Advanced Power Management applet in the Windows 2000 Server Control Panel. **C** is incorrect because the UPS applet was used in Windows NT 4.0, but isn't used in Windows 2000 Server. Instead, the UPS tab in Power Options is used. **D** is incorrect because the UPS tab in Power Options is used to configure a UPS in Windows 2000 Server.

20. ☑ **A** and **B.** Press the self-test button on the UPS or remove external power from the UPS. The self-test will simulate a power failure, but won't disrupt power to any components attached to it. Disconnecting the power to the UPS and then seeing if the equipment plugged into it continues to run is another method. When power is interrupted, there will be some downtime.

☒ **C** is incorrect because if the UPS is shutoff, then no power can be passed to components either from the external power or the battery on the UPS. **D** is incorrect because if the computer is shutoff, it won't tell you anything about whether the UPS itself is properly providing power from battery backup.

LAB ANSWER

1. Apply the latest service pack to the operating system. This will also apply any updates to the agent, if they are available.

2. Use the EISA Configuration Tool to create a configuration file. This tool can use existing .CFG files or can also be used to create new .CFG files for EISA adapters.

3. Use the self-test on the UPS. This will simulate a power loss, but the UPS will continue providing power to the components attached to it.

4. Using the self-test won't allow you to determine how long the battery will provide power to components plugged into it.

Server+
COMPUTING TECHNOLOGY INDUSTRY ASSOCIATION

6

Performance

The best way to handle a problem is to make sure it never happens in the first place. That is the basic concept of this chapter. In dealing with networks, you should ensure that your network is performing as expected, that data is safe and organized, and that any hardware installed on the computers will function as expected.

In this chapter, we'll cover topics that keep the network functioning like a well-oiled machine. We'll discuss monitoring performance and creating baselines so that you will have something to which you can compare the current performance measurements. We will also discuss physical housekeeping, which includes maintenance tasks that must be performed. Finally, we'll look at hardware verification, which consists of identifying the hardware currently on your system and ensuring that new hardware will work properly with it. In performing these tasks, your network will function at a higher level of performance and data will be safer.

CERTIFICATION OBJECTIVE 6.01

Creating a Baseline and Comparing Performance

Performance has always been a major issue for networks. Networks are dynamic, and will grow and change with the company they serve. As new employees are hired, new workstations will be added to the network, more IP addresses will be used, and network traffic will increase. As time passes, more servers may be needed, users will require newer applications and technologies, and your network will be taxed further. As the requirements of an organization change, performance becomes affected.

Regardless of your background with networks, you have probably experienced performance issues on your home computer. Chances are, your computer isn't the same as it was ten years ago. As new versions of your operating system and applications were released, you probably upgraded to the latest version. This may have slowed your computer, so more memory was added. As your hard drive filled with programs and data, you may have needed to install a larger hard disk. You may have even found the need to replace the computer completely, as it became so slow that it couldn't keep up with minimal requirements. The same applies to servers, workstations, and other components making up a network. Changes over time will cause technologies to reach their limits and network performance to slow.

As we've seen from this, there are several areas that will affect performance. These include:

- CPU
- Memory
- Hard disk
- Network

In dealing with performance in these areas, you will need to find the resource that is slowest on your network, speed it up, and then determine whether other areas are affecting speed. This may force you to reconfigure components, upgrade hardware and software, add new technologies, or change your network to meet the needs of users.

Bottlenecks

When you look at a bottle, you'll notice that one end is narrow. When liquid is poured, the neck of the bottle restricts the flow, so that it pours slower than it would if the bottleneck didn't exist. In terms of networking, a bottleneck is a component that restricts the flow of information. Even though the component may be operating at peak efficiency, other components are passing the information at a faster rate. For example, if your computer has a slow processor, then data is forced to wait in memory before it can be passed onto the CPU for processing. In this case, the CPU is a bottleneck. The load on it is too great for its capabilities, and it cannot handle the amount of data that could be passed to it.

To eliminate bottlenecks, you need to find which resource is overloaded, and then relieve the load. This can be done by sharing a component's load with other components, or by replacing the slow component with a faster one. In the case of our CPU example, you could replace the existing CPU with a newer and faster processor, or install a second processor so that multiprocessing is used on that machine. In other cases, performance tuning may be as simple as changing configuration settings, such as those found in Windows Control Panel. In doing this, the bottleneck is eliminated and performance improves.

Finding the source of a performance problem is like solving a mystery. It requires knowledge and deductive reasoning. You need to begin with an understanding of the components that make up an individual computer or a network, so that you know what may be suspect. In some cases, you may find unique programs that aren't installed on workstations that are running properly. In other cases, you will find that certain components can't be a problem. Let's say a user complains that a standalone machine is slow opening and saving files. Because it isn't on the network, cabling or network cards won't be the reason why it is slow accessing data. Understanding the software and hardware installed on a machine will help you realize what software and hardware is suspect and which can be eliminated as the possible source of a problem.

Performance tuning also relies on using the proper tools. Network monitoring tools can be used to measure network activity. This software allows you to determine why two or more computers can't communicate with one another. Whereas network monitors can be used to detect network problems, system monitoring tools can be used to detect problems with servers and workstations. These allow you to determine whether you have bottlenecks with your CPU, hard disks, memory, and other elements of the system. We will discuss each of these types of tools in greater detail later in this chapter.

Baselines

When using network and system monitors, it is important that you don't merely use them when problems occur. If you did, you would have no idea what your system looks like under normal circumstances. For this reason, it is important to create baselines of machines and networks so that you can spot abnormal measurements.

A baseline is a snapshot of your computer or network's performance measurements, which can be used for planning and analysis. To create a baseline, you run a system or network monitoring tool at times when the server, workstation, or network is running normally. These results are logged, so that performance measurements are saved to a file.

In creating a baseline, you will need to run the monitoring tool over a period of time, and at different times of the day, so that you can determine peak hours. This will show you when users and applications are using a server, workstation, or network the most and the least. By this, you will generally see when users are logging in and out of the network at the beginning and end of their shifts. It is important that this information is collected, or your analysis of usage will be skewed. Beyond this, you should gather information throughout the day. It isn't uncommon to set a monitoring program to gather data every minute for three or four days, so that you have an accurate picture of how the network or machine is being used.

Once you've logged this information to a file, you can compare the measurements to those gathered when performance seems sluggish. For example, if your processor had a 40 percent utilization rate in the baseline, and current measurements showed an 80 percent utilization rate, you could see that the processor is under a greater workload or experiencing problems. If a baseline wasn't available, then you might miss the fact that the component was under greater demands or acting abnormally.

exam
ⓦatch

It is important to remember that a baseline must be logged. Performance tools that don't provide the functionality to save results to a log cannot be used for a baseline because the results cannot be referred to at a later date.

Performance Monitoring

There are a number of different monitoring tools available for determining whether a system or network is working properly. Many operating systems include monitoring tools that aid you in this task, thereby saving you from having to incur the cost of purchasing them separately. As we'll see, they enable you to create baselines and help in finding bottlenecks, so that you can improve the performance of machines and networks. In this section, we will look at several such tools that come with Windows operating systems.

System Performance

Windows 2000 provides the Performance Console as a method of monitoring performance on local and remote computers. This console is actually the Microsoft Management Console (MMC) with two snap-ins installed: System Monitor and Performance Logs and Alerts. A *snap-in* is a module that is added to MMC, so that you can perform various functions through a central console program. System Monitor allows you to monitor resource utilization and network throughput, whereas Performance Logs and Alerts allows you to log performance data and set remote notification of performance issues. This allows you to monitor the local computer or remote computers on your network.

Those familiar with Windows NT will recognize the similarities of the Performance Console to that of the Performance Monitor. Performance Monitor (PERFMON.EXE) was a tool used for monitoring performance issues on a Windows NT Server. It provided four methods of monitoring various components of Windows NT:

- **Report view**   Displayed a textual report on the screen.
- **Chart view**   Displayed a graph on the screen.
- **Alert view**   Enabled you to send alerts when certain thresholds had been met.
- **Log view**   Logged areas being monitored to a file.

As we will see, Performance Console is an evolution of this tool. It breaks apart the functionality of Performance Monitor into different snap-ins, while extending the features that were available in its predecessor.

Both versions of this tool allow you to set what is to be monitored by adding items from various categories. These categories include processor, memory, and other elements of your system and network that may experience performance problems. Because each category may have various areas that you'll want to monitor, items are contained under each of them. These items are called counters. They provide data associated with each object that's associated with a particular resource.

When using Performance Console, the System Monitor provides a visual representation of counters being watched. The System Monitor snap-in allows you to view real-time and previously logged data about areas of your system and network. This data can be presented to you in the form of a graph, a histogram, or a report, so that you can analyze it in a way that's meaningful to you. When System Monitor is first opened, it will (by default) open in graph view, but no information will be displayed. This is because counters will need to be added, so that System Monitor knows what to watch. Once counters are added, the data will be displayed in the graph area, in a way similar to that shown in Figure 6-1.

To add counters, you must open the Add Counters dialog box. This is done from the toolbar, by clicking the button that has a plus symbol ("+") on it. When the Add Counters dialog box appears, you will see a section that allows the options of monitoring the local computer or a remote computer. Below this, you will see a drop-down list containing various categories of resources. By selecting objects from this listing, you control what areas you want to monitor. A list of counters associated with the object will appear on the dialog box, which you can use to further narrow what is to be monitored.

Once the counters are added, the timer bar on the System Monitor's graph area will begin to move. This indicates a real-time update, showing the value of the associated counter in both the graph and the value bar below. The value bar is located beneath the graph, and shows the Last, Average, Minimum, and Maximum values of the counter that's currently selected. The Duration value shows the time

FIGURE 6-1 System Monitor in the Windows 2000 Performance Console

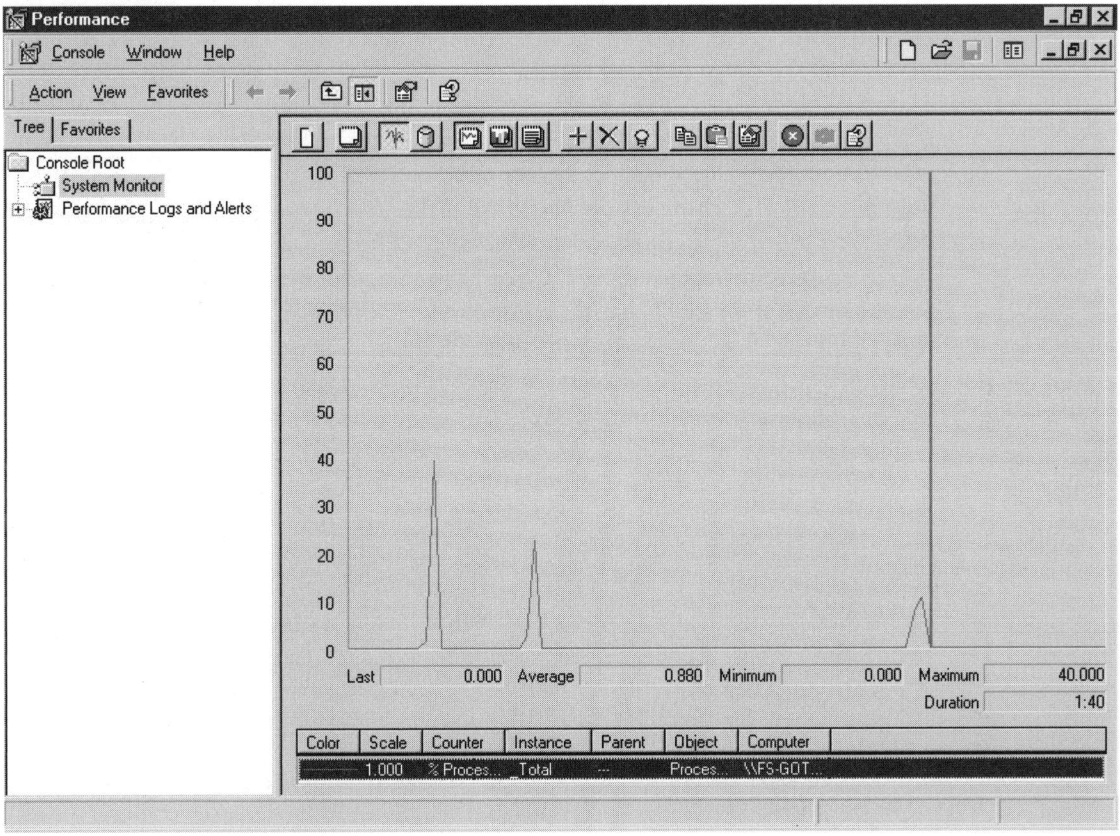

that's elapsed in the graph. Because multiple counters may be used, a legend appears at the bottom on the graph area, informing you of what each colored line in the graph represents.

Although there are many objects that you could monitor, two that often lead to confusion are the PhysicalDisk and LogicalDisk objects. These are used to monitor hard disk performance issues. The PhysicalDisk object monitors physical disk counter data, whereas the LogicalDisk monitors any counter data associated with local drives and storage volumes. By default, the PhysicalDisk object is enabled, but the LogicalDisk object is disabled. To turn the counters for these objects on or off, the diskperf utility must be used. Diskperf is run from the command prompt, and uses switches to control the disk counters. By default, Windows 2000 uses the diskperf –yd command to obtain data on physical drives. However, to obtain data on logical drives, you will need to run diskperf –yv from the command prompt. To disable the counter, you can run diskperf –n at the command prompt. Once you've turned on the counter and rebooted, you will then be able to collect data about the disk.

on the job

It is common for administrators using Performance Console or Performance Monitor to forget that disk counters need to be turned on. In Windows NT, you can turn disk counters on using the diskperf –y command. In Windows 2000, you use the diskperf –yd command for physical drives, and the diskperf –yv command for logical drives. Once rebooted, the disk counters will be able to collect data, and will remain on until the diskperf –n command is used to turn them off. If you are using Performance Console or Performance Monitor, and can't collect hard disk counter data, it is usually because the counters haven't been activated using diskperf.

When creating a baseline, you will need to log the data that's collected. If you don't, then it will only be displayed on the screen, and can't be referenced in the future. Whereas Windows NT's Performance Monitor provided a log view for this, Windows 2000 uses the Performance Logs and Alerts snap-in.

The Performance Logs and Alerts snap-in is loaded automatically when the Performance Console is opened. As shown in Figure 6-2, it has three areas that you can configure:

- Counter Logs
- Trace Logs
- Alerts

Although the Alerts feature is discussed in Chapter 7, we'll look at how you use this snap-in to log data in the paragraphs that follow.

Counter Logs are used to obtain and store data that's collected by the counters you specify. When counter logs are used, data is obtained at specific update intervals. The data can be stored in a comma-delimited or tab-separated format so that it can then be imported into other programs, or stored in a binary log format. This information can be viewed using System Monitor or it can be exported to other programs for analysis or when creating reports. For example, you could export it to a database to store former data collections, or to a spreadsheet program to analyze the results.

FIGURE 6-2   Performance Logs and Alerts as shown in Performance Console

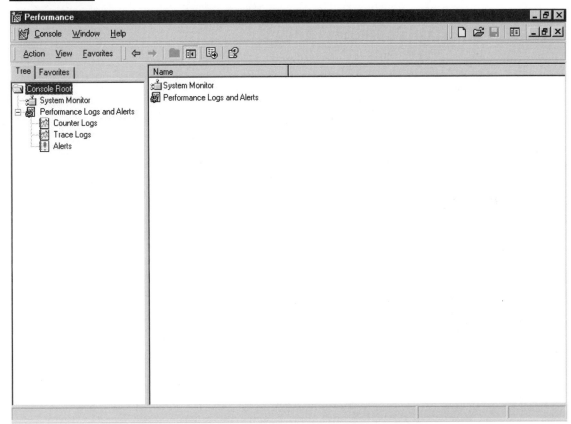

Trace Logs are different from counter logs in that they don't obtain data at regular update intervals. Instead, they log data when certain events occur. For example, they might gather data when a page fault occurs. They monitor the activities you specify, and when one happens, they store the information in a log file.

EXERCISE 6-1

Using System Monitor in Windows 2000 Server's Performance Console

1. From the Start menu, select Programs | Administrative Tools | Performance.

2. When the Performance Console appears, select System Monitor from the left pane. The interface for System Monitor will appear in the right pane.

3. Click the button with the plus symbol ("+") to display the Add Counters dialog box.

4. When the Add Counters dialog box appears, select the Use Local Computer Counters option.

5. Select Processor from the drop-down list of Performance Objects.

6. Select the Select Counters from List option, and then select the % Processor Time item in the list below.

7. Select the Select Instances from List option, and then select the Total item.

8. Click Add.

9. Click Close and watch as the activity for all processors on that computer appears on the graph on your screen. If it often exceeds 90 percent, your processor may be a bottleneck.

Network Performance

Network Monitor is another tool that's available with Windows NT Server and Windows 2000 Server. Using this tool, you can determine why certain computers are unable to communicate and analyze network traffic. The versions that come with these operating systems are limited to analyzing activity on the local network segment. To use the full version of Network Monitor, you will need to purchase and use the one that comes with Microsoft Systems Management Server.

Shown in Figure 6-3, Network Monitor allows you to view data that's transferred in frames across your network. It captures all frames or a subset of frames that are transmitted to or from the local computer. This information is then displayed on the Network Monitor interface, so that overall statistics are shown as well as those for network utilization, broadcasts, multicasts, and total bytes and frames received per second. You can also filter captured frames, so that only certain frames are captured.

| FIGURE 6-3 | Network Monitor for Windows 2000 Server |

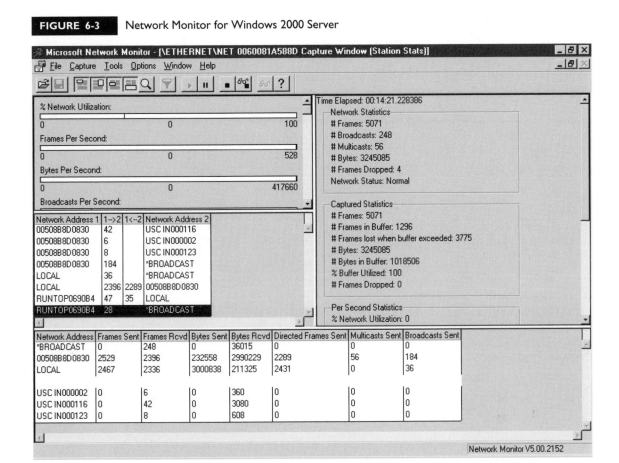

By using Network Monitor, you can identify possible problems and then take measures to deal with them. Improving network performance can be difficult to undertake, and generally involves one of four solutions:

- Reducing network traffic
- Upgrading the network and improving speed
- Splitting the network into subnets
- Dealing with problem components

FROM THE CLASSROOM

Dealing with Performance Issues

Dealing with performance issues follows similar procedures for troubleshooting other problems. What is important to remember is to start with the simplest possible solution first, and work your way to the most complex. For example, if you suspected a bad network card on a particular computer was slowing down your network because it was constantly sending broadcasts, start by removing that computer from the network and seeing if the situation improves. If it does, replace the network card on that computer. All too often,

administrators forget to start with the easy solution, and work through complex problems by starting with the most complex solutions.

It is also important that you understand the tools included with the operating systems being used, so that you can use them effectively when they're needed. If you need to learn a utility when a problem arises, users will need to live with that problem until you're ready to begin the troubleshooting and performance tuning process.

—*Michael Cross, MCSE, MCP+I, MCPS, CNA*

It may seem like a trite suggestion to reduce traffic to speed a network, but there are occasions when this is the answer to your problem. Your network may be using old equipment, users may be using the network in ways you didn't expect, or any number of other reasons may be gobbling up bandwidth. As we'll see in the following paragraphs, there are common situations that can improve your network's performance by simply reducing traffic.

Some users may be bogging down the network, and you will need to identify and determine why this is happening. In some cases, it may be due to users copying large files across the network or performing complex queries that are returning large amounts of data. By getting these users to perform the queries or copy data when network usage is low, the perceived performance of the network by other users will increase.

A number of companies will use diskless workstations, in which hard disks aren't installed on the computers used by network users. The workstation must access their operating system, programs, and data across the network, causing extensive network traffic. To deal with this problem, you should consider installing hard disks on some or all of these machines, so that they boot locally.

Having applications available locally will also improve the performance of the network, as programs won't need to be passed over the network to a workstation. As Citrix, Microsoft Terminal Services, and other application servers become more popular, administrators may find they are compromising network bandwidth for ease of administration. If these are being used, you will need to ensure your current network architecture supports it effectively.

No network is ever complete, and upgrades will need to be performed so that the technologies being used don't become archaic and slow. This may require upgrading network cards and cabling. For example, your network might need to move from Ethernet to Fast Ethernet or Fiber-Distributed Data Interface (FDDI). If subnets of your network are separated by distance, and there are large numbers of users, then using a T1 line to connect them may also be an option. By upgrading the network, you are keeping pace with the changing needs of your organization.

In many cases however, upgrading equipment and the media used to transmit data is a final decision. If there are a large number of users on your network, it may require breaking the network into smaller networks, called subnets. A large network is split into two or more smaller networks and connected with bridges, routers, or servers that provide a routing service. In some situations, you may even put a server on each subnet to decrease the amount of traffic being passed between the subnets when users log on or access data on a central server.

Before taking the major step of breaking your network apart, or purchasing expensive upgrades, you should first consider that problem components are causing performance issues. Bad network cards, poor cabling, or other elements of your network may be causing the performance issues. For example, if your cabling was run beside an elevator or generator, interference may be damaging packets that are being transmitted on the network, causing them to be retransmitted. Such problems can generally be solved without great cost or labor to get your network running effectively.

SCENARIO & SOLUTION

Now that we've discussed performance in such detail, let's look at a number of questions students and professionals have regarding this issue:	
I am using System Monitor, and can't see any results from disk counters. Why?	The disk counters may be turned off. Logical disk counters are turned off by default, so that they aren't constantly using resources. To turn them on, use the DISKPERF utility.
Why would I want to break my network into smaller segments?	This would decrease network traffic because broadcast messages would be limited to the subnet, and traffic meant for computers within one subnet wouldn't be passed to other subnets.

CERTIFICATION OBJECTIVE 6.02

Performing Physical Housekeeping

When you were a kid, your mother may have told you—time and time again—to clean up your room. Being a kid, you probably let it pile up until it became such a problem that you couldn't find anything. If you let it pile up long enough, and your mother got sick-and-tired of it, she may have given in and maintained your room for you. Now that you're older, you probably feel that that you're playing Mom to the users on your network. You tell them to clean up their files, organize folders, and then finally go in and perform the necessary maintenance for them. Welcome to housekeeping.

In terms of computers, the activities of housekeeping deal with maintenance activities that protect the hardware, software, and data residing on it. These activities include:

- Running programs that deal with disk errors and fragmentation
- Clearing out files from the trash, cache, and temporary files directories
- Organizing important files and folders
- Removing programs that are no longer needed

■ Backing up data and protecting against viruses

By performing these actions, which are expanded upon in the paragraphs that follow, the performance and life span of your system will improve.

Disk Errors and Fragmentation

Your data is important to you, and disk maintenance can help to keep it safe. Errors on a disk can cause files to become corrupt and data to be lost. In addition, files can become fragmented, causing performance to be affected. To diagnose disk problems and improve performance, there are a number of tools that can be used.

Error-checking tools can be used to detect bad sectors and errors with your file system. One such tool is Check Disk, which is shipped with Windows 2000. This is similar to the chkdsk tool that shipped with previous versions of Windows NT. It will analyze hard disks to determine if any problems exist, and when possible, will fix them automatically.

In Windows 2000, Check Disk is started from the Properties dialog box for the disk you want to check. In Windows Explorer or My Computer, right-click the hard disk you wish to check, and then select Properties. When the Properties dialog appears, click the Tools tab, and then click the Check Now button. This will open the Check Disk dialog box, where you will see two check boxes: Automatically Fix File System Errors and Scan for and Attempt Recovery of Bad Sectors. Once you've decided what to check, click the Start button to begin the program.

on the *If you are going to have Check Disk automatically fix file system errors, then*
Job *you will need to ensure that all applications or files on that disk are closed. If there are any open files or programs, Check Disk will be unable to acquire exclusive access to the disk. A message box will inform you of this and will give you the option of rescheduling Check Disk to start the next time the computer is restarted.*

Windows 9*x* and Windows ME also provide error-checking software called ScanDisk. You can use this tool to check hard disks for logical and physical errors, and have them automatically repaired. ScanDisk is started from the Start menu by selecting Programs | Accessories | System Tools | ScanDisk. This will open the ScanDisk utility, shown in Figure 6-4.

FIGURE 6-4

ScanDisk

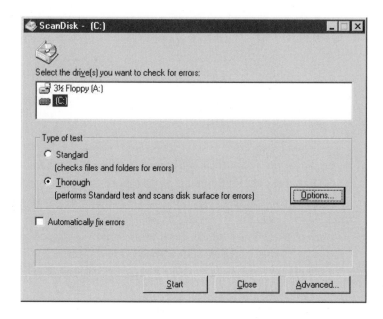

Once this tool is open, you can then choose the level to which ScanDisk will check the disk. There are two types of tests: Standard and Thorough. Standard will check the file system for errors, whereas Thorough will also check the disk surface for errors. By clicking the Automatically Fix Errors check box, you can avoid having to answer message boxes that ask how the program should fix errors each time an error is found. You can further narrow your error checking by clicking the Options button and selecting whether you want to check Data areas, System areas, or both. The Options dialog box will also let you choose whether write testing will be performed, and if bad sectors in hidden and system files will be repaired.

The Advanced button will display a dialog box for ScanDisk's advanced options, which allows you to control how various errors are dealt with. The options listed on this screen are broken into different sections. These sections and their options are as follows:

- **Display Summary** Allows you to set whether a summary of the errors that were encountered is displayed. The options for this section are Always, Never, and Only If Errors Are Found. *Always* will display a summary after scanning is complete, whether errors are found or not. This may cause a problem as it will display a summary after each disk is scanned, thereby stopping any scheduled scans until a user clicks the OK button on the summary and allows it to continue. *Never* will cause ScanDisk not to display a summary, so that you may not know if any errors were encountered or not. *Only If Errors Are Found* will display a summary if ScanDisk encounters any errors during the scan.

- **Log File**   Determines whether a new log file is created or if information is appending to the existing log file. The options for this section are Replace Log, Append to Log, and No Log.

- **Cross-linked Files**   Sets how ScanDisk deals with cross-linked files. Cross-linked files are two or more files that are using the same area of the disk, so that data is only correct for one of the files. In some cases, it may not be correct for either of them, and the data in these files may be lost. The options for this section are Delete, Make Copies, and Ignore.

- **Lost-file Fragments**   Fragments of files that aren't connected to a specific file. As such, although they may contain data, they are usually taking up disk space and contain no viable information. The options for this section are Free and Convert to Files. When you choose to convert them to files, you will have a file containing the data created on your hard disk, which will continue to use up space. You can convert them to files if you think you will be able to identify their origin (such as with documents), and then manually restore the file. In many cases, this isn't the case. By freeing the lost file fragments, you will restore the data, but then be unable to see what they were.

- **Check File For**   Allows you to choose whether ScanDisk will check for Invalid File Names, Invalid Dates and Times, and Duplicate Names.

The final check boxes on this dialog box allow you to choose whether the host drive will be checked before other disks to be scanned, and whether MS-DOS mode name length errors are to be reported. Upon choosing the options you want, clicking OK will return you to ScanDisk's main screen. Clicking Start will begin ScanDisk's analysis and repair of your hard disk.

In addition to experiencing errors, you may find that your system's performance may be suffering due to fragmentation. Files are fragmented when they aren't stored in contiguous spaces on a hard disk. To illustrate this, imagine yourself doing a jigsaw puzzle with the pieces scattered across a table in front of you. Although you may be able to identify the picture, it would be easier to see what it is if all the pieces were in their proper place and organized as they should be. Fragmentation of files is similar, where pieces of the file may be stored in various locations on your hard disk, causing the computer to search and put the pieces together.

exam
Watch

Fragmentation doesn't usually cause any kind of damage to your data, but it will affect performance. Your computer will need to find each of the fragments of a file before loading it, taking greater time in displaying the information you need. To deal with disk fragmentation, use a disk defragmenter program.

Fragmentation can occur when data is added to files and the size of the file grows. Contiguous space on the disk may be used by another file, so part of it must be stored in another location. It can also occur when new files are created. The file is created in the first available space on the disk. If there isn't enough contiguous space to write the entire file in one area, the file becomes fragmented. Fragmentation will continue to get worse as more files are created, moved, and deleted. As fragmentation occurs, the computer needs to perform additional reads and disk head movements to read or write the fragmented parts of the file, which takes longer and decreases performance.

Windows 2000, Windows 9x, and Windows ME all include the Disk Defragmenter tool, which rearranges files on your disk so that they are stored in a contiguous space. This tools was not available in Windows NT. It can defragment volumes that are formatted in FAT, FAT32, and NTFS.

on the
Job

To use Disk Defragmenter, you must have administrator privileges to the workstation or server. Also, you can only run one instance of this program, and defragment volumes located on the local computer. It cannot defragment volumes located on remote computers on your network.

As shown in Figure 6-5, Disk Defragmenter has three panes that provide different forms of information. The top pane displays the volumes on your computer and allows you to select the ones you want to defragment. The middle area displays the analysis of the volume, showing the amount of fragmentation. The bottom area shows the volume during and after defragmentation. In these displays, red lines depict fragmented areas of the volume, blue sections depict contiguous files, green lines depict system files (which can't be moved by Disk Defragmenter), and white areas show free space. When first run, the Analysis Display and Defragmentation display will appear identical. As files are defragmented, you will notice a difference between them.

FIGURE 6-5

Running Disk
Defragmenter

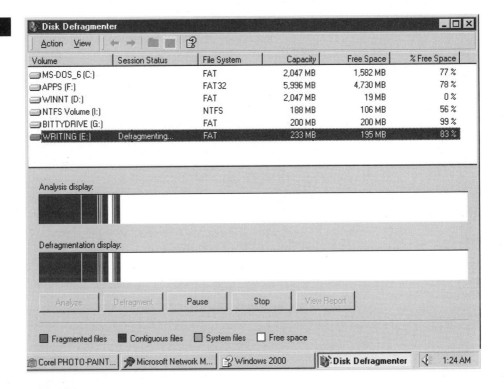

EXERCISE 6-2

Using Disk Defragmenter on Windows 2000 Server

1. From the Windows Start menu, select Programs | Accessories | System Tools | Disk Defragmenter.

2. When the utility appears, select volume C: and click the Analysis button. This will check the drive to see if defragmenting is necessary.

3. When analysis is complete, a message box will appear informing you of whether defragmentation is necessary. Regardless of the results, for this exercise, click the Defragment button to defragment the volume.

4. Upon completion, notice that the Analysis Display and Defragmentation Display are different from when the utility started.

5. Close Disk Defragmenter.

Clearing Files

Just as fragmented files can cause performance problems, so can files that have been deleted, cached, or created temporarily but never deleted. As these files continue to reside on your system after their usefulness has been served, they take up hard disk space. As available hard disk space gets lower, you may notice your system slowing down, increasing the need to clear these files from your system.

Operating systems such as Windows 9x/ME, Windows NT/2000, and Novell NetWare don't immediately remove files from the computer when they are deleted. In the case of files deleted from a Windows operating system, these files are moved to the Recycle Bin. In the case of Novell NetWare, files deleted from a NetWare server are still salvageable, and remain in the directory from which they were deleted. Files that are deleted when a directory is deleted are stored in the DELETED.SAV directory. In both Windows and NetWare, files can still be recovered even though they have been deleted.

NetWare provides methods to purge and salvage deleted files from the server. In the NetWare Administration tool, the Salvage utility can be invoked from the Tools menu. The Salvage utility allows you to view a listing of recoverable files. By selecting one or more of these files, you can then click the Salvage button to restore them, or the Purge button to completely remove them from the system. Deleted files may also be purged automatically if the volume becomes full. In such cases, NetWare will purge recoverable files on a first-deleted basis. In other words, the file that was first deleted will be the first to be purged, then the second, third, and so on. The most recent files will be the last to be purged.

In Windows, files are stored in the Recycle Bin when they are deleted, allowing you to restore them if you delete a file by accident. Files are not purged from the system until you right-click the Recycle Bin and select Empty Recycle Bin. The maximum number of files that can be stored in the Recycle Bin is determined by size, in terms of the amount of hard disk space specified the Recycle Bin's properties. By default, this is set to 10 percent of the volume's disk space. Settings in the Recycle Bin's properties allows you to use all available hard disk space, purge files as soon as they are deleted, or use a setting somewhere in between. As less hard disk space is available, the oldest files are automatically purged from the Recycle Bin first.

exam
Watch

Questions may appear on your exam dealing with files that remain on your system, and thereby continue to use up disk space. Remember that just because a file is deleted, it doesn't necessarily mean that it's removed completely from the system. You may need to purge files for them to be permanently deleted from a server or workstation.

In addition to deleted files, files may be cached to the hard disk, so that they may be used at a later time. For example, when you visit a Web site, the HTML files are first downloaded to a directory on your hard disk and then loaded into your Web browser. The files are cached here, so that when you click the Back button and return to a previous Web page you've visited, it can be loaded from the cache rather than downloaded from the Web site again. Such files may also consist of other temporary files and program files that can be deleted safely.

To remove such files, Windows 9*x*, Windows ME, and Windows 2000 all include a Disk Cleanup program. This can be started from the Start menu by selecting Programs | Accessories | System Tools | Disk Cleanup. When the program appears, you can then select the volume to analyze from a drop-down list, and click OK to begin. Disk Cleanup will look at the volume to determine what can be deleted safely. You will then see how much space can be freed up, and areas where the files reside. Clicking a check box beside each directory containing the files, and then clicking OK will remove them from your disk.

on the
Job

Maintenance should be performed regularly. Scheduling can be configured in many of the programs discussed in this section, so that they can run automatically at certain times. On Windows 9x, Windows ME, and Windows 2000 machines, you can also use the Maintenance Wizard. This will walk you through the process of scheduling programs to run at specific times during the week and month.

Organizing

Organization is an important part of computer housekeeping. As a machine gets used more, it can easily get out of control, and it becomes difficult to find the files you need. This is why it is important to organize your directories early in designing your network or setting up your computer. By having a well-organized directory structure, your system won't become complex and difficult to navigate.

It is also important that you regularly check directories for files and folders that are no longer used. This particularly becomes an issue on networks where users may be removed from a system, but their directories remain after their accounts are deleted. Even though the user is gone, and no one else may be using his or her files, it is common for administrators to leave the files on the server indefinitely. This makes a great waste of hard disk space, and can easily be remedied by contacting others in the former user's department and asking if the files will still be needed.

Occasionally, you should contact users and have them look at the files in their network directories to determine if files are still needed. Many users consider a server to be almost unlimited in the space that can be used. As such, they may have files that haven't been accessed for years and are no longer needed. By deleting these files, considerable space may be recovered.

Another issue that commonly arises is when users move from one area of the network to another, causing the administrator to move that user's files to another server. On Novell NetWare, the NetWare Copy command may be used, so that the user's directory is copied to a new server. However, although the user can now access his or her files from the new server, the original directory still exists on the old server. It is important that such directories are deleted after being copied, as disk space may be used unnecessarily.

Removing Programs That Are No Longer Needed

As time passes, newer and better applications are available to users. Also, time has a way of changing people's needs, making older programs obsolete. If programs are no longer being used, then you will need to determine whether they should be removed from a system.

Determining the programs to be removed can be a matter of balancing policies and laws against users never using software. Some organizations need to hold onto data for a specific period of time, and require programs to remain installed for that time so that they can access the data. For example, although a police department may not use an old database program, they may need it to remain installed on a server so that old police records can be accessed. Although no one is using the software, it needs to remain there, just in case it one day needs to be accessed.

If there is no need to keep a previous program, it is best to remove it from a system. Some programs may conflict with one another, and keeping old software for no reason may create such conflicts. Even if conflicts don't occur, the software is using valuable hard disk space and should be removed so that space can be used for more useful data and applications.

Backing Up Data and Protecting Against Viruses

Protecting your files is an important maintenance routine. If your system were attacked by a virus, fell victim to a fire or other disasters, or simply experienced a hardware failure, you would want to ensure that the information that's valuable to you is safe. For this reason, you should perform backups and virus scans regularly.

Files should be backed up to another form of media, and a backup of your system should be kept offsite. If a disaster occurred, your data would remain safe. We will discuss backups in greater details in the next chapter.

Viruses are programs that attack data and software on your system, so that programs don't run as expected and data is modified, corrupted, or deleted. Some viruses are meant to be humorous, such as playing "Yankee Doodle Dandy" over your system repeatedly. Other viruses may perform such actions as reformatting your hard disk so that all information is lost. Because of the damage viruses can do, you should install a reliable antivirus scanner on your system.

A common mistake many people make is that they don't regularly update their antivirus files. These are files that allow the software to identify and remove viruses from your system. Updated antivirus files are released at least once a month, and should be updated on your system as soon as they come out. If these aren't updated, then a new virus could attack your system.

SCENARIO & SOLUTION

Now that we've discussed computer housekeeping in detail, let's look at some common situations you may encounter:	
I want to run ScanDisk on my Windows NT Server, but can't find it. How can I start the program and check my hard disk for errors?	ScanDisk isn't used on Windows NT. It is included with Windows 9x, Windows ME, and Windows 2000. To check a Windows NT machine for errors, run CHKDSK from the command prompt.
I've heard that I can schedule maintenance on my Windows ME machine. How can I do this?	Run the Maintenance Wizard. This will start a wizard that walks you through the process of scheduling maintenance tasks.

CERTIFICATION OBJECTIVE 6.03

Performing Hardware Verification

A basic tenet of troubleshooting is that the best way to deal with a problem is to ensure that it never happens in the first place. In short, if you get it right the first time, and deal with risks proactively, then you will never have problems. An area where this becomes evident is when hardware is involved.

Hardware verification involves understanding the hardware that's on your system and ensuring that new hardware is verified and tested before it becomes part of a production network. In terms of evaluating current hardware, this means taking an inventory of your network and documenting what routers, bridges, and other equipment is currently being used. It also requires documenting the processors, hard disks, and other components making up your servers and workstations. As for verifying and testing new equipment, it requires researching and testing hardware before it goes "live" on your network, so that you don't find that it doesn't work when users are relying on it.

Evaluating Current Hardware

As mentioned earlier, networks are dynamic. The structure, technologies, and equipment will change over a period of time, and it is important that you understand your hardware environment as changes take place. Operating systems and applications will need hardware that meets minimal requirements. Hardware will reach the end of its lifespan and need to be replaced, and new hardware may be incompatible with existing ones. By evaluating current hardware, you will be better able to plan what changes need to occur in the future, and will have a firm grasp on what components are up to date.

All operating systems and applications have minimal requirements that must be met if they're to work properly. For example, a server being installed on your network may need at least 64MB of RAM, a VGA monitor, and a specified amount of hard disk space if it is to work. Greater requirements may be recommended, so that the server will run more effectively. If your server doesn't meet these requirements, then the software won't be able to function as expected, and installation may be impossible. Before going through the cost and effort of installing applications and operating systems, only to find out you can't use them, you should ensure that these minimal hardware requirements are met before installation begins.

Many companies have a member of the IT staff assigned to be responsible for inventories of equipment. The information on hardware is documented, so that it can be tracked and referred to when upgrades are planned and performed. If an accurate inventory doesn't exist, then two methods can be used to obtain an up-to-date catalog of hardware. One is to create a manual inventory, so that information is stored in a database or on paper documentation. The other method is to use automated inventory capture tools, which can detect what equipment is being used on your network.

Manual Inventories

It may seem like manual inventories are more work than they are worth, but they're invaluable. They are also less work to create than you'd expect. It involves going to each piece of equipment and writing down the relevant information. This may include its make and manufacturer, speed, and so forth. When components are upgraded or replaced, the inventory is updated to reflect these changes. An example of how this information can be cataloged is shown in Table 6-1.

TABLE 6-1	Category	Information
Example Inventory Sheet Used for Cataloging Hardware	Asset #	
	Computer name	
	Make/Model	
	Serial Number	
	Installed Protocols	
	IP Address	
	Operating System	
	CPU	
	Memory (MBs)	
	Hard Disk Size (GBs)	
	Network card	
	Applications (locally installed)	
	Location	

As you might expect, the information you include would depend on the type of equipment being inventoried. In Table 6-1, the categories deal with servers or workstations, and the hardware making up this equipment. The Asset # would be a number identifying the equipment, so it can easily be referred to later. It may also be used to refer to hardware when it is being devalued and used as a deduction from taxes. The computer name is also used in identification, but is more useful in determining which computer it is dealing with on a network. The IP Address also provides this identification, but can be used to control what IP Addresses are currently in use on the network, and thereby can't be used by other computers. Additional protocols should also be documented in case certain programs require a specific protocol or have a conflict with them. The make and model of the computer is documented to determine who manufactured the computer and the type of computer it is. This and the serial number can be used when you need to acquire updated drivers, register the equipment, or call the manufacturer for assistance. Operating systems and applications should be logged to determine what software is in use, licensing information, and for identifying what software requires upgrading or replacement. The remaining information deals with hardware components installed on the computer, and can also be used to determine what needs upgrading or replacement.

Automated Survey Tools

Network management software can also be used to determine what hardware is available on your network. Such tools use various agents and polling processes to evaluate devices on a network. This allows you to view components making up your network. You can then save this information, so that it can be referred to later. By using such tools, you can create an accurate inventory of equipment.

exam
ⓦatch

Hardware verification is an important part of upgrading and installing new components on a network or computer. If hardware isn't properly tested to see if it works with existing software and hardware, then you may experience problems. It is a proactive method of ensuring that equipment works properly when it is placed on a production network.

Testing Hardware

Hardware verification requires testing of equipment before it is added to a production network. Testing minimizes the risks of using various technologies by ensuring they work before being used in a real-world environment. Imagine the problems that could result if a backup device didn't work with a new server, or an operating system was unable to recognize its network card after being upgraded. Rather than taking unnecessary risks, it is important that you confirm that equipment will work.

In determining the level of testing necessary, you will need to evaluate the importance of a particular component. If you were replacing a large number of workstations with new computers, it would be a waste of time and resources to test every single machine before putting them on the network. If one machine didn't work, a user could simply use a different one until his or her workstation was repaired or replaced. On the other hand, a new server that will be used by all users of a network should be tested. If a server became unavailable, users may be unable to logon, access resources, and thereby would be unable to do their work. Also, if the server were to crash, important data might be lost and be unrecoverable.

To test the equipment, you should create a lab that mimics the way your actual network is set up, and allows you to test the hardware under similar conditions. You should simulate real-world conditions, including the protocols being used, storage, operating, and maintenance. This test-lab should also match the environmental conditions that the equipment will be experiencing when it goes live. You should use the same electrical power supply, match temperatures and humidity, and mirror other conditions. In doing this, you will be able to ensure that the hardware will operate properly under normal and possibly abnormal conditions.

Testing doesn't merely have hardware running under normal circumstances. As any administrator will tell you, equipment will often experience conditions that are far from normal. Temperatures may fluctuate if air conditioners fail and network traffic may increase beyond average amounts when users log on and off the network at the beginning and end of the day. If you are testing an uninterruptible power supply (UPS), you can't simply let the power remain on, and use it like a power bar in the lab. Power would need to be shut off to accurately test its abilities. Such factors would need to be included in any test criteria you create.

Hardware Compatibility Tools

In many organizations, there aren't the resources or facilities to create a test-lab that acts as a smaller version of the actual network. Manufacturers of operating systems tend to realize this fact, and perform tests on hardware to determine whether they work correctly with the software. Lists are released, recording the hardware they've found to be compatible. In other instances, software is included with the operating system to analyze hardware and determine compatibility automatically.

Hardware Compatibility Lists (HCLs) should be referenced to ensure that your computer has hardware that functions correctly with software being installed. Companies such as Microsoft, Red Hat Linux, and Novell make these lists available on their Web sites, and may also include them on the installation CDs of operating systems. For example, Microsoft includes a list of devices and hardware that Windows 2000 supports on the installation CD, in a file called HCL.TXT. Before performing an installation, you should compare the components on a machine to those listed in the Hardware Compatibility List. If your hardware doesn't appear in the list, contact the hardware's manufacturer to find out whether it is compatible.

Expect to see questions dealing with Hardware Compatibility Lists (HCLs) on the exam. HCLs are listings of hardware that have been tested and found to work correctly with particular software. Usually this software consists of operating systems.

Windows 2000 also provides another tool for checking hardware compatibility. The Windows 2000 Readiness Analyzer is software that tests your hardware to determine if it is compatible with the operating system. Although included with the Windows 2000 installation CD, it will also run on Windows 95, Windows 98, Windows NT 3.51, and Windows NT 4.0. When run, it will compare your hardware and software with a compatibility list, and then provide output that reveals the results of the test. This allows you to determine if your computer can be upgraded to Windows 2000 without performing any hardware or software modifications.

The Windows 2000 Readiness Analyzer can be launched using the Run command on your Windows Start menu. By typing the following command, you will start the Readiness Analyzer, which will begin to check your system for incompatibilities:

```
WINNT32 /CHECKUPGRADEONLY
```

SCENARIO & SOLUTION

Now that we've discussed hardware verification in such detail, let's look at some common questions asked on this topic:	
I am planning to purchase a new device for the network, but don't have a test network to check whether it will perform as I want with the network operating system. What can I do?	Check the Hardware Compatibility List available for the operating system. This will list hardware that is compatible with that operating system.
I checked the Hardware Compatibility List, but some of my hardware isn't listed. How can I check whether this is compatible before upgrading the server's operating system?	Contact the manufacturer of the hardware. Information may be available on their Web site, or you may have to contact them directly.

EXERCISE 6-3

Using the Windows 2000 Readiness Analyzer

1. Insert the Windows 2000 installation CD into your CD-ROM drive.

2. From the Run command, type the following

   ```
   WINNT32 /CHECKUPGRADEONLY
   ```

3. Wait for the Readiness Analyzer to finish analyzing your machine, then review the results to see if your existing system is compatible to be upgraded to Windows 2000.

CERTIFICATION SUMMARY

Creating a baseline and monitoring performance is important to keeping your system running properly. Baselines are logged performance results, which are taken when your system is running normally. When performance monitoring is done afterwards, you can compare the results to the baseline to determine whether your system is functioning normally or if problems exist.

Physical housekeeping is the maintenance that must be performed so that your system runs properly and its performance continues to be as high as expected. Housekeeping involves such tasks as organizing files, purging deleted files, removing cached and temporary files, regular backups and virus scans, and disk maintenance. There are a number of tools available with operating systems or through third parties that allow you to check your disk for errors and defragment volumes.

Hardware verification is a process of identifying what hardware is on your system and ensuring that new hardware will be compatible with the existing system. It requires comparing your hardware and software to those listed in Hardware Compatibility Lists, and ensuring that hardware will run as expected before it is put on a production network.

✓ TWO-MINUTE DRILL

Here are some of the key points from each certification objective in Chapter 6.

Creating a Baseline and Comparing Performance

❑ Baselines must be logged so that they can be referred to later. By comparing the measurements from the baseline to current performance measurements, you will be better able to detect problems.

❑ Performance Console consists of two snap-ins: System Monitor and Performance Logs and Alerts. These can aid you in detecting reasons why performance on a system isn't up to par.

❑ Network Monitor is a tool used to detect network problems.

❑ Dealing with network and system performance problems may include reconfiguring elements of your system, replacing or upgrading equipment, or changing the architecture of your network.

❑ Disk performance counters may need to be turned on before they can begin collecting data about the hard disk.

Performing Physical Housekeeping

❑ Error-checking tools allow you to determine whether errors exist on your hard disk. By using these tools, you can fix certain disk problems.

❑ File fragmentation occurs when files aren't stored on a hard disk in contiguous spaces. To deal with this, a Disk Defragmenter tool can be used to move files into contiguous spaces.

❑ When files are deleted, they generally remain on the server or workstation, so that they can be recovered by the operating system if the need arises. On Windows machines, they are stored in the Recycle Bin, whereas Novell NetWare will store the deleted files in the DELETED.SAV directory or the directory from which the files were deleted.

❑ Temporary files, cached files, temporary Internet files, and files no longer required by applications can be deleted from your server to reclaim free space.

❑ Antivirus files should be updated regularly to protect your system from viruses.

Performing Hardware Verification

❑ Hardware verification involves understanding the hardware that's on your system, and ensuring that new hardware is verified and tested before it is installed.

❑ Inventories of hardware on your network can be used for planning and performing upgrades.

❑ You should determine what equipment is important to your network, and then test it on a test network before putting it on the production network.

❑ Hardware Compatibility Lists provide a listing of hardware that is compatible with an operating system being installed.

❑ The Windows 2000 Readiness Analyzer can be used to check a system running Windows 9x, Windows NT 3.51, or Windows NT 4.0 so that you can determine that hardware and software is compatible before upgrading to Windows 2000.

SELF TEST

The following questions will help you measure your understanding of the material presented in this chapter. Read all of the choices carefully, as there may be more than one correct answer. Choose all correct answers for each question.

Creating a Baseline and Comparing Performance

1. You have been monitoring a server that has recently begun running slow. You check the current statistics with previous ones. You find that disk activity is generally at 50 percent, and that this has been a regular occurrence since you began recording information on the server. You also find that the processor time has gone from running at 45 percent to 75 percent, and generally runs this high. Finally, you notice that the queue length for the Server Work Queues is generally low but that they occasionally peak at 2. Which of the following is most likely the bottleneck?

   A. The processor
   B. The hard disk
   C. The queue
   D. The entire system

2. You are preparing to create a baseline on a Windows NT Server. Which of the following modes would you use to create this baseline?

   A. Chart
   B. Report
   C. Log
   D. Alert

3. You are preparing to study real-time information on a server that is performing poorly. You assume the problem lies with hardware that will need to be upgraded at a later date. Which of the following will you use to determine what is causing the bottleneck and confirm your assumption that the problem is hardware related?

   A. Network Monitor
   B. Performance Monitor
   C. Performance Logs and Alerts
   D. System Monitor

4. You think there is a bottleneck existing on a Windows 2000 Server, and have decided to check the hard disk counters. After opening the monitoring tool that comes with the operating system, and adding the appropriate counters, you find that information isn't being collected. What is the reason for this?

   A. Windows 2000 has the LogicalDisk counters disabled by default, and they must be enabled by running diskperf –yv.

   B. Windows 2000 has the disk counters disabled by default, and they must be enabled by running diskperf –n.

   C. Windows 2000 has the PhysicalDisk counters disabled by default.

   D. You are using the wrong tool.

5. There is a network problem and you believe that a network card is repeatedly broadcasting messages. Which of the following tools would you use to capture frames and view whether messages are repeatedly being broadcast on the network?

   A. Task Manager

   B. Network Monitor

   C. System Monitor

   D. Performance Monitor

6. You have taken over administration of a network in which security is important. The current network uses diskless workstations, where users log on and their operating system and applications are provided to them over the network. The network backbone has been upgraded to FDDI, but users are complaining that it is slow accessing data and logging onto the network in the morning. Decision-makers are concerned about users being able to take data out of the building, and are hesitant about installing any equipment that would cost a substantial amount of money. All servers and workstations are on a single network, located in one building. There are approximately 200 users on the network at any given time. Which of the following options will you suggest to the decision-makers?

   A. Install hard disks and floppy disks on each of the workstations. Install operating systems and applications on each machine.

   B. Install hard disks on each of the workstations, and install the operating system on each machine. Do not install floppy disks or other methods of saving data to external sources. Use Citrix to provide applications to each machine.

   C. Remove servers and create a peer network.

D. Install hard disks on each of the workstations, and install the operating system on each machine. Do not install floppy disks or other methods of saving data to external sources. Install a T3 line as the backbone of the network, and use Citrix to provide applications to each machine.

Performing Physical Housekeeping

7. Which of the following tools would you use to check for disk errors on a Windows 2000 Server? Choose all that apply

  A. Disk Check

  B. ScanDisk

  C. Task Manager

  D. System Monitor

8. You are checking disk errors on a Windows 98 machine. After running ScanDisk, the user complains that data files are occasionally corrupt. Which of the following could explain why ScanDisk did not work?

  A. ScanDisk isn't used to check a workstation's hard disk for errors.

  B. ScanDisk can detect errors on a hard disk, but cannot fix them.

  C. ScanDisk was running a Standard test and not a Thorough test.

  D. ScanDisk was running a Thorough test and not a Standard test.

9. Files aren't being stored in contiguous spaces on your hard disk, and the computer is accessing data slower. This workstation is running Windows 2000 Professional. Which of the following programs would you run to deal with this problem?

  A. ScanDisk

  B. Check Disk

  C. Disk Defragmenter

  D. System Monitor

10. You are attempting to recover disk space on a Novell NetWare server. You want to purge files that have been deleted by users of the server. Where will you look for such files, so that they can be permanently deleted? Choose all that apply.

  A. The Recycle Bin

  B. The DELETED.SAV directory

    C. The directory that originally stored the files before they were deleted

    D. None of the above. Files are removed from the server when a user deletes them.

11. A Windows 2000 Server has its Recycle Bin set to 10 percent of the volume's hard disk space. Checking the Recycle Bin, you find that it is full of files, totaling 10 percent of the server's disk space. Users of the server use more space, so that less space is available to the Recycle Bin. What will happen to these files in the Recycle Bin?

    A. The first files that were deleted will be emptied from the Recycle Bin.

    B. The last files that were deleted will be emptied from the Recycle Bin.

    C. All files will be removed from the Recycle Bin.

    D. No files will be removed from the Recycle Bin until it is manually emptied.

12. Your computer is running Windows NT Workstation. You want to remove files and folders from your computer's hard disk and free up space. Which of the following should you delete? Choose all that apply.

    A. The TEMP directory

    B. Internet files contained in the Temporary Internet Files directory

    C. Microsoft Word documents ending with the extension .TMP

    D. Files stored in the SYSTEM32 directory

13. A Windows NT Server is running a number of programs, and you are analyzing which should be removed. This server is running Internet Information Server, but you have moved the content for your site to an Apache Web server. The server uses SQL Server, but also has data stored in an older database that hasn't been used for over three years. Due to the Finance department's need to keep tax information, this data hasn't been removed. You have, however, migrated the data into a SQL database. As Windows 2000 Server can be used like a workstation, Microsoft Office has also been installed on this server, although you haven't used it in the time it has been installed. None of these programs appear to be conflicting with one another. Which of the following will you remove?

    A. Internet Information Server

    B. Apache Web Server

    C. SQL Server

    D. As there are no conflicts, none should be uninstalled.

14. A user believes that their system is infected with a virus. A virus scanner was installed on this computer three years ago, and you haven't touched it since then. It runs regularly each night, checking this computer's files for possible viruses. This leads you to believe that the virus scanner has been functioning normally all this time. Which of the following is most likely the reason for this problem?

    A. The virus scanner wasn't installed properly.

    B. Antivirus files haven't been updated.

    C. The antivirus software hasn't been updated.

    D. The antivirus software has always been infected with a file, and is the cause of this problem.

Performing Hardware Verification

15. You are manually creating an inventory of hardware and software on workstations and servers. In creating this inventory, you document the make and model of the computers, serial numbers, operating system, and network card being used, and applications that are installed locally. Which of the following is a problem with this inventory?

    A. Inventories should not include software.

    B. The CPU, hard disk, and memory on servers and workstations haven't been inventoried.

    C. The CPU, hard disk, and network cards on servers and workstations haven't been inventoried.

    D. Inventories should be created with network inventory software that gathers information automatically.

16. Your company is upgrading workstations and servers and other network equipment. There will be two routers added to the network, two servers will be replaced with new ones, and 100 old workstations will be replaced with brand new machines. In addition, you will be upgrading one older server to a more recent operating system. This server will be used as a distribution server, so that all installation CDs will be installed on it, and IT staff can use these files when installing applications. For which of the following will you perform hardware verification on a test network before adding them to the production network? Choose all that apply

    A. The two servers that are replacing old ones.

    B. The old server that is being upgraded.

    C. The workstations.

    D. The routers.

17. You are testing an uninterruptible power supply (UPS) on a test network. You let the UPS run under normal circumstances for a week, then install the UPS so that your server and router are plugged into it. Which of the following is true?

    A. New hardware should be tested for at least a month before being placed on the production network.

    B. You should never plug a router and server on the same UPS.

    C. UPSs never require testing.

    D. The UPS should not only be tested under normal circumstances, but abnormal ones as well.

18. You are preparing to install Red Hat Linux on your computer. Your company can't afford to implement a test network, so you're unsure if the current hardware will work. Which of the following will provide a listing of hardware that is known to work with this operating system?

    A. Red Hat Linux user manual

    B. Hardware Compatibility List

    C. Hardware Incompatibility List

    D. Documentation for the hardware

19. You want to upgrade computers on your network to Windows 2000, and decide to use the Windows 2000 Readiness Analyzer. Which of the following platforms can you check with this tool? (Choose all that apply.)

    A. Red Hat Linux

    B. Windows NT 3.51

    C. Windows NT 4.0

    D. Windows 3.1

20. You want to check clients on your network running Windows 95 and Windows 98 to see if they can be upgraded to Windows 2000 without having to upgrade existing hardware and software. Which of the following will you use to obtain this information? (Choose all that apply.)

    A. Hardware Compatibility List

    B. Windows 2000 Readiness Analyzer

    C. System Monitor

    D. None of the above. Windows 9x machines can't be upgraded to Windows 2000.

LAB QUESTION

You are the new administrator of a network running Windows 2000 Servers and workstations running Windows 98, Windows 2000 Professional, and Windows NT Workstation. The network is currently broken into two segments. One subnet is for the administration on the top floor of a leased three-story building, whereas two departments on different floors use another subnet. You find that users on the subnet for the two departments commonly exchange data among themselves, but occasionally need to access files on the servers running on the administration subnet. There are approximately 100 users logged onto the network during work hours.

   As part of your initial duties in taking over the network, you have decided to create a baseline. Due to the financial situation of the company, you are limited to using tools included with the operating systems.

1. When creating a baseline for the server, what tool will you use?

2. To refer to it later, which tool will you use to view the information collected?

3. To obtain information on activities when they occur, what kind of log should you create?

4. Users in the branch offices are complaining that the network is running relatively slow. Which is the least expensive method of improving their performance?

5. A Windows 98 machine is suffering from file fragmentation. From your Windows 2000 Professional workstation you try defragmenting the volume on the Windows 98 machine, but find you cannot. Why?

SELF TEST ANSWERS

Creating a Baseline and Comparing Performance

1. ☑ **A.** The processor. The processor is generally running high, and has increased its processing time since the baseline was created. This indicates that either the processor usage has increased or that there is a problem with the processor.

   ☒ **B** is incorrect because the disk usage has always been this high and the server has only recently begun to run slow. **C** is incorrect because the queue is generally low, but only peaks occasionally. Because it isn't running high all the time, this indicates that this isn't where the bottleneck exists. **D** is incorrect because bottlenecks on a machine aren't caused by an entire system, but by components of a system that are either in need or upgrade, repair, or replacement.

2. ☑ **C.** Log. To create a baseline, results must be logged so that you can refer to them afterwards. A baseline is a snapshot of your computer or network's performance measurements, which can be used for planning and analysis. To create a baseline, you run a system or network monitoring tool at times when the server, workstation, or network is running normally. These results are logged so that performance measurements can be saved to a file.

   ☒ **A, B,** and **D** are incorrect because each of these fail to log the results to a file. Report view displays a textual report on the screen, chart view displays a graph on the screen, and alert view sends alerts when certain thresholds have been met.

3. ☑ **D.** System Monitor. This is a snap-in that is loaded into the Performance Console and shows real-time displays of performance information. It is used to monitor resource utilization and network throughput, so that you can determine where a bottleneck exists on a Windows 2000 Server.

   ☒ **A** is incorrect because Network Monitor is used to gather information about the network. It doesn't display information on server resources. **B** is incorrect because the server is running Windows 2000, and Performance Monitor is a Windows NT tool. **C** is incorrect because Performance Logs and Alerts allow you to log performance data and set remote notification of performance issues. It isn't used to view real-time data, but to log information for later reference.

4. ☑ **A.** The LogicalDisk monitors any counter data associated with local drives and storage volumes. By default, the LogicalDisk object is disabled, and must be enabled by running diskperf –yv from the command prompt. Once you've turned on the counter and rebooted, you will then be able to collect data about the disk.

☒ **B** is incorrect because to disable the counter, you run diskperf –n at the command prompt. C is incorrect because by default, Windows 2000 has the PhysicalDisk counters enabled. It uses the diskperf –yd command to obtain data on physical drives. **D** is incorrect because if you were using the wrong tool, you wouldn't be able to add the appropriate counters.

5. ☑ **B.** Network Monitor. This tool is available with Windows NT Server and Windows 2000 Server. It is used to analyze network traffic. The versions that come with these operating systems are limited to only analyzing activity on the local network segment. In this case, you would be able to view broadcasts.
☒ **A, C, and D** are incorrect because these tools don't allow you to view frames that are captured off the network.

6. ☑ **B.** Install hard disks on each of the workstations, and install the operating system on each machine. Do not install floppy disks or other methods of saving data to external sources. Use Citrix to provide applications to each machine.
☒ **A** is incorrect because this would allow users to remove data from the building. C is incorrect because a peer network would prevent users from being able to log onto the network and acquire the operating system and applications they need to do their work. **D** is incorrect, because the cost of installing the T3 line would be incredibly high and would be overkill for the users' needs.

Performing Physical Housekeeping

7. ☑ **A and B.** Disk Check and ScanDisk. Both of these error-checking tools can be used to detect bad sectors and errors with your file system. Each of these will analyze hard disks to determine if any problems exist, and when possible, will fix them automatically.
☒ **C** is incorrect because Task Manager is used to monitor applications, processes, and performance statistics. **D** is incorrect because System Monitor is used to monitor performance issues on Windows 2000 Server.

8. ☑ **C.** ScanDisk was running a Standard test and not a Thorough test. ScanDisk allows you to run two types of tests: Standard and Thorough. Standard will check the file system for errors, whereas Thorough will also check the disk surface for errors. As disk errors are continuing to occur, it is probable that there are disk surface errors, which wouldn't have been detected when a Standard test was run.
☒ **A** is incorrect because ScanDisk is an error-checking tool. **B** is incorrect because ScanDisk can fix certain errors on hard disks. **D** is incorrect because ScanDisk running a Thorough test will check the disk surface for errors, but a Standard test will only check files and folders for errors.

9. ☑ **C.** Disk Defragmenter. The situation being discussed in this question is file fragmentation. Files are fragmented when they aren't stored in contiguous spaces on a hard disk. To defragment files, Disk Defragmenter can be used.

   ☒ **A** and **B** are incorrect because ScanDisk and Check Disk both check for errors on the disk. **D** is incorrect because System Monitor is used to monitor possible performance issues on a computer, but isn't used to analyze and fix file fragmentation.

10. ☑ **B** and **C.** The directory that originally stored the files before they were deleted, and the DELETED.SAV directory. On Novell NetWare servers, deleted files are still salvageable, and remain in the directory in which they were deleted. Files that are deleted when a directory is deleted are stored in the DELETED.SAV directory. In both Windows and NetWare, files can still be recovered even though they have been deleted.

   ☒ **A** is incorrect because Windows computers use the Recycle Bin as a storage location for deleted files. **D** is incorrect because files still reside on the server after deletion, until such time as they are purged from the server.

11. ☑ **A.** The first files that were deleted will be emptied from the Recycle Bin. The maximum number of files that can be stored in the Recycle Bin is determined by size, in terms of the amount of hard disk space specified the Recycle Bin's properties. By default, this is set to 10 percent of the volume's disk space. As less hard disk space is available, the oldest files are automatically purged from the Recycle Bin first.

   ☒ **B** is incorrect because it is opposite from the way that the Recycle Bin automatically removes files. **C** is incorrect because all files will not be removed from the Recycle Bin. **D** is incorrect because files will be automatically removed from the Recycle Bin as less free space is available.

12. ☑ **B** and **C.** Internet files contained in the Temporary Internet Files directory and Microsoft Word documents ending with the extension .TMP. Files in the Temporary Internet Files directory contain cached files used by the Web browser. Documents ending with the extension .TMP are temporary files, and can also be deleted.

   ☒ **A** is incorrect because the TEMP directory shouldn't be deleted. Files within this directory can be deleted, but the directory itself shouldn't be. **D** is incorrect because the SYSTEM32 directory contains files used by the operating system.

13. ☑ **A.** Internet Information Server. This Web server isn't being used, and content has been migrated to the Apache Web server.

   ☒ **B** is incorrect because Apache Web server is being used as the Web server. **C** is incorrect because SQL Server contains both the data from the old database software and also new databases. **D** is incorrect because software that no longer serves a purpose and isn't being used should be removed from the server. Even though there are no conflicts, it is still using resources (such as hard disk space).

14. ☑ **B.** The anti-virus files haven't been updated. Because of this, the information on new viruses and how to remove them isn't available to the software. This means the software can't detect and remove new viruses.

   ☒ **A** is incorrect because the virus scanner has been running regularly, and doesn't appear from this to be installed incorrectly. **C** is incorrect, as the antivirus software can continue to run normally so long as updated antivirus files are still available for it. **D** is incorrect because there is no reason to believe that the software is the reason for this problem. If it was, a problem probably would have occurred before now.

Performing Hardware Verification

15. ☑ **B.** The CPU, hard disk, and memory on servers and workstations haven't been inventoried. The information gathered includes very few hardware components. This must be included so that it can be used in planning and performing hardware upgrades and replacements.

   ☒ **A** is incorrect because inventories should include the applications and operating systems installed on servers and workstations. **C** is incorrect because network cards have been included in the inventory. **D** is incorrect because inventories are often created manually.

16. ☑ **A and D.** The two servers that are replacing old ones and the routers. If the servers failed on the production network, users would be unable to logon or access the server's resources. The routers can be placed on the test network for a time and tested before being added to the production network. If either of them fail, they won't affect the network's ability to communicate.

   ☒ **B** is incorrect because this server is going to be used only as a distribution server. If it fails, all of the data is still available on the original installation CDs. **C** is incorrect because there are a considerable number of workstations being added to the network. If one of these failed, a user could use a different workstation until their workstation was repaired or replaced.

17. ☑ **D.** The UPS should not only be tested under normal circumstances, but abnormal ones as well. By merely letting the UPS run, you have no idea whether it will work if there is a power loss. You should unplug it from the power, and then determine if it continues to supply power from the battery to the server and router.

   ☒ **A** is incorrect because there is no set time as to how long hardware should be tested. **B** is incorrect because there is no problem plugging a router and server into the same UPS. **C** is incorrect because a UPS should be tested to ensure that it works correctly before your server or other devices are plugged into it.

18. ☑ **B.** Hardware Compatibility List. This is a listing of hardware that is supported by the operating system and is found to be compatible with it through testing. Before performing an installation, you should compare the components on a machine to those listed in the Hardware Compatibility List. If your hardware doesn't appear in the list, contact the hardware's manufacturer to find out whether it is compatible.

    ☒ **A** and **D** are incorrect because neither the operating systems user manual or documentation for the hardware will provide a listing of all hardware that's compatible with Red Hat Linux. **C** is incorrect because there is no such thing as a Hardware Incompatibility List.

19. ☑ **B** and **C.** Of the platforms offered as choices, the Windows 2000 Readiness Analyzer can be run on Windows NT 3.51 and Windows NT 4.0. It can run on clients using Windows 95, Windows 98, Windows NT 3.51, and Windows NT 4.0.

    ☒ **A** and **D** are incorrect because the Readiness Analyzer won't run on Red Hat Linux or Windows 3.1.

20. ☑ **A** and **B.** The Hardware Compatibility List (HCL) and the Windows 2000 Readiness Analyzer. The HCL is a listing of compatible hardware. The Windows 2000 Readiness Analyzer is software that tests your hardware to determine if it is compatible with the operating system.

    ☒ **C** is incorrect because System Monitor provides no method of checking a client to see if its hardware is compatible with Windows 2000. **D** is incorrect because the Readiness Analyzer can run on clients using Windows 95, Windows 98, Windows NT 3.51, and Windows NT 4.0. If existing hardware and software is compatible, it can then be upgraded to Windows 2000.

LAB ANSWER

1. Performance Logs and Alerts, which is part of the Performance Console. Performance Logs and Alerts is a snap-in, which allows you to log information collected from counters. To create a baseline, information must be logged so that you can refer to it later.

2. System Monitor, which is part of the Performance Console. System Monitor is a snap-in, which you can use to load and view information collected with the Performance Logs and Alerts snap-in.

3. Trace Log. A Trace Log is different from a counter log in that it doesn't obtain data at regular update intervals. Instead, it logs data when certain events occur. It monitors the activities you specify, and when one happens, it stores the information in a log file.

4. Create a subnet for each floor of the building so that the two departments and administration level of the company each work in a different subnet. Because users in these departments commonly exchange data among themselves, this will separate traffic so that it is contained in each subnet. Users on one subnet won't be subject to most of the traffic being caused by the other new subnets.

5. Disk Defragmenter can only defragment volumes located on the local computer. It cannot defragment volumes located on remote computers on your network.

Server+
COMPUTING TECHNOLOGY INDUSTRY ASSOCIATION

7

Backup and SNMP

CERTIFICATION OBJECTIVES

A s a network administrator, the powers-that-be in your company will expect you to have knowledge of everything and the ability to see into the future. If a problem occurs, people will wonder why you didn't know about it sooner, or why measures weren't taken beforehand to deal with such an occurrence. Fortunately, although you may not be the Oracle of Delphi, your network can give you the abilities to know about issues before they become a problem, and to take preventative measures to deal with them.

Protecting data and knowing when problems exist have always been a major part of network administration. This chapter will help you with that. It will help you to ensure that if hell's fury rains down on your network, the data is at least backed up and in a safe location. It will also help you to take steps to be informed of performance issues and other network problems when they occur.

CERTIFICATION OBJECTIVE 7.01

Performing a Regular Backup

Data backups are copies of data that are written to a tape or other storage device. Using a backup program, your files are archived to a medium that can be stored in another location. For example, you may make a backup to a data tape, rewritable CD, or ZIP drive, and then store it in a branch office of your company. When someone deletes a file that can't be recovered, your server's hard disk crashes, or a disaster occurs, you can then recover the data from a backup. Regular backups allow you to keep your data safe and to restore it to a server when a problem occurs.

Performing regular backups is like having insurance. Maybe you haven't fallen victim to a disaster, but what would happen if you did? Would you feel relief at having been prepared, or experience the ultimate loss of losing everything that's valuable to you? By thinking of backups in this way, you'll understand the importance of performing them regularly. Missing backups is like missing a payment on your insurance; if something happens, you won't be covered.

The same way you plan for the future with insurance, you should carefully plan ahead with backups. A common mistake made on new networks is that no planning actually goes into the backup process. An administrator will simply set up the backup program, and let it run with little to no thought over what should really be backed up. This leads to redundant or useless data being backed up regularly, or important data being missed by the backup.

If you are taking over an established network, your predecessor should have already investigated what data needs to be backed up, and set up a backup process. If this is the case, you should determine what is being backed up. In doing so, you may find that the wrong data is being backed up, new data is being missed, or the backup process has been done incorrectly until the time you took over. To find what is being backed up, you can talk with your predecessor, other members of the IT staff, check backup logs, or use available network documentation.

If you can't determine what is being backed up, then take the approach as if no backup is in place. Backtrack the previous administrator's work, and communicate with others as to what data is to be backed up. This involves getting together with department heads and project leaders, and finding what files are important to them. Basically, it is better to start from scratch than to be doubtful about existing practices.

If you are creating a new network, then determining what data needs to be backed up can be easier. Creating a directory structure that suits the security requirements of each department, and units within those departments, will be part of your network's design. From this, you'll know where important data is stored and will be able to determine what directories can be omitted from a backup.

In identifying the data to be backed up, you will need to determine where the files are located. Most of the data should be stored in directories on the server, but some projects may be stored on individual workstations. Workstations will generally contain less data than servers, so you can back up this data across the network. In such cases, you will need to ensure that the workstations are online when the backups take place. If a user shuts down the workstation when backups are scheduled, then the backup will fail.

If servers have larger hard disks, containing significant amounts of data, then you will probably want to have each server to use its own backup device. Media used to back up data have space limitations, so backing up your entire network to one tape will use up the space quickly. In such cases, multiple tapes will be needed to complete a single backup. Also, if servers are located in different geographical areas, then backing up data across a network to a single device will take longer, and will use up network bandwidth. If this is your situation, installing a backup device at each location or on each server will allow backups to complete quickly, and will make it easier restoring data.

on the job

In addition to user files, you will need to determine what other data should be backed up on a regular basis. Administrators will generally remember that user files will be included in backups, but may forget that other data will also need to be archived. For example, SQL Server databases or Web server content may need to be backed up. Users will make use of these, but probably won't mention them when being interviewed on the important files and data used in their work.

Once you've determined what to back up, you will need to determine how often it should be done. This will depend on the importance of the information and how often it changes. For example, if files are archived to a directory for historical reference, and users access them on a read-only basis, then you may only need to backup the data yearly or even as a one-time event. If users are constantly modifying documents daily, then you will probably want to back up this data nightly. As you can see, factors dealing with importance and changes to data would vary from department to department and company to company.

As we'll see later in this chapter, there are different types of backups that can be done. The type of backup allows you to control whether all areas of your system are backed up, or only files that have changed. Generally, companies will perform a full backup of files on a weekly or monthly basis. Each night, they will back up files that have been modified since the last full backup of the system. By doing so, you would then recover the files from the full backup, and then restore the files that have changed. If a user deletes a file, and knows when the file was last modified, then you can restore the file from the backup for that date. This means the user may have only lost a day's work, or won't lose any changes if it has been backed up and no changes have been made since then.

Once you've made the decisions necessary for your backup plan and configured your initial backup process, then you will need to monitor whether backups are running properly. Problems can occur for various reasons, including:

- The backup process has been configured incorrectly.
- All of the components necessary to run the backup program haven't loaded or have loaded improperly. For example, Novell NetWare's Storage Management System requires a number of files to be loaded on the server or it will not run. It needs TSAxxx.NLM, QMAN.NLM, SCSE.NLM, and SBCON.NLM to be loaded. If any of these haven't been loaded, then the backup won't run.

- The device used for the backup isn't running properly. This can be due to hardware problems or because drivers for the backup device haven't loaded properly or been properly installed.

- Problems with the media, such as a bad tape, or the incorrect type of tape being inserted into the device.

- Workstations included in the backup process may be shutdown.

- Network problems may prevent the backup program from connecting to servers and workstations included in the backup process.

Failed backups can be detected in a number of ways. Some backup programs can be configured to send a message to a particular user if the backup fails. If this feature isn't available, or hasn't been configured, then you will still be able to look at the interface for the backup program and see something indicating that the backup has failed. An icon or words stating the failure will generally appear beside the backup job that failed. Finally, checking error logs is crucial for determining whether a backup job completed or not, and the logs will often contain extended information about why the failure occurred. Once you've found that the job has failed, and determined why, it is important that you fix the problem immediately. The longer you wait to fix the problem, the greater the chance that, at some point, some data may need to be restored.

Testing is another important part of the backup process. No matter how many times you back up the data, it will be useless if you can't restore it. Once the data is backing up error-free, you should begin testing whether data can be restored properly. This doesn't mean restoring all the data and overwriting everyone's files, but selecting a directory containing files that can be restored. Creating a directory containing various types of files is an excellent method of testing restores. You can restore that directory on a weekly basis until you're comfortable that it's performing correctly, and then do test restores on a monthly basis after that. If you are restoring a user's data, then you can substitute that for your test restore.

It is important to keep at least one backup offsite. If your business falls victim to fire, flood, or some other disaster, then the backup media at that site may also be destroyed. To prevent losing all of your data under such circumstances, you should make two full backups of your system and keep one of these at a different location. For example, if you were using tape backups, then you could make a full backup each week, and then make a second backup on a different tape immediately afterwards. One of these tapes could then be stored at a separate secure location.

Another common method is to rotate tapes. One week, you would make a full backup of data, and then make nightly backups of files that have changed. At the end of the week, you would then take these backups and store them offsite. During the week that follows, you would use a different set of tapes and repeat this procedure. When that week ends, you would move this set of tapes offsite, and use the previous set of tapes for your backups. We will discuss the rotation of tapes in greater detail later in this chapter.

Tape Backup

Tape backups are the most common method of backing up data. With this method, magnetic tapes are used to store data sequentially. These tapes are similar to those used in microcassette recorders, which require you to fast-forward and reverse the tape to find what you want. This sequential access to archived data makes it slow to restore data, as the device must cue up the tape to where the data is located. However, the cost to purchase such tapes is minimal, with each tape costing a few dollars. This makes tapes a popular method of data recovery.

There are a number of different tape drives available that support different sizes of data and allow an assorted number of tapes. Many tape devices will allow you to insert only one tape at a time. Once the tape is full, you will need to eject the tape and insert another one. For larger companies with a significant amount of data to be backed up, devices with multiple tape magazines are also available. When these are used, when one tape becomes full, it will move on to the next tape in the magazine. This saves you from having to manually replace tapes quite so often.

Two common types of tape drives are Digital Audio Tape (DAT) and Digital Linear Tape (DLT). Each of these were developed in the mid-1980s and use magnetic tape to store data for backups. DAT was created by Sony and Philips for recording music in a digital format, but was found to be useful for recording data in backups. With this method, data is stored on 4mm tapes. In comparison, the DLT method of data storage was originally developed by Digital Equipment Corporation, but is currently owned by Quantum Corporation. It stores data on a half-inch magnetic reel-to-reel tape, in which one reel is contained in the cartridge while the other is stored inside the DLT drive. DAT is not as fast as DLT, and doesn't provide as large of a storage capacity. However, it is less expensive than DLT, which makes DAT a popular method of tape backup.

FROM THE CLASSROOM

Understanding Data Recovery

Having a basic understanding of data recovery can be as problematic as having a poor or nonexistent backup plan. It is important that you don't make shortcuts by allowing backups to continue failing for days or weeks at a time, forgetting to rotate backup tapes and store them offsite, or failing in researching the features available to you.

There are a number of different backup programs available on the market, which either come with operating systems or are available through third parties. If you don't understand the features available through your backup program or the network operating system being used, you may wind up causing more work than necessary for users. For example, Novell NetWare provides a Salvage feature that allows you to restore deleted files without having to restore from a backup. You could compare this to the Windows Recycle Bin, but on a grander scale. When a user deletes a file on a NetWare server, the file isn't completely removed from the server. A copy of it is retained on the system, which can be restored using the Salvage feature. This allows you to restore the exact version of the file that was deleted. If the file were restored from a tape backup, then it would contain only the data that was in the file at the time the backup was performed. If the backup were performed the previous night, then all the user's work for that day would be lost.

You will also need to understand how different programs restore data. Programs such as Microsoft Exchange and SQL Server require more than merely restoring files from a tape. Microsoft Exchange needs to have data restored to a server with the same name that files were backed up from. You can't restore data to a server with a different name, which makes testing backups difficult. Microsoft SQL Server requires you to load database dumps and transaction logs onto the SQL Server for test restores. This means you will need a firm understanding of how SQL Server works.

A good method is to have one or more experts in backups and restores, for different areas of your network. A SQL Server administrator might take responsibility over backing up and restoring data on Microsoft SQL Server, whereas the Webmaster might take over backing up and restoring your Web server and e-mail server. This would leave you, the network administrator, with the responsibility of dealing with network backups and restores. You would also oversee these other members of your IT staff, and confirm they are doing the backups. This not only lessens the network administrator's workload, but it ensures that different areas of your network have experts on different programs doing the backups.

—Michael Cross, MCSE, MCP+I, MCPS, CNA

There are a number of other methods for backing up data, but tape backups are the most popular. There are methods that use 8mm tapes, but these aren't covered on the exam. Understand DAT/DDS and DLT methods of tape data storage, as these will appear on your exam.

DAT uses the Digital Data Storage format (DDS), which uses a process similar to that used in VCRs to store data on the DAT tape. It uses a helical scan, in which read/write heads spin diagonally across a DAT tape. Two read heads and two write heads are used. When data is written, the read heads verify that data has been written correctly to the tape. If it detects any errors, then the data is rewritten. As shown in Table 7-1, there are different formats of DDS available for tape drives, which allow different amounts of storage on a tape.

As shown by this table, there are four different formats of DDS. The original DDS format allowed you to store up to 1.3GB of data, but the next generation increased storage to 2GB of data on a 120-minute cartridge. This data was uncompressed, so less data could be stored on the tape than the other methods allow. DDS-1 was the first to use compression, and allows you to store up to 4GB of data on a 120-minute cartridge. DDS-2 increased compression on a 120-minute cartridge to allow up to 8GB of data. DDS-3 uses a 125-minute cartridge and allows you to store up to 24GB of compressed data. This format also introduced the use of Partial Response Maximum Likelihood (PRML), which eliminates noise so that data is transferred to the tape cleaner and with less errors. Finally, DDS-4 allows 40GB of compressed data to be stored on a 125-minute cartridge. Each of these formats is backward compatible. This means that if you had a DDS-3 device, you could use DDS-1 or DDS-2 cartridges.

TABLE 7-1		
	Type of Format	**Storage Capacity**
DDS Formats for DAT Drives	DDS	2GB
	DDS-1	2/4GB
	DDS-2	4/8GB
	DDS-3	12/24GB
	DDS-4	20/40GB

on the **Job**

Just as cassette or video tapes will wear out after a period of time and force you to buy new ones, DDS cartridges have a limited lifespan. Don't expect DDS cartridges to last indefinitely; keep a few blank ones on hand for replacement. DDS cartridges should be retired after 2000 passes or 100 full backups. After this, you may experience errors in data, or the tape may fail to be accepted by the backup program being used.

As mentioned, Digital Linear Tape is faster than DDS, and provides a higher storage capacity. Using this method, you can put more data on the tape, allowing you to use this media with larger hard disks, and relieving you from having to change tapes quite so often. As shown in Table 7-2, there are different generations of DLT that accommodate different capacities of storage.

Unlike DDS, each version of DLT provides data compression. DLT2000 allows you to store up to 30GB of data, DLT4000 allows up to 40GB of data, and DLT7000 allows up to 70GB of data storage. However, if compression isn't used, then half of this amount can be stored on the tape.

DLT drives store data differently than DAT/DDS drives. With DLT, the data path is made up of parallel tracks recorded in a serpentine pattern. The first track of data is written from one end of the tape to the other. Once it has reached the end, the heads are then repositioned, and the next track is written in the opposite direction. The DLT drive will continue writing data back and forth across the tape until the tape is full.

Tape Automation

Programs that are used for tape backups provide the ability to automate the backup process. Rather than having to go over to the server and backup device each day and start a new back up job from scratch, you can set the program to perform a tape

TABLE 7-2	DLT Type	Capacity
DLT Types and Capacities	DLT2000	15/30GB
	DLT4000	20/40GB
	DLT7000	35/70GB

backup at specified times. By configuring the Backup program to do this, you can set certain backup jobs to:

- Run every day, week, or month.
- Run at specific times. This allows you to set jobs to run when few people are using the server, so that performance isn't effected by the backup job.
- Run a specified number of times, so that one type of backup only runs once, whereas others are performed nightly.

As we'll see in the following section, you can also configure your backup program to run certain types of backups. Rather than backing up every piece of data on the server, including files that haven't been modified since the last backup, you can set the backup to only back up files that have changed. This prevents the tape from filling up quickly with redundant data that has already been backed up onto the tape.

Full, Incremental, and Differential

There are three types of backups that you can use when backing up a computer: full, incremental, and differential. As we'll see in this section, each of these backs up data differently, and may be used in different situations. By using these together correctly, you can ensure that important data has been stored on a tape in the event of a problem.

Full backups are used to back up all of your data. This is used when you want to back up all directories and files on a volume, or all of the volumes on a server. Depending on the amount of data being saved to a server, you will perform a full backup on a weekly or monthly basis. If tapes are filling quickly and important data is changing rapidly, then a full backup should be performed at least once a week.

When a full backup is performed, the file is changed to indicate that it has been backed up. What is changed is called the *archive bit*. The archive bit is an attribute of a file, which indicates whether files need to be backed up or not. The archive bit is set when a file is modified to show that data within it has changed, and thereby needs to be backed up. It is cleared by a full backup to show that the file has been backed up to tape.

The need for the archive bit becomes clear when incremental backups are performed. Incremental backups will back up all files that have been modified since the last full or incremental backup. It will not back up any files that have not been modified. During this type of backup, the backup software checks the archive bit to see whether the file has changed, and if it needs to be backed up to a tape. Once backed up, the archive bit is cleared, so that the next incremental backup doesn't back up the file again if it is unmodified.

To restore data from incremental backups, you first restore files from the most recent backup. Once this is complete, you add the incremental changes that have been saved to the tape by the incremental backups. This ensures that files have been completely restored to a system and are completely up-to-date. If only the full backup was restored, then any changes since the time of that back up would be missed. If only the incremental backup were used, then files that have not changed since the full backup wouldn't be restored.

on the **job**

It is common to use a combination of full and incremental backups. This is more efficient and effective than simply running full backups each day. If full backups were run each day, it would take considerable time and use more tapes than using a combination of methods. The only drawback is, to restore from full and incremental backups, you will need the most recent full backup and every incremental backup tape since the last full backup.

Differential backups will back up all files that were modified since the last full backup, but they do not clear the archive bit when data is backed up. To illustrate this, let's say you ran a full backup on your system, and (among other data) backed up a file called WORK.DOC. After the backup, you changed some information in WORK.DOC, and then ran a differential backup. The differential backup would back up this file, but if no more changes were made to WORK.DOC, each additional differential backup would continue backing up this file. This is different from an incremental backup, which would back up the modified file, clear the archive bit, and not back it up again until the file was modified. Because a differential backup will back up all files modified since the last full backup, the benefit of a differential backup over a incremental backup is that only two backup sets are required. To restore data, you would restore the full backup, and then the differential backup tape.

Differential backups will be slower each time they are performed because the size of the backup will grow with each differential backup. This is because the same data and additional data is being backed up each time. This makes differential backups faster to perform than full backups, but (after the first time a differential backup is performed), slower than incremental backups. Because only modified files are changed, an incremental backup is considerably faster than a full backup (which backs up all files, regardless of whether they've been modified). As the number of files increases on your server, the time it takes to perform an incremental backup will increase as well.

Although you can combine full backups with incremental backups and differential backups, you should never combine differential and incremental backups. It is a waste of time and resources to do so. The differential backup doesn't clear the archive bit, but the incremental backup will. This means that each time you ran an incremental backup, the archive bit would be cleared, as is done when a full backup is performed. If a differential backup were run afterwards, it would find no archive bits set, and assume that no data has changed since the last backup. For this reason, the differential backup would not contain all of the information that has changed since the last full backup.

exam
☾atch

Expect to see a number of questions on the exam dealing with full, incremental, and differential backups. It is important that you memorize these backup types and what they do. In particular, don't get confused between incremental and differential backups. The key to remembering how the backups work is to understand the archive bit and the role it plays.

SCENARIO & SOLUTION

Now that we've discussed the different types of backups available, let's look at some common scenario questions that arise when dealing with backups.

What is the difference between a differential backup and an incremental backup?	Incremental backups will back up data that has changed since the last full or incremental backup. Differential backups will only back up data since the last full backup, regardless of how many differential backups have been performed since that time.
I want to use a minimal number of tapes for performing backups and restoring data. What is the best way to do this?	Run a full backup each week, and then run a differential backup daily. This will mean that you only need two tapes to restore the data.
It is taking considerable time to perform daily backups. Each week I perform a full backup, and then perform a daily differential backup. How can I make backups quicker to perform?	Instead of differential backups, perform incremental backups. This will only back up files that have changed since the last full or incremental backup.

EXERCISE 7-1

Performing a Full Backup on Windows 2000 Server

1. From the Windows Start menu, select Programs | Accessories | System Tools | Backup.

2. When the Backup program starts, you will see several tabs. The default tab that appears should be the Welcome tab. On this tab, click the Backup Wizard button.

3. The first screen of the Backup Wizard is the Welcome screen. Click Next to continue.

4. The next screen allows you to specify what you would like to back up. The first option allows you to back up everything on your computer, the next allows you to specify what to back up, and the third allows you to only back up the System State data. Click the second option, labeled Back Up Selected Files, Drives, or Network Data.

5. When the next screen appears, the left pane will allow you to browse the server and the network to select files and directories to back up. The right pane will show the files and directories to back up. Select the files and directories to back up, then click Next.

6. The screen that appears allows you to specify the media type to back up data to. If you have no backup device installed, then this drop-down list will be disabled, and you can only back up to a file. Select the device, then click Next.

7. The final screen will show what options you have selected through this process. On this screen, there is also an Advanced button, which allows you to specify the type of backup to perform. Click the Advanced button.

8. When the Advanced screen appears, you will see what's shown in Figure 7-1. This screen has a drop-down list containing various types of backups. *Normal* is a full backup, *Copy* will back up all files but won't clear the archive bit, *Incremental* performs an incremental backup, *Differential* performs a differential backup, and *Daily* backs up files that have changed today (and doesn't clear the archive bit). Select Normal as the backup type, and click Next.

9. The next screen allows you to specify whether data should be verified after the backup. This will ensure data is backed up correctly, but will increase the

FIGURE 7-1

The Backup
Wizard

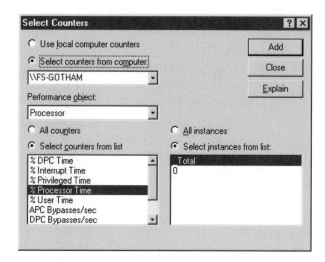

time it takes for the process to complete. Click this check box to select this. The second check box allows you to use compression (if a device supporting compression exists). If this check box is enabled, then compression can be used. Click Next to continue.

10. The next screen allows you to choose Media Options. As shown in Figure 7-2, it allows you to specify whether data should be appended to an existing backup (if it exists) or backup data replaced on the media. Select the first option (to append it), and then click Next.

11. The screen that appears allows you to label the backup job. Accept the default label, then click Next to continue.

12. The next screen allows you to specify whether the job should be started now, or rescheduled for a later time. Select the Now option, and then click Next.

13. At this point, you will return to the final screen. Click Finish to start the job.

Tape Rotation Strategy

Earlier in this chapter, we mentioned the importance of rotating tapes and keeping at least one set of tapes offsite. One popular rotation strategy is the Grandfather-Father-Son Backup, or GFS. It organizes rotation into daily, weekly, and monthly backup tapes.

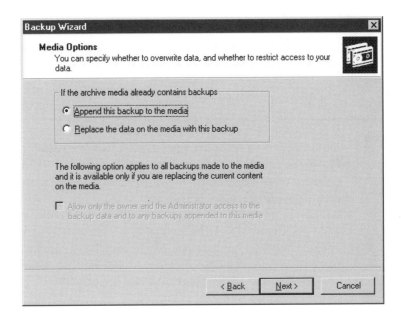

The GFS backup strategy is based on a weekly, seven-day schedule that runs from Sunday through Saturday. In other instances, where the business is only open five days a week, then the strategy runs from Monday through Friday, with no backups being performed on the weekend. During the week, at least one full backup is performed. Backups performed on other days are either incremental or differential. These daily and weekly backup tapes can then be stored offsite, while another set is used through the next week. To illustrate this method, let's look at the following backup schedule.

Sunday	Monday	Tuesday	Wednesday	Thursday	Friday	Saturday
None	Full Backup	Differential	Differential	Differential	Differential	None

In this schedule, no backups are made on weekends because the company is closed so no data is added or modified. Each Monday, the network administrator does a full backup of the server's volumes. A differential backup is made each day after this, on a tape or tapes, that can be reused. This means that only two data sets are needed to perform a restore.

At the end of the week, these tapes can be stored offsite. The tape set for each week in the month is then rotated back into service and reused. In other words, at the beginning of the next month, the tape set for the first week of the previous month is reused. This means you have one set of tapes for each week of the month, with most sets of tapes being kept offsite.

on the **Job** *It is common for the number of tapes being used in a GFS strategy to be minimized. One set is used for a week, while another set is stored offsite. However, if a disaster happens, and there is also a problem with the second tape set stored offsite, then you will experience problems. This is why the GFS recommends one tape set for each week.*

In the Grandfather-father-son scheme, the full backup is considered the "father" and the daily backup is considered the "son." The "grandfather" portion of the name is a full backup that is performed monthly, and stored offsite. The grandfather tape isn't reused, and is permanently stored offsite.

A similar rotation scheme is the "autopilot" strategy, in which software used for the backup keeps a database and expects a certain tape to be inserted each day. Daily, weekly, and monthly backup tapes are used with this strategy, with 20-25 tapes used in a rotation. It is common to use 21 tapes consisting of four daily tapes for each Monday through Thursday in a month, five weekly tapes for each Friday (as some months have five Fridays), and 12 monthly tapes for the last weekday of the month. As stated, what makes this different from the GFS strategy is that the software expects specific tapes each day, saving you from having to manually keep a schedule of what to back up.

Replicating a Folder to a Network Drive

Replicating a folder to a network drive means to copy data to another location. Some operating systems like Windows NT provide replication services in which certain data can be replicated to other servers. This is commonly used to copy files such as logon scripts to another location. In doing so, a user can log on from another location without having to contact a remote server. For example, if a logon script for the London domain were replicated to the Detroit domain, a user who is temporarily working in Detroit wouldn't have to connect to the London server to logon. Although it serves a purpose, replicated data shouldn't be considered a replacement for regular backups.

Replicating folders should only be considered a temporary, secondary solution. If a folder was replicated to a server from a workstation, and both the workstation and server were destroyed in a fire or flood, then both copies of the data would be lost. However, if you want to ensure data is safe while working on a workstation, or that the data will be backed up with the server, it is a viable means of backing up data.

on the **job**

Replicating folders can cause more problems then they are worth. To give a real-life example, an Excel spreadsheet was being used to track items, and the folder was replicated to the server. This folder was accessible to other users in the department, and they began to make copies of the spreadsheet to their local hard disks. Some users modified data in the copy on their hard disk, while others modified the spreadsheet on the server. This caused problems because some data was being duplicated, and other data seemed to be omitted. We soon began receiving help desk calls stating "The data I entered this morning just disappeared," as individuals began using more than one copy themselves!

Removable Media

Removable media are methods of storing data that can be removed from a computer. These include floppy disks, hard disks, tape cartridges, disk cartridges, reel tapes, or optical disks. Because the media isn't permanently attached to your server or other hardware used for backing up data, you can take it out and store it at another site.

When backing up data, you may find that you need to back the data onto more than one media. For example, you may wish to use a rewritable CD to copy data, or create images or backup sets that can then be used on any machine with a CD-ROM drive. In other situations, costs may dictate that some servers will need to use older backup devices while others use newer and more expensive methods. Because most backup programs support different media, and removable media can be stored offline, you may find multiple methods and forms of media are used in your company.

There are two methods for accessing data on removable media devices. The first is sequential access, which we've seen with tape backups. Sequential access requires you to cue up the media to reach the area on the media where the data you want resides. It is similar to fast forwarding a VHS tape on a VCR until you find the point on the tape that you want to watch. The other method of data access is random access. This method is used on hard disks, Zip drives, and other devices, where you can access any of the data on the media immediately. In using various media, you will find that either sequential or random access is used to store and retrieve data.

Table 7-3 lists common removable media devices and the issues dealing with each. For the exam, you should familiarize yourself with the media, as they may be dealt with directly or indirectly in questions.

TABLE 7-3	Device	Description
Comparison of Removable Media Used for Backups	Floppy disk	Floppy disks have the lowest capacity, as floppies allow you to store up to 1.44MB of information on them. They are removable, slow in storing data, and are random access.
	Disk cartridge	Disk cartridges are growing in popularity as their speed and storage capacity increases. There are different disk cartridge drives on the market, including Zip and Jaz. They are random access.
	Tape cartridge	Tape cartridges are the most common medium for backing up data. They are slow in speed, but have a high capacity for storing data. Tape cartridges are sequential access.
	Hard disk	Removable hard disks provide increased speed and capacity for storing data, and use random access for accessing data.
	Reel tape	Reel tapes store data on large reels of magnetic tape. They are an older method of backing up data, and commonly found on mainframe computers. This method is sequential access.
	Optical disk	Optical disks are high quality and have a large storage capacity. As they decrease in price, they are becoming a popular method of backing up data. Optical disks are random access.

CERTIFICATION OBJECTIVE 7.02

Setting SNMP Thresholds

SNMP is the Simple Network Management Protocol. This is a protocol that allows you to monitor network devices and their functions, so that you can manage hardware such as backup devices, routers, servers, and so forth from a single network client. This relieves administrators from having to physically visit each device to view whether it is functioning correctly. It also allows the administrator to view statistics on devices (such as throughput and collisions) and send commands to devices so they can be reconfigured remotely.

As we'll discuss in greater detail later in this chapter, SNMP uses a two-tiered approach. A central management system is software installed on a client computer, which monitors SNMP-enabled devices. This software provides an interface for SNMP, and is used to reconfigure and view information on devices. It connects to SNMP agents, which are programs that execute on the devices and serve information to the management system. A Management Information Base (MIB) for the managed device contains definitions that are specific to a particular agent, and is used to supply or set a value used by the agent. Because it is impossible to monitor the agent through the management system all of the time, a feature is included in SNMP that allows the device to send messages to the administrator. This type of message is called a "trap."

on the
job

SNMP is useful for larger networks, but is rarely used on smaller networks. If devices are located on a single floor of a building, or in a single office, then it is easier to walk to the device than to spend the time, money, and resources to set up SNMP software or pay for SNMP-enabled devices. On larger networks, which are spread over a greater geographical distance, then SNMP is important as it will take time and be more difficult to physically visit the device.

Traps allow devices to automatically notify administrators as soon as a specified event occurs. For example, let's say you set an SNMP agent to send a trap message when a hardware device fails. When this event occurs, the agent will take notice of this, and a message will be sent to a predetermined location. Without the trap, you would need to monitor the device every hour of every day. By using traps, you are automatically informed of a problem.

For traps to work effectively, each managed piece of hardware or software must be configured to issue SNMP traps when a particular event occurs. This requires setting thresholds, which are limits that are monitored. To illustrate this, let's say you're concerned about a server's CPU usage, and you set a threshold of 80 percent. If CPU utilization on the server were to exceed 80 percent, then the threshold would be crossed. The SNMP agent would then send a trap to a specific location, which could include sending e-mail to the administrator or logging the trap to a file.

When using traps, it is important to realize that it is a one-way communication process. The SNMP Agent can only send the trap, and has no way of recognizing whether it was received. If a trap was configured to send a message to a nonexistent IP address, the incorrect name of a computer, or to be written to a log file in a nonexistent directory, then you would have no way of knowing a problem existed. As far as the SNMP Agent is concerned, the message was sent and it did its job correctly. This means that when configuring traps, you will need to take care that the trap destinations are defined correctly and the network is correctly configured and operating.

Community Names

Community names are SNMP's method of providing security. When SNMP is configured, you should create a list of community names that determine who will have access to managed devices. This same community name is entered in the management system, so that it can provide it to the SNMP Agent and thereby gain access. Without the use of community names, anyone could gain access to a device.

Community names are similar to passwords. When a management system attempts to connect to a SNMP Agent, it provides the community name. If this name matches one that is in the SNMP Agent's list, then the management system is allowed to communicate with the SNMP Agent. Community names are case-sensitive, so the names at both ends must be entered identically when configuration takes place. If the community name provided does match, then the management system can view or configure the SNMP device. This is similar to providing a password because, if the community names do not match, then access is denied.

exam
Watch

Community names are case-sensitive. If the same community name is provided in the SNMP Agent and the Central Management System, and access is still denied, the problem may be that the upper- and lowercase letters may not match.

Many systems and applications use the community name *Public* by default. This is seen in Windows 2000, where this community name allows everyone read access to the SNMP Service. Others will use Public, and provide greater access than merely being able to read information. Because the Public community is a common default name, you should remove it immediately upon configuration, because it is easy to guess. Someone would only need to try *public*, *Public*, or *PUBLIC* and guess the community name in three tries or less. In addition to removing or renaming this community name, you should remember to use names that are not easy to guess. This same philosophy should be applied to any other passwords used on your system.

on the
Job

It is wise to use different community names and passwords for different devices. A common security risk is where the same password is used for servers, routers, repeaters, and so forth. In doing so, finding the password for one allows access to other devices and applications across the network.

In addition, you can use security settings for each community name provided. This allows you to provide different levels of access to different communities. Although different SNMP Agents will provide additional settings, there are two levels of access common to SNMP Agents: READ and READ/CREATE. READ allows users to view information, but not reconfigure the Agent. This prevents you from changing settings after you have properly configured them. READ/CREATE gives users the ability to read and write changes to the SNMP Agent. By giving different levels of access to different community names, you can control which users can view information and which can change settings.

SCENARIO & SOLUTION

Now that we've discussed a number of issues dealing with SNMP, let's look at some common scenario questions and answers.	
Which of the components for SNMP are configured?	The central management system and the SNMP agent are configured. The MIB contains definitions used in this process, but doesn't have an interface that you use for configuration.
Why are community names important?	Community names serve the same purpose as passwords and provide a level of security that prevents users from viewing or reconfiguring devices.

Requirements for SNMP Usage

Like anything in networking, SNMP has certain requirements that must be met for it to function. Unlike many other elements of networking however, there are very few requirements for using SNMP. They are:

- Network communication
- Software that uses SNMP
- An SNMP Agent

In terms of network communication, SNMP must be installed. It is installed automatically with TCP/IP. In addition to this, the network must be functioning properly so that the SNMP components can communicate. The SNMP Agent defines the objects or settings that can be managed, whereas the software that uses SNMP provides an interface between the user and the device.

Management Agents

A management agent, or SNMP Agent as we have called it throughout this chapter, acts as a middleman between the management system and your device. It allows the management system to access settings, so that they can be viewed or changed. In short, it provides an interface between the management system and the elements you need to manage.

For SNMP to be used, the agent must be available. The agent can be software that is loaded on a managed device, or may exist as code contained in the device's firmware. It may reside in the firmware because some devices, such as network bridges, may not have the ability to have software loaded into it.

The agent is used to serve information to the management system and provides an access point to the device. Code in the agent defines the parameters available to the management system. This code may be included in the driver for the device or it may exist in a separate application that is loaded on a computer to which the device is attached. The application will communicate with the device through a driver or the device's firmware, and then serve the information to the management system. When reconfiguration of the device is done, the management system passes the changes to the agent, which then controls changes to device settings.

MIB

Management Information Base (MIB) is a database containing information about managed devices. The information in the database defines what can be viewed and modified through SNMP. These definitions of a device are passed to the SNMP Agent, and from there are exposed to the management system. The definitions in the MIB are the properties and functions of objects supported by an SNMP enabled device and information that can be retrieved by the objects.

The information contained in the MIB for one device will not be the same for others. Different elements of a network will have different pieces of information to provide. For example, a CPU would provide information on utilization, whereas a router would provide information on throughput. Because of this, the amount of information in the MIB for each element will vary. One element may provide limited information, whereas others may provide hundreds or thousands of pieces of information.

To deal with complex and large quantities of information, a structured format is used for MIB databases. Information is organized in a hierarchical format, which makes the information more manageable and prevents definitions used by one organization from conflicting with those of another. This hierarchical structure is in a complex tree format, which is based on a numbering system where each MIB is represented by a numeric object identifier. This tree is a global entity, and each vendor or organization (when larger companies are involved) is given its own branch and numbering range to use. This issued numbering range is similar to the way that IP addresses are issued, and the way that IP addressing is structured.

> **EXERCISE 7-2**

Configuring SNMP Agents on Windows 2000 Server

1. Right-click My Computer, and when the context menu appears, click Manage. This will open Computer Management.

2. When Computer Management opens, you will see the screen in Figure 7-3. In the console tree (left pane), open the Services and Applications node, and then click Services. This will display a listing of services in the Details pane (right pane). Double-click the SNMP Service to display its properties.

3. When the SNMP Service Properties appears, click the Agent tab. In the field labeled Contact, type the name of the user or administrator of this computer. In the Location field, enter where this computer is located. This provides contact information that you can use if a trap message is sent.

> **FIGURE 7-3**
>
> Access the SNMP Service from Computer Management

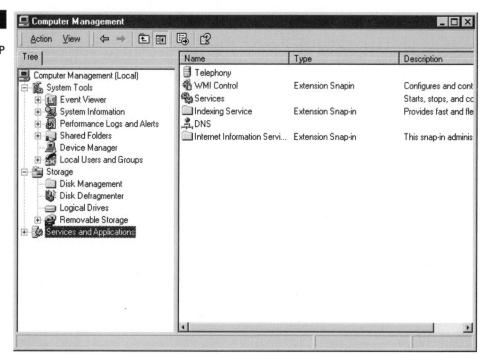

4. Click the Traps tab to view what's shown in Figure 7-4. In the Community Name field, enter the community name to which that trap messages will be sent. Click Add to List.

5. In the Trap Destinations section of this tab, click the Add button. A dialog box will appear, allowing you to enter the IP address, IPX address, or host name to which trap messages will be sent. Click OK.

6. Click OK to confirm your configuration, and exit the SNMP Properties.

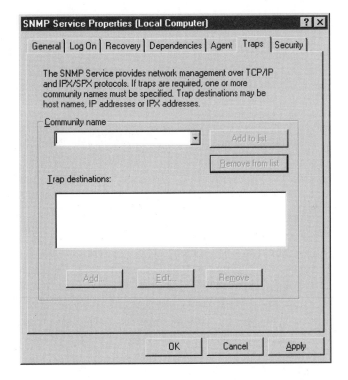

CERTIFICATION OBJECTIVE 7.03

Establishing Remote Notification

Remote notification is a feature that enables a device, a service, or an application to report problems or events to a specific user, such as the network administrator. This allows the user or administrator to take action and deal with any issues that affect the successful completion of a task or event. For example, if an uninterruptible power supply (UPS) had a low battery, a message could be sent notifying the administrator of this problem. The administrator could then replace the battery or temporarily put another UPS in its place. If notification is sent early enough, the administrator could be onsite before the user realizes a problem even exists.

There are a number of different delivery methods available for remote notification. The delivery method is the way in which a user or administrator is notified. These include:

- Pop-up messages
- E-mail
- Log files
- Pagers

Although hardware and software on your network may provide multiple delivery methods, it is important to realize that every device, service, and application doesn't support every method. You will have to examine what methods are available, and then decide which is best for you and members of your IT staff.

Pop-up messages are messages that will pop-up on a user's screen. Such messages may appear on every workstation, or be directed to a specific user. If you can designate where the pop-up message will appear, you may have the ability to direct the message to a specific IP address or a user account. If an IP address is specified, then the pop-up message will appear on a single workstation. If a user account is used, then the message will appear on every machine to which the user is logged on.

E-mail messages may be used to send text-based messages to specified users. The type of e-mail may vary depending on the abilities of the device, service, or application, and the components and services provided on your network. Internal e-mail may be used to send electronic mail to a user or administrator on the local network. This is seen on Novell Networks, when notification is sent to a recipient through GroupWise. If the network is connected to the Internet, then e-mail may be sent onto the Internet. When the recipient opens their e-mail program, they can then read the message sent by the remote notification service. The problem with this method is that—by the time the recipient connects to the Internet or logs on their network and checks their e-mail—it may be too late to deal with the problem.

The same problem applies to log files. With this method, messages are written to a file, which requires that you open the file to view any notifications. It also requires the user to have the proper permissions to access the log file.

Pagers are a new method of remote notification, and are often seen in shutdown software for UPSs. It provides the ability for the device to send a pager message under predetermined conditions. For example, if the power fails then a message can be sent to a specified pager number, immediately alerting the person that a problem exists. This is a valuable feature if the administrator is away from his or her workstation, or if manual intervention is required to restart the system.

To configure a device to use remote notification, special software must be used to set where notification will be sent and the type of notification that will be used. This may consist of setting the path and filename of a log file, the e-mail account to be used, the user account or IP address to send messages, or a pager number to call when a particular event occurs. This software is generally included with the device if remote notification is supported.

Servers often provide a method of notifying designated users of events and problems that are encountered. In Windows 2000, the Alerter service is used for this purpose. This service is used by the server, services running on that server, and devices such as UPSs. It works with the Messenger service, which is used to send messages to users when the Alerter service encounters a specified issue.

If the Alerter service is used by a UPS, it is configured through the UPS applet in the Windows Control Panel. This allows you to send an alert if there are such problems as a main-power failure, low-battery, or if the UPS shuts down. The exact configuration settings for the UPS applet will depend on the device being used. As such, you should check your UPS documentation before configuring it.

Another common reason to send notification to a specific user is when your server has performance or operating issues that affect its ability to function as expected. For this purpose, the Performance Logs and Alerts utility in Windows 2000 can be used. This is the Windows 2000 version of the Performance Monitor tool in Windows NT 4.0 Server. As we saw in the previous chapter, it will monitor your system and report any problems in the form of a message that's sent to a specific user. In Windows 2000, these notifications are called alerts.

SCENARIO & SOLUTION

Now that we've looked at remote notification, let's look at some common scenario questions and answers involving this topic.	
Do all devices provide support for remote notification?	Many devices provide various types of remote notification, but not all of them do. You will need to research the product and determine whether this feature is supported.
I have disabled the Messenger service on Windows 2000. What effect will this have on the Alerter service?	The Alerter service won't be able to send messages dealing with issues it encounters, and which you have specified that you want to be alerted about.

EXERCISE 7-3

Creating an Alert Using Performance Logs and Alerts on Windows 2000 Server

1. From the Run command on the Windows Start menu, type **MMC** and then click OK. Microsoft Management Console will open.

2. From the Console menu, click the item labeled Add/Remove Snap-in. The Add/Remove Snap-in dialog box will appear, and you will notice an Add button. Click this button to open the Add Standalone Snap-in dialog box that lists the available snap-ins to install.

3. As shown in Figure 7-5, select Performance Logs and Alerts from the listing, and then click Add. Click Close to return to the previous menu, then click OK to Add the snap-in.

4. In the left pane, expand the Performance Logs and Alerts node, and then click Alerts.

5. In the Details pane (right pane), right-click the blank area, and then click New Alert Settings from the context menu that appears.

6. A dialog box will appear. Enter the name for this alert in the field on this box, and then click OK.

7. When the dialog box for this alert appears, click the General tab, and then click the Add button.

FIGURE 7-5

Performance Logs
and Alerts

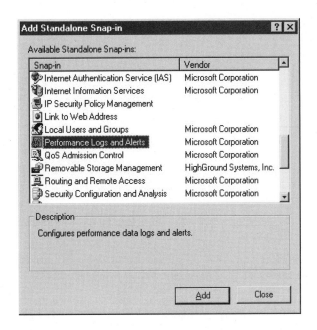

8. A Select Counters dialog box will appear, as shown in Figure 7-6, allowing
   you to select the counters you want to monitor. From the drop-down list
   called Performance Object select the Processor item. Click the Select Counters
   from List option, and then select the % Processor Time counter. Click the
   Add button, and then click Close to return to the properties of the alert.

FIGURE 7-6

Select Counters

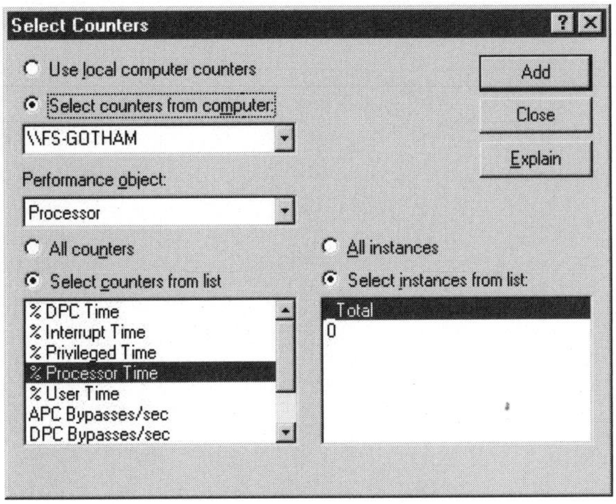

9. Select the counter you just added from the listing on the dialog box. On the drop-down list called Alert When the Value Is, select Over. On the Limit drop-down list, select 80. This will cause an alert to be sent when Processor Time is over 80 percent.

10. Click the Action tab, and then select the Send a Network Message to check box. Enter the user account to which a network message should be sent. Click OK to confirm your selections and exit the dialog box.

CERTIFICATION SUMMARY

Backups are important to keeping your data safe. To back up and restore data, a combination of hardware and software is used. There are many different devices that can be used for backing up data, which provide sequential or random access when restoring the data. Software used to back up the data allows you to perform full, incremental, or differential backups to ensure that the data is backed up in different ways.

SNMP is the Simple Network Management protocol, which is a protocol that allows you to view information about a device and reconfigure it from a remote client. A central management system provides an interface to SNMP and allows the administrator to set thresholds for SNMP agents, which exposes and serves information about the device to the management system. If the device exceeds this threshold, then a trap message can be sent out, informing the administrator of a possible problem.

Remote notification provides a way for devices, services, and applications to contact designated users, and inform them of possible problems or issues. Such messages can be sent in a variety of ways, including e-mail, pagers, log files, or pop-up messages. By sending notification, the administrator is relieved of having to constantly check hardware and software for problems.

TWO-MINUTE DRILL

Here are some of the key points from each certification objective in Chapter 7.

Performing a Regular Backup

❑ Backups make a copy of data to a form of media. If data on a server is corrupt, deleted, or destroyed in some way, it can be recovered from the backup.

❑ There are many different types of media that can be used for backups. These include floppy disks, disk cartridge, hard disk, reel tape, optical disk, and tape cartridge.

❑ Full backups will back up all files to a tape or other media. It doesn't matter what the archive bit is set to with this method. Once completed, the archive bits for backed up files will be cleared.

❑ Differential backups will back up all data that has changed since the last full backup. It won't clear the archive bit once the file has been backed up.

❑ Incremental backups will back up all data that has changed since the last full or incremental backup. Once a file is backed up, it will clear the archive bit, so that unmodified files won't be backed up again.

❑ A rotation scheme should be used with backups; sets of backups are stored offsite and another set is used for backups.

Setting SNMP Thresholds

❑ SNMP is the Simple Network Management Protocol, which allows you to view whether a device is operating, statistics on the device, and to send commands to reconfigure the device.

❑ SNMP uses a two-tier approach to network management. A central management system is used to view and configure the device, and serves as an interface for the administrator. An SNMP agent is used to connect to the management system and provides information to it. Values that can be set or viewed are provided through a Management Information Base (MIB).

❑ Trap messages are a one-way communication process.

❑ Community names act like passwords in SNMP, providing security. They are case-sensitive.

❑ SNMP Agents are also called management agents. They act as an intermediary between the device and the management system. If they aren't loaded or configured, the management system will be unable to view or modify device settings.

Establishing Remote Notification

❑ Remote notification allows hardware and software to contact designated individuals or workstations to inform them of issues or problems that have been encountered.

❑ Notification can use a variety of delivery methods, including e-mail, pop-up messages, log file entries, or even pager messages.

❑ Remote notification is configured through software that comes with the device or through applets and services available on the server operating system.

❑ In Windows 2000, the Alerter service is used to send notification of various problems and events.

❑ Performance Logs and Alerts in Windows 2000 and Performance Monitor in Windows NT both allow you to send alerts when certain performance thresholds are exceeded.

SELF TEST

The following questions will help you measure your understanding of the material presented in this chapter. Read all of the choices carefully, as there may be more than one correct answer. Choose all correct answers for each question.

Performing a Regular Backup

1. You have designed a network for a new company and implemented a process for backing up important data. You have two servers on your network that use tape drives for backing up data. A project has started in which programmers are saving their source code to the local hard disks of their workstations. You are concerned that if one of the hard disks fail, all of this data will be lost. To deal with this possibility, you set up the backup program to back up data on the workstations across the network. After the first night the backup program runs, you notice that the only backup job that failed is the one for backing up data on these workstations. The ones scheduled before and after this job have been successful. All backup jobs on each of the two servers were performed successfully. What is most likely the reason for this?

    A. Backups cannot be performed across a network.

    B. There is a problem with the backup media.

    C. The workstations were shutdown for the night.

    D. A server was shutdown for the night.

2. Your company's IT staff is deciding the best method of performing backups. Your IT manager has read about the benefits of the Digital Data Storage (DDS) format. Which of the following uses the Digital Data Storage format?

    A. DAT tape cartridge

    B. DLT tape cartridge

    C. Optical disks

    D. Removable hard disks

3. Your network server has a 30GB hard disk on which important data is stored. If you were going to back up all of the data on this hard disk, which of the following would you use?

    A. DDS

    B. DDS-2

    C. DDS-3

    D. DDS-4

4. Your network has two servers. One of the servers has a 40GB hard disk, whereas the other server has a 30GB hard disk. You want to use Digital Linear Tape as the media on each of the server's backup devices. Which of the following could you use? (Choose all that apply.)

   A. DLT2000

   B. DLT4000

   C. DLT7000

   D. DLT-ME

5. On Friday, you perform a full backup of your network server. Because you and other employees of the company don't work on Saturday and Sunday, you set up your backup program to perform incremental backups of the server over the weekend. On Monday, you receive a phone call stating that the user accidentally deleted a file from the server. When you attempt to restore the file from the Sunday backup, you find that you cannot restore the file. Why is this? Choose the best answer.

   A. Incremental backups will only back up files that have changed since the last full backup. As such, the file will be on the Saturday incremental backup job. Restore the file from this.

   B. Because the file couldn't have been modified on the weekend, it must be restored from the full backup job.

   C. The incremental backups must be done in reverse. You must run the Sunday, Saturday, and Friday backup jobs in that order to restore the file.

   D. You cannot run full and incremental backup jobs after one another. Due to this, the data has been backed up incorrectly.

6. A document called RESUME.DOC is saved to a network drive. You perform a full backup, so that this file is backed up to a tape drive. You then modify the document afterwards and perform an incremental backup. You want to be especially thorough, so you perform a differential backup immediately afterwards. The next day, you want to restore the file. Which of the backup jobs would contain the most recent version of the document?

   A. Full backup

   B. Incremental backup

   C. Differential backup

   D. The differential and incremental backups

7. Which of the following devices use sequential access methods for restoring data from backups? (Choose all that apply.)

   A. Tape cartridge

    B. Optical disk

    C. Reel-to-reel

    D. Floppy disk

Setting SNMP Thresholds

8. Which of the following is used to view information and configure settings on a backup device so that you can determine if a problem exists?

    A. SNMP Agent

    B. SNMP Mediator

    C. Central Management System

    D. MIB

9. You have configured an SNMP threshold to monitor when disk space on a server's hard disk exceeds a particular size. When this occurs, a trap will be sent, informing the administrator. You configure it so that a message is sent to an IP address, but when the threshold is exceeded, the computer with this IP address is offline. What will occur?

    A. The SNMP Agent will fail to receive confirmation that the trap message was received, and log the trap to a file.

    B. The SNMP Management System will fail to receive confirmation that the trap message was received, and log the trap to a file.

    C. The SNMP Agent will fail to receive confirmation that the trap message was received, and continue sending the trap every 15 minutes until it is received.

    D. SNMP trap messages are a one-way communication process, so it has no way of recognizing whether it was received. As such, no further action will take place.

10. You are configuring SNMP so that you can view information, reconfigure, and be notified if a problem occurs with a device. You configure the SNMP Agent to permit a community name called SNMPAdmin. On the central management system, you configure it to use a community name called SNMPADMIN. You then test it to see whether you can view information, and find that the management system won't connect to the SNMP agent. What is the problem?

    A. A maximum of eight characters are allowed for community names.

    B. The management system must be configured before the agent.

    C. Community names are case-sensitive.

    D. Community names are preset names and cannot be entered manually.

11. Which of the following is a common default community name, which should be removed or renamed when configuring SNMP?

    A. Public

    B. Community

    C. SNMP

    D. Password

12. After configuring an SNMP Agent, you find that a community name called SNMPAdmin can only view information. You wanted to use this community name to reconfigure a device, should the need arise. What is most likely the problem?

    A. SNMP doesn't allow reconfiguration to occur remotely.

    B. SNMP Agents aren't used in reconfiguring devices.

    C. The community name is invalid.

    D. The proper settings haven't been made to the community name.

13. Which of the following serves information about a device to a separate application that you can use to manage the device?

    A. SNMP Agent

    B. Central management system

    C. Device driver

    D. MIB

14. Which of the following is a database containing information on managed devices and defining what can be viewed and modified through SNMP?

    A. SNMP Agent

    B. Central Management System

    C. MIB

    D. SQL

Establishing Remote Notification

15. You have established remote notification for a new UPS that is installed on a network server. As with other servers, you have used your user account to log on the server and have also used this account for backup jobs. You have decided to have pop-up messages sent to any computer

you're currently using. This will enable you to view any problems as they arise. Shortly after installing and configuring the UPS, a power failure occurs. Because the battery hasn't had time to fully charge, notification is sent to inform you of a low battery. Which of the following will occur?

A. The pop-up message will be sent to the first machine it encounters with your user account. As such, it will only appear on the screen of the server using the UPS.

B. The message will appear on every machine on which your user account is used to log on.

C. It will experience a conflict when it determines that your account is used for backups and logged on multiple machines. As such, no message will be sent.

D. Hardware devices cannot use remote notification, and thereby cannot send such messages.

16. You want to use remote notification to inform you of problems on your network. Your thought is that, as soon as a problem occurs, the service using remote notification will send a message to you and you will be aware of the problem immediately (so long as you are logged on the network). Each of the following delivery methods can be used, but which will suit your needs? (Choose all that apply.)

A. Pop-up messages

B. E-mail

C. Log files

D. Pager

17. You have decided to configure Windows 2000 Server to notify you if a UPS attached to the server experiences a power loss, low-battery, or shuts down. When you test the UPS and shut it down, no notification of this is sent across the network. Which of the following services should you check are installed and running properly on Windows 2000 Server to ensure that remote notification is possible? (Choose all that apply.)

A. Alerter service

B. Messenger service

C. Microsoft Outlook

D. Control Panel

18. Which of the following must be used to configure a device to use remote notification? (Choose all that apply.)

A. Server services and applets

B. Software that comes with the device

   C. None. Devices will automatically send notification to whatever user accounts are members of the Administrator group, or to e-mail accounts or pager numbers specified in the user account information.

   D. None. The device must be configured by changing the firmware.

19. You have just installed a UPS on a Windows 2000 Server and want to use remote notification to inform you when a problem occurs. Where would you configure the UPS and set it to send alerts when certain events occur?

   A. The UPS applet in Control Panel

   B. Active Directory Users and Computers

   C. UPS snap-in in Microsoft Management Console

   D. Internet Options in Control Panel

20. Which of the following tools in Windows 2000 can you use to monitor performance counters and issue alerts when performance thresholds have been exceeded?

   A. Performance Monitor

   B. The Performance applet in Control Panel

   C. Perfmon

   D. Microsoft Management Console with the Performance Logs and Alerts snap-in

LAB QUESTION

Your company is open from 9A.M.-5P.M., seven days a week. It has a network consisting of four servers and 200 workstations. You work Monday to Friday, and are on-call during weekends.

   The company has recently started a software development project. All of the source code for this project is saved on a network directory called PROJECT. It is vital that the files in this directory are safe, as hundreds of thousands of dollars has been invested into the development of this software.

  1. You decide to use a Grandfather-Father-Son strategy for performing backups. In using this strategy, you want to make a schedule for what type of backup will be performed each day of the week. In the following table, mark off what types of backups (full, incremental, differential) will be performed during the week:

Sunday	Monday	Tuesday	Wednesday	Thursday	Friday	Saturday

2. When backing up the network, the backup program gives you the choice of performing a full, incremental, or differential backup. You want to use a combination of these backup jobs to back up your system. Which of the following should you not mix?

3. When performing a full backup, all files in the PROJECT directory are backed up. What will happen to the archive bit on each file?

4. You configure an SNMP Service on one of the servers. It currently has a default community name called *public*. You create a new community name *PUBLIC*. What is the problem with this name?

5. When configuring the SNMP Service, you decide to create two other communities. One is called VIEWERS, who will be limited to viewing information. The other will be called MODIFIERS, who will have access to change settings for the SNMP Agent. What security settings will you give each group?

SELF TEST ANSWERS

Performing a Regular Backup

1. ☑ **C.** The workstations were shutdown for the night. If workstations are not online and connected to the network when the backups take place, then the backup jobs will fail. This is because the data on the hard disks cannot be accessed.

   ☒ **A** is incorrect because backups can be performed across the network. This is commonly done with workstations, because workstations generally contain less data than servers, so it will not take significant time or resources to back them up over the network. **B** is incorrect because if there was a problem with the backup media, then jobs after the one that backs up the workstation also would have failed. **D** is incorrect because servers generally aren't shutdown for the night, and if the one responsible for backing up data were shutdown, then the backup job for it also would have failed.

2. ☑ **A.** DAT tapes use the Digital Data Storage format. DDS uses a helical scan, where two read heads and two write heads spin diagonally across a DAT tape. When data is written, the read heads verify that data has been written correctly to the tape. If it detects any errors, then the data is rewritten.

   ☒ **B, C,** and **D** are incorrect because neither DLT tapes, optical disks, nor removable hard disks use DDS.

3. ☑ **D.** DDS-4. This generation of DDS allows 40GB of compressed data to be stored on a 125-minute cartridge.

   ☒ **A** is incorrect because the original DDS format allows only 1.3GB or 2GB of data on a 120-minute cartridge. This is because there was no compression with the first generation of DDS. **B** is incorrect because although DDS-2 used compression, it could hold only 8GB of data on a 120-minute cartridge. **C** is incorrect because DDS-3 stores 24GB of data on a 125-minute cartridge.

4. ☑ **B** and **C.** DLT4000 and DLT7000. If compression is used, DLT4000 allows up to 40GB of data, and DLT7000 allows up to 70GB of data storage. Therefore, each of these could be used to back up the servers.

   ☒ **A** is incorrect because DLT2000 allows you to store up to 30GB of data. **D** is incorrect because (although, you might have expected such a name if Microsoft had developed it) there is no such version of DLT called DLT-ME.

5. ☑ B. Because the file couldn't have been modified on the weekend, it must be restored from the full backup job. Incremental backups will back up all files that have been modified since the last full or incremental backup. It will not back up any files that have not been modified. Therefore, because the file wasn't modified on the weekend, it would only have been backed up by the Friday full backup job.

   ☒ A is incorrect because the Saturday and Sunday jobs would only back up files that have changed since the full backup. Because the company is closed on the weekends, this would mean that no data will be backed up on either of the incremental backups. C is incorrect because incremental backups are not done in reverse. To do a full and complete restore, you would restore data from the full backup job, and then restore each of the incremental backups. D is incorrect because you can use full and incremental backups to back up data.

6. ☑ B. Incremental backup. Incremental backups will back up all files that have been modified since the last full or incremental backup.

   ☒ A is incorrect because the file was changed after the full backup. C is incorrect because when the incremental backup was run, the archive bit would have been reset. For this reason, the differential backup would determine this file hadn't been changed since the last full backup, and fail to backup the file. D is incorrect for this same reason.

7. ☑ A and C. Tape cartridge and reel-to-reel tapes can be used for backups, and use sequential access. Sequential access requires you to cue up the media until you reach the area on the media where the data you want resides.

   ☒ B and D are incorrect because optical disks and floppy disks use random access for accessing data. This allows you to access the data directly, without having to cue the media to a particular spot before being able to restore it.

Setting SNMP Thresholds

8. ☑ C. Central Management System. A central management system is software installed on a client computer, which monitors SNMP-enabled devices. This software provides an interface for SNMP and is used to reconfigure and view information on devices.

   ☒ A is incorrect because the SNMP agent is used to serve information about the device to the management system. B is incorrect because there is no such component as an SNMP Mediator in the SNMP standard. D is incorrect because the MIB contains definitions that are specific to a particular agent, and is used to supply or set a value used by the agent.

9. ☑ D. SNMP trap messages are a one-way communication process, so it has no way of recognizing whether it was received. As such, no further action will take place. As far as the

SNMP Agent that sent the message is concerned, the trap has been sent and no further messages are necessary.

☒ **A, B,** and **C** are incorrect because each of these require confirmation that the trap was received, which does not occur. Trap messages are a one-way communication process.

10. ☑ **C.** Community names are case-sensitive. Because the SNMP Agent uses SNMPAdmin and the management system uses SNMPADMIN, different cases are used for the same name. Therefore, communication cannot be permitted.

☒ **A** is incorrect because community names permit names greater than eight characters. **B** is incorrect because you can configure agents before management systems are configured. **D** is incorrect because you enter the names of community names manually.

11. ☑ **A.** Public. When configuring SNMP, you should rename or remove the Public community name. Because it is a common default name, users might be able to guess it and have access to whatever capabilities the Agent provides.

☒ **B, C,** and **D** are incorrect because these aren't common default community names used by SNMP Agents.

12. ☑ **D.** The proper settings haven't been made to the community name. This name has READ access and should have READ/CREATE (read/write) access to modify the SNMP Agent.

☒ **A** is incorrect because SNMP allows you to connect to devices to view information and change settings. **B** is incorrect because SNMP can be used to reconfigure devices. **C** is incorrect because the name used for the community group is valid.

13. ☑ **A.** SNMP Agent. SNMP Agents are also called management agents, and are used to serve information to the central management system. It allows the management system to access settings, so that they can be viewed or changed. It provides an interface between the management system and the elements you need to manage.

☒ **B** is incorrect because the central management system monitors SNMP-enabled devices. This software provides an interface for SNMP, and is used to reconfigure and view information on devices. **C** is incorrect because the device driver may be used by the SNMP Agent to access the device. **D** is incorrect because the MIB contains definitions that are specific to a particular agent, and is used to supply or set a value used by the agent.

14. ☑ **C.** MIB is an acronym for Management Information Base. It is a database containing information about managed devices. The information in the database defines what can be viewed an modified through SNMP.

☒ **A** is incorrect because the SNMP Agent is used to serve information about the device to the management system. **B** is incorrect because it is software installed on a client computer, which monitors SNMP-enabled devices, allowing you to view or make modifications. **D** is incorrect because (although SQL is a database) SQL isn't used for SNMP.

Establishing Remote Notification

15. ☑ **B.** Pop-up messages are messages that will pop-up on a user's screen. Such messages may appear on every workstation, or be directed to a specific user. If the pop-up message is directed to a specific user account, then the message will appear on every machine on which the user is logged on.
☒ **A** and **C** are incorrect because the pop-up message will be sent to all computers on which you are logged on. It will not experience a conflict when it determines your user account is logged onto multiple machines, or be sent to the first machine it encounters. **D** is incorrect because various hardware devices like UPSs will often include remote notification features. As this UPS was configured to send pop-up messages, this particular UPS must have that ability.

16. ☑ **A** and **D.** Pop-up messages and pager. Pop-up messages can be configured to send messages to your user account, alerting you of problems if you are logged onto the network. If a pager is used, a message will be sent to your pager, also alerting you of any problems.
☒ **B** is incorrect because it requires that you have your e-mail program open, and—if Internet e-mail is used—that you are connected to the Internet at the time the problem occurs. **C** is also incorrect because it requires you to check the log file to view any notifications.

17. ☑ **A** and **B.** Alerter service and Messenger service. Each of these services must be running on Windows 2000 if remote notification is to be used. The Alerter service is used to monitor events and send a message through the Messenger service to a designated user.
☒ **C** and **D** are incorrect because Microsoft Outlook and Control Panel aren't services, and aren't required for remote messages to be sent across the network.

18. ☑ **A** and **B.** Server services and applets, or software that comes with the device. Some server operating systems provide services that allow you to configure the device, and specify where (and the type of) notification will be sent. Devices also generally come with software that allow you to configure remote notification features.
☒ **C** is incorrect because devices must be configured before remote notification can be used. **D** is incorrect because devices are configured through software, not by changing firmware in the device.

19. ☑ **A.** The UPS applet in Control Panel. This is used to configure your UPS and set up alerts to be sent when certain events occur.
☒ **B** is incorrect because Active Directory Users and Computers isn't used to set up remote

notification for a UPS. **C** is incorrect because there is no UPS snap-in in Microsoft Management Console. **D** is incorrect because the Internet Options applet in Control Panel is used to configure your options when connecting to the Internet.

20. ☑ **D.** Microsoft Management Console with the Performance Logs and Alerts snap-in. The Performance Logs and Alerts snap-in allows you to monitor performance counters and issue alerts when thresholds have been exceeded.
    ☒ **A** and **C** are incorrect, as both of these are the same program. PERFMON.EXE is the executable to start Performance Monitor. This was the previous incarnation of Performance Logs and Alerts that was available in Windows NT Server 4.0. **B** is incorrect because there is no Performance applet in Control Panel.

LAB ANSWER

1. The Grandfather-Father-Son (GFS) backup strategy is based on a weekly, seven-day schedule that runs from Sunday through Saturday. With this strategy, a monthly full backup is performed and stored offsite. During the week, at least one full backup is performed. Backups performed on other days are either incremental or differential. These daily and weekly backup tapes can then be stored offsite, while another set is used through the next week. From this, a backup schedule would look similar to the following:

Sunday	Monday	Tuesday	Wednesday	Thursday	Friday	Saturday
INC	FULL	INC	INC	INC	INC	INC

In this schedule, INC refers to incremental backups. Differential backups could also be used. Because you only work Monday to Friday, you would perform a full backup during the week, and then have automated incremental or differential backups performed during the other days of the week.

2. Incremental and differential. When an incremental backup is performed, the archive bit is cleared. If a differential backup were performed, it would see that the archive bit was cleared, and by this, determine that the file hasn't changed since the last full backup. This makes it pointless performing the differential backup when the incremental backup has been performed. You should use either incremental or differential backups with full backups, but not both.

3. When a full backup is performed, the archive bit is cleared. When data is modified, the archive bit on the file is then set. This allows incremental and differential backups to determine what files have been modified since the full backup, and which should thereby get backed up.

4. Public is a common default community name on SNMP Agents. Community names are case-sensitive, allowing you to create a new community name PUBLIC. However, because the name is still a common default, it is easy to guess and may be used to gain access to the agent.

5. VIEWERS should have READ access, while MODIFIERS should have READ/CREATE. This will allow the VIEWERS community name to view information, and the MODIFIERS community name the ability to change SNMP Agent settings.

Server+

COMPUTING TECHNOLOGY INDUSTRY ASSOCIATION

8

Environment

Administrators will spend a significant amount of time dealing with servers, workstations, and cabling, but forget the environment where the equipment resides. This can be a dire mistake. The same way the cleanliness, temperature, and security of your home will affect you, a bad environment will affect various systems on your network. Dust can clog machinery, high temperatures can burn out components, and poor security can make your computers and other network devices vulnerable. By having an optimal environment, your systems will last longer and experience fewer problems.

CERTIFICATION OBJECTIVE 8.01

Recognizing and Reporting on Physical Security Issues

You may have implemented network passwords, access control on files, and a number of other security measures, but have you considered that someone could still pick up the server and walk away with it? Electronic security is a wonderful thing, but it doesn't protect your equipment from deliberate and accidental threats of a physical nature. To protect your equipment, and the data on it, you need to develop methods of recognizing and reporting on such security issues.

Physical security is controlling access to equipment. It is the protection of this equipment and the data it may contain. When you think of the number of tangible components making up a network, you can see that this covers a wide variety of areas. Servers, workstations, cabling, routers, repeaters, bridges, and so forth, can all be damaged. The primary rule is to limit the number of people who may have access to the equipment, even on a cursory level.

exam
⑩atch

Physical security is an important part of the exam and your workplace. The important thing to remember is that you want to restrict access to servers and other important equipment. This is stressed in this chapter. You will also want to remember that the more you restrict access, the harder it may become to perform certain tasks.

What Are You Protecting and from Whom?

The first step in designing a physical security system is to identify what will need protecting and from whom you will be protecting it. For example, a hotel may have an outdoor Web camera that displays a live feed of its bar on the Internet. This would be more susceptible to public vandalism, and drunks throwing bottles at the equipment, than (hopefully) a server inside your organization would be. By identifying what threats equipment may be exposed to, and whom you're protecting it from, you will be able to customize security measures to specific areas.

exam
ⓦatch

Remember that physical security is controlling who has access to servers and other equipment. The fewer people who can physically touch this equipment, the more secure your network.

You should begin by looking at an inventory of equipment and determining what is of specific value. This includes hardware, software, data, media, and other elements of your network. The value of the equipment should be based on both cost and how hard it would be to replace. Although data on a computer may have very little monetary value, it may cost a considerable amount to replace or it may have future monetary value. For example, if a computer's hard disk holds the great American novel, it may not be worth much now, but it would be impossible to replace and may be worth millions of dollars when it is published. Conversely, cabling used to connect a computer to the network may have a monetary value, but is relatively cheap and easy to replace. Once you've determined what you're protecting, you can determine if the items are organized into a centralized location, or will need to be.

A centralized location is important because it is easier to secure your servers in a single, locked room than it is to deal with them scattered across a building. The equipment stored here would consist of your servers, routers, repeaters, patch panels, and other primary components for your network. In addition to a room, it is also common to have your major equipment stored in a closet that can be secured.

In terms of whom you're protecting this equipment from, you should keep in mind that there is less chance that a burglar will break in and steal your equipment than there is that someone in your organization will. A burglar would have to get past the security of your building, but employees are already inside this security parameter. Being inside, they have the ability to cause problems, intentionally or otherwise.

Over the last number of years, computer theft has become a growing problem. Corporate theft is a major problem that collectively costs companies millions of dollars each year. Although there is less of a chance that someone will walk out of your offices with a server under their arms, it isn't uncommon for people to steal the components that make up a computer. This includes CPU chips, RAM, CD ROMS, and so forth.

on the
Job

One school I worked at had a problem with people (presumably students) stealing components. A few times a month, a student would try to turn on a computer, only to find it had no processor or memory. In other cases, spare hardware went missing. By implementing security measures, you can avoid such thefts from occurring in your organization.

A more common problem that your organization may experience is honest users who cause damage by accidents or out of curiosity. Such problems may occur when someone decides to see what a particular button does, or decides to "help" you by modifying settings on a computer. Other problems may consist of hardware accidentally being knocked over or a power cable being knocked out of a plug. By keeping equipment secure, these problems can also be avoided.

Physical Security

Physical security requires you to limit access. This can be done in a variety of ways, with the methods ranging from basic common sense to implementing high-tech security. This is the next step in implementing a security plan: evaluating the different ways in which you can secure your equipment. Cost, available facilities, and other limitations may restrict your organization from using some of these methods, but they are good to know.

You should limit access to areas containing servers. You don't want employees outside of your IT staff having access to a server room or closet, as this can lead to problems. Keeping this in mind, one of the easiest methods of securing equipment is to keep it behind a locked door. Servers should be locked in a cabinet or a room that isn't accessible to the public. This area should be well ventilated so that the equipment doesn't overheat (which is one of many environmental issues discussed later in this chapter).

When limiting the number of people who have access to servers and other equipment, you will want to restrict them from entering these areas with food or drinks. The last thing you want is a repairman spilling a can of soda pop on a keyboard or into a printer or server. To protect workstations, the same no "food or drink" rule might also be applied to work areas. However, trying to tell your boss not to have a morning coffee at a workstation might cause more problems than a keyboard is worth.

If you are unable to store your server in a dedicated server room or closet that can be locked, then you should consider storing the server in a rack or cabinet that can be locked. By being locked, it will prevent people from accessing the server components. There are a number of racks and cabinets on the market that are used to store such equipment and prevent people from accessing what's inside without a key.

It is important that regardless of whether a server is kept in a cabinet, closet, or a dedicated room, the equipment is kept off the floor. Being at ground level, it could be accidentally kicked or be susceptible to floods that would damage the equipment. This could inadvertently bring down the system, and may damage data on the server.

Backups should also be kept in a secure location, such as in the server room with the other equipment. In addition to keeping your current set of tapes secure, you should also keep a full backup of your server offsite. Such backup tapes could also be stored in a locked cabinet or safe at a branch office, or in a safe deposit box. Remember that if someone obtained these tapes and restored them on another computer, they would have access to all your data. Essentially, this would be the same as if they'd stolen the entire server. For this reason, you should consider the security of the backup tapes with the same degree of attention as the servers themselves.

While your mind may be focusing on hardware, you should also include software in your physical security plan. Software is expensive, and companies must purchase licenses for the use of copies installed on computers. As such, the number of installations must be monitored so that you know how many licenses must be purchased. Installation CDs for software used in your company should be kept in a secure location where users will be unable to access them. If users are able to access them, they could make pirate copies or install them on other computers (such as the ones at home), thereby violating licensing agreements.

FROM THE CLASSROOM

Physical Security

It is important to remember that security is a tradeoff. When implementing security measures, you will have to remember that the more secure something is, the less easy it is to do your work. If someone has to find keys to open locks, enter multiple passwords, or go through various steps to access something, it will add to the time and difficulty of performing a task.

When designing the physical security measures for your network, keep in mind that you and others will still have to work effectively with this equipment. The more secure a system is, the more difficult it will be to access. If it is too difficult to access certain equipment, it may deter people from doing some of the work they should do.

—*Michael Cross, MCSE, MCP+I, MCPS, CNA*

Theft Deterrents

In addition to securing the location that the equipment resides in, you may also consider methods that secure the equipment directly. There are a number of tools and techniques that can be used to prevent people from damaging or stealing network components. Depending on the security level desired, these options may be useful in your organization.

Workstations and servers may benefit from having physical locks placed on their power switches, floppy disk drives, CD-ROM drives and so forth. Unless someone has a key to open the lock, they will be unable to access that device. This will prevent users from saving sensitive data to a floppy disk or a rewritable CD, or installing their own unauthorized programs on the machine.

Many organizations go further than merely locking the floppy disk drives and CD-ROM drives on their workstations and remove them completely. This ensures that users will be unable to leave the workplace with data files or install unauthorized programs. If data does need to be stored on a floppy disk or a CD-ROM, then users must do so through specific workstations that are controlled by trusted users (such as supervisors). If programs need to be installed, they can only be installed over the network by IT staff. This increases control over what goes on and comes off of your network.

Many portable computers also have a lock slot on their back panel, where you can attach a heavy cable that locks the computer to a desk or workspace. These cables can't be removed from the computer without damaging the case, unless you have the key. This means that the hardware cannot be moved, unless you want it to be moved.

Users can also do significant damage by using a keyboard. They could inadvertently or deliberately change settings, delete important files, or perform other actions that will damage data on the server. To protect the server from such actions, you could hide the keyboard in a locked drawer. However, this only acts as a deterrent, as a user could simply hook up the keyboard from their workstation. You could also lock the keyboard, preventing users from entering data through the keyboard. Finally, if the desk for the server has a keyboard tray, you could lock the tray so that it can't be opened without a key.

Permanent stickers are another method of protecting your equipment. Such stickers may act as asset stickers by identifying to whom the component belongs and by having a number that can be used when inventorying. Such stickers are an inexpensive deterrent. Some stickers will also leave an indelible marking if they are removed, identifying that it is stolen property.

A recent method of security involves software that can be used to recover stolen computers. Two such programs are Computer Sentry Software's CyberAngel and Absolute Software's CompuTrace. If the software is used, and your server or workstation is stolen, you can call a toll-free phone number to inform the company that developed the software. When the stolen computer is connected to a modem and phone line, it dials into the security company, who then traces the call. This allows the company to contact the police, who then go to where the computer is located, recover your property, and arrest the culprits.

Locking Computers with Passwords

Passwords are a common method of controlling access. If the password that is entered doesn't match the one stored on the system, access is denied. Although you're probably familiar with using them for network access, you might not have considered other methods of password protection.

Computers often provide a screen saver mode with password protection. This is seen on Novell NetWare servers, where a password-protected screen saver can be activated by entering the following at the command prompt of the server:

```
SCRSAVER ACTIVATE
```

Once activated, the server cannot be accessed unless the proper username and password is entered.

Other standalone machines and workstations also provide password-protected screen savers. For example, on Windows machines, you can set password protection through the Display applet. Once set, anyone attempting to access the machine will need to enter a password first.

Windows NT and Windows 2000 machines can also lock the workstations by pressing CTRL-ALT-DEL, and then clicking the button on the dialog that appears to lock the workstation. If another user attempts to use the machine, they will need to enter your username and password (or an administrator account's username and password) to unlock the machine. Unfortunately, if a username and password other than the one currently logged on is used, any open programs and files used by the current user (who locked the machine) will be closed. This could be a major problem, depending on what the user had open when he or she locked the machine.

Some applications also provide the ability to password protect data. For example, applications in Microsoft Office provide the ability to password protect documents created with its programs. If a user attempts to open such a file, they will need to enter the proper password or they will be unable to view or modify it.

In using such passwords, you should remember some basic guidelines for secure passwords:

- Use hard-to-guess passwords. If you use a common word, name, or number for your password, users will be able to guess it quickly.

- Use a combination of letters, numbers, and special characters.

- Do not share your passwords with others, as this defeats the purpose of password-based access.

EXERCISE 8-1

Preventing Access to a Workstation Using Password-Protected Screen Savers

1. From the Start menu, select Settings | Control Panel.

2. When Control Panel opens, double-click Display.

3. Click the Screen Saver tab, and then select the Password Protected check box.

4. Click the Change button and set your password.

5. When the computer goes into screen saver mode, press the SPACEBAR. A dialog box should appear, asking for your password.

Smart Cards

Smart cards are another method of providing a measure of security to your network. Smart cards are small plastic cards that have a microchip and/or a memory module embedded in them that can store a significant amount of information. The cards are generally inserted into a special reader that reads information on the card, although some readers can scan the cards from a distance. They can come in formats that are disposable or reprogrammable, making them useful for whatever your needs may be.

exam
ⓦatch

The Server+ exam expects you to have a basic knowledge of smart cards, in that they can be used to secure facilities and systems. If you're confused about smart cards, think of them as an evolution of the cards you currently use with magnetic strips. You've probably used the cards with the magnetic strips for banking, credit cards, and so forth. Unfortunately, the problem with magnetic cards is that they can be easily be demagnetized or stolen. With smart cards, the information on them can be updated, and they don't demagnetize. To prevent information on the card from being modified or stolen, an encryption method is used to protect what's stored on the smart card.

Smart cards can store identification credentials on them so that you can't gain access without the card. Some keyboards are available that include a slot for the smart card, so that users can't gain access to a system unless their smart card contains the proper permissions. Many companies currently use them for access to restricted areas. Such applications of the technology makes smart cards a viable solution for physical security.

Biometrics

Biometrics is another useful tool for physical security. In this technology though, "physical" is truly part of the package. Biometrics uses measurements of a person's characteristics to allow or deny access to a system. These characteristics may include fingerprints, voice patterns, facial patterns, eye retinas, and so forth. These measurements are stored, analyzed, and used to authenticate people.

Biometrics has become a replacement for access methods such as passwords and keys, which can be stolen and used by another person. Elements of the person can be scanned and compared to a stored measurement in the system. If the voice, fingerprints, or other elements being used do not match, then access is denied. To give an example, a sealed door to a server room may have a scanner or reader attached to it. By placing your finger on it, your fingerprint is scanned and converted into a digital form. This will be compared to stored biometric data, where specific points in the fingerprint are compared to those stored in the database. If your fingerprint identifies you as someone who may enter the server room, then the door will unlock. If not, then you won't be able to enter the room.

Promoting Security Awareness

Making people understand why security is in place is an important part of implementing physical security measures in your company. If employees don't understand why security is important, they may feel untrusted and have animosity toward you and other members of the IT staff. Unless this is made clear, you may find yourself in a difficult situation, explaining to a superior why he or she can't enter a restricted area. Additionally, if members of your IT staff don't understand how the security works, then they may inadvertently disrupt it and become security risks themselves.

SCENARIO & SOLUTION

Now that we've discussed physical security issues in such detail, refer to the following Scenario & Solution for some common questions and situations that you may encounter.

I have implemented smart cards, biometrics, and many other methods that are explained in this chapter. Now I am finding it difficult and/or time consuming to do common tasks. What should I do?	The cardinal rule of security is that it is a tradeoff. The more you protect information and equipment, the more defenses you'll have to go through. After all, the data and equipment that has the ultimate security can't be accessed by anyone. Unfortunately, this means it's also unusable. A good security system balances the need for access with the need for security. You should always evaluate how sensitive and important data and equipment is and determine what level of security is required to protect it. If security is stringent, you will need to either get used to it or lighten security measures so that you can get your work done.
The company I work for is small but growing. Traditionally, security has been lax, due to the familial relationships in the office. I have implemented a new security plan, but I'm concerned about the reaction of other employees. What can I do?	Inform employees of the company that a new security policy is in place and explain the reasons behind it. In wording it, remember to not sound like you're accusing people of wrongdoings, but protecting equipment from accidental damage and any malicious damage that could occur from break-ins or other situations. You can inform them by memo, through your intranet, or by having department heads explain it to their staff.
I have implemented a regular backup schedule, but the company I work for has only one office. There is no place to keep a copy of the backup offsite. What should I do?	Keeping backups offsite is important. If there is a fire or other disaster, then any backups onsite may be destroyed. If you don't have a place to store backups offsite, there are a number of options. Since backup tapes are small, you could keep them in a safe deposit box at a bank. Security guard and alarm companies may also be used. For a fee, they may provide a service to store your backups in their offices (such as in a safe).

Recognizing and Reporting on Server Room Environmental Issues

Computers and other components of your network can be affected by a variety of environmental issues. Temperature, humidity, electrical interference, vibrations, and other factors may have an adverse impact on your hardware, causing failures and shortening the lifespan of equipment. In this section, we'll discuss these issues and how to recognize and avoid problems that may result from them.

Temperature

Variations in temperature can have dire effects on hardware, just as they can on anything else. If a computer is too hot or too cold, it can damage the hardware, causing your server to experience failures. It is for this reason that it is important for a server room to be a steady, cool temperature.

Heat has always been a problem for computers. The inside of a running computer can be as much as 40 degrees hotter than it is on the outside of it. This excess heat is caused by the hardware running in the computer, which raises the interior temperature. This is why computers have heat sinks, fans, and an internal airflow that cools the power supply, processors, adapters, and other components. To avoid damage from heat, it is important to keep these fans running in good order, so that the interior temperature of the computer is kept at less than 110 degrees. Above this, components of your system can overheat and be permanently damaged.

Combinations of hot and cold are also a problem. Consider what happens to the pavement in your driveway as summers and winters roll by. Heat causes it to expand, and the cold causes it to contract, until you finally wind up with cracks. Although you won't see cracks appearing from temperature in your computer case, other components will be affected by temperature variations. One such effect is called "chip creep," which occurs when the expansion and contraction of the circuit boards cause movement in the computer chips. Chips in your computer gradually begin to lose contact with the sockets they're in, so that they can't send and receive signals properly.

By controlling temperatures in your server room, you can keep such problems from occurring. It is important that the area containing your servers and other important network components is air-conditioned, so that temperatures are kept at a constant level of cool. Alarms can also be used, alerting you if temperatures in the server room exceed 80 degrees, which may cause equipment to suffer from the heat. In some models, these alarms can be attached to the server and will automatically shut it down if it gets too hot.

Air Flow and Air Quality

The flow and quality of air is another issue. Remember that computers take air in through fans, circulate it through the computer to cool components, and then force it back out. If the quality of the air or the ability to force this air through the computer is poor, then your hardware may pay the price for it.

Temperatures may rise in a computer if the flow of air is hindered in some way. You may have removed a hard disk or CD-ROM drive from a drive bay and didn't have a face plate to cover the opening. In other cases, you may have removed an adapter card and left the back of the computer open because you didn't have a spare cover. Rather than covering these openings as soon as possible, you may have left them open, thinking the openings would let air in and that this would be good for the computer. Unfortunately, the opening keeps air from circulating in the computer as it's designed to. Airflow is lost through the opening, causing temperatures to rise rather than drop.

Just as leaving areas of the computer open is bad, it is also bad for the computer when certain areas are blocked. Computers have air vents, which take in air and let it back out again. If these are blocked, temperatures can rise. This may be caused by placing the equipment in areas that aren't well ventilated, or by blocking the air intake and outflow on the computer. Such blockages may occur by covering the computer or by putting objects in from of the vents.

on the **Job**

Animal hair is another major cause of blockages for air intakes and outflows. If animals are around the area of the computers, then their hair can get into these and prevent the computer from properly being cooled. For this reason, it is important that you either keep animals away from the systems or vacuum these rooms regularly and thoroughly.

Air quality is another issue with computers that can block intake and outflow vents. Fans in a computer will circulate the air it takes in. However, if the air is of poor quality, then particles in the air are also circulated. Dust, smoke, hair, thermal insulation, and other elements can damage components in the computer and block the vents as they build up. To alleviate this problem, it is important to vacuum out these vents and the inside of the computer occasionally, and use filtration devices that take pollutants out of the air.

ESD

Electrostatic discharge (ESD) is caused by static electricity. Static electricity will build up a charge on an object over time, until it comes in contact with another object. At this time, electrons are discharged (that is, transferred) between the objects until both of them have an equal charge. When a human is one of the objects, the result can be a small shock. You've probably experienced this when you walked across a dry carpet and then got a shock touching another person. If you gave such a shock to a processor or other computer component, the ESD could cause significant damage.

Damage can occur even if the electrostatic discharge is mild. For a person to feel an electrostatic discharge, the ESD must be around 3000 volts. If you saw a spark from the discharge, then it would be in the vicinity of 20,000 volts. For a chip to be damaged, the ESD can be as low as 20 or 30 volts. By not taking precautions, you can render a component inoperable.

Damage caused by ESD can be immediate or over time. As mentioned, even if you don't feel a shock, the electrostatic discharge may have occurred and damage may be present. This may cause catastrophic damage, so that the component becomes inoperable right away. In other cases, the performance and functionality of the component may degrade over a period of time, until it finally has to be replaced.

exam
ⓦatch

Questions may appear on your exam that deal with electrostatic discharge. It is important to remember that ESD wristbands and mats may be used to protect against ESD, and that damage can occur gradually, over a period of time.

To control ESD, it is important to understand how it may occur, and then deal with the possibility of it occurring accordingly. In addition to generating a charge yourself by walking across the room, ESD may be caused by unclean conditions and humidity. Dust and dirt particles are capable of carrying a charge. If the particles are on a component, they may build this charge up over time, discharge it, and continue this cycle again and again. Humidity can add to this problem, as a humidity level below 50 percent can make dry conditions that increase ESD. Conversely, if humidity is too high, then water particles (which are an electric conductor) may condense and stick to components. By keeping humidity levels between 70-90 percent, you can prevent such problems from occurring.

There are a number of ways to prevent ESD from occurring. Antistatic bags can be used when storing components or transporting them. These bags protect components stored in them. Electrical charges are collected on the outside of the bag, so that they are separated from what's inside the bag. These should also be used when shipping components, so that other packing materials (such as Styrofoam) don't cause a discharge and damage equipment before its even used.

ESD wristbands (or wrist straps) are a common method of dealing with electrostatic discharge when you're working on computers or other electronic equipment. They are used to ground you so that you can't produce a discharge. ESD wristbands are straps that wrap around your wrist. They are made of insulated material with a metal button on it. The button is attached to a wire that generally has an alligator clip on the other end. This allows you to connect the wire to an electrical ground. Because the wires on the wristbands are generally quite long, you are able to move about your work area with little hindrance while protecting yourself and equipment from ESD.

Another tool is an ESD mat. Like the wristband, the ESD mat is made of an insulated material. The mat has two wires attached to it, which have alligator clips on the ends of them. One wire is clipped to an electrical ground, while the other is clipped to the computer that you're working on. By laying the computer component on the mat and grounding it by attaching one of the wires, any static charge it holds will be bled away and the component will be grounded.

on the
job

You should avoid allowing anyone to touch you when you're working on equipment. Although you may be grounded using an ESD wrist strap or mat, the other people in the room may not be. By allowing yourself to be touched, they can pass an electrostatic discharge, which will then be passed through you. If you're touching a processor or other component, the charge will pass through you to it, possibly causing damage.

In using ESD wristbands, it is important that you don't use them when working on monitors and other pieces of equipment that are labeled with high voltage stickers. Using a wristband when working on such equipment may not only damage the equipment, but most importantly, *it can kill you!* By using the ESD wristband or mat with high voltage equipment, you can create a live circuit between yourself and the equipment. In other words, you are setting yourself up to be electrocuted.

In recent years, sprays have appeared on the market that can be used on carpets and fabrics, so that any static charges are reduced. In using these, ESD is also reduced. You can also reduce such charges by wearing shoes or boots with rubber soles, which will insulate you from build ups that would otherwise occur as you walk around.

EMI and RFI

EMI is electromagnetic interference, whereas RFI is radio frequency interference. Each of these can cause major problems on a network, as they can corrupt data being transmitted across cables on your network. Basically, the signals from radio frequencies and electromagnetism interfere with the transmissions going across your network. Their signals overlap with those being sent across the cable. You can compare this to when someone tries talking over you in a conversation, so that the information you're trying to convey gets lost in the conversation. In a network, however, the interruptions can cause messages to become corrupted and need to be repeated. As is the case with the person talking over you, the name for this interference of network transmissions is called *noise*.

Electromagnetic interference is a common source of problems for networks and may be caused by a wide variety of sources. EMI sources include heavy machinery (such as elevators), lights, industrial equipment, and so forth. Network cabling near these sources can be affected by the electromagnetic interference, so that data being transmitted across the cables is corrupted.

Radio frequency interference can also be caused by a number of sources. RFI sources may include microwaves, appliances, furnaces, and, of course, radio transmission. The cables used to transmit data can stretch for a long distance and act as an antenna, picking up such interference.

To deal with EMI and RFI, you should ensure that cabling used by your network is shielded in some way and not laid close to EMI and RFI sources. Computers and other equipment should also be separated from electrical equipment, large magnets, and other sources of interference. By keeping a distance from such sources and ensuring that cabling uses some form of shielding, RFI and EMI can be kept to a minimum.

Vibrations and Physical Impacts

Vibrations and physical impacts are other environmental issues that can have negative effects on computers and other components of your network. A violent shock (such as the computer being kicked or dropped) can break adapters, motherboards, and so forth. Such impacts and vibrations can also loosen chips and adapters from their sockets. It is important that you keep equipment away from sources of vibrations and physical shocks so that you don't need to repair or replace the equipment.

exam
Watch

You will find that a number of the environmental questions on the exam will require common sense more than technical knowledge. You aren't required to know how to install temperature alarms, fire suppression, or other equipment. You will, however, be expected to know and understand what is needed if your server room is to be a good environment for equipment.

Protecting Your Server Room from Disasters

Disasters are a major consideration when planning a positive server room environment. A number of disasters can occur that will do limited to massive damage to your network. Some disasters have the ability to destroy a server room, whereas others will cause limited downtime.

exam
Watch

Downtime is an important problem for networks. If a network goes down for a period of time, users will be unable to do their work. The company will still have to pay these users, and may have to pay overtime as they catch up on their work when the network returns to service. Any decisions that require you to take servers offline or lose network resources should also take the effects of downtime into consideration.

Server rooms should have some method of fire suppression that will put out a fire, but not damage the equipment in the room. In other words, don't use a room that has water released into the room to combat a fire. There are a number of methods that can be used, including foam and having oxygen depleted in the room through chemicals released into the air.

You should also keep your computers off the floor, so that if a flood occurs, your servers and other equipment won't be destroyed. Even a small amount of water can short out the computer and cause rust and other problems that will damage the equipment. Keeping computers off the ground will also reduce the amount of dust and dirt that will get into the equipment and will safeguard them from accidentally being kicked.

Air conditioning is not only a maintenance consideration, but also preparation against disasters. Heat waves cause high temperatures, which can damage your equipment. Because you don't want your air conditioner conking out on a hot summer day, you should have backup air conditioning for the server room. If a problem occurs, the equipment in the room will be protected from rising temperatures.

Power should also be a consideration. If there is a power failure, users will be unable to do the work on their computers and servers may shut down improperly. If the server doesn't shut down gracefully, then data on the server can be corrupted. There are a number of methods that can be used to provide power when your regular source fails.

Backup generators are a common method of providing power to a building when the electric company is unable to. Backup generators run on gasoline and can be started up relatively quickly when standard power sources become unavailable. Once started, the backup generators will provide power until they run out of fuel or the regular power is returned.

In using backup generators, you should run regular tests. Such tests should be done on a monthly basis, so that you don't find out whether it works or not during an emergency. In the test, you should switch the building from normal power sources to running on the generator. If power is supplied properly, then you can consider the test a success. However, you will need to remember that testing uses fuel, so you will want to replenish it after the test.

Uninterruptible power supplies (UPSs) are another method of providing power during a power outage. When power fails to be passed to the UPS, sensors in the UPS will detect the change in voltage and the battery in the UPS will take over. Although the primary benefit of a UPS is that it provides backup power through a battery, it also provides other benefits. UPSs often provide surge protection and they filter noise, so that components using the UPS don't suffer from power spikes or electromagnetic interference. For more information on UPSs and how to upgrade them, refer to Chapter 5 of this book.

During a power failure, turn off any workstations and equipment that isn't necessary. Although power may continue to be supplied to a building through a backup generator, you don't want to drain or overload the generator by having unnecessary equipment draining power. After all, you don't know how long you're going to have to rely on that backup power.

If a disaster is bad enough, it may not matter what measures you took to protect against it. An example of this would be an earthquake that levels the building or a fire that destroys everything in your server room. For this reason, it is important that the data isn't lost with the equipment. When backing up data onto tapes or other media, you should remember to keep a copy of this data offsite. If the servers are destroyed, then the data can be restored onto new machines. Such a procedure may make the difference between a company losing some computers or losing its business completely.

Backing up data is covered in great detail on the exam. For detailed information on this, refer to Chapter 7 of this book.

Cleanliness

As mentioned throughout this chapter, it is important for your server room to be clean. By vacuuming and dusting the room regularly, you can improve the lifespan of equipment and their performance. However, cleaning the server room is something that you will generally have to do yourself, as you don't want janitorial staff having free access to the equipment.

Anyone who's had a help desk call from a user who can't access the network or turn on their computer, and then found that the network or power cable has been kicked loose by janitorial staff, will understand why you don't want custodians in the server room. You want to restrict access to the room so that the chances for accidents and malicious acts are lessened. The last thing you want is a janitor kicking over a mop bucket and flooding the equipment nearby.

When cleaning the room, a vacuum is a must. Dust and dirt can get into vents in the equipment and cause damage. Because of this, you should not only vacuum the room, but also use a vacuum designed for computers to suck out the dust from such vents and the inside of your computer.

When cleaning equipment, you should always refer to the manufacturer's guidelines. This will tell you whether it's recommended to use liquid cleaners, alcohol, or other cleaners on a component. In some cases, none of these will be useful and you will have to rely on simply vacuuming out the dust.

SCENARIO & SOLUTION

Now that we've discussed server room environmental issues in such detail, let's look at a few scenario questions and situations that you may experience with this topic.

Our company has custodial staff to clean our offices. Can I just have them take care of cleaning the server room?	If you do have janitors clean your server room, you should monitor their activities. You don't want them accidentally kicking the cable out of a server's network card or getting the equipment wet with mop water. However, it is better if you keep the server room as a restricted area, so that only IT staff are permitted entry. Due to the sensitivity of the equipment, it is better to maintain the environment yourself, so that you know what is being done and that the work is done properly.
I have just had a new server delivered. Are there any environmental issues I should consider before setting up the server?	You should wait for the equipment to reach the same temperature as the server room before setting it up. If it is wintertime and cold outside or summertime and hot outside, then the new server will also be hot or cold. By allowing the machine to reach the temperature of the server room, it won't experience the stress of starting up cold or hot. Also, the heat generated by the computer as it runs won't change the internal temperature as drastically, causing components to expand quickly or overheat (and thereby become damaged).

CERTIFICATION SUMMARY

Physical security requires controlling access, so that only those who require access to components of your network are able to physically interact with it. This can be done through a variety of methods, including smart cards, locks, passwords, biometrics, and so forth. By restricting access, you enhance the security of your network.

Environmental issues in a server room can have a great impact on hardware. Factors such as vibrations, electrostatic discharge, and high and low temperatures can affect hardware and shorten its lifespan. You should store equipment and media in an environment that is cool, well ventilated, and free of electrical interference. You should also perform proper preventative maintenance; cleaning equipment and the area it's stored in, and storing equipment properly.

TWO-MINUTE DRILL

Here are some of the key points from each certification objective in Chapter 8.

Recognizing and Reporting on Physical Security Issues

❑ Physical security deals with limiting access to important equipment, such as servers, routers, and UPSs.

❑ Servers and other important equipment should be kept in a locked room or cabinet that is well ventilated.

❑ When evaluating security threats, you should remember that you're not only protecting your system from people outside of your company, but also from employees within the organization.

❑ Backups should be stored in a locked cabinet or safe, and a set of backups should also be stored offsite.

❑ Workstations without floppy disk drives or CD burners prevent users from leaving the building with sensitive data. Locks can also be applied to the drive or CD burner for this reason.

❑ Smart cards are small plastic cards that have a microchip embedded in them and can store a significant amount of information.

❑ Smart cards are commonly used to store credentials, which can be read by a special reader. Together, they authenticate the cardholder and allows or denies access to a security system on the computer or facility.

❑ Biometrics uses measurements of a person's characteristics to allow or deny access to a system. These characteristics may include fingerprints, voice patterns, facial patterns, and eye retinas.

❑ You will need to develop a training plan that informs IT staff members of security measures and tells employees why they are in place and important.

Recognizing and Reporting on Server Room Environmental Issues

❑ Environmental factors are issues that affect the surroundings of computers and equipment. This includes such issues as temperature, electrostatic discharge, cleanliness, and so forth.

❑ It is important that a server room is kept cool and computers are well ventilated. The inside of a running computer can be as much as 40 degrees hotter than it is on the outside of it, so high external temperatures or a lack of air flow can cause them to overheat.

❑ Airflow is another issue that can affect a server. If air cannot flow through a computer properly, components inside may overheat.

❑ Electrostatic discharge (ESD) can cause damage to a processor and other components in a computer. The damage can be caused immediately or over time.

❑ ESD wristbands, ESD mats, antistatic bags, sprays, and wearing rubber-soled shoes are all methods of reducing the possibility that an electrostatic discharge will occur.

❑ Never wear an ESD wristband when working on high voltage equipment, as it can cause you to be electrocuted.

❑ Noise can be caused by electromagnetic interference (EMI) or radio frequency interference (RFI). Noise can corrupt data in network transmissions.

❑ Vibrations and physical impacts can loosen components and damage equipment.

❑ A UPS provides battery backup power and will also provide protection from power surges and spikes.

SELF TEST

The following questions will help you measure your understanding of the material presented in this chapter. Read all of the choices carefully, as there may be more than one correct answer. Choose all correct answers for each question.

Recognizing and Reporting on Server Room Environmental Issues

1. You are planning to upgrade physical security for your network. Which of the following will you need to consider when planning this security? (Choose all that apply.)

   A. Protocols

   B. Creating an inventory of equipment that is valuable to the network

   C. Identifying who is a possible security threat

   D. Whether Windows 2000 Servers are authenticating properly

2. You have a server stored in a closet, which has no locking mechanism. Because you can't get permission to modify the door to this closet by putting a lock on it, you have decided to secure the machine itself. You attach a thick cable to the case and lock the other end to a bolt in the wall. When the server is up, you remove the mouse and keyboard and take it with you as a deterrent. The server itself has a locking plastic door that prevents people from accessing the CD-ROM and floppy disk drives, unless they have a key for them. You then place the server high on the shelf of a metal rack. Which of the following physical security risks still exist? (Choose all that apply.)

   A. Hardware inside the server is still at risk.

   B. People can remove the server.

   C. People can knock over the server.

   D. People will still be able to access the server and add components to the computer. In doing so, they can enter commands and modify data.

3. The company you work for has limited facilities and a limited budget. It can't afford to dedicate space for a server room. At present, the servers are stored in a corner of an unlocked storage room that is used to store old files for historical purposes. Which of the following other options may be used to secure your servers?

   A. Install locks on the storage room that use biometrics, which will allow users to access the room only if they physically meet the criteria of the biometric lock.

B. Remove the storage materials from this room so that no one has a need to access this room except IT staff.

C. Install a standard door lock on the storage room. If anyone needs access to it, they will need to have you open the door.

D. Leave servers where they are. Train users on why equipment is important and that they shouldn't touch it.

4. Which of the following hardware components should be included in a physical security plan? (Choose all that apply.)

A. Software installation CDs

B. Mouse

C. Keyboard

D. Backup tapes

5. Which of the following methods can be used for recovery of stolen equipment?

A. Removing serial numbers from computer cases

B. Smart cards

C. Permanent stickers

D. Biometrics

6. You are thinking of implementing password protection on a NetWare file server. This will prevent users from accessing the server and the data stored on it. Which of the following can passwords be used on, so that the server and its data are secured? (Choose all that apply.)

A. Documents

B. Screen savers

C. System files

D. Files currently open

7. A user named Joe works in the finance department. He has come to you with several ideas for a password that he will use, but wants your input on which one to use. Which of the following is a secure password?

A. joe

B. password

C. finance

D. jf*981

8. Which of the following best describes a smart card?

   A. They are small plastic cards that have a microchip embedded in them that is used to store information.

   B. They are small plastic cards that have a magnetic strip, which is used to store information.

   C. They are a type of adapter card that is installed on a computer and used to prevent users from accessing data on the computer.

   D. They are a type of plate that is attached to the computer. Using a keypad on the card, it can accept input that authenticates the user.

9. In which of the following ways can you use smart cards to provide physical security for your network?

   A. They can store a schedule of your backup routines, which you can refer to on the card's display screen.

   B. They are used to lock computer cases to protect components inside of them.

   C. They are attached to the computer, providing information on whether the computer has been stolen or not.

   D. They can be used to prevent users from using the computer unless they have the proper credentials in their smart card.

10. Which of the following is used for authenticating a person if biometrics is used as a security measure? (Choose all that apply.)

    A. Voice patterns

    B. Passwords

    C. Information stored on a card

    D. Fingerprints

Recognizing and Reporting on Physical Security Issues

11. Which of the following is chip creep?

    A. When combinations of hot and cold expand circuit boards, cause movement in the computer chips, and begin to lose contact with sockets.

    B. When combinations of hot and cold expand circuit boards, cause movement in the computer chips, and cause them to crack.

    C. When combinations of hot and cold expand circuit boards, causing motherboards and adapters to crack.

D. When combinations of humidity and dryness cause movement in the computer chips which begin to lose contact with sockets.

12. Each of the following choices provides a scenario. Which of the following involve factors that can affect a computer's airflow, which may cause it to overheat?

A. A computer is put in a locked closet that is air-conditioned. A pile of boxes blocks the air vent on the computer.

B. A computer has a sheet of plastic covering it as contractors repair a ceiling.

C. An adapter card has been removed and there are no back plates to cover the opening.

D. A CD-ROM drive has been removed from a computer. There are no spare face plates to cover the opening to the drive bay.

E. All of the above.

F. None of the above.

13. At what voltage can electrostatic discharge cause damage to components such as processors in your computer? Choose the minimal voltage.

A. 30

B. 3000

C. 20000

D. 30000

14. Your server room is air-conditioned and has humidity levels kept below 50 percent. It has a lock on the door preventing users from accessing the room without a key. The only people who have copies of this key are you, a security officer who patrols the area at night, and a janitor who cleans the server room nightly. You have an alarm installed to alert those within earshot of whether the temperature has dropped below the level it should be. Which of the following are environmental problems exist with this situation?

A. The room is kept clean by a janitor.

B. The humidity is too high.

C. The humidity is too low.

D. The alarm will not alert anyone, because no one is there at night.

15. Which of the following can prevent ESD from damaging equipment?

A. Dust

B. Low humidity

C. High humidity

D. Antistatic bags

16. Which of the following methods should you use to reduce ESD when working on high voltage equipment in a server room? (Choose all that apply.)

A. ESD wristband

B. ESD wrist strap

C. Antistatic sprays on the carpets leading into the server room

D. Wear rubber soled shoes

17. Which of the following are sources of EMI or RFI? (Choose all that apply.)

A. Someone building up static by walking across a dry carpet

B. Radar emissions from a nearby airbase

C. Data being transmitted across a network cable

D. An elevator starting up

18. In the next few days, construction workers will be removing concrete walls on the other side of your server room. To do this, the workers will be using sledgehammers and jackhammers. No work will be done on the electrical systems and the walls being affected are not the ones separating the two rooms. Which of the following should you do while construction is underway?

A. Install heavy padding in the server room so that all walls are fully covered and protected.

B. Remove the servers from the room and move them to a temporary location so that they are away from the vibrations.

C. Remove the servers from the room and move them to a remote location so that they won't be affected by the EMI of the sledgehammers.

D. Inform the workers that the server room is on the other side, so that they can account for this in their work.

19. You have decided to place tables in your server room to keep the servers off of the floor. Which of the following benefits will result from this? (Choose all that apply.)

A. Protection from flooding

B. Protection from physical shock

C. Protection from dust and dirt

D. Improved ventilation by keeping the server higher in the air

20. You want to protect your system from power surges and spikes, as well as provide backup power in case of a power failure. Which of the following can you use for this purpose?

    A. Backup generators

    B. Power supplies

    C. Power bars

    D. UPS

LAB QUESTION

You are the new network administrator of a medium-size network. This network has five servers, which are all located in the same building. On the top floor, a server is locked in a closet that has a vent in it that's connected to the air-conditioning system, whereas another is locked in a cabinet that has no openings for air. The server in this cabinet is in a room where humidity has been kept below 50 percent, and air conditioning is used. On the second floor, the Web server for the local intranet is stored under a table near your office. The final two are locked in the basement in the boiler room, for which you have arranged to have the only key.

Your company is the only business that rents space in the building, and a high-tech security system has been installed to keep the public from entering. If a visitor comes to do business, they are met by an employee and accompanied directly to that person's office. Repairmen and janitors are given passes so that they can move freely through the building and fix whatever they are repairing or cleaning.

    1. Who will you need to consider as a possible physical security threat when designing the security?

    2. Which of the servers is in an insecure location?

    3. Which of the servers is in locations that have environmental problems?

    4. What effect will the humidity levels of the one server's location have on the server?

SELF TEST ANSWERS

Recognizing and Reporting on Server Room Environmental Issues

1. ☑ **B** and **C**. Creating an inventory of equipment that is valuable to the network, and identifying who is a possible security threat. Your plan will need to take into account an inventory of equipment and determine what is of specific value. This includes hardware, software, data, media, and other elements of your network. The value of the equipment should be based on both cost and how hard it would be to replace. You will also need to identify whom you are protecting this equipment from, so that you can limit their access.
☒ **A** and **D** are incorrect because although protocols and authentication provide electronic security, they aren't involved in physical security.

2. ☑ **A** and **D**. Hardware inside the server is still at risk, and people will still be able to access the server and add components to the computer. Although no one can steal the entire computer, they can still open the case and remove hardware inside the computer. Although you took the keyboard and mouse with you, there is nothing stopping someone from hooking up another mouse and keyboard. In doing so, they can enter commands and modify data.
☒ **B** is incorrect because the server is attached to a bolt in the wall with a heavy cable.
C is incorrect because people can't easily knock over the server, as it is high on a rack shelf.

3. ☑ **C**. Install a standard door lock on the storage room. If anyone needs access to it, they will need to have you open the door. This will control access and is a low cost solution.
☒ **A** is incorrect because biometric locks are expensive and the company has a limited budget.
B is incorrect because the company has limited facilities, and because of this, can't afford the space for a dedicated server room. **D** is incorrect because telling users not to touch equipment does nothing to restrict access.

4. ☑ **A** and **D**. Backup tapes and software installation CDs. Backup tapes should be considered as part of your physically security plan, as they contain all data on a server or servers in your company. Software can be expensive and licensing needs to be controlled. Therefore, you should also keep software in a secure environment.
☒ **B** and **C** are incorrect because a mouse and a keyboard are inexpensive. If they are stolen or damaged, they can be replaced easily and cheaply.

5. ☑ **C**. Permanent stickers. Such stickers are an inexpensive deterrent. They provide a method of identifying ownership of equipment, and some will leave an indelible marking if they are removed, identifying that it is stolen property.

☒ **A** is incorrect because removing serial numbers from computer cases will also remove a method of identifying your computer if it is recovered. **B** and **C** are incorrect because although smart cards and biometrics are useful for physical security, they aren't used for recovering stolen equipment.

6. ☑ **A and B.** Documents and screen savers can both use passwords to restrict access. Documents created with programs such as Microsoft Office can have passwords associated with them that control who can open them. Screen savers are another common method for controlling who can access a computer, as they may allow you to set a password that will control access.
☒ **C** is incorrect because system files cannot be password protected. **D** is incorrect because if the files are currently open, then they have already been opened using a password.

7. ☑ **D.** jf*981 is a good password because it combines letters, numbers, and special characters that will be hard to guess.
☒ **A** is incorrect because the user's name is easy to guess. **B** is incorrect because *password* is a common word that is also easy to guess. This particular password is a problem one because many users will actually use *password* as their password. **C** is incorrect because this is the department the user works in, and is thereby easy to guess.

8. ☑ **A.** They are small plastic cards that have a microchip embedded in them that is used to store information. The cards are inserted into a special reader, or scanned from a distance by a reader, which can be used to authenticate credentials stored on the card.
☒ **B** is incorrect because smart cards don't use magnetic strips. **C** is incorrect because smart cards aren't adapter cards installed in the computer. **D** is incorrect because smart cards aren't attached to the computer or directly accept input through the card itself.

9. ☑ **D.** They can be used to prevent users from using the computer unless they have the proper credentials in their smart card. Smart cards can store identification credentials on them, so that you can't gain access without the card. Some keyboards are available that include a slot for the smart card, so that users can't gain access to a system unless their smart card contains the proper permissions.
☒ **A** is incorrect because smart cards don't provide a display (such as palm-top computers do), so that you can refer to scheduling information that you program inside of it. **B** is incorrect because smart cards aren't used to lock computer cases. **C** is incorrect because smart cards aren't attached to a computer to provide information on whether it has been stolen.

10. ☑ **A and D.** Voice patterns and fingerprints may be used in biometrics to control access. Biometrics uses measurements of a person's characteristics to allow or deny access to a system. These characteristics may include fingerprints, voice patterns, facial patterns, eye retinas, and so

forth. These measurements are stored, analyzed, and used to authenticate people.
☒ B is incorrect because passwords are not used in biometrics. C is incorrect because information stored on a card isn't used for biometrics. It is, however, used with smart cards.

Recognizing and Reporting on Physical Security Issues

11. ☑ A. When combinations of hot and cold expand and contract circuit boards, causing movement in which the computer chips begin to lose contact with the sockets they're in, so that they can't send and receive signals properly.
☒ B is incorrect because the effect of chip creep isn't circuit boards or chips cracking. C is incorrect because the effect of chip creep isn't motherboards and adapters cracking. D is incorrect because humidity and dryness doesn't cause chip creep. They can however be contributing factors to electrostatic discharge, which can also damage computers.

12. ☑ E. All of the above. Airflow is the flow of air through a computer. Computers take air in through fans that circulate it through the computer to cool components and then force it back out. If there are openings in a computer, such as when back or face plates aren't covering drive bays, this keeps air from circulating in the computer as it's designed to. Airflow is lost through the opening, causing temperatures to rise rather than drop. Air vents being blocked are another reason why airflow is affected, as this blocks air intake and outflow on the computer. Such blockages may occur by covering the computer and putting objects in front of the vents. All of the scenarios involve restricted airflow.
☒ F is incorrect because all of the scenarios involve causes for problem airflow.

13. ☑ A. 30. For a chip to be damaged, the ESD can be as low as 20 or 30 volts. This damage can be immediate, leaving the component inoperable, or gradually occur over time.
☒ B, C, and D are incorrect because the question is looking for the minimal voltage at which damage can occur. At 3000 volts, a person to feel an electrostatic discharge. At 20,000 volts, the discharge is visible; you can see a spark.

14. ☑ C. The humidity is too low. A humidity level below 50 percent can make dry conditions that increase ESD. This will commonly occur during winter, when atmospheric conditions cause the environment to be dry. Humidity levels between 70 and 80 percent are a good range to work with.
☒ A is incorrect because the server room should be clean. A janitor should not have access to this room anytime he or she wants, but this is a physical security issue, not an environmental issue. B is incorrect because the humidity isn't too high, but is too low. D is incorrect because the security officer patrols the area at night and will thereby be able to hear the alarm go off.

15. ☑ **D.** Antistatic bags. These are used to transport and store components and protect them from getting an electrostatic discharge.

    ☒ **A** is incorrect because dust and dirt particles are capable of carrying a charge. If the particles are on a component, they may build this charge up over time, discharge it, and continue this cycle again and again. **B** is incorrect because low humidity can cause ESD. A humidity level below 50 percent can make dry conditions that increase ESD. **C** is incorrect because if humidity is too high, then water particles may condense and stick to components. As water is a conductor of electricity, then problems with ESD can occur from this.

16. ☑ **C** and **D.** Wearing rubber soled shoes and spraying the carpets leading into the server room will both reduce ESD.

    ☒ **A** and **B** are incorrect because ESD wrist straps and wristbands are the same thing, and using them when working on high voltage equipment can kill you. The use of them can create a live circuit between you and the equipment, causing you to be electrocuted.

17. ☑ **B** and **D.** Radar emissions and elevator motors are both sources of EMI or RFI. EMI is electromagnetic interference, whereas RFI is radio frequency interference. Other EMI sources include heavy machinery (such as elevators), lights, and industrial equipment. Other RFI sources may include microwaves, appliances, furnaces, and radio transmissions.

    ☒ **A** is incorrect because building up static is what causes electrostatic discharge (ESD). **C** is incorrect because EMI or RFI can affect data being transmitted across a network cable.

18. ☑ **B.** Remove the servers from the room and move them to a temporary location so that they are away from the vibrations. These vibrations could damage your computer and loosen chips and adapters from their sockets. It is important that you keep equipment away from sources of vibrations and physical shocks so that you don't need to repair or replace the equipment.

    ☒ **A** is incorrect because a padded room is never a good solution for you. Also, if the walls were fully covered then you wouldn't be unable to plug in your equipment. **C** is incorrect because the sledgehammers will be separated from your servers by a wall and some distance (as they'll be working on other walls in the neighboring room). Your worries should be with vibrations in this instance. **D** is incorrect because the workers will be unable to do anything about the vibrations and probably won't care about your problems or concerns.

19. ☑ **A, B,** and **C.** Protection from flooding, protection from physical shock, and protection from dust and dirt. You should keep your computers off the floor, so that if a flood occurs your servers and other equipment won't be destroyed. Keeping computers off the ground will also reduce the amount of dust and dirt that will get into the equipment and safeguards them from accidentally being kicked.

    ☒ **D** is incorrect because ventilation doesn't improve just because the server is raised higher.

20. ☑ **D.** UPS stands for uninterruptible power supply. When power fails to be passed to the UPS, sensors in the UPS will detect the change in voltage and the battery in the UPS will take over. Although the primary benefit of a UPS is that it provides backup power through a battery, it will also protect components plugged into it from power spikes and surges.

    ☒ **A** is incorrect because although a backup generator will provide electricity during a power outage, it doesn't protect systems from power surges and spikes. **B** is incorrect because a power supply is installed in a computer and used to provide power to components in the computer. If external power fails, then it will be unable to pass the electricity onto these components. **C** is incorrect because although power bars may provide protection from surges and spikes, they don't provide electricity during power failures.

LAB ANSWER

1. Employees, repairmen, and janitors are possible physical security threats. You should prevent them from having access to servers and other network components.

2. The Web server that is stored under a table near your office. Each of the other servers are physically secure, as they are locked away securely. Although many of these servers have environmental problems associated with them, they are physically secure.

3. There are three servers experiencing environmental problems. The server locked in a cabinet that has no openings for air has ventilation problems. The final two are locked in the basement in the boiler room, which will make them vulnerable to high temperatures.

4. The humidity levels are below 50 percent, making the area dry. This increases the chances that electrostatic discharge may occur and damage components.

Server+
COMPUTING TECHNOLOGY INDUSTRY ASSOCIATION

9

Troubleshooting and Problem Determination

CERTIFICATION OBJECTIVES

Problems with a network's server can have serious implications for the network and its users. If the server provides resources or a single service to the network, as in a file server or mail server, that resource or service will be unavailable. If the server manages the network's access and security, the entire network may become unavailable. As most organizations cannot afford extensive network downtime, it is important that server problems be resolved as efficiently as possible.

The information in this chapter will help you to accurately and quickly pinpoint and resolve server problems. The chapter begins with some basic observation and questioning techniques you can use to determine the nature of server problems.

Next, the chapter covers basic tools, utilities and procedures you can use to diagnose and troubleshoot problems. It then concludes with a discussion of how to use these tools, utilities, and procedures to pinpoint and resolve bandwidth, configuration, and hardware and software issues.

CERTIFICATION OBJECTIVE 9.01

Performing Problem Determination

All computer problems can be resolved. Sometimes this resolution involves adjusting configurations or replacing a hardware component. It can even include replacing the computer altogether. To resolve any computer problem, you must first determine its source. In many cases, however, a computer can behave in a way that does not easily lead you to the component or subsystem causing the trouble. In such cases, you need to use a combination of the computer's symptoms and its history, as well as information from the computer's user or other network users to diagnose the problem.

Observing the Environment

If you are performing onsite troubleshooting, observing the environment around you can be crucial to problem solving. Such observations can give you clues as to a problem's cause, and just as important, may alert you to potential trouble down the road.

Take note of the room's environment; items such as the temperature. Most computer components do not work well in the presence of heat. Furthermore, very high or low humidity can cause condensation or electrostatic discharges, respectively, both of which can lead to hardware problems. A safe humidity level is between 50 and 80 percent. Likewise, be aware of nearby devices that could cause Electro Magnetic Interference (EMI).

Notice the way components are plugged into wall outlets and determine if the outlets are overburdened with plugs. Observe how electrical and network cables are arranged. For example, do people have to step over the cable from the server to the hub? Such setups can lead to loose or disconnected cables.

Finally, notice the way people use their computers. Though you are not onsite to tutor people in applications or use of shortcuts, it's prudent to be on the lookout for rough handling of the equipment. If the user "bangs" on the keys, this could explain a faulty keyboard. In addition, some users tend to triple- and quadruple-click icons on the screen in an attempt to hurry things along, a practice that often leads to computer lock-ups.

It is important not to assume your observations are linked to the problem at hand before questioning the customer. For example, you may notice a loose network cable on the floor and reattach it. Think of how embarrassing it would be to find out the cable was removed on purpose and that the problem actually lies with the computer's hard drive.

Questioning the Customer

When you have a chance to speak with the user, start by asking about the nature of the problem. This will give you clues as to whether the problem is network-wide or localized on the server. Once you've determined what the problem is (its symptoms, not its cause), get some basic history from the user. Ask if the problem occurred at random or in response to a user action. An error that occurs "out of the blue" is different than an error that pops up every time the user tries to access a particular file.

Ask the user to try to replicate the problem. For example, if users complain they can't access a particular file on the server, have them try to access it again. Watch closely as the user performs the task. Take note of any error messages or unusual computer activity they might not have noticed. This over-the-shoulder approach also gives you a chance to see the process from beginning to end. For example, if a user is having difficulty logging in, watching them log on might reveal problems such as an activated Caps Lock button on the keyboard. Also, keep a sharp eye on how the user carries out the task. They may not be doing it properly. For example, a file access error could be the result of the user trying to open a file for which the workstation has no host application.

Of course, when the user tries to replicate the problem, it may not recur. In this case, it is likely another process prevented the action from taking place. For instance, an inability to access the Internet may have been caused by the external Web server's failure to provide the browser's startup page. It could turn out that the next time the user tries to access the Internet, the page is served.

Be very aware of your personal interactions with the user at this point. This can be a common occurrence, and a user's initial reaction is often embarrassment.

You should also find out about any recent changes to the computer and/or the surroundings. For example, ask if a new component or application has recently been installed. If one has, ask if the feature or device has worked at all since the new installation. The answer to this question could lead you to important information about application or device conflicts, as well as other misconfigurations. For example, if the user tells you the automatic backup utility hasn't worked since a new hard drive was installed, you can suspect the two events—the installation of the new hard drive and the backup utility failure—are related. Use the steps in Exercise 9-1 as a basic question and answer checklist when performing onsite troubleshooting.

EXERCISE 9-1

Questioning the Customer

Use the following questions as a guideline for determining the nature of the problem:

1. What happened to indicate there is a problem?

2. Were there any error messages?

3. Can you reproduce the problem?
   a. If yes, how do you reproduce the problem?
   b. If no, how often does the problem happen? Does the problem occur more frequently at different times of the day?

4. Are there any other problems or unusual behaviors?

5. When did the problem start happening?

6. Has anything changed recently on the system?

Once you have gathered information about the problem, determine whether the problem is limited to the current computer, or is occurring elsewhere on the network. If the computer cannot access a network resource, check to see if other computers can access it. If not, the problem probably lies with the resource itself, not the individual computers. Note that network access problems can often be caused by problems with cabling, routers, or other network devices. This chapter focuses only on problems caused by the server itself.

CERTIFICATION OBJECTIVE 9.02

Using Diagnostic Resources and Procedures

Once you have determined the cause of a server problem, the solution will probably seem obvious. For example, if you determine a server's connectivity problem is caused by an incorrect TCP/IP configuration, you will undoubtedly conclude that you must reconfigure the TCP/IP settings.

In order to resolve problems, then, you must first make an accurate diagnosis of the problem's cause. This section describes some of the tools, utilities, and procedures you can use to make these diagnoses. Diagnostic resources, such as hardware tools, software utilities, OS errors, and previous documentation are described, as well as how to gather the proper resources once the problem has been located, and how to shut down the server and perform remote troubleshooting. Specific troubleshooting procedures for resolving bottlenecks, configuration, and hardware and software problems are discussed in subsequent sections in this chapter.

Diagnostic Utilities

There are a myriad of third-party diagnostic utilities that can help you locate a computer's point of failure. However, some very useful utilities included with TCP/IP and the OS can help you determine network connectivity and allow you to view the network configuration of individual computers.

exam
ⓦatch

The utilities described in this section are a major focus of the Server+ troubleshooting questions.

PING

The PING (Packet InterNetwork Groper) utility allows you to determine basic TCP/IP connectivity between two networked computers. To use the PING utility, enter the following at the command line and press ENTER:

```
ping host
```

where "host" is the IP address or domain name of another computer. Your computer will send several echo packets to the specified host using the Internet Control Message Protocol (ICMP) and will return information about packet loss and packet delivery time. PING is a common TCP/IP utility, and can be used in Windows, Unix/Linux, Novell Netware, and OS/2. The result of a PING command, issued in Windows, is shown in Figure 9-1.

These results indicate there is network connectivity between your computer and the specified host. By default, the PING utility will send four 32-byte echo packets with a timeout interval of 2 seconds. Use the –n option with the PING command to set a specific number of packets, and use the –w option to increase or decrease the timeout interval.

If there is no network connectivity, the PING utility will return results similar to those shown in Figure 9-2. Failed PING results indicate your computer could not communicate with the specified host in the allotted time.

If a PING command fails, you may be able to continue using the PING utility to narrow down the problem. For example, the ability to ping a host using its IP address, but not its domain name, indicates a name resolution failure. When this is

---

FIGURE 9-1

The PING utility is used to determine network packet loss and transfer time

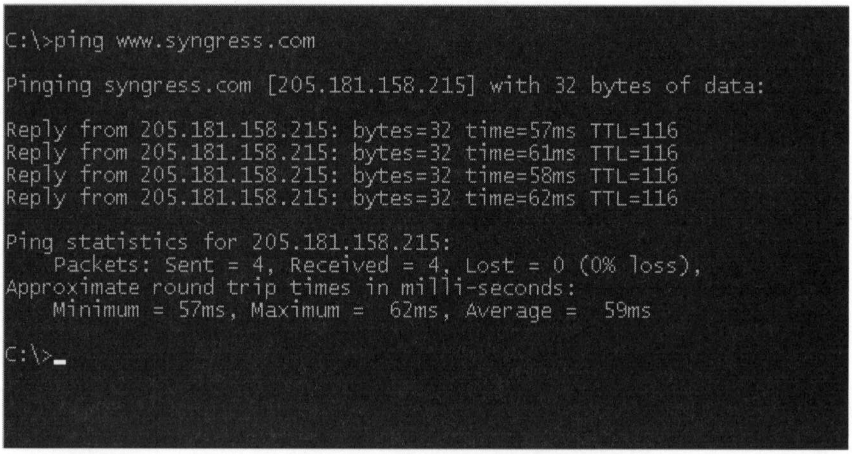

```
C:\>ping www.syngress.com

Pinging syngress.com [205.181.158.215] with 32 bytes of data:

Reply from 205.181.158.215: bytes=32 time=57ms TTL=116
Reply from 205.181.158.215: bytes=32 time=61ms TTL=116
Reply from 205.181.158.215: bytes=32 time=58ms TTL=116
Reply from 205.181.158.215: bytes=32 time=62ms TTL=116

Ping statistics for 205.181.158.215:
    Packets: Sent = 4, Received = 4, Lost = 0 (0% loss),
Approximate round trip times in milli-seconds:
    Minimum = 57ms, Maximum =  62ms, Average =   59ms

C:\>_
```

FIGURE 9-2

A 100% packet loss may indicate a failed network connection

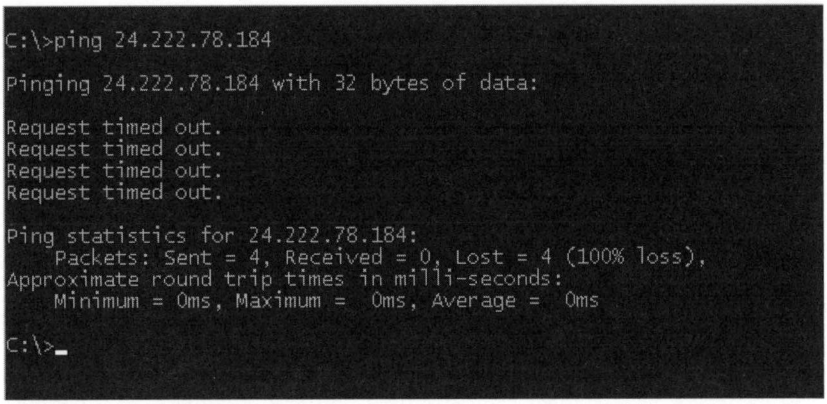

```
C:\>ping 24.222.78.184

Pinging 24.222.78.184 with 32 bytes of data:

Request timed out.
Request timed out.
Request timed out.
Request timed out.

Ping statistics for 24.222.78.184:
    Packets: Sent = 4, Received = 0, Lost = 4 (100% loss),
Approximate round trip times in milli-seconds:
    Minimum = 0ms, Maximum =  0ms, Average =  0ms

C:\>_
```

the case, you should focus your attention on the network's name resolution service. You may also be able to locate a bandwidth problem by increasing the PING timeout interval. That is, if the PING command fails at 2 seconds, but is successful with a 10 second timeout interval, there is likely a bandwidth problem, rather than a connectivity problem.

If the PING utility continues to return failed results, use the command to determine whether the problem lies with the current computer or the specified host. Start by pinging your own computer. A failed result means the problem lies within your computer, or in the network between your computer and the host.

If your computer has connectivity, continue by trying another host. If successful, the problem may lie externally, with the initial remote host. Finally, use the PING command with a local machine to determine if the network's routers or gateways are at fault. A router or gateway problem may be indicated if you can ping a computer on your local network, but cannot ping a computer on another network.

ARP

Network Interface Cards (NICs) use the ARP (Address Resolution Protocol) to resolve IP addresses to hardware MAC addresses. To minimize address resolution requests (and overall network traffic), each workstation using the ARP protocol will generate an ARP cache, containing recently resolved IP–MAC relationships. The ARP utility can be used to view a computer's ARP cache, and possibly pinpoint and resolve network connectivity problems. For example, if a single local computer does not have network connectivity, use the ARP command on another computer to determine if the problem lies with the failed machine's IP address. Like PING, ARP is part of the TCP/IP suite, and can be used on Windows, Unix/Linux, Novell Netware, and OS/2.

To view the ARP cache, enter the following at the command prompt:

```
arp -a
```

The results, as shown in Figure 9-3, can be used to locate problems stemming from duplicate or incorrect IP addresses.

To remove an incorrect ARP entry, use the following command:

```
arp -d host
```

where "host" is the domain name or IP address of the computer whose ARP entry you wish to remove. To manually add an ARP entry, use the following command:

```
arp -s ipaddress macaddress
```

Where "ipaddress" is the computer's IP address and "macaddress" is the computer's NIC MAC address. Note that the ARP cache retains the most recently accessed IP addresses. This means that the contents of the ARP cache are dynamic, and are continuously being removed, replaced, and updated. When you manually add an ARP entry, a static entry is created, and it will not be removed from the cache or updated. Figure 9-4 shows a static entry (as indicated in the "Type" column).

NETSTAT

The TCP/IP utility, NETSTAT, can provide you with information about each of a computer's active network connections. To use the NETSTAT utility, enter the following at a Windows, Unix/Linux, Novell Netware, or OS/2 command prompt:

```
netstat
```

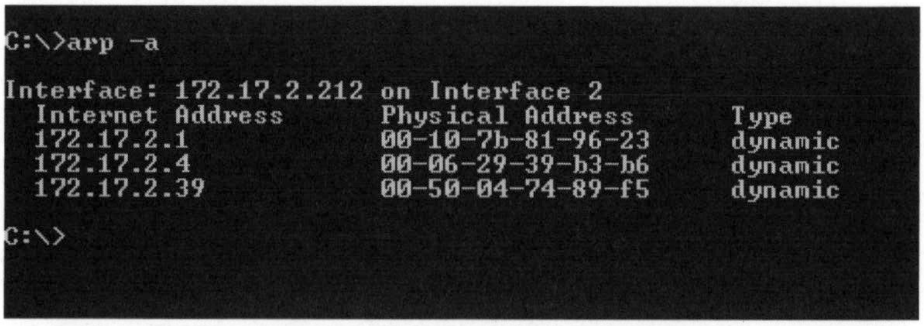

FIGURE 9-3

The ARP command can be used to show IP/MAC address relationships

```
C:\>arp -a

Interface: 172.17.2.212 on Interface 2
  Internet Address        Physical Address       Type
  172.17.2.1              00-10-7b-81-96-23      dynamic
  172.17.2.4              00-06-29-39-b3-b6      dynamic
  172.17.2.39             00-50-04-74-89-f5      dynamic

C:\>
```

FIGURE 9-4

Manually added
ARP entries are
listed as "static"

```
C:\>arp -a

Interface: 172.17.2.212 on Interface 2
  Internet Address        Physical Address      Type
  172.17.2.4              00-06-29-39-b3-b6      dynamic
  172.17.2.46             00-15-14-93-56-b2      static

C:\>
```

The protocol, local address/port, foreign address and state will be displayed for each active connection. A typical NETSTAT result, run from Windows, is shown in Figure 9-5. On some platforms, a send queue or receive queue column will also appear, indicating the number of bytes waiting in the send or receive queue. If this number is higher than 0, it indicates that data is not being transmitted properly. The state "ESTABLISHED" indicates an open and active connection. The state "TIME_WAIT" indicates the connection is closed, but that the network is still handling undelivered packets from that connection in the network. A large number of "TIME-WAIT" results could mean an internal network error. "CLOSED" and "CLOSE_WAIT" indicate that the connection is not currently being used.

To view all socket connections (including those that are not active), use the –a option. The "LISTEN" status indicates that the connection listening for incoming connections is not active.

When you use the –e option, NETSTAT will display information about the computer's Ethernet card (NIC). This includes the number of bytes sent and received, as well as a breakdown of errors and discarded bytes. Figure 9-6 shows the

FIGURE 9-5

The NETSTAT
utility provides
information about
each active
connection

```
C:\>netstat

Active Connections

  Proto  Local Address        Foreign Address        State
  TCP    mailsrvr:1052        205.181.158.215:80     TIME_WAIT
  TCP    mailsrvr:1053        205.181.158.215:80     TIME_WAIT
  TCP    mailsrvr:1054        205.181.158.215:80     TIME_WAIT
  TCP    mailsrvr:1055        205.181.158.215:80     TIME_WAIT
  TCP    mailsrvr:1057        209.191.172.130:80     TIME_WAIT
  TCP    mailsrvr:1065        207.254.119.234:80     ESTABLISHED
  TCP    mailsrvr:1066        207.254.119.234:80     ESTABLISHED
  TCP    mailsrvr:1067        207.254.119.234:80     ESTABLISHED
  TCP    mailsrvr:1068        207.254.119.234:80     TIME_WAIT

C:\>
```

FIGURE 9-6

The –e
NETSTAT option
displays statistics
for the Ethernet
card (NIC)

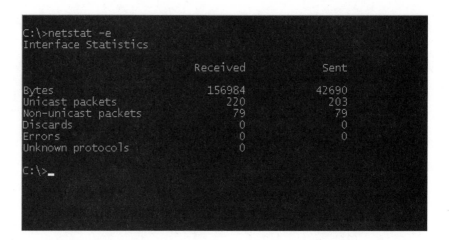

```
C:\>netstat -e
Interface Statistics

                                   Received              Sent

Bytes                                156984             42690
Unicast packets                         220               203
Non-unicast packets                      79                79
Discards                                  0                 0
Errors                                    0                 0
Unknown protocols                         0

C:\>_
```

results of the NETSTAT command run with the –e option. As you can see, there
appear to be no communication problems stemming from this Ethernet card.

By using the –i option, you can view the number of packets received (Ipkts),
errors received (Ierrs), packets sent (Opkts), errors sent (Oerrs) and network
collisions (Coll). This can help you pinpoint communication problems. For
example, if there are a high number of errors received from all remote hosts, the
problem may lie with your system. If errors are received from only one of the listed
hosts, chances are that the host itself is responsible. If the Opkts number is low and
the Oerrs number is high, there may be an I/O resource conflict within the current
computer. In this case, you will need to reconfigure some of the computer's
hardware.

Finally, by using the –r option, you can use the NETSTAT utility to view the
computer's current routing table. The output (Figure 9-7) contains the IP address,
Netmask, Gateway, Interface, and number of hops (Metric) for each connection.
This information can be used to pinpoint routing table errors.

exam
watch

*PING, ARP, and NETSTAT are TCP/IP tools and are therefore common to all
operating systems using TCP/IP.*

Trace Route

Route tracing utilities allow you to view the entire route between your computer and
a specified remote host. When you trace a route, your computer issues ICMP echo

The –r NETSTAT option displays the current machine's routing table

```
C:\>netstat -r

Route Table
===========================================================================
Interface List
0x1 ........................... MS TCP Loopback interface
0x2 ...00 02 55 70 0f a5 ...... IBM 10/100 EtherJet PCI Adapter
===========================================================================
Active Routes:
Network Destination        Netmask          Gateway       Interface  Metric
          0.0.0.0          0.0.0.0       172.17.2.1    172.17.2.212       1
        127.0.0.0        255.0.0.0       127.0.0.1       127.0.0.1       1
       172.17.2.0    255.255.255.0    172.17.2.212    172.17.2.212       1
     172.17.2.212  255.255.255.255       127.0.0.1       127.0.0.1       1
   172.17.255.255  255.255.255.255    172.17.2.212    172.17.2.212       1
        224.0.0.0        224.0.0.0    172.17.2.212    172.17.2.212       1
  255.255.255.255  255.255.255.255    172.17.2.212    172.17.2.212       1
===========================================================================

Active Connections

  Proto  Local Address          Foreign Address         State
  TCP    AMYT:1025              localhost:1051          ESTABLISHED
  TCP    AMYT:1051              localhost:1025          ESTABLISHED
  TCP    AMYT:1987              owa.corenetworks.com:nbsession  ESTABLISHED
  TCP    AMYT:2156              owa.corenetworks.com:1059  ESTABLISHED
  TCP    AMYT:2160              owa.corenetworks.com:1070  ESTABLISHED
  TCP    AMYT:2164              owa.corenetworks.com:1059  ESTABLISHED
  TCP    AMYT:2168              owa.corenetworks.com:1070  ESTABLISHED
  TCP    AMYT:4840              corebug.corenetworks.com:nbsession  ESTABLISHED
  TCP    AMYT:4844              home-v2.websys.aol.com:80  CLOSE_WAIT
  TCP    AMYT:4851              home-v2.websys.aol.com:80  CLOSE_WAIT
  TCP    AMYT:4855              home-v2.websys.aol.com:80  CLOSE_WAIT
  TCP    AMYT:4856              home-v2.websys.aol.com:80  CLOSE_WAIT
  TCP    AMYT:4858              home-v2.websys.aol.com:80  CLOSE_WAIT

C:\>
```

packets to the specified address and generates a report of the hops (computers, routers, and so on) between your computer and the host.

To trace a route in Windows 9*x*/NT/2000, use the **TRACERT** command:

```
tracert host
```

Where "host" is the IP address or domain name of the remote host. Figure 9-8 shows a typical result of the TRACERT command. As you can see, there were 14 hops between the local computer and the remote host. The asterisks indicate that the connection failed to reach the host. Using route tracing, you can also use the time information to locate slow data transfers (bottlenecks).

If you are using the Unix/Linux platform, you can trace a route using the **TRACEROUTE** command. In Novell Netware, use **IPTRACE**, and in OS/2, use **TRACERTE**.

9x/NT/2000   TRACERT
UNIX/LINUX   TRACEROUTE
NOVELL   IPTRACE
OS/2   TRACERTE

FIGURE 9-8

The TRACERT
utility displays the
number of hops,
as well as the
transmission time
to a remote host

```
C:\>tracert www.syngress.com

Tracing route to syngress.com [205.181.158.215]
over a maximum of 30 hops:

  1    24 ms    26 ms    24 ms  gw-5.accesscable.net [24.138.5.1]
  2    29 ms    28 ms    23 ms  CDR7-3.accesscable.net [24.138.7.3]
  3    26 ms    29 ms    28 ms  CDR7-153.accesscable.net [24.138.7.153]
  4    30 ms    30 ms    28 ms  205.150.223.33
  5    49 ms    46 ms    48 ms  119.at-5-0-0.XR2.MTL1.ALTER.NET [152.63.131.70]

  6    48 ms    48 ms    55 ms  292.at-2-0-0.TR2.MTL1.ALTER.NET [152.63.128.222]

  7    53 ms    59 ms    60 ms  117.at-6-1-0.TR2.NYC9.ALTER.NET [152.63.7.150]
  8    65 ms    65 ms    65 ms  186.ATM6-0.XR2.BOS1.ALTER.NET [152.63.20.201]
  9    61 ms    65 ms    65 ms  190.ATM7-0.GW3.BOS1.ALTER.NET [146.188.177.221]

 10     *         *         *    Request timed out.
 11    65 ms    65 ms    66 ms  lynn2-br1-s8-0-0.wharf.shore.net [207.244.95.13]

 12    64 ms    64 ms    66 ms  lynn2-cr2-f0-0-10.wharf.shore.net [207.244.95.68
]
 13    65 ms    66 ms    65 ms  infoboard.f0-0.shore.net [204.167.97.74]
 14    65 ms    66 ms    66 ms  syngress.com [205.181.158.215]

Trace complete.

C:\>_
```

exam
ⓦatch

PING and route tracing utilities use ICMP echo packets to initiate application-independent communication with a remote host.

Viewing TCP/IP Configuration

TCP/IP configuration utilities allow you to view and modify the current TCP/IP configuration, including the IP address, subnet mask, and network servers. To view the TCP/IP configuration in Windows 9x/NT/2000, use the **IPCONFIG** command at the command prompt. Results similar to those shown in Figure 9-9 will be displayed.

You can view more configuration details by using the /all option with the IPCONFIG command (Figure 9-10). To manually release an adapter's IP address, use the /release option, and to renew the IP address, use the /renew option.

Windows 9x includes a graphical utility for viewing the TCP/IP configuration, called **WINIPCFG**. To use this utility, enter WINIPCFG at the Run line. Results similar to those in Figure 9-11 will be displayed.

NT/2000/XP IPCONFIG
WIN 9x   WINIPCFG
LINUX/OS/2 IFCONFIG
NOVELL   CONFIG

FIGURE 9-9

The Windows IPCONFIG utility displays TCP/IP configuration information

```
C:\>ipconfig

Windows 98 IP Configuration

0 Ethernet adapter :

        IP Address. . . . . . . . . : 0.0.0.0
        Subnet Mask . . . . . . . . : 0.0.0.0
        Default Gateway . . . . . . :

1 Ethernet adapter :

        IP Address. . . . . . . . . : 0.0.0.0
        Subnet Mask . . . . . . . . : 0.0.0.0
        Default Gateway . . . . . . :

2 Ethernet adapter :

        IP Address. . . . . . . . . : 24.138.5.212
        Subnet Mask . . . . . . . . : 255.255.255.0
        Default Gateway . . . . . . : 24.138.5.1

C:\>_
```

To view or modify the TCP/IP configuration in Linux and OS/2, use the **IFCONFIG** utility at the command prompt. In Novell Netware, use **CONFIG** at the command prompt.

FIGURE 9-10

The ipconfig /all command displays detailed configuration information

```
2 Ethernet adapter :

        Description . . . . . . . . : USB/Ethernet Link
        Physical Address. . . . . . : 00-10-4C-11-B7-17
        DHCP Enabled. . . . . . . . : Yes
        IP Address. . . . . . . . . : 24.138.5.212
        Subnet Mask . . . . . . . . : 255.255.255.0
        Default Gateway . . . . . . : 24.138.5.1
        DHCP Server . . . . . . . . : 24.138.9.2
        Primary WINS Server . . . . :
        Secondary WINS Server . . . :
        Lease Obtained. . . . . . . : 04 22 01 7:24:57 AM
        Lease Expires . . . . . . . : 04 23 01 9:48:17 AM
```

FIGURE 9-11

The WINIPCFG
utility is a
graphical view of
the IPCONFIG
utility

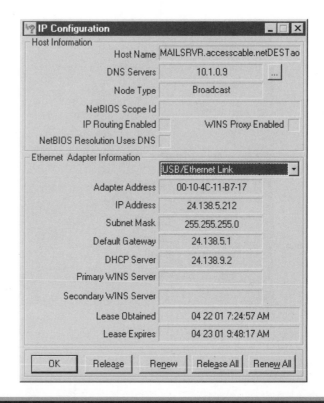

SCENARIO & SOLUTION

A good knowledge of the utilities previously described is important in identifying server problems. Therefore, you will likely see a number of questions about them on the Server+ exam. Before continuing with this chapter, test your knowledge by answering the following Scenario & Solution questions.

Which TCP/IP utility should you use to test for basic TCP/IP connectivity?	PING
How can you view the route between your computer and a remote host?	Use a route tracing utility (TRACERT, TRACEROUTE, IPTRACE or TRACERTE)
Which utility allows you to view recently used IP/MAC address relationships?	ARP
Which utility will display address and status data about a computer's current connections?	NETSTAT

Hardware Diagnostic Tools

Some computer and network problems cannot be pinpointed using connectivity utilities or experience alone. The following hardware tools can help you determine the exact location of a physical failure in the network or server.

Hardware Loopback Adapter

A hardware loopback adapter is a device that allows you to test the operational status of a computer's NIC, serial, or parallel ports. When plugged in, the adapter will indicate whether the port is able to transmit and receive data. A failed loopback test indicates the port itself, or its hardware configuration, is at fault.

Fox and Hound

The Fox and Hound system is a set of hardware tools used to perform continuity tests on phone and network cables. The "Fox" (also called a tone generator) is a hand-held device attached to one end of the cable, typically via alligator clips. The "Hound" (also called a tone locator or induction locator) is normally a probe-shaped device placed near the other end of the cable. The Fox will generate a tone that is sent along the cable. If the Hound receives the signal, you will hear the tone on the Hound's internal speaker. Failure of the tone to reach the far end indicates a break or fault in the cable.

The tone generator can also be used to locate the correct end of a cable. For example, it can be used to determine which cable in a group of many cables, such as a wiring closet, is attached to a particular outlet or computer.

TDR

A time domain reflectometer (TDR) sends a signal down the cable. When the signal reaches the end of the cable, it is reflected back to the TDR. The TDR then calculates the distance the signal traveled, before being reflected, by measuring the amount of time it took for the signal to be returned. If this distance is less than your overall cable length, it means there is a break in the cable at the specified distance from your location.

Oscilloscope

An oscilloscope is a device that can convert cable frequencies into graphical output. By attaching an oscilloscope to a cable and reading its output at different points along the cable, you can determine if there are crimps, breaks, or attenuation.

Interpreting Errors

The use of error messages in determining the cause of a problem was discussed earlier in the chapter. The nature of the error, along with your knowledge of the computer's subsystems or Operating System can help you pinpoint the problem. In fact, when errors are indicated by the server, they are often the first and best piece of information for pinpointing the problem.

Some errors, such as those generated by the OS, will automatically be displayed. Other errors are logged by the Operating System, and are not displayed automatically. When viewed, these logs can help you determine when and where a system error was generated. The following subsections discuss how to use errors and error logs to determine the cause of server problems.

Operating System Errors

In many cases, an Operating System error is the first sign of trouble in a computer system. These errors can be quite descriptive, leading you immediately to the cause of the problem. For example, the Windows error "A: is not accessible" indicates there is no disk in the floppy drive, or that a disk is present, but is unreadable. Other error messages are equally helpful. For example, if you receive a missing Operating System error, you can use your knowledge of the boot process to narrow down the problem to a corrupt master boot record, a failed hard drive, or a corrupt system file. A "bad command or filename" error indicates a missing file or typo. Some error messages will even indicate a course of action, such as "Incorrect Printer Driver, please Install Correct Driver."

Unfortunately, some error messages are more cryptic and do not immediately lead you to the source of the problem. For example, if you receive the message "Error Code 12452," you will likely have to look in the manufacturer's documentation to determine what a 12452 error code means. Linux machines typically give the following message when an error occurs "Internal Server Error. The server encountered an internal error or misconfiguration and was unable to complete your request." Any time you receive an error you do not understand, look for a description in the system's Help files or in the manufacturer's documentation. Failing that, visit the manufacturer's Web site, or look the error code up elsewhere on the Internet.

Critical Errors

For the purposes of this chapter, a critical error refers to an event that halts the operation of an entire system or a currently running application. Critical errors include General Protection Faults and Illegal Operations in Windows and ABENDs (ABnormal ENDs) in Novell Netware. Some critical errors cause the computer to lock up, giving no indication about the cause of the problem.

If the error halts an application, close the application and look at the system's error logs (discussed next) to pinpoint the root of the problem. If the error halts the entire system, use the shutdown procedures described later in the chapter. The text accompanying the error can typically be used to locate the source of the problem. If the error text seems vague, refer to the manufacturer's documentation or Web site.

Error Logs

Many Operating Systems keep event logs helpful in reviewing recent activities. When a problem occurs, you can search the event logs to determine when the problem first started or which file or subsystem is at fault.

Windows NT/2000   Windows NT and 2000 include a utility called the Event Log service. This service starts automatically when Windows loads, and keeps three separate activity logs; a system log, application log, and security log. The system log records system-related events, such as driver loading and display changes. The application log records application-specific activities, such as loading, saving, and file access. The security log is available only to system administrators, and records events such as logon attempts and failures, in addition to network resource access attempts.

Each logged event is accompanied by the date and time, as well as the event type (error, warning, information, success or failure notations). In the event of a problem, you can use the Event Viewer to read these logs and track the events and tasks leading up to the problem. To open the Event Viewer, select Start | Programs | Administrative Tools | Event Viewer.

In addition to reading the event logs, you can use the Event Viewer to set the log size, save logs, clear full logs, and select what happens when the log becomes full. In most cases, older events are replaced in the logs by newer events as they occur.

However, you can configure the log service to display an error message when the log is full. This allows you to save the log before old items are overwritten with new items.

Novell Netware   Netware includes an error log called SYS$LOG.ERR, which keeps track of non-critical errors and warnings in the system. The log is kept automatically by the OS, and can be viewed as a regular text file.

Unix/Linux   By default, Linux creates several logs of system activities, including the boot.log, cron, and netconf.log. These logs do not pinpoint errors, but will log all activities associated with the specified system (system boot process, network configuration, and so on). If you are familiar with the normal system processes, it's easier to spot errors in the log.

OS/2   The OS/2 error log file is called SYSLOG, and is enabled by entering the following lines in the CONFIG.SYS file:

```
run=c:\os2\epw.exe on
run=c:\os2\eprout.exe -1
```

where "c:\os2" is the path for the epw.exe and eprout.exe files.

Using Previously Written Documentation

In order to maintain a smoothly running system, it is imperative you keep adequate documentation of everything from computer specifications and recent upgrades to a list of known issues and resolved problems concerning each server on your network. When something goes wrong, this documentation can be an invaluable resource for pinpointing and resolving problems.

Incorrect Configuration

Documentation is particularly helpful when a computer has been configured incorrectly. With a large group of support personnel, it may be difficult to determine who was the last to configure a certain server. Determining who is responsible is not the same thing as finding someone to blame when something goes wrong. Support personnel often configure servers and network devices in a unique way, without sharing that information with the rest of the group. By documenting the modifications to the server, you can determine what has changed and whether that change is the cause of a problem. If the person responsible for configuring this server or network device is unavailable, you will have the existing documentation to determine what was changed, without having to contact the person.

All documentation should include the technician's name, as well as the date the upgrade or modification took place. This is helpful in establishing a chronological order of events, which can be traced in the event of problems.

Future Administrators or Engineers

Documentation provides a set of instructions for the next administrator or engineer. Each network administrator or engineer has countless secrets they keep to themselves regarding the network they support. Every day they are configuring, adding, and modifying servers, workstations, printers, and devices on the network. Each one of these experiences may require custom configuration or troubleshooting in order to be installed correctly. Network support personnel can spend hours, if not days, getting something to work correctly, yet they rarely spend the time documenting their findings for future use. If they leave the company, this information goes with them. The next administrator or engineer may find himself spending as much or more time than the first person trying to get the same problem resolved. If the previous person had documented his efforts, it would have made the second person's job much easier.

Device Inventory

Proper documentation includes an accurate inventory or record of each device on the network. Documenting devices on the network gives you a running record replete with countless details about these devices. For example, you can document the amount of physical memory a system has, its hard disk capacity, IP address, processor speed, MAC address, and serial numbers. This information can be stored in a centralized database for all computer support personnel to use. Many companies are very strict about keeping accurate, up-to-date information for their network. It is strongly recommended you adhere to these documentation standards. If no standards currently exist, it is urged you start a project to inventory the network using as much information as possible. You will be surprised how often you consult this information when it comes to locating devices, determining which need upgrades, or when performing remote managing and software distribution.

Using External Resources to Resolve the Problem

Once you have determined the cause of the server problems, you must generate a course of action for resolving the difficulty. In many cases, the solution may be obvious, such as replacing a bad cable. In other cases, additional solutions may be required, such as a software patch, registry change, or special configuration. The following subsections describe some valuable troubleshooting resources.

TechNet

TechNet is a huge searchable database of all of Microsoft's product-related articles and documentation, and is available on CD to certified members. Many TechNet articles deal with support issues, such as locating and resolving problems, tuning a system, or creating specialized configurations. If you find a problem with a Microsoft product, there is a good chance someone else has already found and addressed the same problem in TechNet.

Manufacturer Web Sites

The Internet is a valuable resource for troubleshooting. It allows users to find up-to-the-minute information on both hardware and software, and uncover answers to common (or sometimes obscure) problems. When faced with a problem you cannot diagnose, or when looking for external resources (such as a software patch), check the manufacturer's Web site. In addition to discussing patches and troubleshooting information, most manufacturer sites suggest ways of resolving common problems, often listing technical support e-mail addresses and phone numbers as well.

Resource Kits and Documentation

Resource kits provide technical information about your Operating System unavailable anywhere else. Resource kits contain additional documentation on the OS too detailed to cover in standard documentation. Whenever you are faced with a problem you cannot solve, check the resource kit—your problem (and its solution) may already be documented there.

Trade Publications and White Papers

Other excellent sources of information are trade publications and white papers. These documents provide valuable information on current techniques and new practices that often cannot be acquired anywhere else. Look for these on the Internet, particularly on manufacturer Web sites, or get them by contacting the manufacturer directly.

Telephone Technical Support

Often, after you have exhausted your resources, such as vendor Web sites, resource kits, and documentation, it is common to open up a technical support incident with the vendor to solve the problem. Chances are, support personnel have already encountered the specific problem with their own software/hardware and documented available fixes. A problem that baffles you may be a very common tech support call for these professionals. To improve the speed and accuracy of your technical support incident, make sure you have the following ready to assist the support technician:

- Details concerning the hardware and software environment, such as the operating system you are running
- Version numbers of affected hardware or software
- Serial numbers
- A detailed account of the problem
- Troubleshooting steps taken so far, and their results

Vendor CDs

Vendor-provided CDs that come with hardware and software are very important references for installation, configuration, and troubleshooting. Many technicians overlook these CDs and spend countless hours troubleshooting on their own. You should make it a practice to consult vendor CDs before product installation, as the CD may provide pre-installation tips and warnings critical for smooth installation and operation. The vendor-provided CDs may also have a technical information base, similar to Microsoft's TechNet, with a number of common problems and their resolutions. Other CDs have tutorials, documentation, and software patches.

Shutting Down the Server

In some cases, to properly troubleshoot a server, it is necessary to turn the server off. The shut down of a server can have extensive ramifications on a network, so it must be done with a great deal of planning and preparation. If the server provides a non-essential service (such as an e-mail or application server), inform all network users of the pending shut down, and make sure they save all related work. If the server provides security, or manages the network, inform all users that the network will be temporarily unavailable. Have them save all work and log off. Next, follow the procedure outlined for the appropriate OS that follows. If the server hangs, or otherwise does not shut down, use the computer's power button to manually turn the computer off.

Windows 9x/NT/2000

After preparing the network's users, shut down a Windows system by clicking the Start button in the Windows taskbar. Select Shut Down. When prompted on the confirmation screen, select Shut Down and click OK. If any users are still logged in, you will be informed and given an opportunity to continue or cancel the shut down procedure. Once you have confirmed the shut down procedure, wait until the server displays the message "It is now safe to shutdown." Use the power button to turn the computer off. Note that in many newer computers, the OS will turn the power off automatically once Windows is shut down.

If you intend to restart the computer instead, select Start | Shut Down and select Restart on the confirmation screen. Windows will automatically shut itself down and reboot. If the computer is locked up, press CTRL-ALT-DEL. The Task Manager window will open. In Windows 9x, press CTRL-ALT-DEL again to restart the computer. In Windows NT/2000, select Shutdown, then select Shutdown and Restart.

Novell Netware

To shut down a Netware server, use the DOWN and EXIT commands at the System Console. The appropriate steps for accessing the console and performing the shut down procedure are explained in Exercise 9-2.

Shutting Down a Netware Server

1. Use ALT-ESC on the keyboard to toggle through each open application, shutting down each in turn.

2. Access the System Console by pressing CTRL-ESC on the keyboard. A list of current screens will appear. Select the System Console by entering its number and pressing ENTER on the keyboard.

3. A command prompt will be displayed. Enter the following command:

   ```
   down
   ```

   The server will properly shut down all active modules.

4. When the server has closed all open modules, a "Type 'exit' to return to dos" message will appear. Enter the following command:

   ```
   exit
   ```

5. The DOS interface will be displayed. Turn the server off using the computer's power button.

To restart a Netware server, enter the RESTART SERVER command at the prompt, rather than EXIT.

Unix/Linux

To shut down a Linux server, follow the steps outlined in Exercise 9-3.

Shutting Down a Linux Server

1. Enter the following command at the command prompt:

   ```
   shutdown -h now
   ```

2. Wait until you see the message "Safe to Power off or Press any key to reboot."

3. Use the power button on the computer to turn it off.

To restart a Linux server, use the –r option (rather than –h) with the SHUTDOWN command. You can delay the shutdown or restart option by replacing the NOW option with a number value. Finally, you can broadcast a message to any remaining users by adding it in quotes to the end of the SHUTDOWN command. For example, to restart the server in 30 seconds and broadcast a warning to all users, enter the following command:

```
shutdown -r +30 "System is restarting. Please log off."
```

OS/2

To shut down an OS/2 server, click Task List in the filebar and select Shutdown System (or right-click the background and select Shut down). Click OK when prompted to confirm the shutdown procedure. Use the power button to turn the server off. Like Windows, you can restart a hung OS/2 machine using the CTRL-ALT-DEL key combination.

Remote Troubleshooting

Remote troubleshooting refers to the ability to troubleshoot and resolve computer problems without having to physically sit at that computer. In many cases, you can use one server on a network to troubleshoot another server on the network. There are a number of services available for remote troubleshooting, such as Windows Remote Access Service (RAS) or third-party applications. These types of services provide the interface and tools for managing, configuring, and troubleshooting remote computers.

It is not necessary, however, to install a sophisticated remote service application to gain remote access to a computer. All that is required is a communication link between computers and the appropriate communications protocol. Most Operating Systems can be accessed remotely using the Point-to-Point Protocol (PPP), Simple Network Management Protocol (SNMP), Serial Line Internet Protocol (SLIP), or Telnet. The remote machine must also be configured to allow remote access.

When troubleshooting a remote computer, use the local machine to access the remote machine, using the LAN, WAN, Internet, or modem. Once you have access to the remote machine, you can use the diagnostic utilities described earlier in the chapter to determine the nature of the problem. You can also access the remote computer's OS and files as if you were sitting in front of that computer. For example, you can use a local computer to view and change OS configuration files or remove a problem application from a remote computer, as if you were actually using the remote computer.

The procedures for setting up remote access, and the protocol commands used to manage and configure the remote machine are beyond the scope of the Server+ exam. However, make sure you are familiar with the concept of remote troubleshooting, as well as the wake on LAN and remote alert features described next.

Wake on LAN

Because remote troubleshooting is such a valuable procedure for system administrators, a number of remote access features have made their way into the computer industry. Some computers contain a "wake on LAN" feature that allows administrators to turn a remote computer on so they can troubleshoot it or perform maintenance. For example, suppose an administrator needs to run a nightly anti-virus scan on all network workstations. Rather than have all users keep their workstations turned on all night, the administrator can wake up the workstations, perform the anti-virus scan, then turn the workstations off, all from a remote location.

To make use of the wake on LAN feature, the remote computer's motherboard and NIC must be designed to support it and the computer must be accessed via the network (rather than a modem). When enabled, the remote computer's NIC uses minimal power (typically supplied by a battery) to monitor incoming traffic for a "wake up" packet. Using remote management software, the local computer sends the wake up packet, which is passed through the remote NIC to the computer's motherboard. The motherboard then initiates the boot process, as if the power button had been physically turned on.

Remote Alert

Another feature that can help in remote troubleshooting is remote alerts. Remote alerts are generated by the remote computer, and are typically sent to a specified computer via the network or a modem. The alert can also be sent via phone lines to a phone or pager, alerting system administrators to a problem condition. Remote alerts are typically used to warn of hardware overheating, failed processes, or security breaches.

Identifying Bottlenecks

A bottleneck is a service or component that causes an entire system to slow down. For example, suppose a server has insufficient RAM to process requests as fast as they are received. In this case, the lack of RAM is causing the entire system to wait, therefore the lack of RAM is considered a bottleneck. Network bottlenecks can occur in network devices (such as routers), network cabling, individual workstations, or the server itself.

This section will focus on server bottlenecks and how to detect and resolve them. That is, the focus is on bottlenecks *not* caused by network devices, cabling, or workstations. Each subsection to follow describes a server component that may be responsible for a bottleneck. Within each of these subsections is a discussion about the utilities you can use to pinpoint or rule out various component that might be the cause of the problem. In most cases, once you have identified the component causing the bottleneck, you will need to upgrade, replace, or reconfigure that component. The procedures for replacing components, resolving misconfigurations, and performing upgrades are described later in the chapter.

Pinpoint the Server

When you suspect a bottleneck, narrow down the source of the problem by using one of the route tracing utilities described earlier (TRACERT, TRACEROUTE, IPTRACE, or TRACERTE). This can give you valuable information about which network segment is causing the delay. If the utility uncovers delays, you will have narrowed down your search, especially if multiple route traces all point to delays involving one particular server. You can also use the NETSTAT utility to view the number of errors (if any) being generated by a particular computer on the network. When communication errors occur, data must be present, resulting in extra network traffic and overall performance degradation.

on the
Job

A bottleneck is not a network or system failure, but rather a decrease in speed. For this reason, an error message usually won't appear. In most cases, you will be alerted to a bottleneck when users start complaining a particular service, or the entire network, is running slow.

Network I/O

Once you have identified the server as the source of the bottleneck, identify or rule out the server's network I/O as the cause of the problem. That is, look to see whether the server's ability to transmit or receive data is at fault. If so, you may need to replace or reconfigure the NIC (these procedures are described in more detail later in the chapter). It may also help improve performance if you remove all unused protocols from the system. This decreases the amount of RAM reserved for network I/O operations, which can lead to an overall system improvement.

The TCP/IP ARP utility can be helpful in determining whether the NIC is at fault. If the server's receive queue is quite full, it means data is being sent to the server faster than it can be passed by the NIC to the server's CPU for processing. On the other hand, a full transmit queue can indicate the server is processing and trying to transmit data faster than the network can accept it. In this case, look elsewhere on the network for the source of the problem. Run the NETSTAT –e command as well to determine if the NIC is experiencing input or output errors. The following are some additional OS-specific tools you can use to determine whether a server's network I/O is the source of a bottleneck.

Windows NT/2000 and OS/2

If you are using a Windows or OS/2 system, you can use the Performance Monitor utility to detect network I/O problems. The Performance Monitor allows you to view charts, logs, and alerts pertaining to system components such as the processor, RAM, hard disk, and virtual memory. To view live data for the Network Interface object (NIC), follow the steps in Exercise 9-4. Note that these steps are specific to Windows NT 4.0 and that the menu options will differ slightly for Windows 2000 and OS/2.

EXERCISE 9-4

Using Performance Monitor to View Live Network Interface Statistics

1. Select Start | Programs | Administrative Tools | Performance Monitor.

2. From the View menu, select Report.

3. From the Edit menu, select Add to Report.

4. Select Network Interface from the Object drop-down list. A list of NIC-related measurements will appear in the Counter box.

5. Select a measurement to monitor, for example "Bytes Received/sec" and click Add.

6. Repeat Step 5 for each measurement you wish to view.

7. Click Done to close the Add to Report dialog box. The on-screen values will be updated continuously to reflect the current status.

You can also use the Performance Monitor to keep a historical data log. Select the Performance Monitor's Log view, select a name and location for the log and start logging. Later, you can use the Performance Monitor to open the log and view historical network activity.

When using the Performance Monitor to detect bottlenecks, keep an eye on the Output Queue Length, as this will indicate if there is data waiting to be sent. If so, it means the network itself, not the server's NIC, is at fault. Also, keep your eye on the statistics indicating the number of bytes and packets received. If this number starts to get higher than normal, or starts to approach the bandwidth, it may indicate the server is reaching its capacity, and may require an additional NIC to share the load. Finally, look for inbound and outbound errors, which may indicate a sporadically functioning NIC.

Novell Netware

Novell Netware includes a performance monitoring utility, called MONITOR. This utility will retrieve and display statistics about the server, including CPU usage,

RAM usage, hard disk information, and NIC status. To run MONITOR.NLM, place the following entry at the end of the AUTOEXEC.NCF file, or enter it at the command prompt:

```
load c:\monitor.nlm
```

Where c:\ is the path in which the monitor.nlm file resides.

The initial screen will display general information, such as the CPU utilization, number of current disk requests and current connections. If the number of current disk requests or connections is higher than normal, it indicates heavy network traffic. This may suggest the current server cannot handle the load, but it does not specifically indicate a server network I/O problem.

To view specific details about the network I/O, select LAN/WAN from the activity list at the bottom of the screen. Choose the appropriate network device from the list (if there is more than one). Statistics for that device will be displayed, such as the number of packets transmitted and received, and the number of failed transmissions and receipts. Check the "Receive discarded, no available buffers" number. In this case, a buffer is a queue used to hold incoming data until the server can process it. This number should be 0. If not, you may need to increase the NIC's Packet Receive Buffers (PRBs). If you are already using the maximum number of PRBs, you may need to look at other ways to speed up the server so it processes incoming data more quickly.

Unix/Linux

Linux does not have a comprehensive performance monitoring utility, but rather, includes a set of utility commands used to monitor various parts of the system. The NFSSTAT command will provide you with a summary of the server's I/O activities, including number of rejected calls, retransmissions, and time-outs. All of these activities mean data had to be resent, resulting in increased network traffic.

Memory Performance

If you still suspect the server as the cause of a bottleneck, but have ruled out the server's network I/O performance, focus your attention on the server's RAM. A lack of RAM will cause a general decrease in server performance, and can use up more

CPU resources than necessary. Furthermore, if the server "misses" incoming data because the RAM cannot keep up, the data will have to be resent, resulting in greater overall network traffic. A basic rule of thumb with RAM is that more is better. However, before you install more RAM in the system, use the following utilities to determine if the RAM is really the problem. If so, use the procedures described later in this chapter to add more RAM to the server.

Windows NT/2000 and OS/2

Again, you can use the Performance Monitor utility in Windows and OS/2 to observe memory usage. First, select the Memory object, and add the appropriate memory statistics. In particular, pay attention to the "% Committed Bytes in use," "Available Bytes," and "Page Faults/sec," as these indicate the amount of free/used virtual memory and how often data is retrieved from the swap file instead of from main memory. If the virtual memory is reaching its capacity, you may need to increase the size of the swap file (or better yet, add more RAM to the system). If the computer is experiencing excessive page faults, you should consider increasing the amount of RAM in the system.

Novell Netware

If you are using a Netware system, use the System Resources option within the MONITOR utility to view memory usage statistics. This section will display information such as the total system memory and amount of free memory. Pay particular attention to the "Total Cache Buffers" information, as this indicates the amount of free memory. A value below 20 to 40 percent indicates low resources, and you should consider adding more RAM to the system. You can use the Resource Utilization option in the MONITOR utility to view more detailed information about how the system's memory is being used.

Unix/Linux

In a Linux system, use the VMSTAT command to view virtual memory statistics, including the total amount of virtual memory, number of page faults, and amount of data being swapped into virtual memory. Excessive swapping indicates you need more virtual memory, and excessive page faults indicate you should add more RAM to the system.

To view details about RAM-specific memory usage, use the SAR command with the –wpgr option. The SAR utility will report statistics such as the number of transfers into memory per second, number of RAM pages available to user processes and number of transfers from RAM to virtual memory. A high instance of swap-outs indicates excessive use of virtual memory.

Processor Performance

If the server's bottleneck is not being caused by a lack of memory, focus your attention on the server's processor. If the processor is inadequate, the server will be inadequate, and the network will suffer for it. Use the following OS utilities to monitor the processor's performance, and if necessary, upgrade or replace the processor, or add additional processors to the system (if the motherboard allows it).

Windows NT/2000 and OS/2

Use the Performance Monitor to view CPU usage in Windows and OS/2. Select the Processor object, and pay particular attention to the "% Processor Time" statistic. This number indicates how busy the processor is. By itself, however, the % Processor Time value does not indicate a CPU bottleneck. The CPU can run at 99%, but as long as it keeps up with system requests, it will not cause a bottleneck. If, however, a high Processor Time is accompanied by a large data count in the processor's queue, it means the processor can't keep up with requests, and must queue data until sufficient resources are available.

Novell Netware

In a Netware system, use the MONITOR utility to view processor usage, such as the percentage of time the processor is busy (Utilization). If the processor Utilization remains above 80%, consider replacing the CPU with a faster one, or adding another CPU to the system.

Unix/Linux

Linux includes a processor monitoring utility, called PS. By entering the PS command at a command prompt, you can view the current processes, including current state, priority, amount of virtual memory required, and CPU utilization. Be on the lookout for processes that have the status "S" or "X", which indicate the process is waiting for I/O resources or available memory, respectively, before it can be executed. Be aware of processes that use up excessive processor time, as indicated in the "TIME" column. If these processes are causing other processes to suffer, stop them (if possible), or assign them a lower priority.

Disk I/O

Hard disk I/O is one of the slowest activities within a computer system. That is, one of the slowest parts of any computer operation is the time it takes to retrieve data from or write data to the hard disk. If a network server is required to make a large number of disk reads/writes to fulfill user requests, the hard disk itself may become a serious bottleneck. One of the most obvious indications of disk activity is the hard drive light on the front of the server. However, a busy hard drive is not always a sign of a bottleneck. That is, a hard drive can be busy 100% of the time, but as long as it is writing and retrieving data as fast as it is requested, the hard drive is not creating a bottleneck.

When the server has a disk I/O bottleneck, consider using the RAID techniques described in Chapter 2 to add additional hard drives to the system for load balancing. If the disk is performing excessive I/O processes for memory page swapping, consider adding more RAM to the system (thereby reducing the amount of disk I/O caused by accessing disk-resident information in the swap file).

Before troubleshooting a disk I/O problem, determine whether the hard disk is really the root of the problem. What follows are some utilities you can use to monitor disk I/O activity and determine an appropriate course of action. In systems with more than one hard drive, pay particular attention to the distribution of activity among the disks. For example, if all users in a network need to access files on one disk, but not another, one disk will be quite busy, while the other goes largely unused. In this case, moving some of the commonly accessed files to one of the relatively idle disks can help divide the workload and speed up disk I/O operations.

Windows NT/2000 and OS/2

The Windows and OS/2 Performance Monitor can display statistics about the hard disk activity in the system. Monitor the % Disk Time value. If it runs consistently higher than 60%, you may have a hard disk bottleneck. Another indication of a disk I/O bottleneck is a high or full disk queue. This indicates the disk is receiving requests faster than it can handle them.

Novell Netware

The Netware MONITOR utility can display information about disk activity. A high "Current disk requests" value indicates the server is receiving a large number of requests to read from/write to the disk, and may allow you to pinpoint the disk as the bottleneck.

Unix/Linux

In a Linux system, use the IOSTAT command to monitor the volume of disk activity. The SAR –d command will provide you with a report of each disk in the system, and can be handy in determining whether one disk is handling the majority of I/O requests.

SCENARIO & SOLUTION

This section contains a lot of detailed information about monitoring server components using different operating systems. Use this information to answer the following Scenario & Solution questions.	
Which utility should I use to monitor the…	
Network I/O in Windows NT?	Performance Monitor
Memory performance in OS/2?	Performance Monitor
Processor performance in Linux?	The PS command
Disk I/O in Netware?	MONITOR

CERTIFICATION OBJECTIVE 9.04

Identify and Correct Misconfigurations

TCP/IP configurations are a common source of server connectivity problems. If a server is unreachable, or is intermittently accessible, it may have an incorrectly configured NIC or IP address. As with other network problems, start by narrowing down the problem to a single computer. For example, if a server is inaccessible from one workstation, try to access the server from another workstation. If the server is still inaccessible, focus your attention on the server rather than the workstations.

When a server resource appears unavailable, use the PING utility to determine whether it has basic TCP/IP connectivity. This will help you determine whether the problem lies with the server itself, or with the resource being accessed. For example, suppose users cannot retrieve a particular file from the server. A successful PING in this case indicates the server can communicate, so you should focus your attention on the file in question or on the server's hard disk. An unsuccessful PING, however, indicates the server does not have connectivity, so you should focus your attention on the server's network I/O.

If you suspect a network I/O problem, view the server's TCP/IP configuration using one of the configuration utilities described earlier in the chapter (IPCONFIG, WINIPCFG, IFCONFIG, or CONFIG). First, ensure the server's IP address and subnet mask match those specified on the workstations attempting to connect to it. You can change the server's IP address and subnet mask using the Network Properties applet in Windows, the LOAD INETCFG command in Netware or the IFCONFIG command in Linux and OS/2.

If the TCP/IP addressing is not the problem, focus your attention on the server's NIC. The ARP –e command described earlier can indicate Ethernet card communication errors. If the NIC has no (or very low) received and sent bytes, check the configuration of the NIC to ensure it is being used properly by the server. For example, make certain it is using the proper computer resources (IRQ, I/O address) and ensure a proper driver is loaded. If the NIC is properly configured, consider that the NIC itself may simply not be working. Use the procedures described in the next section to replace the NIC. The steps for identifying and resolving TCP/IP misconfigurations are summarized in Exercise 9-5

Identifying and Resolving TCP/IP Configuration Problems

1. Use PING to determine basic ICP/IP connectivity. If the PING is successful, look elsewhere for the source of the problem. If the PING is not successful, proceed to Step 2.

2. View the server's TCP/IP configuration. If the IP address or subnet mask is incorrect, enter the appropriate address. If the IP address and subnet mask are not at fault, proceed to Step 3.

3. Use ARP –e to view statistics about the NIC. If necessary, resolve the NIC's hardware configuration or replace the NIC.

SCENARIO & SOLUTION

Test your knowledge of the concepts presented in this section by answering the following Scenario & Solution questions.

The server is experiencing connectivity problems and you suspect a TCP/IP misconfiguration. What does it indicate when…	
You can successfully PING the server?	The server has connectivity and you should look elsewhere for the source of the problem.
You cannot successfully PING the server?	The server does not have TCP/IP connectivity. Focus on the server to resolve the problem.
The server's IP address is incorrect?	You should configure the server with the correct address. This will likely resolve the problem.
The server's IP address is correct?	The IP address is not at fault. You should focus on the server's NIC configuration.
The NIC's hardware configuration is incorrect?	Enter the appropriate hardware settings for the NIC.
The NIC's hardware configuration is correct?	You may need to replace the NIC.

CERTIFICATION OBJECTIVE 9.05

Hardware, Software, and Virus Problems

In some cases, server problems occur because the server itself is simply not working properly. Consider a problem in which workstations cannot access files on a file server. While this may be caused by a connectivity problem, it may also be the result of a faulty hard drive on the server. Furthermore, problems accessing a network service, such as network mail, may be caused by a faulty application on the server, rather than an inability to establish a server connection. This section discusses how to determine when the server's hardware or software is at fault, and how to resolve hardware and software problems when they occur. In the following subsections, a hardware problem is considered to include the device as well as its resources, configuration files, and device drivers. Software problems include applications, OSs, and utilities.

Most hardware devices can be used by a number of applications, and vice versa. Therefore, you can narrow the search by trying to access more than one type of device from the suspect application or using more than one application to access the suspect device. Suppose, for example, you are unable to access the server's hard drive using a particular application. Use a different application to access the hard drive. If it works, you can conclude the hard drive is physically sound and turn your attention to the configuration or reinstallation of the original application. If, however, the hard drive does not work in another program, use the original program to access another device, such as the printer.

Continue combining applications with hardware devices to try to rule out one or the other. Keep in mind that this method will not always lead you to a definitive conclusion. For example, suppose a printer can't be accessed by any application. Although it would appear the printer is at fault, it might be that each application is set to access the wrong printer by default. This is a software, not a hardware, problem.

Once you have followed these procedures and determined the device or subsystem at fault, you should restart the server using the procedures described earlier in the chapter. In many cases, restarting the computer releases resources that a device or application needs to use which may be currently tied up with another device or application. Restarting the computer also forces the computer to reestablish the presence of existing devices and clear information out of its memory.

Hardware Problems

If you have determined that a server problem is hardware-related, either using the previous procedures, or when troubleshooting a bottleneck or misconfiguration problem, you must next turn your attention to finding the device at fault. If restarting the computer doesn't solve the problem, determine if this symptom is familiar to you. For example, if you know the NIC connection often comes loose from a particular computer, you should look there first when the NIC stops working. If the problem is unfamiliar to you, use the information in this section to help you further narrow your search.

Locating the Failed Device

Always check the connection of a suspect device to the computer, and make sure the device is properly configured to use system resources and a driver. If the answer is not apparent, you need to focus your search on the components of the failed system or subsystem. For example, if there is no computer display, there is no need to check the components of the network subsystem.

When examining a subsystem, always start with the parts that are easiest to access or see. In the example of a nonfunctioning display, check the monitor before you take the computer apart to inspect the adapter card. For any subsystem, start with the most accessible part and work your way into the computer. A good knowledge of the system's components will help you determine which devices belong to which subsystems. It is especially important to note whether the device is local or accessed through the network. A problem using a printer, for example, could actually be caused by the computer's inability to make a network connection.

If everything in the current system *appears* to be okay (in other words, everything is powered on and properly attached and there are no resource conflicts), suspect the devices themselves. To identify or rule out a device as the cause of the problem, swap it with another. Take a spare component (one that you know functions correctly) and use it in place of the suspect component. If the new component works, you have discovered the problem.

If the new component doesn't work, there must be a problem elsewhere. In this case, don't assume the original component works; it, plus another component, could have failed at the same time. Install the original component in another system to determine its functionality. For example, assume a video system has a bad adapter card *and* a bad monitor. You swap the monitor with another and get no response, so you assume the monitor is not the cause of the problem and reattach it. When you get the adapter working, there is still no video, because you are using the original bad monitor. Always swap one component at a time. To take another example, suppose a computer can't use a particular scanner. You switch ports, swap the cable, and swap the scanner, all at the same time. If the computer is then able to scan correctly, you will not be able to determine whether it was the port, the cable, or the scanner that caused the problem in the first place.

Again, working your way into the computer, swap out each component with a working one. This includes the problematic device itself and any cables attached to it. If the device is external, try plugging it into another port or try attaching a different device to the suspect port. If the device is internal, switch it to another expansion slot.

If you have tested the attachment and configuration of each device and still have not solved the problem, look at the underlying hardware within the computer itself. That is, test components that are responsible for the computer's performance as a whole, including the BIOS, the CMOS battery, the processor, RAM, and the system board.

Replacing/Swapping Suspect or Failed Devices

When replacing or swapping hardware components, always ensure the computer's power is turned off. If the device is external, simply unplug the device and plug in the new device. Many servers contain removable hard drives that can be pulled out and replaced without having to open the computer case. Note that when replacing hot swappable devices, such as FireWire or USB, the computer does not have to be turned off.

If you are replacing an internal component, make sure you prevent any Electrostatic Discharge (ESD) from getting into the computer by discharging static from your body. Do this by using a properly grounded wrist strap. Locate the device and gently remove any cables, noting their position and any markings that will help you reconnect it properly. Remove all screws being used to secure the component to the computer chassis.

Gently remove the component. If you are removing a drive, simply slide the drive out of the bay. To remove expansion cards, grasp the card by its top corners and pull gently (you may have to rock the card slightly from end to end to remove it from its slot). To remove memory modules, push out on the retaining clips at each end.

Install devices by reversing the uninstallation procedures. Follow the steps outlined in Exercise 9-6 to replace an internal hard drive.

EXERCISE 9-6

Replacing an Internal Hard Drive

1. Shut down the computer and discharge yourself by wearing an ESD strap.

2. Open the computer case. This procedure will vary, depending on the computer itself, and may involve removing retaining screws, pressing retaining clips, or simply sliding the case off.

3. Locate the hard drive and remove the power and ribbon cables. Make sure you grasp the plastic connectors, not the wires themselves. If the connector doesn't come out easily, try gently rocking it lengthwise from side to side (never front to back) while you pull it out.

4. Remove the retaining screws that attach the drive to the drive bay (these are usually located on the sides of the drive).

5. Slide the drive out of the drive bay.

6. To install a hard drive, reverse the preceding steps, ensuring the red stripe on the ribbon cable is lined up with pin 1 on the drive.

Software Problems

If you have determined the problem is software related, and rebooting the computer did not resolve it, you should turn your attention to the configuration of the application. Most applications or utilities include a Preferences, Tools, or Options feature, through which you can configure its operation and the devices it can access.

You can also try uninstalling the application, then reloading it. Some application installations contain errors that affect only one or a small number of its functions. Use the Uninstall utility that came with the application rather than deleting the program's files.

Check to make sure the computer meets the application's minimum requirements. It is possible the computer simply will not support the application. Check the application manufacturer's Web site for patches and updates. Perhaps this user is experiencing a problem caused by a flaw in the application itself. Most manufacturers release patches that can remedy discovered problems.

Viruses

Some viruses cause telltale results that should immediately alert you to their presence (see the From the Classroom sidebar). For example, sporadic results, nonsense error messages, and elaborate auto-executions are often caused by viruses. Unnecessary or excessive disk access and excessive processor/memory or other resource usage can also indicate the presence of a virus.

FROM THE CLASSROOM

No, the Computer Is Not Possessed...

Computer viruses are no fun to deal with and can often be very frustrating. Although some viruses are simply destructive, others are quite creative and, if they didn't result in computer damage and lost files and time, would probably be considered awfully clever. Take, for example, the I Love You virus. This virus is transmitted via a Visual Basic e-mail attachment with the subject line "I Love You." When the attachment is opened, the I Love You virus destroys multimedia files, such as JPG and MP3 files, then sends itself to every user in your e-mail address book. Pretty clever.

Virus creators have also come up with a number of interesting activation methods. Some viruses are activated when their host

application is activated; others are time-sensitive. For example, the Michelangelo virus of 1992 was automatically activated when the computer's date rolled to March 6, Michelangelo's birthday. Other viruses are activated when you use a particular key combination or access a certain feature.

Some viruses require you to play games. For example, one virus turns your mouse pointer into a graphic of a block of cheese. Out of nowhere comes a pack of mice, who follow the cheese wherever you move it. If you click the mouse, the cheese turns into a mousetrap, and "squishes" any mice it touches. Once all the mice have been caught with the mousetrap, the computer returns to normal. The Oreo virus displays a message, stating "I want a cookie," which prevents the user from using their computer until they enter the word "Oreo." The message then goes away, but is repeated 15 minutes later, then 10 minutes later, then 8 minutes later, and so on.

Here's an example of one of the cleverest viruses. It's called the "Good Times" virus and is said to have devastating effects on a computer's system files. Recently, a "watchdog" group issued this warning via e-mail: "If you receive an email message with the subject line "Good Times," DO NOT read the message and delete it immediately." Being helpful by nature, people circulated this e-mail all over the world until—guess what? It was found that the Good Times virus didn't even exist. The punch line is that this virus hoax caused a tremendous amount of worry, preparation, increased traffic and wasted time, and the originator didn't have to do an ounce of coding.

—*Amy Thomson, A+ Certified Technician, MOUS Master*

If you suspect a virus, you should immediately remove the server's network connection (to prevent its spread through the network) and run an anti-virus utility, such as those available from Norton, Symantec, or McAfee. These utilities are designed to locate and remove known viruses. However, an anti-virus utility is only able to deal with viruses it knows about. It is therefore very important you keep the utility current with updates from the manufacturer.

CERTIFICATION SUMMARY

Because servers play such an important role in the network, it is imperative you quickly identify and resolve server problems. Start by making observations about the environment, and by questioning the customer about the nature of the problem and the events surrounding it.

Use TCP/IP, route tracing, and configuration utilities to accurately diagnose the source of communication problems, such as those stemming from bottlenecks and incorrect TCP/IP configurations. If the problem resides within the server itself, narrow down the problem to the hardware or software. Replace or upgrade faulty hardware, and resolve software issues by reinstalling it, reconfiguring it, or using patches and upgrades.

TWO-MINUTE DRILL

Here are some of the key points from each certification objective in Chapter 9.

Performing Problem Determination

❑ Observe the environment to help identify or prevent problems.

❑ Ask the customer about the nature of the problem, the presence of error messages, and the history of the system. Have them try to reproduce the problem.

Using Diagnostic Resources and Procedures

❑ The PING, ARP, NETSTAT, and route tracing utilities can provide you with important TCP/IP connection information.

❑ Make use of error messages when trying to determine the nature and source of a problem.

❑ Use existing documentation to identify problems, and be sure to keep records of your changes for future use.

❑ When shutting down the server, ensure all users are notified, shut down all running applications, and follow the appropriate shut down procedure for the OS you are using.

❑ Remote alerts can inform administrators of problems by phone or pager, and wake on LAN allows administrators to power up the computer for remote troubleshooting.

Identifying Bottlenecks

❑ When troubleshooting a bottleneck, start by using NETSTAT or a route tracing utility to locate the machine or network segment responsible for the problem.

❑ In Windows and OS/2, use the Performance Monitor to view Network I/O, memory, processor, and disk I/O performance.

❑ In Netware, use the MONITOR utility to view Network I/O, memory, processor and disk I/O performance.

❑ Linux includes a set of utilities (commands), such as NFSSAT, SAR, PS, and IOSTAT, that allow you to monitor system performance.

Identify and Correct Misconfigurations and/or Upgrades

❑ When troubleshooting a TCP/IP misconfiguration, start by using PING to determine basic TCP/IP connectivity.

❑ Use a configuration utility (IPCONFIG, IFCONFIG, or CONFIG) to view the server's TCP/IP configuration.

❑ Use the ARP –e command to view statistics about the NIC.

Hardware, Software, and Virus Problems

❑ When there is a hardware problem, use your knowledge of the server's subsystems to locate the failed component.

❑ Hardware problems are resolved by upgrading, replacing, or reconfiguring the failed component.

❑ Resolve software problems by reinstalling, upgrading, or reconfiguring the software.

❑ Use up-to-date anti-virus utilities to locate and remove viruses from the system.

SELF TEST

The following questions will help you measure your understanding of the material presented in this chapter. Read all the choices carefully, as there may be more than one correct answer. Choose all correct answers for each question.

Performing Problem Determination

 1. You are onsite to troubleshoot a problem with a customer's server. Which observation about the surroundings may alert you to the problem (or a future problem)?

   A. The lighting is dim.

   B. The air is dry.

   C. The temperature is cool.

   D. All of the above.

 2. Which should you do first when performing onsite troubleshooting for a server problem?

   A. Ask the user about the server's history.

   B. Narrow down the problem to a single machine.

   C. Ask about the nature of the problem.

   D. Use diagnostic utilities to locate the source of the problem.

Using Diagnostic Resources and Procedures

 3. Which utility can you use in Netware to quickly determine basic TCP/IP connectivity?

   A. PING

   B. ARP

   C. NFSSTAT

   D. CONFIG

 4. A user is trying to open a remote Microsoft Word file on the server. The user is receiving error messages and cannot open the file. Which TCP/IP utility can you use to quickly determine whether the problem is connectivity-related?

   A. MONITOR

   B. IPCONFIG

C. Performance Monitor

D. PING

5. Which of the following statements about the ARP utility is true?

   A. You can use it to create static IP/MAC address associations.

   B. It can only be used in Windows and OS/2.

   C. You can use it to view the status of a computer's active connections.

   D. You can use it to view the computer's routing table.

6. Which utility should you use in Linux to identify the location of a bottleneck between your computer and a remote host on the Internet?

   A. PING

   B. TRACEROUTE

   C. NETSTAT

   D. IPTRACE

7. Which of the following can you use to view the Windows 2000 system log?

   A. System Viewer

   B. Performance Monitor

   C. SYSLOG

   D. Event Viewer

8. What is the name of the default OS/2 error log file?

   A. System log

   B. SYS$LOG.ERR

   C. SYSLOG

   D. NETCONF.LOG

9. One of your coworkers informs you that a customer needs to shut down the server. This same coworker tells you to use the following procedure: access the system console, enter the "down" command, followed by the "exit" command. Which operating system is the server using?

   A. Windows NT

   B. Windows 2000

   C. Netware

   D. Linux

10. Which command should you enter to shut down a Linux server?

- A. shutdown
- B. down
- C. exit
- D. exit to dos

Identifying Bottlenecks

11. Users on a Linux WAN are complaining of slow data retrieval. Which of the following can you use to pinpoint the network segment or server that is causing the bottleneck?

- A. PING
- B. TRACEROUTE
- C. IPTRACE
- D. CONFIG

12. You have determined that a Netware server is causing a network bottleneck. Which utility should you use to determine the hardware component responsible?

- A. Performance Monitor
- B. MONITOR
- C. CONFIG
- D. NFSSTAT

13. You suspect that a network server's network card is causing a bottleneck. Which NETSTAT statistic may confirm your suspicion?

- A. A high receive queue value
- B. A high transmit queue value
- C. A high instance of page faults per second
- D. A high CPU utilization percentage

14. A high network output queue may indicate that:

- A. The network card cannot keep up with data requests.
- B. The current computer is causing a bottleneck.
- C. The current computer's NIC has an incorrect hardware configuration.
- D. There is heavy network traffic.

15. A server is creating a bottleneck because it is experiencing excessive use of virtual memory. All of the following may help you to resolve the bottleneck except:

    A. Adding more RAM to the system

    B. Implementing disk load balancing

    C. Adding a second NIC to the system

    D. Adding a second processor to the system

Identifying and Correcting Misconfigurations and/or Upgrades

16. Which of the following utilities can you use to identify the presence of an incorrect TCP/IP configuration on a Windows 2000 network?

    A. PING, IPCONFIG, ARP

    B. NETSTAT, CONFIG, ARP

    C. PING, IPCONFIG, MONITOR

    D. PING, IPCONFIG, TRACERTE

17. You have narrowed down an OS/2 connectivity problem to the TCP/IP configuration. Which utility can you use to view and change the current configuration?

    A. CONFIG

    B. IPCONFIG

    C. WINIPCFG

    D. IFCONFIG

18. A Windows NT server cannot access the network, and you suspect it has been misconfigured. You have already determined the server is using the appropriate IP address and subnet mask. Which command should you use next to identify the source of the problem?

    A. ARP -a

    B. IPCONFIG

    C. NETSTAT –e

    D. ARP –e

Hardware, Software and Virus Problems

19. A server is generating error messages when the anti-virus software attempts to write a log to the primary hard drive. Which of the following should you do first to determine whether this is a hardware or software problem?

    A. Reinstall the anti-virus software.

    B. Use a different application to access the primary hard drive.

    C. Restart the computer.

    D. Use a different application to access the secondary hard drive.

20. You suspect the server has a virus, but the anti-virus utility does not report the presence of any viruses. What should you do next?

    A. Assume there is no virus and begin alternative troubleshooting procedures.

    B. Reinstall the affected application(s).

    C. Obtain an update from the anti-virus utility's manufacturer.

    D. Delete the affected files.

LAB QUESTION

Workstations on a network cannot access files from a file server, and you suspect the server has an improper TCP/IP configuration. Using the information presented in this chapter, describe the procedure you should use to identify and resolve the problem. Discuss the utilities you can use, as well as their possible results and how you can use those results to troubleshoot the problem.

SELF TEST ANSWERS

Performing Problem Determination

1. ☑ **B.** You may be alerted to a potential problem if the air is dry. Dry air can lead to electrostatic discharge, which is harmful to computer components. The humidity should be kept between 50 and 80 percent.
☒ **A,** the lighting is dim, is incorrect. A lack of bright light will not affect the proper functioning of computer components. Conversely, lights that are too powerful may cause harmful electromagnetic interference. **C,** the temperature is cool, is also incorrect. It is heat, not cool air, that can lead to computer problems. **D** is incorrect because it suggests that all of the answers are correct.

2. ☑ **C.** When troubleshooting a server problem, you should first ask the user about the nature of the problem. That is, ask what happened. Without knowing what occurred, you cannot begin to identify and resolve the problem.
☒ **A,** asking about the server's history, **B,** narrowing down the problem to a single machine, and **D,** using diagnostic utilities, are all incorrect. Although these are all important troubleshooting steps, they should be performed only after you have been informed of the problem condition and can focus your attention on the appropriate areas.

Using Diagnostic Resources and Procedures

3. ☑ **A.** In Netware, use PING to determine basic TCP/IP connectivity. When you use PING, several ICMP echo packets will be sent to the specified host, and the utility will report on the ability to connect, as well as the time it took to send and receive data. PING is a platform-neutral utility, so it can be used in Netware, Windows, OS/2, and Linux, as long as the TCP/IP protocol is being used.
☒ **B,** ARP is incorrect, because this utility will provide you with recently used IP/MAC address relationships, but will not provide data regarding the computer's ability to connect to the machines with those IP/MAC addresses. **C,** NFSSTAT, is incorrect because this is a Linux utility for monitoring network I/O performance, and is not available in Netware.
D, CONFIG, is incorrect because this is the Netware utility for viewing the NIC's configuration. It provides no data on whether the configuration is correct, thereby enabling network connectivity.

4. ☑ **D.** You can use PING to quickly determine whether the problem is connectivity-related. If the PING fails, it indicates the user cannot open the file because the computer cannot

communicate with the server. If the PING is successful, it means the problem lies elsewhere, perhaps with the Word application, with the server's hard drive, or with the file itself.

☒   **A,** MONITOR is incorrect because this is a Netware utility used to monitor system performance, such as processor, memory or disk usage. It will not help in determining network connectivity. **B,** IPCONFIG, is incorrect because this is the Windows NT/2000 utility for viewing and changing the computer's TCP/IP configuration. If the problem in question is connectivity-related, you may have to use IPCONFIG to resolve it, but IPCONFIG will not help you determine whether the workstation can communicate with the server. **C,** Performance Monitor, is incorrect because this is the Windows and OS/2 utility for viewing the system's performance, much like the MONITOR utility in Netware.

5.   ☑   **A.** You can use the ARP utility to create static IP/MAC address associations. By itself, the ARP utility will display recent entries in the ARP cache, consisting of IP/MAC address associations of other computers on the network. By using the –s option, you can create static entries in the ARP cache.

☒   **B** is incorrect because it suggests that ARP can only be used in Windows and OS/2. ARP is a TCP/IP utility, so it can used on any platform that uses TCP/IP. **C** and **D** are incorrect because the ability to view the computer's active connections and routing table are provided by NETSTAT, not ARP.

6.   ☑   **B.** You should use TRACEROUTE to identify the location of a bottleneck between your computer and a remote host on the Internet. This utility will send several ICMP packets to the remote host, reporting on each hop between your computer and the host, as well as the time it took to transfer data to each. If a single hop is reported as taking excessive time, you will have narrowed down the bottleneck to that hop.

☒   **A** is incorrect because the PING utility will report on the total transfer time between your computer and a remote host, but will not indicate which hop took the longest. **C,** NETSTAT, is incorrect because this utility will provide the status of each active connection, but will not indicate transfer times. **D,** IPTRACE, is incorrect because this is the Netware route tracing utility. IPTRACE cannot be used in Windows.

7.   ☑   **D.** Use the Event Viewer to view the Windows 2000 system log. Windows NT and 2000 include an automatic logging service, called Event Log, which keeps logs about system, security, and application activities. Although the Event Log keeps the logs, the Event Viewer must be used to view the logs.

☒   **A,** System Viewer, is incorrect because this is not a valid Windows utility. **B,** Performance Monitor, is incorrect because this utility allows you to view current system performance in Windows, but does not allow you to view the system log. **C,** SYSLOG, is incorrect because this is the OS/2 error logging utility.

8. ☑ **C.** The default OS/2 error log is called SYSLOG. It can be run manually from the command prompt, or run automatically with the appropriate entries in the CONFIG.SYS file.
☒ **A**, system log, is incorrect because this is the name of the system activity log in Windows NT/2000. **B**, SYS$LOG.ERR, is incorrect because this is the Netware error log file. **D**, NETCONF.LOG, is incorrect because this is a network configuration log used in Linux.

9. ☑ **C.** The server is using Netware. To properly shut down a Netware server, access the system console by pressing CTRL-ESC. At the console command prompt, enter "down" (without the quotes). The system will close all open modules. Enter "exit" (without the quotes) to exit Netware and return to DOS. When the DOS command prompt appears, it is safe to turn the computer off.
☒ **A**, Windows NT, and **B**, Windows 2000, are incorrect. To shut down a Windows server, select Shut Down from the Start menu on the taskbar. Turn off the computer when the system tells you it is safe to do so. **D**, Linux, is incorrect. To shut down a Linux server, use the shutdown command at the command prompt. Turn off the computer when the system tells you it is safe to do so.

10. ☑ **A.** You should use the shutdown command to shut down a Linux server. Enter the command at the command prompt, then wait until the system tells you it is safe to turn the power off.
☒ **B**, down, and **C**, exit, are incorrect, as these are the Netware commands to close all modules and exit to DOS, respectively. **D**, exit to dos, is incorrect, as this is not a valid Linux command.

Identifying Bottlenecks

11. ☑ **B.** You can use the TRACEROUTE utility to pinpoint the Linux network segment or server responsible for a bottleneck. TRACEROUTE will trace the route from your computer to a specified remote host. The transfer time to each hop along the route will be reported. Take note of excessive transfer times.
☒ **A**, PING, is incorrect because this command will help establish whether there is connectivity between your computer and a remote host. It will not, however, indicate which part of the connection may be causing a bottleneck. **C**, IPTRACE, is incorrect because this is the route tracing utility used in NetWare. **D**, CONFIG, is incorrect because this utility will allow you to view a Netware computer's TCP/IP configuration, but will not help you locate the network segment or server responsible for a bottleneck, and cannot be used in Linux.

12. ☑   **B.** You can use the Netware MONITOR utility to determine which component is responsible for a server bottleneck. MONITOR allows you to view the system's network I/O, memory, CPU, and disk I/O performance. The data you receive may help you determine whether the NIC, RAM, CPU, or hard disk is at fault.

   ☒   **A,** Performance Monitor, is incorrect because this is a performance monitoring utility in Windows and OS/2, and is not available in Netware. **C,** CONFIG, is incorrect because this utility is used in Netware to view and modify the TCP/IP configuration. It will not indicate TCP/IP performance. **D,** NFSSTAT, is incorrect because this is a Linux utility, used to monitor network I/O performance, and cannot be used in Netware.

13. ☑   **A.** A high receive queue value may confirm your suspicion that the server's network card is causing a bottleneck. A high receive queue value indicates that the NIC is receiving data faster than it can pass the data onto the CPU for processing. Data in the queue must wait for the NIC to catch up before it can be processed. When this is the case, consider upgrading the NIC or adding another NIC to the server to handle part of the load.

   ☒   **B,** a high transmit queue value, is incorrect. This statistic indicates the server is trying to send data faster than the network can handle it. This may be due to heavy network traffic, or a bottleneck external to the server. **C,** a high instance of page faults per second, is incorrect. This statistic indicates the server is making frequent use of virtual memory, which is much slower than RAM. This indicates the bottleneck may be caused by the memory, not the network card. **D,** a high CPU utilization percentage, is incorrect. This statistic indicates how busy the CPU is. A high percentage may indicate the CPU cannot keep up with processing requests.

14. ☑   **D.** A high network output queue may indicate there is heavy network traffic. Data in the output queue has been processed by the computer, but is waiting until the network can receive it. This may be caused by heavy network traffic (a busy network).

   ☒   **A** is incorrect because it suggests a high output queue is caused when the network card cannot keep up with data requests. In fact, the opposite is true; a high output queue typically means the network cannot keep up with the NIC. When the NIC cannot keep up with data requests, the result is usually a high input queue value. **B** is incorrect because it suggests the current computer is responsible for the bottleneck. Again, a high output queue indicates the computer is processing and trying to transmit data faster than the network can handle it. In this case, the network, not the current computer, is causing the bottleneck. **C** is incorrect because it suggests that the NIC has an incorrect hardware configuration. However, if the NIC is improperly configured, the computer will not be able to communicate with it, let alone give it data to hold in the output queue.

15. ☑ **C.** Adding a second NIC to the system will not help to resolve a bottleneck caused by excessive use of virtual memory. When the computer runs out of RAM, it uses a swap file, located on the hard drive, for temporary storage of data. Because hard drive access is slower than RAM access, excessive use of the swap file can cause a bottleneck within the server. Adding a second NIC to the system may increase the speed at which the computer can receive network data, but it will do nothing to speed up the server's ability to process that data.

☒ **A,** adding more RAM to the system, is incorrect. The computer uses virtual memory only when there is no free RAM. The more RAM the system has, the less it will have to make use of the swap file, thus speeding up overall processing time. **B,** implementing disk load balancing, is also incorrect. Remember that the swap file resides on the hard disk. The busier the hard disk is, the longer it will take for swap file requests to be carried out. By adding another disk to the system, you can take part of the overall disk I/O load off of the disk containing the swap file, allowing it to carry out swap file requests more quickly. **D,** adding a second processor to the system, is also incorrect. Data is stored in memory until it can be processed by the processor. By adding another processor, you reduce the amount of data that must be held in memory.

Identify and Correct Misconfigurations and/or Upgrades

16. ☑ **A.** You can use the PING, IPCONFIG, and ARP utilities to identify the presence of an incorrect TCP/IP configuration on a Windows 2000 network. Use PING to establish basic TCP/IP connectivity. Use IPCONFIG to determine whether the computer in question is using the proper IP address and subnet mask. Use ARP with the –e option to determine whether the computer's NIC is able to send and receive data.

☒ **B,** NETSTAT, CONFIG, ARP, is incorrect because NETSTAT is used only to report on active network connections. It will not provide information about why a particular computer does not have network connectivity. Furthermore, CONFIG is a Netware command, and cannot be used in Windows. **C** is incorrect because it suggests using MONITOR, which is a Netware performance monitoring utility. **D** is incorrect because it suggests using TRACERTE, which is a route tracing utility used in OS/2, but not available in Windows.

17. ☑ **D.** Use the IFCONFIG utility to view and change the TCP/IP configuration in OS/2. You will be provided with information about the current IP address, subnet mask, and default gateway.

☒ **A,** CONFIG, is incorrect because this is a Netware utility that cannot be used in OS/2. **B,** IPCONFIG, and **C,** WINIPCFG are incorrect because these utilities allow you to view the TCP/IP configuration in Windows NT/2000 and Windows 9*x*, respectively, but not in OS/2.

18. ☑   **C.** You should use NETSTAT –e next. Once you have determined the TCP/IP configuration is correct, turn your attention to the NIC. The NETSTAT –e command will provide you with statistics about the NIC's recent activities. If no data has been sent or received, it indicates the NIC is not functioning properly.

☒   **A**, ARP –a, is incorrect because this command will list the contents of the ARP cache (IP/MAC address associations). An empty cache indicates a connectivity problem, but will not help you determine whether the problem is TCP/IP or hardware-based. **B**, IPCONFIG, is incorrect because this is the Windows utility used to view the system's TCP/IP configuration (remember, you have already determined the TCP/IP configuration is not at fault, and you probably used IPCONFIG to do it). **D** is incorrect because the ARP utility will not help pinpoint the cause of the problem. Furthermore, -e is not a valid ARP option.

Hardware, Software and Virus Problems

19. ☑   **B.** You should use a different application to access the primary hard drive. If successful, you can rule out the hard drive as the source of the problem, and focus your attention on the anti-virus utility itself.

☒   **A**, reinstall the anti-virus software, is incorrect. Although this may be the ultimate resolution to the problem, you should first determine whether the software is, in fact, at fault before reinstalling it. **C**, restart the computer, is incorrect. Although this may resolve the problem, it will not help you identify whether the problem was the result of the hardware or software. **D** is incorrect because it suggests using a different application to access a different hard drive. If successful, you will still not know whether the primary hard drive or the original application was the cause of the problem.

20. ☑   **C.** You should obtain an update from the anti-virus utility's manufacturer. An anti-virus utility can only detect and remove viruses it knows about. Obtain regular updates from the manufacturer so the utility can properly locate and remove recently released viruses.

☒   **A** is incorrect because it suggests assuming there is no virus. Again, an anti-virus utility cannot deal with viruses it has not been instructed to recognize. Get a manufacturer update to ensure your utility can deal with newly released viruses. **B** and **D** are incorrect because they suggest removing the affected applications and files. This is not likely to remove the virus from the system, so the virus can continue to affect other files and spread from your computer to others.

LAB ANSWER

Start by using the PING utility. This will allow you to determine whether the server has basic TCP/IP connectivity, regardless of the application being used, or the files and hard drive being accessed. If you can successfully PING the server, it means the server's TCP/IP connection has been configured correctly. In this case, focus your attention on the application, files, or hard drive.

If the PING is unsuccessful, focus your attention on the server's TCP/IP configuration. Use a configuration utility (IPCONFIG, IFCONFIG, or CONFIG) to view the server's IP address and subnet mask. Ensure these addresses match those being accessed by the network workstations. If they do not, enter the appropriate addresses and test your solution.

If the server is using the proper IP address and subnet mask, focus your attention on the server's NIC. Use the ARP –e command to determine whether the NIC is able to pass network traffic. If so, turn your attention to other parts of the network, or begin bottleneck troubleshooting procedures.

If the NIC is not able to pass network traffic, focus your attention on its hardware configuration, as this may be an indication that the server itself is unable to use the NIC. Make certain there are no resource conflicts, such as IRQ or I/O addresses, and ensure a proper driver is loaded. If the NIC has an incorrect hardware configuration, reconfigure it and test your solution. If the NIC is properly configured, it may be that the NIC itself is simply not working. In this case, replace the NIC with a known working one.

Server+

COMPUTING TECHNOLOGY INDUSTRY ASSOCIATION

10

Disaster Recovery

CERTIFICATION OBJECTIVES

Organizations are increasingly dependent upon their network servers to support their business productivity. In the case of businesses that depend on Internet Web sites for a portion (or all) of their income, servers *are* their business productivity. These organizations must protect their servers from all types of disasters in order to continue doing business.

Disasters never happen the way you expect them to. Most do not completely ruin an entire network. Instead, parts of the network or even parts of servers will fail, but the rest either continue functioning or are recoverable. Even if a power surge interrupts network connectivity, the data loss that results may equate to thousands of dollars worth of income or productivity.

When you plan for a disaster, you need to take into account every type that might occur—from water damage to fire damage, or from failure of the entire network to failure of a single component. You need to define what failures will constitute a disaster. From there, you can determine what the necessary preventive measures are to keep damage at a minimum.

CERTIFICATION OBJECTIVE 10.01

Planning for Disaster Recovery

The key to disaster recovery planning is making certain disaster recovery costs are commensurate with the losses that could be incurred. You would not want to spend more money on prevention than might be lost in a disaster. Nor would you want to spend so little on disaster recovery that you cannot recover the business in a timely fashion. Imagine a business that generates $10,000 per minute through transactions on a set of servers all located in the same building. In another building, there might be a server that provides archive storage space for non-critical files. When you plan for the disaster recovery of these different servers, it does not make sense to pay as much for a system to protect the archive server as would be paid for the transaction servers. Consequently, you should analyze the risks before developing a disaster recovery plan.

Some of the elements you will encounter during a risk analysis include:

- **Determining what threats can cause a disaster.** These include (but are not limited to) fire, flood, weather, power failure, power surges, virus attacks, hack attacks, heat, and the failure of various components.

- **Determining what vulnerabilities exist in your environment that could lead to the threat of disaster.** For example, if you live in Phoenix, Arizona, you would know that heat is a very likely problem, while a tornado is rare. But if you were in Detroit, Michigan, these dangers are reversed.

- **Determining what countermeasures can be taken for each vulnerability.** There are a variety of ways to handle them:

  - You can monitor for threats and trigger events to control them. For example, you can put in a smoke alarm for a fire, or you can install a utility that monitors a RAID array to ensure all the disk drives are in working order.

  - You can use deterrents to protect against deliberate attacks, such as installing firewalls.

  - You can prevent some disasters. For example, you can prevent data loss during a power failure by installing a UPS.

  - You can provide corrective measures for some disasters that cannot be controlled. For instance, if a server fails, you can restore its data from a tape backup and continue doing business.

Figure 10-1 depicts the interactions of these threats with your systems.

on the
Job

When I am hired by a business to conduct an assessment for disaster recovery, I always put the costs up front. When management understands the amount of money at risk by not having a disaster recovery plan, they are better prepared to make decisions about that plan—such as whether to implement a hot site, or put RAID storage systems on their servers. If management does not understand the costs of a disaster risk, they can make decisions that are either too costly up front, or too costly after the fact.

Planning for Redundancy

Redundancy is a preventative measure. You can plan redundancy at any level in your network. You can also plant redundant components inside the server. Examples of redundant components are:

■ **Redundant power supplies** If one power supply fails, the other takes over. You may be able to configure both power supplies to share the load, or keep one dormant until a failure occurs.

Countermeasures for disasters

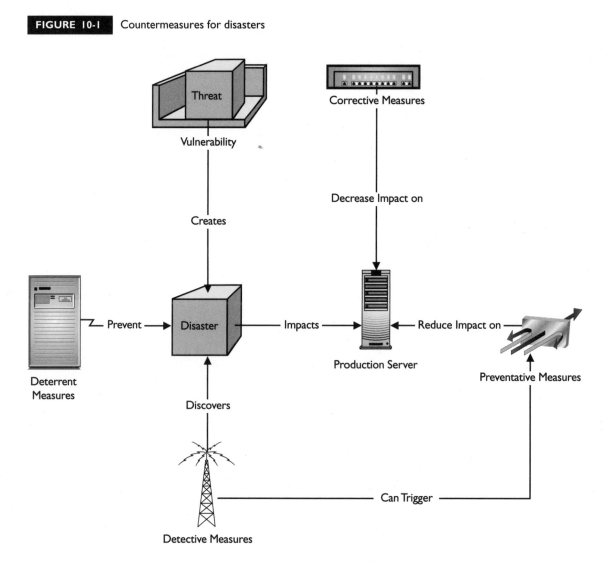

- **Redundant array of inexpensive disks (RAID)**   RAID1, mirroring, is a set of redundant hard disks. Duplexing is a set of redundant hard disks connected to redundant controllers. RAID5, disk striping with parity, establishes a redundant set of disks (between 3 and 32) in which any one of the disks can fail yet allow the array to continue functioning.

- **Redundant network adapters**   If one network adapter fails, the other takes over. You can configure multiple adapters to share the traffic load, or leave one dormant.

- **Error correcting memory**   A redundant memory module provides error correction if a memory error occurs.

You can also establish redundancy at a larger level. You can create redundant servers, such as clusters, shown in Figure 10-2. Clusters are a group, or cluster, of servers that provide services to clients as though they were a single server. If one server fails, another takes over. Clusters generally share traffic load transparently, so end-users aren't aware which server actually provides the service, or that there is more than one physical server.

A cluster uses a *shared nothing* model, so each server owns and manages its own devices, and common devices (such as an external storage system) are not "owned" by a single server at any one time. The servers are connected to each other so they can determine when a failure occurs, and thereby monitor cluster status.

A cluster can be configured to share the load or act as a failover. In the shared load configuration, all the servers in the cluster are performing concurrently by providing services to end-users. In the failover configuration, which is generally a two-server configuration, one server provides services on the network while the second server is configured as a standby. If the second server detects a failure, it takes over and provides services.

exam
ⓦatch

Redundant features, such as RAID or cluster servers, are key elements to a disaster recovery plan because they help prevent disasters from occurring.

FIGURE 10-2   A cluster

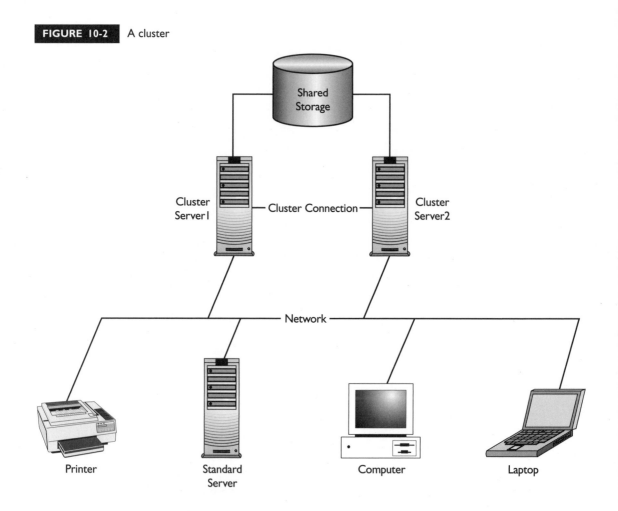

Using Hot Swap, Warm Swap, and Hot Spare to Ensure Availability

You can extend the reliability of a system through methods by which components can be replaced. There are four categories of component replacement:

- cold swap
- warm swap
- hot swap
- hot spare (also known as automatic swap)

You can use these methods, along with a variety of components such as network interface cards, fans, and power supplies. Hard disks in RAID arrays are the most common components that use these methods.

In a cold swap, system power must be shut off before the failed component is removed and replaced. This method produces a significant level of downtime. To reduce the amount of downtime, some systems support warm swap, where the I/O operations must stop, but power remains on while the failed component is replaced. If I/O operations continue while the failed component is replaced, then you have performed a hot swap. A hot swap enables the server to continue running, with absolutely no downtime. The only thing better than a hot swap is using a hot spare. A hot spare is an unused component configured to automatically replace an identical component if the first component fails. In this scenario, the hot spare automatically swaps for the failed component.

EXERCISE 10-1

Installing a Hot Swap Drive

In order to replace a hot swappable disk drive without interrupting server operations, the drive must be part of a RAID1 or RAID5 array.

1. Examine the drive and the manufacturer's documentation to become familiar with the indicator lights and latches.

2. If the drives are not exposed, open the cover.

Check the indicator lights to determine which hard drive has failed. Otherwise, select a drive to replace as part of this exercise.

1. Remove the failed hard drive according to the system's instructions.

2. Slide the hot swap drive into the backplane slot and seat it firmly on the backplane.

3. Lock the drive into place.

Verify that all the drives are aligned and that all status indicators show the drives are ready. If the new drive is not ready, you may need to reset it with the manufacturer's management utility.

4. Close the cover.

Using the Concepts of Fault Tolerance and Fault Recovery to Create a Disaster Recovery Plan

When you are developing your disaster recovery plan, you should focus on both preventative and corrective measures. Preventative measures are usually implemented in the form of fault tolerance. Fault tolerance is the ability of a component, or an entire system, to continue normal operations even in the event of a hardware or software failure. Usually, fault tolerance is implemented through redundant components. Thus, the disaster is prevented even though a failure has taken place.

Corrective measures are a matter of fault recovery. You can recover by rectifying the damage, or by restoring the system to a previously "known good" state. In order to restore the system to a previous known good state, you will need to take periodic "snapshots" of the system. The more recent the snapshot, the less extensive will be the loss of data. Typically, fault recovery is handled through backups.

FROM THE CLASSROOM

Determining Your Need for Fault Tolerance

When determining your need for fault tolerance, you should understand two metrics: mean time between failures (MTBF) and mean time to recover (MTTR). MTBF is the mean time until the device is expected to fail. MTTR is the time it takes to recover once the device has failed.

A component's expected downtime is measured by the ratio MTTR/MTBF. Take a component that has a 5-year MTBF and a 5-minute MTTR. This means that your expected downtime is 1 minute per year for that component. A server's expected downtime is the sum of the expected downtime of all of its parts. Therefore, if the server has three components, each with expected downtimes of 10 minutes per year, then the server's expected downtime is 30 minutes per year.

Consider a server that uses a UPS. Most people consider only the possibility of an external power failure. If you discovered that

the MTBF for the server's power supply is 8 months, and that the MTTR is 8 hours, you might think about building redundancy by adding a secondary power supply.

Many manufacturers will list MTBF values for their hardware, while some even list the MTTR values. You should look for MTTR values close to zero, and MTBF values that are as long as you can afford. However, it becomes expensive to find components with long MTBF values. Plus, there are some disasters—such as those produced by Mother Nature—that do not pay any attention whatsoever to MTBF values. You could end up paying an immense amount for a piece of equipment that is irretrievably ruined by a flood or tornado. Therefore, when you select a piece of equipment, you should consider external methods of system recovery, in addition to the MTBF and MTTR values.

—Melissa Craft, MCSE, CCNA, Network+, MCNE, Citrix CCA

When you develop your disaster recovery plan, you can decide minimum fault tolerance features for current and future servers. These standards may include:

- Uninterruptible power supplies (UPS), surge protectors, noise filters
- Internal power supply redundancy
- RAID
- Clusters
- Redundant fans
- Network adapter redundancy
- Replication of data
- Distributed services

These last two items, data replication and distributed services, need to be configured across multiple servers. Data replication creates a redundancy in actual data by creating copies on multiple servers, then synchronizing those servers on a periodic basis. This process can overwhelm network traffic if the amount of data is extensive and if synchronization is executed during high-usage business hours. You can configure distributed services, such as DNS or DHCP by designating multiple servers to work as secondary servers in a variety of locations. When you distribute services across a number of servers, you will be less likely to suffer a loss of network connectivity for the entire network if a single server fails.

on the
job

Not all disasters are caused by fire or flood. I worked on a client's network a couple of years ago where an IT group had decided to completely centralize all services in the Midwest. One day, I was paged with an emergency because no one could log on to the network. It turned out that the WAN link to the Midwest location had failed because the WAN provider had problems. But that should not have caused logon failures for every single end-user in the West. It turned out that the IT group's centralization project had removed all DHCP servers from every facility (except the Midwest). When the WAN link failed, no computer could obtain an IP address and users were prevented from logging on all over the country. It didn't take too long to install DHCP on a couple of Windows NT servers, but the damage was already done—2 hours of no productivity cost more than a hundred thousand dollars. This was one small disaster that could have been completely avoided by distributing services or by creating a backup link to the Midwest office.

Developing a Disaster Recovery Plan

Any disaster recovery plan should discuss strategies for all possible disasters. Since all catastrophes are not equal, the method of recovering from one type might be completely different than recovering from another type.

At the server level, you should consider a disaster as constituting the failure of one or more components within the server. For example:

- Hard disk failure
- Power supply failure
- Network adapter failure
- Processor failure
- Memory failure

The next level of disaster you should consider is a failure external to the server. It could be the failure of another network component, or a disaster on a much larger scale. For example:

- Building power failure
- Hub or switch failure
- Router failure
- WAN link failure
- Fire, flood, or other disaster that damages equipment

An ounce of prevention is worth a pound of cure. For each of these possible disasters, you should then consider what is necessary to prevent them. For example, you could keep a power supply failure from causing the server to go down by purchasing a server platform with a redundant power supply.

Next, you should think about how to reduce your losses if such a failure occurred. In this case, your losses are tied to downtime. To reduce downtime, keep spare parts on hand, keep a spare server, hub, and router on hand, or only use a full backup scheme.

Finally, you should consider how to recover from a disaster that causes the location to become unusable. This part of your plan is difficult to prepare. You need to know how much each site produces, and how long the business can survive without the site's production. Then, decide what types of site recovery are needed for each site. As you consider a disaster that might affect an entire site, you should prioritize the needs of the business in terms of equipment, location, staff, and especially data and services, that will be required to continue productivity. Then decide how to bring that data up, providing those services as part of the recovery plan.

SCENARIO & SOLUTION

Refer to the following Scenario & Solution when asking yourself questions that might help in developing a disaster recovery plan.

How long could your site operate without servers, physical space, or full staffing?	Using manual processes, the site could operate for 5 days at a 60 percent staffing level without impacting productivity by doubling up at another site.
How much impact would a loss of computing during a crucial time period have on the business?	In the accounting department, a loss of computing during annual statements—its busiest time—will cause an increased need for personnel, resulting in an approximate $250,000 cost per week.
What are the high priority tasks if there is a disruption in service lasting longer than one business day?	Obtaining alternate equipment, space, and staffing would be the chief tasks. Setting up telephone service, restoring data and applications from backup, connecting to the corporate network and/or Internet, and training staff regarding business processes would be other concerns.
What non-essential activities would a disruption in service fail to impact?	Running the monitoring systems; human resource applications.
What is the minimum equipment needed in the event of a disaster?	CAT 5 cabling and Ethernet Network adapters. 3 servers, a switch, a router, 22 workstations, 5 modems, and 12 laptops.
What reference manuals are required for applications and network operations?	The accounting and manufacturing application manuals are essential. The network operations manuals are required to reconnect to the corporate WAN.
What are the current backup procedures for servers and workstations?	Servers are backed up; workstations are not. There is a full backup on Fridays, and incremental backups Monday through Thursday.
What services can continue without computing?	Accounting and human resources can continue for a short period of time.
Who will be in charge in the case of a disaster?	The IT Manager will be in charge of computing resources, while the Accounting Manager will be in charge of all accounting issues.

The critical elements of your disaster recovery plan should include the following:

■ Safety of individuals—including escape routes, alternate routes, and evacuation procedures

■ Applications required for ongoing operations

■ Systems required to support the applications

■ Data required for ongoing operations

■ Alternate procedures if computing is unavailable for a period of time

■ A process to restore computing, including obtaining equipment and offsite backup tapes

■ Inventory of items essential to operations

■ Inventory of forms, manuals, contracts, legal documents, and other critical documentation

■ A crisis management team

■ Vendors of services and supplies (should include alternate vendors if the disaster affects them as well)

Identifying Types of Backup Hardware

Before you select the type of backup hardware to use, you should ask the following questions. Answers to these questions will help determine the speed, capacity, and location for your backup hardware.

1. Where will applications be stored?

2. Where will data be stored?

3. How much disk capacity (for back up purposes) is there on the server(s) and workstation(s)?

4. Do users store their personal data on workstations or servers?

5. How much time are you given to complete backups?

6. Who will perform the backups—a centralized administrator group, or multiple decentralized administrators?

7. Where can the backup device(s) be located?

You should determine how much data will need to be backed up. If your server holds 8GB of data, and it has 30GB of total disk storage capacity, you must have a future backup capacity of 30GB for that single server. Since most backup devices and backup software support some measure of data compression, you can use media that has less space than the data that must be backed up. It is best to plan for backups without using compression, however.

The amount of time it takes to back up your data is another consideration. If you have a Web server that must be backed up, and the backup process reduces the performance of the server, you will want to back up that server as quickly as possible, and during times when the Web server is least accessed. To determine the length of time needed to back up the data, consider a Web server with 30GB of data. If you use an AIT tape device, the transfer rate will be 60 Mbps. It will then take:

```
(30 GB* 1024 MB/GB)/(60MB/s) = 512 seconds / (60 seconds/minute) = 8.53 minutes.
```

Once you know how much capacity is available on your backup media, as well as how quickly you are required to back up the data, and whether you can select more than one backup device or location, you can then select the most appropriate backup device. Table 10-1 lists some common backup hardware devices to help you in your decision.

exam
ⓦatch

AIT is a high-capacity, high-speed, backup device that functions well for backing up enterprise servers.

Identifying Types of Backup and Restoration Schemes

After you have selected your backup hardware, you next need to develop an effective backup strategy. This requires you select a backup scheme and a method of restoration that will efficiently back up data and effectively restore it. You should also select one or more administrators to be responsible for backing up the data, rotating tapes, sending tapes offsite to a storage facility, and for restoring data as needed.

The goal for your backup system is to be able to quickly recover data if there is some form of data loss. To meet this goal, you should back up an entire volume so you can restore data after a disk failure. You can back up server system files and configuration information in order to restore the server in the event of a server failure involving system data loss.

| TABLE 10-1 | Backup Devices |

Backup Device	Capacity	Speed	Reliability	Optimal Location	Ideal For
Floppy disk	1.44MB	0.1 Mbps	Poor	Distributed throughout network	Workstation
High capacity floppy	120MB	0.6 Mbps	Fair	Distributed throughout network	Workstation
Zip	100MB	0.4 Mbps to 1.4 Mbps	Fair	Distributed throughout network	Workstation
CDR/CDRW	650MB	0.3 Mbps to 1.2 Mbps	Good	Distributed throughout network	Workstation
JAZ	1GB to 2GB	6.7 Mbps	Fair	Distributed throughout network	Workstation
AIT (Advanced Intelligent Tape)	50GB per cartridge	60 Mbps	Excellent	Centralized	Server or multiple servers/wkstns
Tape Library	Use with AIT, 8mm, DLT	Depends on type of device	Excellent	Centralized	Multiple servers/wkstns
DAT (Digital Audio Tape)	2GB, 4GB, 12GB or 20GB	.1 Mbps to 2.5 Mbps	Good	Centralized	Server
DLT (Digital Linear Tape)	10GB to 40GB	50 Mbps	Excellent	Centralized	Server or multiple servers/wkstns
8mm	2.5GB to 40GB	1 Mbps	Excellent	Centralized	Server
MO (Magneto-Optical)	3.5" disk holds 1.3GB, or 5.25" disk holds 5.2GB	1 Mbps to 2 Mbps	Excellent	Distributed throughout network or centralized	Server
DVD-RAM	2.6GB per side	1 Mbps	Good	Distributed throughout network	Workstation

Backup software can be limited by open files. That is, if there is a file that is being used, then the file cannot normally be backed up. Most backup software will list all files that are not backed up for this reason in a log file. You should always check log files to ensure that critical data is backed up. For example, if you have a database server with a large database, and a user leaves his workstation running during the evenings keeping that database open, then you may never actually back up the database file due to that user's habits. This could be a tremendous problem if you need to restore the database and it hasn't been backed up appropriately. One option is to look for a backup system that can accommodate open files. Another is to require an offline backup on a periodic basis, where all users are disconnected from the server, during which the file can be backed up.

Rotation schemes are important to keeping recent copies of data both onsite and offsite. Before you decide the rotation scheme, you should choose the type of backups you want to perform.

- **Full backup** A backup of all data, system files, and applications on a given storage system. After the backup, all files have an archive bit removed. If all backups are full backups, then only the last full backup tape needs to be restored.

- **Incremental backup** A backup of all data that has changed since the last backup. These files are marked with the archive bit. After the incremental backup, those files have their archive bit removed. Incremental backups are usually mixed with full backups. In order to restore data from these, the last full backup and all incremental backups since that last full backup must be restored. This system takes the longest to restore.

- **Differential backup** A backup of all data that has changed since the last *full backup*. All files that have changed since the last full backup are backed up, and the archive bit is not removed. Differential backups are usually mixed with full backups. In order to restore data to them, only the last full backup and differential backup must be restored. This system requires only two tapes to be restored.

- **Copy backup** A full backup of all data is completed but no archive bits are changed. A copy backup does not affect any current backup system or rotation schedule you are using.

In order to make certain you restore the correct tapes, you should log each backup's date and type, regardless of the rotation. Backup media are fragile, so you should store them in an environmentally controlled location, and maintain multiples. Most people select tape cassettes for their backup media. Since tapes wear out, you should replace them every six months with new tapes to ensure the data is viable. When you rotate media, only a minimum number of them will be necessary to provide data redundancy. Table 10-2 discusses the types of media rotation schedules you might select.

exam
ⓦatch

The Tower of Hanoi rotation schedule is based in a mathematical puzzle where a series of disks are stacked in order of descending size on three poles. The object is to move all disks to one pole, moving one disk at a time with only smaller disks on top of larger disks. In order to win the game, the top disk is moved every other time and the bottom disk moved only once. Likewise, when adding a new tape set to the group, you will use it most frequently—every other day—while the other sets are used less frequently.

TABLE 10-2 Types of Media Rotation Schedules

Rotation	Description	Advantages	Disadvantages
No rotation	Use a new tape for each backup. Only execute full backups.	Always have a snapshot of data every day.	Expensive to purchase and store all those tapes.
Grandfather, Father, Son (GFS)	Use one tape for each workday. Back up data on separate tape each workday. Use three weekly tapes. Back up a weekly tape on the final workday and store each weekly tape. Use 14 monthly tapes. Back up a monthly tape after four weeks and store each monthly tape.	Maintain a monthly snapshot of data for one year, a weekly snapshot of data for one month, and a daily snapshot of data for one week.	Requires labeling. Also, because daily tapes are frequently used, they need frequent replacement.
Tower of Hanoi	Each tape set is used a different number of times. When a new tape set is added to the group, it is used every other rotation. The next oldest tape set is used every fourth rotation; the next oldest after that is used every eighth rotation, and so on. Set rotations are performed daily or weekly.	Maintain several copies of data, several week-old copies of data, and a few monthly copies of data, with at least one year-old copy. Uses fewer tapes than the GFS method.	It is a complex rotation schedule that should be managed by an automated scheduler in order to perform it correctly.

EXERCISE 10-2

Performing a Full Backup on Windows 2000

1. Log on as Administrator of the Windows 2000 Server, or as a member of the Backup Operators group.

2. Click Start | Programs | Accessories | System Tools | Backup.

3. Click the Backup Wizard button, as shown in Figure 10-3.

4. Click Next at the Welcome screen.

5. Select the option to Back up everything on my computer, then click Next.

6. Select the backup media type, and the name of the media. Click Next.

FIGURE 10-3   Backup Wizard

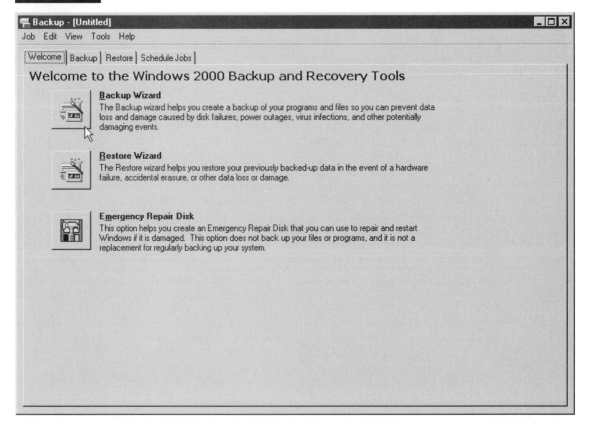

7. Click the Advanced button on the Summary screen, as shown in Figure 10-4.

8. Click the down arrow on the Select the type of backup operation to perform drop-down box. Note that you can select Normal, Copy, Differential, Incremental, and Daily. Select Copy so you do not interrupt normal backup operations on this server. Click Next.

9. Check the boxes to Verify data after backup, and Use Hardware Compression, if available. Click Next.

10. Select the option to Replace the data on the media with this backup, as depicted in Figure 10-5. Click Next.

11. Type in the appropriate backup label and media label, then click Next.

12. Select Later from the When to Back Up dialog box and provide the name and password of an administrator or member of the Backup Operators group. Click OK. Provide a name for the job, then click the Set Schedule button to select the date and time to start the backup.

13. The Schedule Job dialog box is shown in Figure 10-6. Select Once and a time to start ten minutes from now. Click OK, then click Next.

14. Review the summary and click Finish.

FIGURE 10-4

Advanced backup options

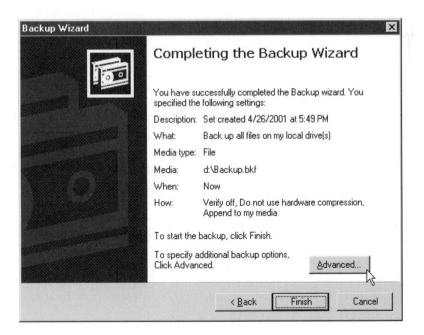

FIGURE 10-5

Replacing data on
your media

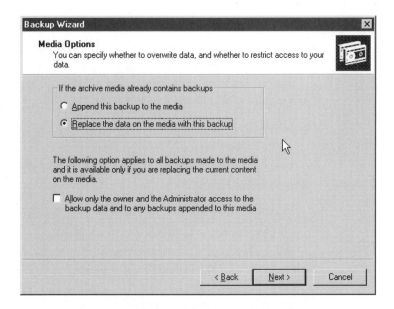

FIGURE 10-6

Scheduling a job

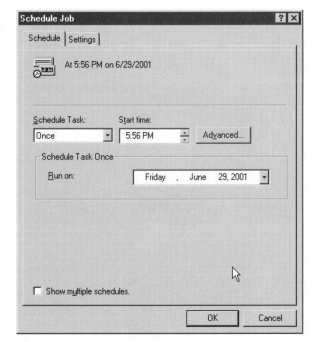

One of the best practices for tape backup is to verify the backup after it has completed. This ensures the backup is good, and that it is more likely to be restored if needed.

Confirming and Using Offsite Storage for Backup

An offsite storage facility is vital to ensuring data restoration. If you store all your tapes in the same location as your servers, and a natural disaster struck, then the data would be lost on both the tapes and the servers. However, if you send tapes offsite periodically, you will be able to restore data even if your facilities and servers are obliterated in some unforeseen cataclysm.

When selecting a storage facility, you should consider the same environmental factors that affect where you place your servers and tapes in your office. For example, you will want to know about:

- **Security** Who has access to your data? Will it be locked up? Will your data be protected from a person who calls up the storage facility and falsely claims to be a member of your organization?

- **Fire protection** Will the tapes be placed in fire-protected storage boxes? What other fire protection does the storage facility have?

- **Air conditioning and heating** What are the temperature variations in the area? Does the storage facility depend on air conditioning or heating to maintain a constant temperature?

- **Moisture control** Will the tapes be protected from moisture?

- **Availability** How quickly can you access your tapes if you need them? Can the facility provide access to your data online, given a set of procedures?

You should visit the storage facility to ensure that it is adequate, and that its delivery vehicles are secure and environmentally controlled. You would not want to select a storage facility that delivers your tapes to you in a pickup truck using open-lidded boxes. Once you have established offsite storage, you should test the offsite procedures to ensure they will work in the event of a disaster.

Documenting and Testing the Disaster Recovery Plan

After deciding on plans for disaster recovery, you should write them down and keep them in a place easily accessible. It is best to keep copies in your office, at satellite offices, and in offsite storage locations. The document itself should cover the following sections:

- **Plan introduction** This section should discuss the reason for the disaster recovery plan and when it should be used.

- **Business impacts** This section should discuss the impact a disaster might have on the business, listing not only those business areas at greatest risk, but also those that will have the greatest financial impact on the company. A matrix of the business areas listing their risks versus their financial impact will make this section easy to understand.

- **Roles and responsibilities** This section should discuss who will perform which functions should a disaster occur. You should list titles as well as names and contact information. Alternates for each role should also be documented.

- **Recovery strategies** This will be your longest section. You should include subheadings for the types of disasters and the approaches you will take from both a preventative and corrective standpoint. Each subheading should discuss the decision points you will make. Another subheading should discuss your escalation plans.

- **Disaster recovery checklists** This section consists of "To Do" lists. You should compose multiple checklists for the types of systems, locations, and staffing that will be needed.

- **System information** This section lists current information about the systems on your network as well as the strategies designed to replace or restore them if they are damaged. System information includes the operating system, updates installed, server names, recovery passwords (if any), IP addresses and protocol settings, services provided, directory services configurations, storage configurations, backup software versions, and applications.

- **Plan administration** This section of the plan discusses who will be in charge of ensuring ongoing disaster recovery "readiness." Such tasks will comprise updating the plan when the organization undergoes changes, ensuring backup and offsite storage management, disaster recovery plan testing, and any other administrative processes your organization requires.

Once the document is complete, you should conduct periodic testing of the plan to ensure you are prepared for any disaster. Tests should make certain the following items are handled:

- Each person understands his or her responsibilities.

- The disaster recovery plan is distributed to key personnel.

- Offsite storage facilities are accessible.

- Backups are tested and verified, and a test restore procedure is conducted.

- Substitute servers are tested and verified, and a test install and data restore procedure is conducted.

- Additional workstations are tested and verified, and a test install and data restore procedure is conducted.

- Personnel are able to carry on their activities at another facility.

- The disaster recovery plan test is evaluated for success or failure and updated accordingly.

CERTIFICATION OBJECTIVE 10.02

Restoring

Disaster recovery hinges on being able to get the business up and running again as quickly as possible. In some cases, you can restore each server to its original state. In other cases, you will need to replace servers. In yet others, you may be forced to restore your data using completely different servers, some that may even be in different physical sites, and reconfigure applications to access that data from a new place. Sometimes you may even need to "double up" data by consolidating servers just to get the business back on its feet. Regardless of the type of disaster—in the event of a failure of a server or of a server's storage system, the data must be restored *somewhere* in order for the business to return to a state of productivity.

Restoration procedures are not as easy as installations. Configuration information is not static and is usually placed in a file or database designated as part of the system. In order for a network operating system or application to remain stable, system files and configuration information should be such that they are not easily tampered with. Various protection mechanisms are put into place, such as marking the files read-only or hidden, or keeping them "open" so they cannot be replaced while the server is operating. As a result, these files are not easily restored if you've installed a new operating system and/or applications and wish to restore the previous configuration rather than re-configure the entire database. This is one of the main reasons you should not only devise a method of restoration, but test it to ensure it works.

Databases can be troublesome, even though they have been designed using an architecture that should make them easy to restore. In many cases, the data restoration is based not on the database file itself, but on transaction logs. Transaction log files improve database performance because all changes can be quickly recorded to a log file, and afterwards, applied to the database file. If a power failure occurs, data can be recovered up to the last transaction committed to the transaction log file. This further prevents a corrupted database file. When a database using transaction logs is recovered, the transaction log file is scanned to see if any transactions have not yet been applied. This is good if you have restored the latest version of the transaction logs. However, if you only restore the database file and do not restore the most recent transaction logs, you will not have a complete restoration of your data. In some cases, you may have a corrupt database file. In order to recover it to the latest transaction, you need only restore the database file and use the current transaction logs to apply the missing data.

exam
ⓦatch

When restoring data to a database server, make certain to restore the most recent transaction logs, as well as the latest non-corrupted database file.

Sometimes, you encounter a minor disaster in which someone has accidentally deleted a subset of data, where only that subset needs to be restored. For example, an administrator might delete a mailbox from an e-mail database server, which rates as a disaster only for the mailbox's owner (and a disaster for the administrator if that mailbox happens to be owned by the CEO). In this case, you should check the database server's documentation regarding single item recovery. There is generally a procedure that can be used to restore recently deleted items. If not, the next option is to restore the entire database file that contained the deleted subset. This is not as optimal as single item recovery since the remaining data will only be as recent as the last backup. A final option is to use a secondary recovery server. In this scenario, you would do the following:

1. Prepare a recovery server to use the same operating system and database application, including the same level of service pack updates, as the production server.

2. Make certain the recovery server does not join the production network server(s) or participate in any replication of data. For many database applications, this server should be identical to the one the information was deleted from. This process will require a topology similar to Figure 10-7.

FIGURE 10-7 Recovery Network is different from Production Network

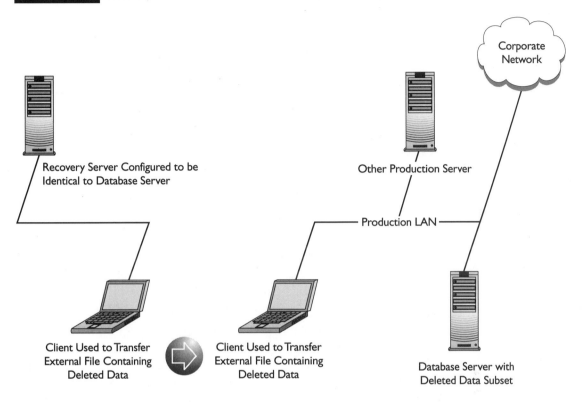

3. Restore the latest database file containing the deleted data subset on the recovery server.

4. Perform database consistency checking to ensure the data is restored and viable.

5. Export the data subset to a common file type. Most databases support comma delimited files. Others support a proprietary file structure, such as local e-mail repositories for e-mail services.

6. Copy the exported data file to a workstation or server.

7. Using the database client or administrative console, depending on how the database imports data files, import the data file into the database.

8. Verify the data has been imported.

9. Apply any permissions to the data subset and verify that the end-user can access the data.

Identifying Hardware Replacements

In order to survive a server failure, you should first determine whether the server needs replacement parts. This may not be an easy task. If the server will not power up, you may surmise the power supply needs to be replaced. However, after replacing the power supply you might find the RAM has been damaged, and must then replace that component, and so on.

One way of handling server failure is to use a temporary recovery server, so you can return the business to operational status at the earliest opportunity. Afterward, you can concentrate on repairing the failed server. Another strategy is to consolidate the data on another production server.

If your network uses strict standards for servers, you may be able to pre-identify a standard set of hardware parts that can be used on multiple servers in case of disaster. Then you can either store the parts offsite or keep them "on hold" at the vendor.

Identifying Hot and Cold Sites

Some business locations are so vital that a business cannot continue operations without them. These locations should consider using either a cold site or hot site for recovery of operations should a disaster arise. A cold site is one which is offline and unused, but which contains the needed equipment and office supplies to continue operations. If a cold site is identified, it must be maintained by the disaster recovery plan administrator so it will is ready when needed. If a disaster strikes, data must still be migrated to the cold site before it can be used. Cold sites are somewhat expensive to maintain, since they require monthly rent, as well as additional equipment and supplies that must be upgraded whenever the production network is upgraded.

A hot site is one which is online and connected to the production network. It holds a copy of data and can take over operations following a disaster, with little or no data loss. Hot sites are more expensive than cold sites because they require onsite administration and daily (or even more frequent) data migration from the production network.

on the Job

During monsoon season, a local hospital called up and asked for assistance in handling a problem with their network. A monsoon had hit that Monday, and since then no one could log on to the network or access its servers and printers. Status lights, however, were running on all the equipment and it seemed to be working fine. Over the phone, I asked the network administrator to turn off all the hubs and switches, then restart them. He refused, stating hospital policy required the equipment remain running at all times. The hospital called me back three days later—another consultant had worked all week trying to fix the problem, with no luck. I was able to run over during a lunch break from another client site. I had the network administrator take me to the room holding all the networking equipment. As I looked at the lights on the switches, I noticed they were pulsing—you could actually see a power surge running through the system. I told the administrator to turn around and not look, during which I turned off each piece of equipment then turned it back on again. Immediately, the administrator's pager went off. People were buzzing him to let him know they could log on to the network again. I then recommended the hospital protect their networking equipment with a UPS that could withstand power surges. Though they were lucky no equipment was damaged, they still lost four days of work due to the power surge.

Implementing the Disaster Recovery Plan

Even before a disaster strikes, you need to begin implementing your disaster recovery plan. The fault tolerance minimum standards for servers you place in the plan will need to be applied to all current and future servers. Depending on the standards you set, and comparing those standards to the existing servers on the network, this process may be an extensive project. After attaining a baseline for disaster recovery, you must maintain the plan and ensure that data backups and migrations are handled accordingly. Plan maintenance should include:

- Updates to the disaster plan documentation
- Annual disaster plan reviews
- Management of server standards
- Management of offsite data storage and/or server parts
- Testing of the plan, including retrieval of data from offsite and practice restorations
- Ensuring availability of a hot or cold site, should the need arise
- Conducting annual inspections of the offsite storage locations and hot or cold sites

SCENARIO & SOLUTION

Daily practices in your information technology department can greatly reduce costs when a disaster actually occurs. The following Scenario & Solution questions and answers will help you decide which practices make sense for your organization.

How can we ensure data is recoverable from a backup tape?	You can create and verify your daily backups, review your backup logs, and resolve all errors as soon as you are aware of them. Make certain all the data you need, including system files and configuration data, is being backed up.
How can we ensure backups can be restored to a server?	Make certain the equipment you use for server recovery is compatible or identical to the backup equipment used in your production network. Tape formats, in particular, should be consistent throughout your network.
What is the best way to protect equipment from fire?	Your building probably has a sprinkler system to put out fires. But water can cause as much, or more, damage to networking equipment than fire. You should invest in protective racks and rack-mounted servers to house the equipment, which will protect it (somewhat) from water. You should also maintain fire extinguishers in the server room. If you can afford to spend more, server rooms can be engineered to release dry chemicals necessary to suppress fires. Also, ventilation systems can be installed to move the smoke away from the room, reducing heat damage.
How do you prepare for a disaster?	Perform fire drills on an annual basis (at least). These drills should step through every process, from moving to a hot or cold site, to retrieving data, to obtaining recovery equipment and performing restoration.
What should be on an installation checklist to ensure a new server can be recovered just the same as existing ones?	Review the location. Make certain there is enough power. Ensure that tape backup equipment and tape formats are consistent with existing ones. Use standard server equipment. Update the disaster recovery plan to include the new server.
How do you explain the importance of a disaster recovery plan to management?	Determine the costs for downtime, either in dollars or in some productivity measurement, such as lost orders/minute. Perform a short risk analysis of the types of disasters that can cause downtime. Provide the risks and costs to management to support the need for disaster recovery planning.

Restoring Active Directory

Active Directory is a directory service for Windows 2000. You must be using a Domain Controller in order to perform this exercise, which is an authoritative restore, and should only be executed on a test server for the purposes of learning the process. If your test server is part of a multiserver domain, you should wait until all servers have synchronized, about 15 minutes in a single test LAN, between the steps of creating and deleting. Deleted items require authoritative restores. If you require a non-authoritative restore due to a server failure, you can restart the server when first prompted (shown in the exercise as Step 9).

You should already have a backup for this server. If not, create a backup as described in Exercise 10-2.

1. Click Start | Programs | Administrative Tools | Active Directory Users & Computers.

2. Right-click on the Domain and select New | Organizational Unit. Name the OU "**DeleteMe.**"

3. Right-click on the DeleteMe OU and select New | User. Fill out the minimal details and Create the user. Repeat this process for as many users as you wish to test restoring.

4. Right-click on the DeleteMe OU and select Delete.

5. Shut down the server and boot into Directory Services Restore Mode, by pressing F8 at the server startup, selecting Safe Mode and Other Startup Options, and then selecting Directory Services Restore Mode.

6. Log on to Windows 2000 with a local administrator's account and confirm OK to the Safe Mode dialog box.

7. Click Start | Programs | Accessories | System Tools | Backup, then select the Restore Wizard.

8. Click Next at the Welcome screen. At the What to Restore dialog box, expand your most recent backup and checkmark the System State data. Click Finish.

9. At the prompt to restart the computer, click No. Then close the Backup application.

10. Click Start | Run and type **CMD**. Press ENTER to open a command prompt.

11. Type **NTDSUTIL** and press ENTER.

12. Type **AUTHORITATIVE RESTORE** and press ENTER.

13. Type **RESTORE SUBTREE OU=DeleteMe,DC=yourdomainname,DC=COM** and press ENTER. Replace yourdomainname with your actual domain name. You may need to replace com, if you are using a .org or .local name for your domain.

14. A message should appear telling you the restore completed successfully. Type **QUIT** twice to change prompts and then **EXIT** to close the Command prompt window.

15. Restart the server and verify the DeleteMe OU has been restored by looking in the Active Directory Users and Computers console.

CERTIFICATION SUMMARY

As organizations depend increasingly on their information technology infrastructure investments to provide the core of their business, that IT infrastructure becomes more valuable. A disaster recovery plan is geared towards protecting that investment, as well as providing a method of returning the business to a productive state as soon as possible.

One of the major tasks in disaster recovery is simply to protect data from accidental loss through preventative measures. Hardware failures, power issues, software corruption, and natural disasters can all contribute to data loss. Preventative measures range from installing Uninterruptible Power Supplies (UPS) to using redundant hardware components.

Another major task is to enable data recovery through corrective measures. Regardless of the problem that caused the data loss, an administrator should be able to restore the data to a system that can provide the business function. Corrective measures include conducting daily backups of the data, planning for server replacement, or even finding alternate locations (hot or cold sites) if the worksite is damaged enough that the business must move in order to continue operations.

Disaster recovery plans require ongoing maintenance and management. An administrator should conduct annual drills, continuously update the plan with new information, and ensure ongoing backups are performed. Restoration is more difficult than installation, so it should be practiced long before a real disaster requires it to be performed.

✓ TWO-MINUTE DRILL

Here are some of the key points from each certification objective in Chapter 10.

Planning for Disaster Recovery

❑ Before starting your disaster recovery plan, you should determine what a disaster would cost for each server and site, as well as the risk of certain disaster types likely to occur.

❑ There are four ways of handling disasters: monitor for threats of disasters, deter disasters, prevent disasters, and correct disasters. Most disaster recovery plans consist of preventative and corrective measures.

❑ You can plan redundancy for internal server components such as network adapters, power supplies, and RAID.

❑ You can plan redundancy at the server level by implementing clusters.

❑ A hot swap is when you can replace a component, such as a hard drive, without shutting down power or I/O on the server.

❑ Fault recovery is the method of restoring a system to a previously "known good" state.

❑ A disaster recovery plan should account for disasters of all sizes, whether it be the failure of a single server or an entire location.

❑ Tape libraries are ideal for backing up multiple servers and/or workstations.

❑ An incremental backup only backs up new items or those that have changed since the last backup.

❑ An offsite storage facility should have the same environmental qualities you expect of your server locations.

❑ Disaster recovery plans should be tested and maintained.

Restoring

❑ The main goal of restoration is to get the business back to a state of productivity.

❑ The latest transaction logs will recover database files to the most recent transaction.

❑ A recovery server used temporarily can speed up business recovery while you identify and replace hardware components.

❑ A hot site is one which is *live* and online at the same time as the production network. If there is a disaster, staff simply transfers to the hot site.

❑ The disaster recovery plan should be maintained on an ongoing basis and periodically tested.

SELF TEST

The following questions will help you measure your understanding of the material presented in this chapter. Read all the choices carefully, as there may be more than one correct answer. Choose all correct answers for each question.

Planning for Disaster Recovery

1. Which of the following is a Redundant Array of Inexpensive Disks (RAID) helpful for in disaster prevention?

   A. Monitoring and event triggering

   B. Deterrent measures

   C. Preventative measures

   D. Corrective measures

2. You have been tasked with developing a disaster recovery plan. Which of the following duties do you tackle first?

   A. Test a server restore.

   B. Set up weekly backups.

   C. Determine whether a ZIP drive should be used to back up your server.

   D. Determine what threats will cause costly downtime.

3. Which of the following components should *not* be redundant in the server?

   A. UPS

   B. Storage

   C. Power supply

   D. Network adapter

4. Your company operates a database application that contains information about every one of its customers. Without this database, no one can conduct a sale or provide service without undergoing lengthy manual processes. Which of the following redundant systems is most appropriate to protect this database application?

   A. Network adapter

   B. Cluster server

   C. Power supply

D. AIT tape backup device

5. Which describes a system where a component can be physically replaced without shutting down the server power, and without discontinuing I/O?

   A. A cold swap

   B. A warm swap

   C. A hot swap

   D. A hot spare

6. You are developing a disaster recovery plan. Your analysis finds that a hard disk failure causes you nine hours of downtime, which costs $20,000 per hour, or a total of $180,000 for Server1, and costs $150 per hour, or a total of $1050 for Server2. Which of the following preventative measures should be instituted for Server2?

   A. A tape backup at a cost of $1000

   B. Redundant network adapters at a cost of $250

   C. RAID5 for a cost of $12,000

   D. RAID1 for a cost of $550

7. Which of the following does not constitute a disaster?

   A. Hard disk failure causing the server to go down.

   B. Memory failure causing the server to go down.

   C. Software error causing database corruption.

   D. A fire in the janitor's closet which is immediately put out.

8. You are developing a disaster recovery plan for your network. Which of the following should you include in your plan?

   A. Office floor plans for use in evacuation routes

   B. Phone numbers to local office supply stores

   C. Sprinkler system layout

   D. Names of all end-users

9. Your database server has a 20GB database. How long will it take to back up the database with a Digital Linear Tape drive that has a 50Mbps transfer rate?

   A. 20 minutes

   B. 6.83 minutes

C. 4 minutes

D. 42.67 minutes

10. Which of the following backup hardware devices is best for backing up multiple servers with 30GB of data?

A. Floppy disk

B. AIT

C. JAZ

D. Magneto-Optical

11. In your disaster recovery plan, you have specified that all servers should have full backups performed. You are reviewing your backups and note that some of your most critical files are not being backed up. Why might this be happening?

A. The backup has been configured to skip these files.

B. The tape device does not have the capacity to back them up.

C. Users have kept the files open during backup.

D. The backup type is incremental and the files have not been changed since the last backup.

12. Which of the following types of backups only back up files that have been changed since the last full backup, even if partial backups have taken place since that last full backup where the archive bit was not changed?

A. Full backup

B. Differential backup

C. Incremental backup

D. Copy backup

13. You have been instructed to select an offsite storage facility for backup tapes. What should you verify about the offsite storage facility?

A. That the facility uses RAID on its servers.

B. That the location is near your office.

C. That you can have a Web cam pointed at your tapes.

D. That the offsite storage facility uses air conditioning.

14. Janelle is the backup operator for the network. She has just resigned and will be replaced by Gary. What is your next task as the disaster recovery plan administrator?

   A. Perform a drill of the disaster recovery plan.

   B. Change the backup methods.

   C. Update the plan with the new contact information.

   D. Check your offsite facility for environmental controls.

Restoring

15. An administrator has accidentally deleted an entire section of a database. Which of the following files should be restored?

   A. The database file

   B. Boot logs

   C. Backup logs

   D. System state data

16. A mailbox has been deleted from the mailserver. You have been tasked with restoring the mailbox. One of the Web applications you use is run from the e-mail server, so you have been asked to restore the mailbox without interrupting the e-mail system. How can you do this?

   A. You should take the server down and perform an authoritative restore.

   B. You should run a service that undeletes files.

   C. You should restore the e-mail data onto a recovery server, export the mailbox to a file and import it to the server.

   D. You should perform a differential backup.

17. Which of the following can be used to quickly restore the business to productivity, regardless of which hardware components on a failed server must be repaired?

   A. A full backup

   B. A differential backup

   C. An extra network adapter

   D. A recovery server

18. Your company is solely based on the Internet. All sales and services are provided by Web applications. You are selecting a method for disaster recovery. Your business impact, if your site were to fail, will be a complete loss of all business, which is estimated at more than a million dollars per month. Which of the following should you consider for your disaster recovery plan?

    A. A spare site

    B. A hot site

    C. A cold site

    D. A warm site

19. Which of the following practices will make certain your tapes can be restored?

    A. Using identical tape backup devices with identical formats.

    B. Performing only incremental backups.

    C. Using the latest backup device.

    D. Storing tapes in an offsite storage facility.

20. What will help you persuade upper management to develop a disaster recovery plan?

    A. Providing upper management with a business impact analysis.

    B. Running the company through a fire drill.

    C. Purchasing an extra server for recovery purposes.

    D. Selecting a hot site.

LAB QUESTION

You have a Windows 2000 Domain Controller that will not turn on. There is no indication that power is running to the server, even though the power outlet and UPS both seem to be working fine. The server also holds the main SQL Server database for your company's ongoing operations. You have another server in your lab with similar capabilities. How do you proceed with a restoration?

SELF TEST ANSWERS

Planning for Disaster Recovery

1. ☑ **C.** RAID acts as a preventative measure against hard disk failure. If a hard disk fails, then server failure is prevented because the RAID system can tolerate a hard disk failure.

☒ **A** is incorrect because monitoring and event triggering is a method simply alerting the administrator that a threat of disaster *can* occur. **B** is incorrect because a deterrent measure protects against human-initiated threats. **D** is incorrect because a RAID array cannot correct a failure that has already taken place.

2. ☑ **D.** You should determine what threats of disaster exist for your environment, and whether they will cause downtime. Furthermore, you will want to determine how much downtime the threats may cause.

☒ **A** is incorrect because you would test a server restore only after you had a disaster recovery plan established. **B** is incorrect because you may discover that a daily backup is more appropriate for your disaster recovery plan. **C** is incorrect because you have not determined what type of risks your company is exposed to, and therefore don't know what hardware would be best used to back up your server.

3. ☑ **A.** A UPS should not be redundant in the server. It is not an internal component, and as a battery backup device it does not require redundancy.

☒ **B, C,** and **D** are incorrect because you should consider redundant components for your storage, power supply, and network adapters.

4. ☑ **B.** A cluster server is the most appropriate of the available choices to protect the database application since it provides the most redundant features. It is also a good idea to place the database on a RAID-based storage system, too.

☒ **A** is incorrect because two network adapters cannot ensure as much protection as a cluster. **C** is incorrect because two power supplies offer less protection than a cluster. **D** is incorrect because an AIT backup device is not a redundant system.

5. ☑ **C.** A hot swap allows you to replace a component while the server continues operating.

☒ **A** is incorrect because a cold swap requires the server power be shut off, which means that I/O cannot continue. **B** is incorrect because a warm swap allows the power to continue, but I/O must be discontinued. **D** is incorrect because a hot spare does not need to be physically replaced, it automatically switches over.

6. ☑ **D.** You can prevent a hard disk failure from causing you downtime by implementing a mirrored drive, or RAID1, on Server2. The cost of $550 is less than the amount of money that would be lost if there was a hard disk failure.

   ☒ **A** is incorrect because tape backup is not a preventative measure, it is a corrective measure. **B** is incorrect because redundant network adapters will not prevent a hard disk failure from causing downtime. **C** is incorrect because RAID5 is too costly a measure for Server2. RAID5, however, would be an appropriate preventative measure for Server1, especially if implemented with a hot spare.

7. ☑ **D.** A fire in the janitor's closet which is immediately put out does not constitute a disaster, because it did not cause an interruption in business productivity.

   ☒ **A, B,** and **C** are incorrect because database corruption and servers going down for any reason will cause an interruption in business productivity.

8. ☑ **A.** You should include office floor plans for use in evacuation routes since end-user safety is a high priority in disaster recovery planning.

   ☒ **B** is incorrect because you can obtain office supply store phone numbers at any time, if needed. **C** is incorrect because the sprinkler system layout will not change your disaster recovery plans. **D** is incorrect because the names of all end-users are not necessary to disaster recovery.

9. ☑ **B.** It should take
   (20GB * 1024MB/GB) / (50Mbps) = 409.6 seconds / 60 seconds/minute = 6.83 minutes.

   ☒ **A, C,** and **D** are incorrect time choices.

10. ☑ **B.** An Advanced Intelligent Tape (AIT) backup device, because it has high capacity and a fast transfer rate, is the best choice of these four options for backing up multiple servers with 30GB of data.

    ☒ **A** is incorrect because a floppy disk is never good for backing up a server, nor does it have the capacity for even 1GB of data. **C** is incorrect because a JAZ drive is not appropriate for server backups and does not have the capacity. **D** is incorrect because Magneto-Optical disks do not have the capacity for 30GB of data, as compared to AIT.

11. ☑ **C.** If a file is open, it might not be backed up. You can review the backup logs to determine if files were open during the backup procedure. You should also look for a method of disconnecting users from the server and closing files during backups to prevent this from happening in the future.

    ☒ **A** is incorrect because a full backup does not skip files. **B** is incorrect because it is highly unlikely. Most tape devices will simply ask for another tape after a previous tape has been filled to capacity. **D** is incorrect because full backups were specified in the question.

12. ☑ **B.** A differential backup will back up any file that is new or has been changed, as designated by the archive bit, since the last full backup. A differential backup does not change the archive bit.

    ☒ **A** is incorrect because a full backup will back up every file on the server regardless of whether it is new or has been changed since the last backup. **C** is incorrect because an incremental backup will only back up files that are new or have been changed since the last backup, even if it was an incremental backup. **D** is incorrect because a copy backup backs up all files regardless of previous backups.

13. ☑ **D.** You will want to verify that the offsite storage facility has environmental controls similar to that used in your server room.

    ☒ **A, B,** and **C** are incorrect because none of these items affect how well your data is protected and managed.

14. ☑ **C.** Whenever a person who plays a role in the disaster recovery plan has changed positions, you should update the roles and responsibilities section of the plan with the new contact information.

    ☒ **A, B,** and **D** are incorrect because none of these tasks relates to the backup operator position change.

Restoring

15. ☑ **A.** The database file should be restored. The most recent transaction logs will update the database file with the latest transactions.

    ☒ **B, C,** and **D** are incorrect because boot logs, backup logs, and system state data will not be useful for a database restore.

16. ☑ **C.** You can perform a mailbox restoration using a separate recovery server, where you can export the mailbox, and import it into the production server without interrupting the e-mail system.

    ☒ **A** is incorrect because taking the server down does not keep the e-mail system running. **B** is incorrect because the mailbox is probably not a separate file, but a part of a database. **D** is incorrect because a differential backup will not restore the data.

17. ☑ **D.** A recovery server can be used to take the place of a production server until you can identify and replace the server's damaged parts.

    ☒ **A, B,** and **C** are incorrect because backups and a network adapter will not, by themselves, quickly restore the server if the server has failed hardware components.

18. ☑ **B.** Given the extensive reliance of the business on the server data, and the value of that business, a hot site is the optimal choice for disaster recovery.

    ☒ **A** and **D** are incorrect because neither a spare site nor a warm site exist. **C** is incorrect because a disaster would cause an interruption in business during the time it takes to get the cold site up and running.

19. ☑ **A.** If you use identical tape backup devices with identical formats for the tapes, then you will be more assured of restoring the data.

    ☒ **B** is incorrect because an incremental backup does not ensure that the data can be restored. **C** is incorrect because the age of the tape backup device does not affect whether the data can be restored. **D** is incorrect because storing the tapes in an offsite storage facility will not ensure they can be restored.

20. ☑ **A.** A business impact analysis listing the types of disaster threats and the cost to the business will help persuade upper management to develop a disaster recovery plan.

    ☒ **B, C,** and **D** are incorrect because these options are elements that you might place in a disaster recovery plan, but will not persuade management to develop a disaster recovery plan.

LAB ANSWER

First, determine what the cause of the problem is. You may correctly surmise the problem is related to the power supply.

1. After obtaining a new power supply for the server, you will find that the server starts, but that it will take too many days to order other parts that need to be installed.

2. Since the server is vital to the organization, you should restore the data to the lab server on a temporary basis.

3. Start by installing Windows 2000 Server as a Domain Controller in the same domain configuration as the previous Windows 2000 Server.

4. Install all the Service packs for the operating system.

5. Install SQL Server.

6. Install any applications and application service packs.

7. Restart the server in the Directory Services Restore Mode.

8. Open the Windows 2000 Backup application. Perform a full restore, including system state data, from the last full backup.

9. Restart the server.

A

About the CD

T his CD-ROM contains the CertTrainer software. CertTrainer comes complete with ExamSim, Skill Assessment tests, and the e-book(electronic version of the book). CertTrainer is easy to install on any Windows 98/NT/2000 computer and must be installed to access these features. You may, however, browse the e-book directly from the CD without installation.

Installing CertTrainer

If your computer CD-ROM drive is configured to autorun, the CD-ROM will automatically start up upon inserting the disk. From the opening screen you may either browse the e-book or install CertTrainer by pressing the *Install Now* button. This will begin the installation process and create a program group named "CertTrainer." To run CertTrainer use START | PROGRAMS | CERTTRAINER.

System Requirements

CertTrainer requires Windows 98 or higher and Internet Explorer 4.0 or above and 600 MB of hard disk space for full installation.

CertTrainer

CertTrainer provides a complete review of each exam objective, organized by chapter. You should read each objective summary and make certain that you understand it before proceeding to the SkillAssessor. If you still need more practice on the concepts of any objective, use the "In Depth" button to link to the corresponding section from the Study Guide.

Once you have completed the review(s) and feel comfortable with the material, launch the SkillAssessor quiz to test your grasp of each objective. Once you complete the quiz, you will be presented with your score for that chapter.

ExamSim

As its name implies, ExamSim provides you with a simulation of the actual exam. The number of questions, the type of questions, and the time allowed are intended to be an accurate representation of the exam environment. You will see the following screen when you are ready to begin ExamSim:

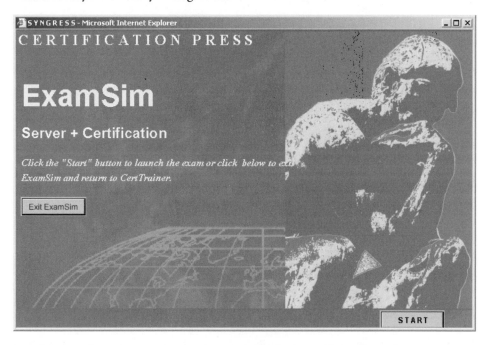

When you launch ExamSim, a digital clock display will appear in the upper left-hand corner of your screen. The clock will continue to count down to zero unless you choose to end the exam before the time expires.

Saving Scores as Cookies

Your ExamSim score is stored as a browser cookie. If you've configured your browser to accept cookies, your score will be stored in a file named *History*. If your browser is not configured to accept cookies, you cannot permanently save your scores. If you delete this History cookie, the scores will be deleted permanently.

E-Book

The entire contents of the Study Guide are provided in HTML form, as shown in the following screen. Although the files are optimized for Internet Explorer, they can also be viewed with other browsers including Netscape.

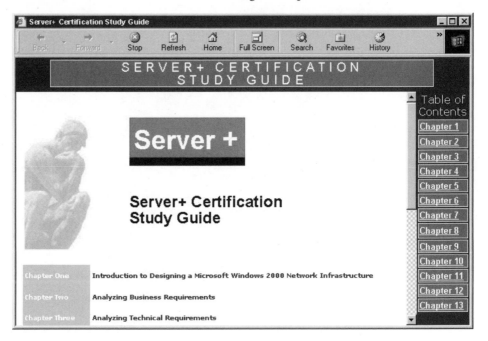

Help

A help file is provided through a help button on the main CertTrainer screen in the lower right hand corner.

Upgrading

A button is provided on the main ExamSim screen for upgrades. This button will take you to www.syngress.com where you can download any available upgrades.

Server+

COMPUTING TECHNOLOGY INDUSTRY ASSOCIATION

B

About the Web Site

A t Access.Globalknowledge, the premier online information source for IT professionals (http://access.globalknowledge.com), you'll enter a Global Knowledge information portal designed to inform, educate, and update visitors on issues regarding IT and IT education.

Get *What* You Want *When* You Want It

At the Access.Globalknowledge site, you can:

- Choose personalized technology articles related to your interests. Access a news article, a review, or a tutorial, customized to what you want to see, regularly throughout the week.

- Continue your education, in between Global courses, by taking advantage of chat sessions with other users or instructors. Get the tips, tricks, and advice that you need today!

- Make your point in the Access.Globalknowledge community by participating in threaded discussion groups related to technologies and certification.

- Get instant course information at your fingertips. Customized course calendars show you the courses you want, and when and where you want them.

- Obtain the resources you need with online tools, trivia, skills assessment, and more!

All this and more is available now on the Web at:

http://access.globalknowledge.com

Visit today!

Glossary

Active terminator   Uses a voltage regulator to normalize the termination voltage.

Address Resolution Protocol (ARP)   A utility that resolves TCP/IP addresses to the MAC address of the network adapter.

Advanced Technology Attachment (ATA)   This architecture integrates the disk controller onto the drive itself. IDE supports up to two drives on a 16 bit interface and PIO modes 0, 1, and 2. Other drives based on the ATA standards include ATAPI (typically associated with CD-ROM drives), Fast-ATA, and Ultra-ATA. ATA is also known as IDE. *See also* Fast ATA.

Advanced Technology Attachment Packet Interface (ATAPI)   This architecture is the specification for IDE tape drives and CD-ROMs.

Agent   Agents may be installed as software that is loaded on a managed device, or it may be part of a device's firmware. It will often be installed as software when you are managing something like a server, or some other piece of equipment that uses software. The agent may also reside in the firmware of a device, as is the case with network bridges and other devices that don't support software being loaded into them. *See also* Management agent.

Agent code   The agent code defines all of the parameters available to the management system. They can either be written into a device's software driver or incorporated as a separate application. This separate application will communicate with the device either through its driver or firmware to provide these parameters to the management system. Compaq has chosen to use the separate-application approach in their management agent software.

Alerter service   In Windows 2000, the Alerter service provides a method of notifying designated users of events and problems that are encountered. This service is used by the server, services running on that server, and devices like a UPS. It works with the Messenger service, which is used to send messages to users when the Alerter service encounters a specified issue.

Application   *See* Management application.

Archive bit   When a full backup is performed, the file is changed to indicate that it has been backed up. What is changed is called the *archive bit.* The archive bit is an attribute of a file, which indicates whether files need to be backed up or not. The archive bit is set when a file is modified to show that data within it has changed, and thereby needs to be backed up. It is cleared by a full backup to show that the file has been backed up to tape.

ARP   *See* Address Resolution Protocol.

Array   *See* Redundant Array of Inexpensive Disks.

Array controller   An array controller is an interface card that connects to both hard disks using a SCSI cable and has the configuration information on the logical disk that is created.

ATA   *See* Advanced Technology Attachment.

ATAPI   *See* Advanced Technology Attachment Packet Interface.

Autopilot backup   A tape rotation scheme (similar to GFS) is the "autopilot" strategy, in which software used for the backup keeps a database, and expects a certain tape to be inserted each day. Daily weekly, and monthly backup tapes are used with this strategy, with 20-25 tapes used in a rotation. It is common to use 21 tapes consisting of four daily tapes for each Monday through Thursday in a month, five weekly tapes for each Friday (as some months have five Fridays), and 12 monthly tapes for the last weekday of the month. What makes this different from the GFS strategy is that the software expects specific tapes each day, saving you from having to manually keep a schedule of what to backup.

Backup   *See* Autopilot backup; Copy backup; Data backup; Differential backup; Full backup; Incremental backup; Tape backup.

Ballast   Racks are filled with heavy equipment, and if they are tilted, they can fall over easily. If you have a single, free standing rack, obtain the stabilizing "feet," or *ballast*, from the rack manufacturer and attach it so that it will be difficult to push over.

Baseline   A baseline is a snapshot of your computer or network's performance measurements, which can be used for planning and analysis. To create a baseline, you would run a system or network monitoring tool at times when the server, workstation and/or network is running normally. These results are logged, so that performance measurements are saved to a file. *See also* Server baseline.

Basic Input/Output System (BIOS)   The BIOS is a small chip inside the computer that is responsible for informing the processor(s) about which devices are present in the system and how to communicate with those devices. Whenever the processor makes a request from a component, the BIOS steps in and translates the request into instructions that the required component can understand. All communication to the computer's components must go through the BIOS. If the BIOS cannot communicate with a component, the computer, in effect, cannot make use of that component. If you install a device with which the computer seems unable to communicate, you might need to upgrade or replace the existing BIOS. If the BIOS chip cannot be upgraded, then you must consider replacing either the motherboard or the entire server. *See also* Flash BIOS.

Biometrics   Biometrics is another useful tool for physical security. In this technology though, "physical" is truly part of the package. Biometrics uses measurements of a person's characteristics to allow or deny access to a system. These characteristics may include fingerprints, voice patterns, facial patterns, eye retinas, and so forth. These measurements are stored, analyzed, and used to authenticate people.

BIOS   *See* Basic Input/Output System.

Blackouts   Blackouts are a total loss of power, which may be caused by anything from a blown circuit breaker to a loss of power from the electric company.

Bottleneck   In terms of networking, a bottleneck is a component that restricts the flow of information. Even though the component may be operating at peak efficiency, other components are passing the information at a faster rate. Once the bottleneck is eliminated, the performance will improve.

Brownouts/sags   Brownouts or sags are temporary reductions in power, which may occur when large machinery starts up, or when the electric company drops the electricity to an area (such as when a transformer blows out, or there is a high demand for power in a particular area). Brownouts are a problem, because if a computer loses power for longer than 50 milliseconds, they will generally reboot themselves.

Buffer   Some memory module designs (usually those involving large numbers of chips) require a device to re-drive or amplify the signals. On EDO modules this device is called a buffer; on synchronous modules this device is called a register.

Cable SELect (CSEL) method   CSEL is another method of cabling IDE drives. CSEL has been a part of the ATA specification for quite some time but has never been fully implemented. CSEL is implemented using a special cable that has one connector with pin 28 not connected. This disconnected ping indicates to the drive that it is the slave. To implement CSEL both drives must support it and be jumpered accordingly, a CSEL cable is used and the host adapter supports CSEL. An adapter that supports CSEL will have pin 28 grounded. Though most hard drives support this configuration, it is rare to find the cable or a BIOS that supports it. CSEL may become more prevalent as the PnP (Plug and Play) initiative becomes more prevalent.

Cache memory   Cache memory is a small amount of fast SRAM that resides between the CPU and the main memory. Cache memory comes in three sizes: 256KB, 512KB, 1024KB and 2048KB. *See also* Primary cache memory; Secondary cache memory.

Catastrophic damage   When ESD causes the immediate malfunction of a device, it is considered *catastrophic*. As unlikely as it might seem, catastrophic damage can be less harmful to the system than degradation. When a device suffers catastrophic damage, the result is immediate and typically quite obvious, so the device will most likely be replaced right away.

Cathode Ray Tube (CRT)   Most desktop computers use CRT monitors. CRTs use an electron gun to activate phosphors behind the screen.

Central Processing Unit (CPU)   A CPU is a chip that has a number of transistors and is used to move and calculate data within the personal computer (PC).

CGA   *See* Color Graphics Adapter.

Check Disk   Error checking tools can be used to detect bad sectors and errors with your file system. One such tool is Check Disk, which is shipped with Windows 2000. This is similar to the chkdsk tool that shipped with previous versions of Windows NT. It will analyze hard disks to determine if any problems exist, and when possible, will fix them automatically.

Cluster   A cluster can be configured to share the load or act as a failover. In the shared load configuration, all the servers in the cluster are performing concurrently by providing services to end-users. In the failover configuration, which is generally a two-server configuration, one server provides services on the network while the second server is configured as a standby. If the second server detects a failure, it takes over and provides services.

CMOS   *See* Complementary Metal Oxide Semiconductor.

Coaxial cable   Coaxial cable is similar to what we use today for television and VCR connections. Coaxial cable is made up of two conductors that share a common axis. This is where the name comes from. The inside of the cable is made up of a solid or stranded copper wire typically surrounded by foam. Next is an outer wire mesh tube that further protects the signal traveling along the inner wire. The outside is a tougher plastic encasement that protects all the inner components.

Color Graphics Adapter (CGA) monitor   CGA monitors are an older type and can display combinations of red, green, and blue at different intensities, resulting in 16 different colors. The maximum resolution of a CGA monitor is 640 x 200 pixels in monochrome mode and 160 x 100 pixels in 16-color mode.

COM *See* Component Object Model.

Community name A good way to look at a community name is as a password. When configuring SNMP, you provide a list of community names that will have access to the managed objects on the system. Community names are SNMP's security solution. The same community name must be supplied in the management application. If the community names match, the application will be permitted to communicate with the management agent. If the names do not match, then access will be denied and no exchange of information will take place. An important detail to note here is that community names are case-sensitive. This is often the cause of many communication problems between the management agent and the management application, for those new to the process. For each community name provided, two potential security settings exist. The first option is READ and the second is READ/CREATE (read/write).

Complementary Metal Oxide Semiconductor (CMOS) An energy saving chip used in battery powered laptops and a variety of applications. CMOS is also used in desktop computers to hold the date, time, and other startup parameters.

Component Object Model (COM) Microsoft's component architecture software. It creates a structure to aid in constructing routines to be retrieved and executed.

Controller Most controllers are either fibre channel arbitrated loop (FC-AL) interfaces or SCSI devices.

Copy backup A full backup of all data are completed but no archive bits are changed. A copy backup does not affect any current backup system or rotation schedule you are using.

Counter Log Counter Logs are used to obtain and store data that's collected by the counters you specify. When counter logs are used, data are obtained at specific update intervals. The data can be stored in a comma-delimited or tab-separated format, so that it can then be imported into other programs, or in a binary log format. This information can be viewed using System Monitor, or it can be exported to other programs for analysis or when creating reports.

CPU   *See* Central Processing Unit.

Cross-linked files   Cross-linked files are two or more files that are using the same area of the disk, so that data are only correct for one of the files.

Crosstalk   Crosstalk is when two wires in close proximity inadvertently share information due to interfering with each other.

CRT   *See* Cathode Ray Tube.

CSEL   *See* Cable SELect.

DAT   *See* Digital Audio Tape.

Data backup   Data backups are copies of data that are written to a tape or other storage devices. Using a backup program, your files are archived to a medium that can be stored in another location.

DDS   *See* Digital Data Storage.

Degradation   When ESD causes a gradually worsening problem in a device, it is referred to as *degradation*. Degradation, on the other hand, can cause a component to malfunction sporadically, sometimes working and sometimes not. This makes it harder to pinpoint the problem, so the problem itself can persist for a longer period of time. Additionally, a total failure of one component will typically not affect the usability of other components. However, degradation can cause a component to fail in ways that also result in the failure of other components.

DHCP   *See* Dynamic Host Configuration Protocol.

Diagnostic partition   A diagnostic partition is a specially protected section of the hard disk, which is used to store setup and diagnostic utilities that are used by your computer. The setup software is used to configure your system, change security settings, and configure power management. The diagnostic software is used to test and analyze the computer, to determine if problems exist. Not all computers use diagnostic partitions, as many will use a CMOS setup routine. However, many computers — such as those manufactured by Compaq—use a hidden drive on the hard disk.

Diagnostic tools   Diagnostic tools are used to troubleshoot your computer, and detect possible problems. Such tools may be included with the computer itself, available through the operating system installed on it, or added separately as utilities and software packages. Due to the various ways diagnostic tools are available to you, the methods in which they are used and upgraded vary.

Differential backup   Differential backups will back up all files that were modified since the last full backup but doesn't clear the archive bit when data are backed up. A differential backup is different from an incremental backup, which would backup the modified file, clear the archive bit, and not back it up again until the file was modified. Since a differential backup will backup all files modified since the last full backup, the benefit of a differential backup over a incremental backup is that only two backup sets are required. To restore data, you would restore the full backup, and then the differential backup tape.

Differential signaling system   "Balanced" SCSI bus. Uses one return line for every outgoing line thus doubling the amount of wires from an SE method. HVD is more expensive than SE but is less likely to accept interference and extends the cable length to 25 meters. Also called High Voltage Differential (HVD).

Digital Audio Tape (DAT)   The DAT drive was created by Sony and Philips for recording music in a digital format, but was found to be useful for recording data in backups. With this method, data are stored on 4 mm tapes. DAT is not as fast as DLT, and doesn't provide as large of a storage capacity. However, it is less expensive than DLT, which makes DAT a popular method of tape backup.

Digital Data Storage (DDS)   The DDS format uses a process similar to that used in VCRs to store data on the DAT tape. It uses a helical scan, in which read/write heads spin diagonally across a DAT tape. Two read heads and two write heads are used. When data are written, the read heads verify that data have been written correctly to the tape. If it detects any errors, the data are rewritten.

Digital Linear Tape (DLT)   The DLT method (in contrast to DAT) of data storage was originally developed by Digital Equipment Corporation but is currently owned by Quantum Corporation. It stores data on a half-inch magnetic reel-to-reel tape, in which one reel is contained in the cartridge while the other is stored inside the DLT drive. Digital Linear Tape is faster than DDS, and provides a higher storage capacity. Unlike DDS, each version of DLT provides data compression.

DIMMs   *See* Dual inline memory modules.

Direct Memory Access (DMA)   DMA channels allow devices to write data directly into memory without first being asked by the processor. Other devices can read this data directly from memory without asking the processor for it.

Disaster recovery plan   Any disaster recovery plan should discuss strategies for all possible disasters. Since all catastrophes are not equal, the method of recovering from one type might be completely different than recovering from another type. At the server level, you should consider a disaster as constituting the failure of one or more components within the server. The next level of disaster you should consider is a failure external to the server. It could be the failure of another network component, or a disaster on a much larger scale. Finally, you should think about how to reduce your losses if such a failure occurred. In this case, your losses are tied to downtime. To reduce downtime, keep spare parts on hand, keep a spare server, hub, and router on hand, or only use a full backup scheme.

Disk Defragmentor   Windows 2000, Windows 9x and ME all include the Disk Defragmenter tool, which rearranges files on your disk so that they are stored in a contiguous space. This tool was only available to Windows NT as a third party tool. Windows 2000 includes a light version of that third party tool as a built in utility. It can defragment volumes that are formatted in FAT, FAT32, and NTFS.

Disk preparation   The RAID array, or hard disk, is configured—the disk is partitioned and a file system applied. In some NOSs, like NetWare, you can configure software-based mirroring. In other NOSs, such as Windows 2000, you must wait until after the NOS is fully installed before you configure software-based disk configuration options. Disk preparation is sometimes incorporated into the NOS's Setup program; otherwise, you must prepare the disk separately using FDISK and FORMAT commands.

Disk striping with parity   Disk striping (with parity), also known as RAID 5, provides the performance of RAID 0 but with fault tolerance. Disk striping consists of data being written in stripes across a volume that has been created from areas of free space. These areas are all the same size and spread over an array of 3 to 32 disks. The primary benefit of striping is that disk I/O is split between disks, improving performance, although improvements do not exceed the I/O capabilities of the disk controllers. Fault tolerance functionality is added to disk striping with the addition of parity information in one of the stripes. The parity stripe is the exclusive OR (XOR) of all the data values for the data stripes in the stripe. If no disks in the stripe set with parity have failed, the new parity for a write can be calculated without having to read the corresponding stripes from the other data disks.

Diskperf   Diskperf is run from the command prompt and uses switches to control the disk counters. By default, Windows 2000 uses the diskperf -yd command to obtain data on physical drives. However, to obtain data on logical drives, you will need to run diskperf -yv from the command prompt.

Display system   The server's display system relies on the proper function of the monitor and the internal video card. The video card's function is to create the images that will result in the picture you see. The monitor simply displays the images sent to it by the video card.

DLT   *See* Digital Linear Tape.

DMA   *See* Direct Memory Access.

DNS   *See* Domain Name System.

Domain Name System (DNS)   Because the actual unique IP address is in the form of a number difficult for humans to use, text labels separated by dots are used instead. The DNS is responsible for mapping domain names to the actual IP numbers in a process called resolution.

DRAM   *See* Dynamic RAM.

Dual inline memory modules (DIMMs)   Similar to SIMMs except in the way the pins are wired. DIMMs provide twice the circuit path over SIMMs.

Duplexing   Of all the types of RAID, you will find that RAID 1, or mirroring, and RAID 5 are the most often implemented. When you configure RAID 1, you install two disks and either one or two controllers. When you use two controllers, it is called *duplexing*. Duplexing ensures fault tolerance not just with your hard drives, but also with your disk controller. With traditional mirroring there is one disk controller. If the controller fails then the server is down until that component is replaced. Duplexing gives you a second controller.

Dynamic Host Configuration Protocol (DHCP)   This software assigns IP addresses to clients (at their stations) logging onto a network using TCP/IP.

Dynamic RAM (DRAM)   RAM chips that must be constantly electronically refreshed because the capacitors in them (holding the electrical charge) eventually lose their charges.

ECC   *See* Error Correcting Code.

ECU   *See* Extended Industry Standard Architecture Configuration Utility.

EDO RAM   *See* Extended Data Output RAM.

EGA   *See* Enhanced Graphics Adapter.

EIDE   *See* Enhanced IDE.

EISA   *See* Extended Industry Standard Architecture.

Electromagnetic interference (EMI)   These are waves coming from an electrical device.

Electronically Erasable Programmable Read Only Memory (EEPROM)
    See Flash BIOS.

Electro-static discharge (ESD) One of the most prevalent threats to a computer component is electro-static discharge (ESD), also known as *static*. Static is all around us, especially when the humidity is low. ESD is caused when two objects of uneven charge come in contact with one another. Electricity has the property of traveling to areas with lower charges, and the static shock that you feel is the result of electrons jumping from your hand to the metal screw in the light switch plate. The same process can occur within the computer. ESD mats look like vinyl placemats but have a wire lead and an alligator clip. *See also* Hidden ESD.

Elements The objects that a management application makes available are called elements. The most common elements on a network are servers, workstations, printers, and network devices such as routers, bridges, and switches. Vendors can also define elements that are subsystems of these devices. For example, not only can a server be defined as an element, but devices such as the processor, hard disks, network adapters, and drive controllers can also be defined as elements.

EMI *See* Electromagnetic interference.

Enhanced Graphics Adapter (EGA) EGA monitors are capable of generating up to 64 colors, of which 16 can be displayed at any one time. EGA monitors have a maximum resolution of 720 x 350 when displaying text only and 640 x 350 in graphics mode.

Enhanced IDE (EIDE) A standard built on the original IDE specifications. EIDE increases the previous maximum disk size from 504 MB to over eight gigabytes, more than doubles the data transfer rate over the original IDE specification, and doubles the number of drives (to four) a PC can contain. IDE and EIDE interfaces can support a maximum of two devices.

Error *See* Operating System error.

Error Correcting Code (ECC) ECC allows data that is being read or transmitted to be checked for errors and, when necessary, single bit errors are corrected "real-time". ECC differs from parity-checking in that errors are not only detected but also corrected. ECC is increasingly being designed into data storage and transmission hardware as data rates increase.

Error log   Many Operating Systems keep event logs helpful in reviewing recent activities. When a problem occurs, you can search the event logs to determine when the problem first started or which file or subsystem is at fault.

ESD   *See* Electro-static discharge.

Ethernet   A networking protocol linking up to 1,024 nodes in a bus topology. Has been used by DEC and 3Com. *See also* Fast Ethernet.

Event log   During any point in time after the server installation, you can check the event logs to verify event messages. Most event logs are simply files of text written to the hard disk. Almost always, an event log is saved in the partition that is most easily available if the network operating system didn't boot. This is usually the system partition for the server. In the case of NetWare, you can find log information stored on the DOS partition.

Expansion slot   Expansion slots are the means through which adapters and expansion cards communicate with the rest of the computer and are used to attach cards to the motherboard. Several types of expansion slots exist, and the slot type must match the card type. One of the most common card/slot types is ISA (Industry Standard Architecture). ISA devices are 16-bit. EISA (Extended ISA) devices are 32-bit the slots are backward compatible with ISA devices.

Extended Data Output RAM (EDO RAM)   Extended data output (EDO) RAM is a type of random access memory chip that improves the time to read from memory on faster microprocessors such as the Intel Pentium. EDO RAM was initially optimized for the 66 MHz Pentium. For faster computers, different types of synchronous dynamic RAM are recommended. EDO is capable of speeds of about 50MHz. It holds its last requested data in a cache after releasing the data.

Extended Industry Standard Architecture Configuration Utility (ECU)   The EISA Configuration Utility (ECU) is a utility that reads a card's configuration file, which describes the card's characteristics and system resource requirements. It is used each time an EISA or ISA expansion card is added, removed or repositioned on a system. Because the utility assigns resources for the system and adapters (a precursor to plug-and-play), this spares the administrator from having to keep a list of all of the resources that have already been assigned.

Extended Industry Standard Architecture (EISA)   A bus standard that doubles the ISA bus from 16 bits to 32 bits. EISA also provides bus mastering.

Fast ATA   Created by the Small Form Factor Committee, to increase the capacity of the ATA interface. Also known as Enhanced IDE (EIDE) and Fast ATA, ATA 2 supports PIO modes 3 and 4, DMA modes 1 and 2, block transfers and LBA (Logical Block Transfers).

Fast Ethernet   A LAN access method that runs at 100 Mbps. Ethernet runs at 10 Mbps, and Gigabit Ethernet runs at 1000 Mbps.

Fast Page Mode (FPM)   FPM works by sending the row address just once for many accesses to memory in locations near each other, improving access time.

Fault tolerance   Fault tolerance is the ability of a component, or an entire system, to continue normal operations even in the event of a hardware or software failure. Usually, fault tolerance is implemented through redundant components. Thus, the disaster is prevented even though a failure has taken place.

FDDI   *See* Fiber Distributed Data Interface.

Fiber Distributed Data Interface (FDDI)   Fiber optic networks running at 100 Mbps, utilizing wiring hubs as prime servers for network monitoring and control devices. Also a standard for transmitting data on optical fiber cables and is 10 times faster than Ethernet but only twice as fast as T3 lines.

Fiber-optic cable   Fiber-optic cable, the most expensive cable, is made up of glass or plastic fibers. Distinctly different from both twisted-pair and coax, fiber-optic cable is made up of a light-conducting glass or plastic core. More reflective material, called cladding, surrounds the core, and the outer plastic sheath protects the inside.

Fibre Channel Fibre Channel is one of the newer interfaces and is faster than SCSI. A Fibre Channel interface uses a Fibre Channel arbitrated loop (FC-AL) to enable multiple devices to connect to a single server. The main benefit of Fibre Channel is its speed. Fibre Channel technology provides unsurpassed transfer speeds for demanding high-bandwidth transactions, such as High Definition TV or imaging. Fibre Channel specifies a one gigabit per second data transfer technology that can operate over fibre optic cables (hence the name *fibre* channel), or even over copper wires. The fibre optic cables can be up to 10 kilometers (roughly four miles) in length, whereas copper can be up to 30 meters in length. Logically, Fibre Channel is a bi-directional point-to-point serial data channel between multiple ports.

Firewire *See* IEEE 1394.

Firmware revisions These revisions are created to correct bugs from previous versions and add new features. Often, an incompatibility with an operating system is quickly fixed by checking to ensure that the hardware is at its most current revision.

Flash BIOS Newer types of BIOS chips (Flash BIOS) have been introduced in which the chip's instructions can be overwritten. Flash BIOS, or Electronically Erasable Programmable Read Only Memory (EEPROM), chips can be electronically upgraded using a floppy disk supplied by the chip's manufacturer. The disk contains a program that automatically "flashes" (updates) the BIOS so that it can recognize new hardware types or support different configuration options. The BIOS then retains the new settings, so it has to be flashed only once.

Forced Perfect Termination (FPT) FPT uses diode switching and biasing to force the impedance of the cable to match each device. Forced perfect termination actively monitors the bus to ensure that no signal reflection occurs.

Fox and Hound The Fox and Hound system is a set of hardware tools used to perform continuity tests on phone and network cables. The "Fox" (also called a tone generator) is a hand-held device attached to one end of the cable, typically via alligator clips. The "Hound" (also called a tone locator or induction locator) is normally a probe-shaped device placed near the other end of the cable. The Fox will generate a tone that is sent along the cable. If the Hound receives the signal, you will hear the tone on the Hound's internal speaker. Failure of the tone to reach the far end indicates a break or fault in the cable.

FPM   *See* Fast Page Mode.

FPT   *See* Forced Perfect Termination.

Fragmentation   Fragmentation can occur when data are added to files, and the size of the file grows. Contiguous space on the disk may be used by another file, so part of it must be stored in another location. It can also occur when new files are created, in which the file is created in the first available space on the disk. If there isn't enough contiguous space to write the entire file in one area, the file becomes fragmented. Fragmentation will continue to get worse as more files are created, moved and deleted. As fragmentation occurs, the computer needs to perform additional reads and disk head movements to read or write the fragmented parts of the file, which takes longer and decreases performance.

Full backup   Full backups are used to backup all of your data. This is used when you want to backup all directories and files on a volume, or all of the volumes on a server. Depending on the amount of data being saved to a server, you will perform a full backup on a weekly or monthly basis. If tapes are filling quickly and important data are changing rapidly, then a full backup should be performed at least once a week. When a full backup is performed, the file is changed to indicate that it has been backed up.

GET command   The GET command should be considered the read function of SNMP. When a management application needs to retrieve information from the agent, it uses the GET command to do so. As with the SET command, the GET is a two-way process.

GFS   *See* Grandfather-Father-Son.

Grandfather-Father-Son (GFS)   One popular tape rotation strategy is the GFS backup. It organizes rotation into daily, weekly, and monthly backup tapes. The GFS backup strategy is based on a weekly, seven-day schedule that runs from

Sunday through Saturday. In the GFS scheme, the full backup is considered the "father" and the daily backup is considered the "son." The "grandfather" portion of the name is a full backup that is performed monthly, and stored offsite. The grandfather tape isn't reused, and is permanently stored offsite.

Hard disks   Hard disk technology is constantly being updated. The storage capacity of the hard disks being increased, and the form factor of the hard disks is changing. Because a hard disk that takes up a smaller physical space can help conserve costs, it is more desirable to have smaller disks. Therefore, the form factor of hard disks is becoming more compact and has more available space.

Hardware Compatibility List (HCL)   An HCL states what hardware at what firmware revision is compatible with the operating system (OS). Microsoft is good about issuing this. The HCL lists what types of RAM is compatible. Hardware Compatibility Lists should be referenced to ensure that your computer has hardware that functions correctly with software being installed.

Hardware loopback adapter   A hardware loopback adapter is a device that allows you to test the operational status of a computer's NIC, serial, or parallel ports. When plugged in, the adapter will indicate whether the port is able to transmit and receive data. A failed loopback test indicates the port itself, or its hardware configuration, is at fault.

Hardware RAID   Hardware RAIDs are the most flexible and usually higher performance. They also allow for more levels of RAID and have the least overhead on the OS.

Hardware verification   Hardware verification involves understanding the hardware that's on your system, and ensuring that new hardware is verified and tested before it becomes part of a production network. In terms of evaluating current hardware, this means taking an inventory of your network, and documenting what routers, bridges and other equipment is currently being used. It also requires documenting the processors, hard disks, and other components making up your servers and workstations. As for verifying and testing new equipment, it requires researching and testing hardware before it goes "live" on your network, so that you don't find that it doesn't work when users are relying on it.

HCL   *See* Hardware Compatibility List.

Hidden ESD   Because it takes such a small charge to damage a computer component, you might be unaware of its occurrence. This is referred to as *hidden ESD*. Hidden ESD can also come from a dust buildup inside the computer. Dust and other foreign particles can hold an electric charge that slowly bleeds into nearby components. Hidden ESD can cause more serious problems than ESD that you can feel.

High Voltage Differential   *See* Differential signaling system.

Hot Swap   Replacement of a device while the computer is still functional.

Hound   *See* Fox and Hound.

ICMP   *See* Internet Control Message Protocol.

IDE   *See* Integrated Drive Electronics.

IEEE 1394   IEEE 1394 is more expensive than USB and much faster (up to 400Mbps). IEEE 1394 is typically used for devices that require fast transmission of large amounts of data, such as video cameras and digital versatile disk (DVD) players. IEEE 1394 is often referred to as *Firewire*, the trademarked name given to Apple Computer's IEEE 1394 systems. IEEE 1394 is also referred to by other manufacturer-specific names, such as *i.link* or *Lynx*.

Incremental backup   Incremental backups will back up all files that have been modified since the last full or incremental backup. It will not backup any files that have not been modified. During this type of backup, the backup software checks the archive bit to see whether the file has changed, and if it needs to be backed up to a tape. Once backed up, the archive bit is cleared, so that the next incremental backup doesn't backup the file again if it is unmodified.

Industry Standard Architecture (ISA)   An expansion bus that accepts plug-in boards connected to various peripherals. Originally called the AT bus. *See also* Extended Industry Standard Architecture.

Input/Output (I/O) address   One type of computer resource is the I/O address. When the computer is started, the BIOS loads into RAM device-specific information about the existing devices, including their drivers and other rules of communication. Whenever the processor needs to communicate with a device in the computer, it first checks RAM for the entries pertaining to that device. Without an I/O address, components would appear nonexistent to the processor.

Integrated Drive Electronics (IDE)   IDE and EIDE interfaces can support a maximum of two devices. Because IDE drives are built on ATA technology, the term *IDE* is often used to refer to any non-SCSI drive type. *See also* Enhanced IDE.

Integrated NIC   Some server platforms include network adapters as part of the motherboard. These are sometimes called integrated NICs. Even if the NIC is integrated, you may still need to install another adapter. Each NIC is designed for a specific network protocol and cable type. Integrated NICs are designed for the most common network protocol and cable types only—in most cases they are Ethernet or Fast Ethernet network adapters using Category 5 unshielded twisted-pair copper cabling. If you have a network that uses Token Ring over shielded twisted-pair copper cabling, then the integrated Ethernet NIC will not work.

Interleaving   *See* Memory interleaving.

Internet Control Message Protocol (ICMP)   A protocol employed to send error and control messages within TCP/IP.

Internet Protocol (IP)   The protocol used to execute the network layer of communications (layer three). This protocol accepts packets from layer 4 (transport layer) and sends them to layer 2 (data link layer). *See also* Transmission Control Protocol/Internet Protocol.

Internetwork Packet eXchange (IPX)   A communications protocol (designed for NetWare) to route messages between nodes.

Interrupt ReQuest (IRQ)   A computer instruction designed to interrupt a program for an I?O.

I/O address   *See* Input/Output address.

IP   *See* Internet Protocol.

IPX   *See* Internetwork Packet exchange.

IRQ   *See* Interrupt ReQuest.

ISA   *See* Industry Standard Architecture.

Keyboard   A *keyboard* connects to the serial port of your computer and enables you to type data. Because the keyboard is the primary input device, you rely on the keyboard more than you think. The keyboard contains certain standard function keys, such as the ESC key, TAB key, cursor movement keys, SHIFT keys, and CTRL keys, and sometimes other manufacturer-customized keys, such as the Windows key.

Keyboard Video Mouse (KVM)   The combination of the three peripherals.

KVM   *See* Keyboard Video Mouse.

LAN   *See* Local Area Network.

Local Area Network (LAN)   A system using high-speed connections over high-performance cables to communicate among computers within a few miles of each other. *See also* Wake on LAN.

LogicalDisk object   The LogicalDisk monitors any counter data associated with local drives and storage volumes. This is used to monitor hard disk performance issues. By default, the PhysicalDisk object is enabled, but the LogicalDisk object is disabled.

Logical Unit Number (LUN)   LUNs are actually sub units of SCSI devices. Each SCSI device can have up to 8 LUNs and LUNs can also have sub units called LSUNs (Logical Sub Unit Number) up to 255 devices per LUN. SANs use LUNs to tell the Fibre Channel HBA which partition on the SAN to attach to and use.

Look-Aside   Look-aside caches mean that the cache sits on the same bus as the main memory and is accessed at the same time. Because the cache sits on the same bus, it is limited to the speed of memory. It has faster response times to cache miss cycles, a lower cost and is fast for standalone applications.

Look-Through   In this architecture the cache sits in serial with the system memory and the CPU requiring the CPU to look-through to the RAM. It reduces the system bus utilization, allows system concurrency, completes write operations in zero wait-states, and has higher performance in systems with multiple bus masters. A request to main memory will only be made if there is a cache miss.

Low Voltage Differential (LVD) signaling system   All Ultra-2 SCSI devices use LVD to provide up to 80MBps with 16 bit and 40MBps with 8bit buses. LVD is backward compatible with SE and can co-exist on a SE bus by switching to SE mode. LVD and Ultra SCSI are used interchangeably.

LUN   *See* Logical Unit Number.

LVD   *See* Low Voltage Differential.

Management agent   A management agent, or SNMP agent, is a software application that resides on the managed device. This component defines the information made available to the management application. Compaq Insight Agent is an example of a management agent. It is important to note that the management agent is not always installed on a computer. Many network devices, such as routers and switches, run a form of an SNMP-configurable agent. The management agent contains all of the parameters that are available to the SNMP client.

Management application   A management application is a program that provides us with the interface to communicate with an agent. Compaq Insight Manager is a perfect example of a management application. The objects that a management application makes available are called elements.

Management Information Base (MIB)   It is a database containing information about managed devices. The information in the database defines what can be viewed an modified through SNMP. The MIB for the managed device contains definitions that are specific to a particular agent and is used to supply or set a value used by the agent. These definitions of a device are passed to the SNMP Agent, and from there exposed to the management system. Each MIB is represented by a numeric object identifier. This tree (based on a complex numbering system) is actually a global entity with each vendor (or on a larger scale, each organization) being given its own branch and numbering range to use. This is done much the same way IP addressing is structured.

Master/slave configuration   The hard drive or CD-ROM drive controller's function is to receive commands to the drive and control the action of the drive itself. The technology incorporated in IDE and ATA devices allows one controller to take over the function of more than one drive. This means that you can install up to two drives on a single ribbon cable. This setup is called a *master/slave configuration* because one drive's controller directs the activities of both drives. Most computer systems can support a mixture of IDE and ATA drives.

Mean Time Between Failures (MTBF)   MTBF is the mean time until the device is expected to fail.

Mean Time To Recover (MTTR)   MTTR is the time it takes to recover once the device has failed.

Memory   Considered the primary storage area on a computer. *See also* Cache memory.

Memory interleaving   The process of dividing system memory into multiple sections so the CPU can access several sections at once.

MIB   *See* Management Information Base.

Microsoft Diagnostics (MSD)   One of the most popular diagnostic tools for Microsoft operating systems is MSD, or Microsoft Diagnostics. MSD is a DOS based program called MSD.EXE that can be run from the command prompt. It allows you to view information about your system, even when you're having to boot it from a floppy disk. In recent versions of Windows, MSD moved away from being a DOS based program and became a graphical Windows tool. Like its predecessor, the diagnostics tool for Windows NT provides information about your system and it's resources.

Microsoft Management Console (MMC) Windows 2000 provides the Performance Console as a method of monitoring performance on local and remote computers. This console is actually the Microsoft Management Console (MMC) with two snap-ins installed: System Monitor and Performance Logs and Alerts.

Mirroring One of the more common ways to back up your data is to create a mirrored copy of the data on another disk. The mirroring system utilizes a code that duplicates everything written on one hard disk to another hard disk, making them identical. The best way to incorporate disk mirroring is at the hardware level with what is known as an array controller.

MMC *See* Microsoft Management Console.

Modem *See* Modulator/demodulator.

Modulator/demodulator (modem) Modems are responsible for transmitting data to and from the computer. They can be the cause of a server bottleneck. When this is the case, you will need to upgrade the modem to support the demands of remote users.

Monitor The function of a *monitor* is to produce visual responses to user requests. Most desktop computers use cathode ray tube (CRT) monitors. CRTs use an electron gun to activate phosphors behind the screen. Each dot on the monitor, called a *pixel*, has the ability to generate red, green, or blue, depending on the signals it receives. This combination of colors results in the total display you see on the monitor. Monitors are available in a wide array of colors and resolutions. The word *resolution* refers to the size and number of pixels that a monitor can display. Higher resolutions display more pixels and have better visual output. Lower resolutions result in grainy displays. *See also* Color Graphics Adapter; Enhanced Graphics Adapter; Super VGA; Virtual Graphics Array.

MONITOR   Novell NetWare includes a performance monitoring utility, called MONITOR. This utility will retrieve and display statistics about the server, including CPU usage, RAM usage, hard disk information, and NIC status.

MSD   *See* Microsoft Diagnostics.

MTBF   *See* Mean Time Between Failures.

MTTR   *See* Mean Time To Recover.

NAS   *See* Network attached storage.

NetBEUI   *See* NetBIOS Extended User Interface.

NetBIOS Extended User Interface (NetBEUI)   The transport layer for NetBIOS.

NETSTAT   The TCP/IP utility, NETSTAT, can provide you with information about each of a computer's active network connections. The protocol, local address/port, foreign address and state will display for each active connection. On some platforms, a send queue or receive queue column will also appear, indicating the number of bytes waiting in the send or receive queue. If this number is higher than zero, it indicates that data are not being transmitted properly.

NetWare   NetWare is unique in that it does not load directly upon server boot up. Instead, NetWare loads after a version of DOS. This means that with NetWare, you must configure a partition (no more than 1GB is necessary, and usually less than 100MB is required) that boots DOS. Then you can install NetWare on the remaining free space on the hard disk.

Network adapter   *See* Network Interface Card.

Network attached storage (NAS)   NAS offers a storage system that connects directly to the network, rather than directly to individual servers. These storage systems are self-contained and intelligent, enabling clients and servers to store and share data on them. When you are planning your server, you should determine whether the server will be storing data on an NAS device.

Network cabling   Cable media use electronic signals or light conducted across copper or glass to communicate from one end to the other. There are three main types: twisted-pair cable, coaxial cable, and fiber-optic cable.

Network configuration   First, you must configure the network adapter to be able to access the network media. This means that you should have the correct driver for the network adapter, and that you have configured the correct parameters for it. Second, you must configure the protocols so that the server can communicate with other hosts on the internetwork. Although there are a lot of protocols available, there is only one that is used universally: TCP/IP. TCP/IP is prevalent in most networks because of its use on the Internet.

Network Fault Tolerance (NFT)   NFT occurs when you install two NICs; one of which is the active NIC and the other that only becomes active upon failure of the first NIC.

Network Interface Card (NIC)   A network adapter is also referred to as a Network Interface Card (NIC). You can configure multiple NICs in a single server to access the same local area network if the hardware and the network operating system support it. Some server platforms include network adapters as part of the motherboard. These are sometimes called integrated NICs. *See also* Integrated NIC.

Network Load Balancing (NLB)   NLB occurs when you install two or more NICs, all of which are active on the same LAN, simultaneously sharing the network traffic load.

Network Monitor   Network Monitor is another tool that's available with Windows NT Server and Windows 2000 Server. Using this tool, you can determine why certain computers are unable to communicate, and analyze network traffic. The versions that come with these operating systems are limited to only analyzing activity on the local network segment.

Network operating system (NOS)   A 32-bit network operating system (NOS) can address up to 232 bytes of memory at any one time. New NOSs rarely support all the available hardware either. Some network operating systems allow you to configure multiple disks as RAID arrays. Every network operating system has its own unique installation process.

NFT   *See* Network Fault Tolerance.

NIC   *See* Network Interface Card.

NLB   *See* Network Load Balancing.

Noise   Noise occurs when outside interference effects the flow of electricity. There are two kinds of noise that can effect the alternating current of an electrical line: electromagnetic interference (EMI) and radio frequency interference (RFI). EMI is caused by other electrical components, such as lighting, generators, and so forth. RFI is caused by radio transmissions, which are picked up by the cables like antennas would.

Noise filter   To combat noisy or dirty current, you should use a *noise filter*. Noise filters are designed to condition the flow of electricity by removing EMI. Like suppressors, noise filters can be used as individual devices or as part of a UPS.

Online UPS   A more expensive but more efficient type of UPS is an *online UPS*, which is located between the computer and the power supply. Incoming power keeps the UPS battery charged, and all power to the computer comes from the battery. When the power goes out, the UPS simply continues to provide the computer with power from the battery's reserve. This means there is no "break" in the power, as there is in an SPS.

Operating System (OS) error   In many cases, an Operating System error is the first sign of trouble in a computer system. These errors can be quite descriptive, leading you immediately to the cause of the problem. Other error messages are equally helpful. For example, if you receive a missing Operating System error, you can use your knowledge of the boot process to narrow down the problem to a corrupt master boot record, a failed hard drive, or a corrupt system file. A "bad command or filename" error indicates a missing file or typo. Some error messages will even indicate a course of action, such as "Incorrect Printer Driver, please Install Correct Driver."

Oscilloscope   An oscilloscope is a device that can convert cable frequencies into graphical output. By attaching an oscilloscope to a cable and reading its output at different points along the cable, you can determine if there are crimps, breaks, or attenuation.

Packet Internet Groper (PING)   If you are using TCP/IP, one of the utilities that you can use when verifying network connectivity is PING. All network operating systems that use TCP/IP have some form of PING available to them. PING is a TCP/IP utility. To test whether you can contact other network hosts, type PING *ip_address* where ip_address is the IP address of another host on the internetwork. You can also type PING *dns_hostname.* PING is a common TCP/IP utility, and can be used in Windows, Unix/Linux, Novell Netware, and OS/2.

Pager   Pagers provide the ability for the device to send a pager message under predetermined conditions. For example, if the power fails then a message can be sent to a specified pager number, immediately alerting the person that a problem exists. This is a valuable feature if the administrator is away from his or her workstation, or if manual intervention is required to restart the system.

Partial Response Maximum Likelihood (PRML)   PRML eliminates noise so that data are transferred to the tape cleaner and with fewer errors.

Passive terminator   Uses an array of resistors but does not work for some higher performance drives.

PCI   *See* Peripheral Component Interconnect.

Performance Logs and Alerts   Performance Logs and Alerts allows you to log performance data and set remote notification of performance issues. This allows you to monitor the local computer, or remote computers on your network. The Performance

Logs and Alerts snap-in is loaded automatically when the Performance Console is opened.

Performance Monitor (PERFMON)   PERFMON is a tool used to for monitoring performance issues on a Windows NT Server. It provided four methods of monitoring various components of NT: Report View, Chart View, Alert View, and Log View.

Peripheral Component Interconnect (PCI)   Another common slot/card type is the PCI. PCI architecture is 64-bit and is faster and newer than ISA and EISA architecture. PCI slots are smaller than ISA and are white (where ISA slots are black). PCI slots can be used by PCI cards only.

PhysicalDisk object   The PhysicalDisk object monitors physical disk counter data. This is used to monitor hard disk performance issues. By default, the PhysicalDisk object is enabled, but the LogicalDisk object is disabled.

PING   *See* Packet Internet Groper.

Pixel   Each dot on the monitor, called a *pixel*, has the ability to generate red, green, or blue, depending on the signals it receives. This combination of colors results in the total display you see on the monitor.

Platform   At the highest level, we have the management platform. This can be defined as the system on which the management application and agent will function.

Plug and Play (PnP)   A standard that requires add-in hardware to carry the software to configure itself in a way to be supported by the computer's OS.

PnP   *See* Plug and Play.

Point-to-Point Protocol (PPP)   A standard for dial-up telephone connections of computers to the Internet.

Pop-up message   Pop-up messages are messages that will pop-up on a user's screen. Such messages may appear on every workstation, or be directed to a specific user. If you can designate where the pop-up message will appear, you may have the ability to direct the message to a specific IP address or a user account.

POST   *See* Power On Self Test.

Power On Self Test (POST)   The internal test encoded in ROM and performed whenever a computer is started or reset.

PPP   *See* Point-to-Point Protocol.

Primary cache memory   This memory is L1 or Level 1 cache and is small (4KB to 16KB) and built directly in the CPU.

PRML   *See* Partial Response Maximum Likelihood.

Processor upgrade   Processor architectures include many different speeds per design. Upgrading a CPU can be easy if upgrading within the same processor family. These types of upgrades usually involve no more than a physical replacement. Depending upon the motherboard, the new CPU could be automatically recognized or the motherboard may require jumpers to be changed to accommodate the new speed by utilizing a frequency selection and a multiplier.

Racks   Racks include rails so that you can slide components in and out of the rack to work on them. You must install half of each rail on the equipment, and the other half of the rail on the rack itself. You then slide the equipment onto the rails and attach the brackets to the equipment and affix it to the rack, so that the equipment does not accidentally slide out.

Radio Frequency Interference (RFI)   RFI is caused by radio transmissions, which are picked up by the cables like antennas would. Radio frequency interference can also be caused by a number of sources. RFI sources may include microwaves, appliances, furnaces, and of course radio transmission. The cables used to transmit data can stretch for a long distance, and act as an antenna, picking up such interference.

RAID *See* Redundant Array of Inexpensive Disks.

RAM *See* Random access memory.

Rambus Direct RAM (RDRAM) The future type of RAM to improve performance. RDRAM uses 16-bit wide Rambus Inline Memory Modules (RIMMs). Data are read in small packets at high clock speeds. DRDRAM works on a narrower 16 bit bus than the 64 bit DRAM bus, but it operates at much higher speeds to achieve increased performance. Like SDRAM, it uses a serial presence detect chip to inform the motherboard of its characteristics. RDRAM promises to transfer up to 1.6 billion bytes per second.

Random-access data access This method is used on hard disks, Zip drives, and other devices, where you can access any of the data on the media immediately.

Random access memory (RAM) The lower limit for RAM should never be the minimum required to run an operating system (OS). You can choose whether to install Extended Data Output (EDO) RAM or Synchronous Dynamic RAM (SDRAM) although usually you can't install both. Generally, memory falls under either dynamic RAM (DRAM) or static RAM (SRAM) categories. DRAM must be refreshed constantly—every few milliseconds. SRAM holds the data without needing to be refreshed, and can react much faster. RAM speed is measured in nanoseconds (ns). *See also* Extended Data Output RAM; Synchronous Dynamic RAM.

RDRAM *See* Rambus Direct RAM.

Readiness Analyzer *See* Windows 2000 Readiness Analyzer.

Redundancy Redundancy is a preventative measure for hardware and/or software backups. You can plan redundancy at any level in your network. You can also plant redundant components inside the server. Examples of redundant components are: redundant power supplies; RAID; redundant network adapters, and error-correcting memory.

Redundant Array of Inexpensive Disks (RAID)   Redundant Array of Inexpensive Disks (RAID) is a form of storage that was created to provide redundancy and increased storage so that data loss was minimal in case of a hard disk failure. RAID technology minimizes the loss of data when problems occur with accessing data on a hard disk. RAID is a fault-tolerant disk configuration in which part of the physical storage contains redundant information about data stored on the disks. When there are multiple hard disks configured in a RAID, it is called an *array* and is often housed in an external unit called a *subsystem*. Server platforms usually come with optional hardware RAID arrays that are managed with a specific RAID array adapter interface, and use identical disks that most vendors provide as hot-plug units. Hardware-based RAID is managed from its own BIOS application. *See also* Disk striping with parity; Hardware RAID; Software RAID.

Register   *See* Buffer.

Remote alert   Remote alerts can help in remote troubleshooting. Remote alerts are generated by the remote computer, and are typically sent to a specified computer via the network or a modem. The alert can also be sent via phone lines to a phone or pager, alerting system administrators to a problem condition. Remote alerts are typically used to warn of hardware overheating, failed processes, or security breaches.

Remote notification   Remote notification is a feature that enables a device, service or application to report problems or event to a specific user, such as the network administrator. This allows the user or administrator to take action, and deal with any issues that effect the successful completion of a task or event.

Remote troubleshooting   Remote troubleshooting refers to the ability to troubleshoot and resolve computer problems without having to sit at that computer. In many cases, you can use one server on a network to troubleshoot another server on the network. There are a number of services available for remote troubleshooting, such as Windows Remote Access Service (RAS) or third-party applications. These types of services provide the interface and tools for managing, configuring, and troubleshooting remote computers.

Removable media   Removable media are methods of storing data, which can be removed from a computer. These include floppy disks, hard disks, tape cartridges, disk cartridges, reel tapes, or optical disks. Because the media are not permanently attached to your server or other hardware used for backing up data, you can take them out and store them at another site.

Resolution   Monitors are available in a wide array of colors and resolutions. The word *resolution* refers to the size and number of pixels that a monitor can display. Higher resolutions display more pixels and have better visual output. Lower resolutions result in grainy displays.

RFI   *See* Radio Frequency Interference.

Route tracing   Route tracing utilities allow you to view the entire route between your computer and a specified remote host. When you trace a route, your computer issues ICMP echo packets to the specified address and generates a report of the hops (computers, routers, and so on) between your computer and the host.

Sags   *See* Brownouts/sags.

Salvage   The Salvage utility allows you to view a listing of recoverable files. By selecting one or more of these files, you can then click the Salvage button to restore them, or the Purge button to remove them completely from the system. Deleted files may also be purged automatically if the volume becomes full.

SAN   *See* Storage area network.

ScanDisk   Windows 9x and ME also provide error-checking software called ScanDisk. You can use this tool to check hard disks for logical and physical errors, and have them automatically repaired.

SCSI   *See* Small Computer System Interface.

SCSI Trade Association (STA)   This association, among its many duties, defines many of the sub-types of SCSI drives.

SDRAM   *See* Synchronous Dynamic RAM.

SE   *See* Single Ended.

Secondary cache memory   This memory is L2 (or Level 2) and is external to the CPU but sometimes on the same chip. It is fast, operating from 12ns to 25ns and ranges in size from 256KB to 2048KB. Sometimes, Level 2 cache is on the motherboard and may be upgradeable.

Sequential access   Sequential access requires you to cue up the media, until reaching the area on the media where the data you want resides. It is similar to fast forwarding a VHS tape on a VCR, until you find the point on the tape that you want to watch.

Serial Line Internet Protocol (SLIP)   A standard for how a workstation or PC can dial up a link to the Internet and defines the transport of data packets through an asynchronous telephone line.

Server baseline   A server baseline documents the status of the server's performance as a snapshot. You can document these snapshots on a periodic basis to keep track of the way the server is functioning. Server baselines can reveal problems before a failure takes the server down. For example, if you documented a server's baseline and found that the server's CPU performance had suddenly spiked from a steady 30 percent utilization to a 90 percent utilization, you can then discover what was causing the CPU spike and prevent a possible server failure.

Server platforms   Server platforms are shipped with a BIOS already installed. The BIOS version may not be the latest, so you should make certain to have the latest version available to update the hardware. Hardware components, such as SCSI interfaces and a subsystem, will have their own BIOSs.

Service tools   Service tools are programs that allow you to configure and monitor your system, thereby allowing you to detect and fix possible problems. These include the setup programs and diagnostic tools that are available at bootup, and control how your system functions. Many service tools are available from the computer manufacturer and may be stored in special areas of the hard disk. In some cases, special versions of diagnostic and setup software are also available for different operating systems or may be provided by the manufacturer of the operating system.

Without these tools, you would be unable to run your computer, or detect problems when the operating system fails to load.

SET command   The SET command is the first of two commands used by the management application. This command is used to perform the write function of the SNMP protocol. It is used to change, or set, the parameters available in the management agent. The SET is actually a two-way communication.

Shared nothing model   A model in which each server owns and manages its own devices, and common devices (such as an external storage system) are not "owned" by a single server at any one time.

Shielded twisted pair (STP)   Shielded twisted pair has enhanced protection with a foil wrap and extra shielding outside the individual twists inside the cable. The considerations for STP are cost, installation, capacity, attenuation, and interference.

Signaling system   *See* Differential signaling system; Low Voltage Differential signaling system; Single Ended signaling system.

SIMMs   *See* Single inline memory modules.

Simple Network Management Protocol (SNMP)   SNMP defines a set of commands that a management application uses to retrieve or change the values made available by a management agent. In simpler terms, it provides a means of communication between a device that we want to manage and the system we want to use to manage it. SNMP has emerged as the industry standard and is used as the protocol of most standards-based management platforms. SNMP requirements are rather simple. To function, it needs only a network to communicate across, an application that utilizes SNMP, and an agent that defines the objects (elements) to be managed. To perform its function, SNMP uses a set of commands (called SET and GET) to communicate with information made available to it by the management agent. SNMP communicates over the TCP/IP network protocol. This allows for SNMP's use across many network systems and devices.

Single Ended (SE) signaling system   SE devices are the most common signaling method used. They are unbalanced electrically using a common return line for all the outgoing signals. This "unbalanced" technique makes SE more susceptible to interference so the cable length is limited to 6 meters, and there should be 12 inches of cable between devices.

Single inline memory modules (SIMMs)   A circuit board with memory chips that typically plugs into the motherboard. SIMMs were updated by DIMMs.

SLIP   *See* Serial Line Internet Protocol.

Small Computer System Interface (SCSI)   SCSI is most prevalent (and preferred) interface in servers. An SCSI 2 interface can host seven devices using a single interrupt. SCSI Wide, a 16-bit controller, can host 15 devices. SCSI is superior to other interfaces because it manages its own power, freeing the CPU from that type of overhead. SCSI also has its own basic input/output system (BIOS). Unlike the IDE drive, the SCSI drive must be terminated if it is the last device on the bus. These older-style SCSI drives requiring a physically separate termination resistor are slowly being replaced by the drives with built-in termination.

Smart cards   Smart cards are another method of providing a measure of security to your network. Smart cards are small plastic cards that have a microchip and/or a memory module embedded in it, which can store a significant amount of information. The cards are generally inserted into a special reader that reads information on the card, although some readers can scan the cards from a distance. They can come in formats that are disposable or reprogrammable, making them useful for whatever your needs.

SMP   *See* Symmetric Multi-Processing.

Snap-in   A snap-in is a module that is added to MMC, so that you can perform various functions through a central console program.

SNMP   *See* Simple Network Management Protocol.

Software RAID   Software RAIDs are implemented in the OS and take a larger toll on OS performance. They usually do not allow for Hot Swap functionality so if a drive fails, the server must be taken offline to replace it.

Spikes   Spikes are a sudden increase in voltage, such as when lightning strikes a power line.

SPS   *See* Standby Power System.

SRAM   *See* Static RAM.

SSU   *See* System Setup Utility.

STA   *See* SCSI Trade Association.

Standby Power System (SPS)   One type of UPS is a Standby Power System, which is attached to the computer. The UPS enables its battery power when it detects a loss of electricity. Unfortunately, there can be a brief lapse in power during the time it takes for the UPS to detect a power problem and switch to battery power.

Static   *See* Electro-static discharge.

Static RAM (SRAM)   SRAM is fast and does not require the refresh technology of DRAM. However, it is expensive and takes about four time the silicon area to create. It uses a serial presence detect chip to inform the motherboard of its characteristics.

Storage area network (SAN)   A SAN is a group of storage systems connected through Fibre Channel interfaces directly to a storage network. The SAN uses either Fibre Channel switches or Fibre Channel hubs to connect multiple storage units. Servers on the regular network are configured to access the data on the storage network.

Striping   The striping of data is a way to spread the data out across the disks. This can improve performance. To do striping properly you need a minimum of three hard disks. Three or more different hard disks all acting to get a piece of the data will make the input/output (I/O) faster. Striping also gives you the option of adding parity to the drive set. *See also* Disk striping with parity.

STP   *See* Shielded twisted pair.

Subsystem   Subsystems hold multiple disks, which you can configure as separate disk drives, or as a single RAID array, or some combination of these. A storage subsystem will occupy its own space in the rack. You should place the subsystem next to—either immediately below or immediately above—the server to which it will provide storage. After mounting the subsystem, you will attach it to the adapter card in the server with an appropriate cable. Next you install each disk into the subsystem. *See also* Redundant Array of Inexpensive Disks.

Super VGA (SVGA)   SVGA monitors introduce yet another improvement: They also use analog input and can provide resolutions as high as 1280 x 1024. Some SVGA monitors can provide even higher resolutions. SVGA monitors can display up to 16 million colors at once, referred to as *32-bit true color*. Because the human eye can distinguish only approximately 10 million different colors, it is likely that monitor technology will focus on improving resolution only.

Suppressor   To prevent problems resulting from power surges and power spikes, you can use a *suppressor*. Suppressors are designed to "smooth out" the flow of electricity by removing excess voltage caused by power surges and spikes. Suppressors are available as individual devices or integrated with a UPS.

Surges   Surges are a power surge is also an increase is voltage, but is one that lasts more than $1/20^{th}$ of a second. This commonly occurs when large machinery is shut down, causing excess voltage to be spread across a circuit.

Symmetric Multi-Processing (SMP) units   Many server platforms support more than one processor. These SMP units. Symmetric indicates that these servers distribute a symmetrical load across the processors in the machine. Each vendor's SMP server platforms have different percentages of actual contributed processing power as more CPUs are added.

Synchronous Dynamic RAM (SDRAM) Synchronous DRAM is a generic name for various kinds of dynamic random access memory. SDRAM is synchronized with the CPU speed and thus provides better performance. SDRAM is rated in MHz rather than nanoseconds to more easily compare the CPU speed to the RAM speed. Mounted in 64-bit wide 168 pin DIMMs. SDRAM has an access time of eight nanoseconds to 12 nanoseconds.

System Monitor System Monitor allows you to monitor resource utilization and network throughput. The System Monitor provides a visual representation of the counters being watched. The System Monitor snap-in allows you to view real-time and previously logged data about areas of your system and network.

System monitoring agents System monitoring agents are programs that monitor your system for changes that indicate possible problems. Agents are generally part of a larger software package, where these small programs have a specific task of gathering information, and passing it back to a larger management system.

System Setup Utility The System Setup Utility (SSU) allows you to perform configurations to your system. On some machines, such as many Compaq machines, the SSU is located on the diagnostics partition. On many other machines, it is located in the ROM BIOS (Read Only Memory Basic Input Output System). When your system boots up, you can access the information in the SSU by pressing the delete or F10 keys on your keyboard.

TAG RAM If the L2 cache uses parity, it requires a chip called TAG RAM. The TAG RAM helps the locate the data inside the cache and is also responsible for delaying data transfer from cache to main memory.

Tape backup Tape backups are the most common method of backing up data. With this method, magnetic tapes are used to store data sequentially. These tapes are similar to those used in micro-cassette recorders, which require you to fast-forward and reverse the tape to find what you want. This sequential access to archived data makes it slow to restore data, as the device must cue up the tape to where the data are located. However, the cost to purchase such tapes is minimal, with each tape costing a few dollars. This makes tapes a popular method of data recovery.

TCP/IP   *See* Transmission Control Protocol/Internet Protocol.

Telnet   A virtual terminal protocol that interfaces terminal devices with terminal-oriented processes.

Terminators   *See* Active terminators; Passive terminators. *See also* Forced Perfect Termination.

Time Domain Reflectometer (TDR)   A TDR sends a signal down the cable. When the signal reaches the end of the cable, it is reflected back to the TDR. The TDR then calculates the distance the signal traveled, before being reflected, by measuring the amount of time it took for the signal to be returned. If this distance is less than your overall cable length, it means there is a break in the cable at the specified distance from your location.

Tower of Hanoi (rotation scheme)   Each tape set is used a different number of times. When a new tape set is added to the group, it is used every other rotation. The next oldest tape set is used every fourth rotation; the next oldest after that is used every eighth rotation, and so on. Set rotations are performed daily or weekly.

Trace Log   Trace Logs are different from counter logs in that they don't obtain data at regular update intervals. Instead, it logs data when certain events occur. For example, it might gather data when a page fault occurs. It monitors the activities you specify, and when one happens, it stores the information in a log file.

Tracing   *See* Route tracing.

Transmission Control Protocol/Internet Protocol (TCP/IP)   A set of communication standards to connect different types of computers in networks. TCP/IP is prevalent in most networks because of its use on the Internet.

Trap   Another way SNMP communicates is by using a trap. A trap is SNMP's means of notifying or alerting us of a specific condition. The SET and GET commands use traps to function. Unlike the SET/GET commands, a trap is a one-way communication process.

Troubleshooting   *See* Remote troubleshooting.

Twisted-pair cable   Twisted-pair cable is a series of individual copper cables encased in plastic. Twisted-pair cable is the most common type of cable used today in computer networking. Used heavily in LAN systems, twisted-pair cable uses a series of individually-wrapped copper wires encased in a plastic sheathing. Each cable is individually encased in plastic, and the overall outer shell is plastic as well. Each cable inside is twisted together with another. Most cable today comes with eight cables or wires, making four pairs. The cable is twisted to cut down on crosstalk. Typically, twisted-pair cable consists of RJ-45 or RJ-11 ends. RJ-11 ends are what you see for most telephones. Twisted-pair cabling is made up of 22- or 26-gauge copper wire. There are five types of twisted-pair cabling as ranked by the Electrical Industries Association (EIA). *See also* Shielded twisted pair; Unshielded twisted pair.

Uninterruptible Power Supply (UPS)   A UPS is a large battery. In the event of a power failure, the UPS kicks in and supplies power to the server. Instead of plugging your server into a power outlet, you plug it into the UPS, which then plugs into the power outlet. Most UPS units have a software application that runs on your server's network operating system. Because the UPS is nothing more than a big battery, it will eventually run out of power. To protect the server's data, you can configure the software application to communicate with the UPS and perform a server shutdown after a power failure event and a certain time period have passed. To determine whether the UPS will support the equipment, you must determine what the VA consumption is for each piece of equipment that connects to the UPS, then add all the VA figures together. *See also* Online UPS.

Universal Serial Bus (USB)   USB technology allows the user to add multiple external peripherals, ranging from printers, hard disks, modems, scanners, to just about anything, to a single port without the conflicts associated with serial and parallel connections of the past.

Unshielded twisted pair (UTP)   UTP is the more common of the two types of twisted-pair cable. Unshielded twisted pair is a series of pairs of wires twisted together with their own distinct plastic insulation, and the group of wires is encased in a plastic sheathing that holds all the other wires together.

Updates One of the things you need to do after installing your server is to update the drivers to the latest ones available from the manufacturer. By doing this, you will be able to use all the features of the hardware components in your server.

USB *See* Universal Serial Bus.

UTP *See* Unshielded twisted pair.

VGA *See* Virtual Graphics Array.

Virtual Graphics Array (VGA) VGA monitors were the first to use analog rather than digital output. Instead of creating displays based on the absence or presence of a color (as in digital CGA and EGA monitors), VGA monitors can display a wide range of colors and intensities. They can produce around 16 million different colors but can display only up to 256 different colors at a time. This color setting is often called *16-bit high color.* VGA monitors have a maximum resolution of 720 x 400 in text mode and 640 x 480 in graphics mode.

Virus A sabotage or prank program that attaches itself to other programs to carry out unwanted and sometimes damaging operations.

VMSTAT In a Linux system, use the VMSTAT command to view virtual memory statistics, including the total amount of virtual memory, number of page faults, and amount of data being swapped into virtual memory. Excessive swapping indicates you need more virtual memory, and excessive page faults indicate you should add more RAM to the system.

Wake on LAN Because remote troubleshooting is such a valuable procedure for system administrators, a number of remote access features have made their way into the computer industry. Some computers contain a "wake on LAN" feature that allows administrators to turn a remote computer on so they can troubleshoot it or perform maintenance.

WAN *See* Wide Area Network.

Wide Area Network (WAN)   A network using high-speed long-distance common-carrier circuits or satellites to cover a large geographic area.

Windows Internet Name Service (WINS)   A name resolution software that converts NetBIOS names to IP addresses.

Windows 2000 Readiness Analyzer   The Windows 2000 Readiness Analyzer is software that tests your hardware to determine if it is compatible with the operating system. Although included with the Windows 2000 installation CD, it will also run on Windows 95, Windows 98, Windows NT 3.51 and Windows NT 4.0. When run, it will compare your hardware and software with a compatibility list, and then provide output that reveals the results of the test. This allows you to determine if your computer can be upgraded to Windows 2000 without performing any hardware or software modifications.

WINS   *See* Windows Internet Name Service.

Write-Back   Changes are not copied into main memory until necessary.

Write-Through   Data writes occur simultaneously to the cache and the main memory. Write-through cache is faster than write-back but may cause data loss if power fails.

INDEX

Monitor
  installing, 34-36
  network, 230-231
  system, 225-230
Monitoring agents, 178-181, 206

N

NAS, 12
NETSTAT, 354-356, 388
NetWare 5.1, installation, 65-67
Network
  adapter, 15, 148
  configuration, 68
  connectivity, 68-69
  management, 180
  monitor, 230-231
Network attached storage. *See* NAS
Network interface card. *See* NIC
NIC, 15
  installing, 148-149
  upgrading, 148, 170-171
Noise, 195
Noise filters, 31

O

Operating system. *See* OS
OS
  errors, 362-363
  upgrade, 112-114
Oscilloscope, 362

P

Packet InterNetwork Groper. *See* PING
Passwords, 319-321
Performance
  baselines, 88-91, 224-225, 251
  bottlenecks, 223-224, 372-379
  issues, 222-223, 232
  logs and alerts, 225, 228-229, 293-296
  monitoring, 225

network, 230-233
processor, 377-378
system, 225-230
Performance console, 225-228, 243
Performance monitor, Windows 2000, 88-90
Peripherals
  configuring, 69-70
  upgrading, 152-156, 161-162, 173-174
PING, 352-353, 388, 395-396
Plug and play, 155, 156
Power loss, 191-192, 330-331
Power supply, 15-16
Power supply, redundant, 406
Power-on sequence, 36-37
Problems
  determining, 388
  resources, 366-367
  software, 385-386
  TCP/IP configuration, 379-380
  troubleshooting, 348-351
  utilities, 351
Processor
  cache, 110-111
  compatibility, 108-109
  speed, 109-110

R

Radio frequency interference. *See* RFI
RAID
  adapter, 150-151, 172
  configuring, 63, 95
  disaster recovery, 407
  duplexing, 61
  firmware, 55-56
  hardware, 124
  implementation, 46
  levels, 55, 124
  mirroring, 60-61
  software, 124
  striping, 62-63
RAM, 7-9, 46
  increasing, 126-128, 133

INTERNATIONAL CONTACT INFORMATION

AUSTRALIA
McGraw-Hill Book Company Australia Pty. Ltd.
TEL +61-2-9417-9899
FAX +61-2-9417-5687
http://www.mcgraw-hill.com.au
books-it_sydney@mcgraw-hill.com

CANADA
McGraw-Hill Ryerson Ltd.
TEL +905-430-5000
FAX +905-430-5020
http://www.mcgrawhill.ca

GREECE, MIDDLE EAST,
NORTHERN AFRICA
McGraw-Hill Hellas
TEL +30-1-656-0990-3-4
FAX +30-1-654-5525

MEXICO (Also serving Latin America)
McGraw-Hill Interamericana Editores S.A. de C.V.
TEL +525-117-1583
FAX +525-117-1589
http://www.mcgraw-hill.com.mx
fernando_castellanos@mcgraw-hill.com

SINGAPORE (Serving Asia)
McGraw-Hill Book Company
TEL +65-863-1580
FAX +65-862-3354
http://www.mcgraw-hill.com.sg
mghasia@mcgraw-hill.com

SOUTH AFRICA
McGraw-Hill South Africa
TEL +27-11-622-7512
FAX +27-11-622-9045
robyn_swanepoel@mcgraw-hill.com

UNITED KINGDOM & EUROPE
(Excluding Southern Europe)
McGraw-Hill Education Europe
TEL +44-1-628-502500
FAX +44-1-628-770224
http://www.mcgraw-hill.co.uk
computing_neurope@mcgraw-hill.com

ALL OTHER INQUIRIES Contact:
Osborne/McGraw-Hill
TEL +1-510-549-6600
FAX +1-510-883-7600
http://www.osborne.com
omg_international@mcgraw-hill.com

Custom Corporate Network Training

Train on Cutting Edge Technology   We can bring the best in skill-based training to your facility to create a real-world hands-on training experience. Global Knowledge has invested millions of dollars in network hardware and software to train our students on the same equipment they will work with on the job. Our relationships with vendors allow us to incorporate the latest equipment and platforms into your on-site labs.

Maximize Your Training Budget   Global Knowledge provides experienced instructors, comprehensive course materials, and all the networking equipment needed to deliver high quality training. You provide the students; we provide the knowledge.

Avoid Travel Expenses   On-site courses allow you to schedule technical training at your convenience, saving time, expense, and the opportunity cost of travel away from the workplace.

Discuss Confidential Topics   Private on-site training permits the open discussion of sensitive issues such as security, access, and network design. We can work with your existing network's proprietary files while demonstrating the latest technologies.

Customize Course Content   Global Knowledge can tailor your courses to include the technologies and the topics which have the greatest impact on your business. We can complement your internal training efforts or provide a total solution to your training needs.

Corporate Pass   The Corporate Pass Discount Program rewards our best network training customers with preferred pricing on public courses, discounts on multimedia training packages, and an array of career planning services.

Global Knowledge Training Lifecycle   Supporting the Dynamic and Specialized Training Requirements of Information Technology Professionals

- Define Profile
- Assess Skills
- Design Training
- Deliver Training
- Test Knowledge
- Update Profile
- Use New Skills

College Credit Recommendation Program   The American Council on Education's CREDIT program recommends 53 Global Knowledge courses for college credit. Now our network training can help you earn your college degree while you learn the technical skills needed for your job. When you attend an ACE-certified Global Knowledge course and pass the associated exam, you earn college credit recommendations for that course. Global Knowledge can establish a transcript record for you with ACE, which you can use to gain credit at a college or as a written record of your professional training that you can attach to your resume.

Registration Information

COURSE FEE: The fee covers course tuition, refreshments, and all course materials. Any parking expenses that may be incurred are not included. Payment or government training form must be received six business days prior to the course date. We will also accept Visa/MasterCard and American Express. For non-U.S. credit card users, charges will be in U.S. funds and will be converted by your credit card company. Checks drawn on Canadian banks in Canadian funds are acceptable.

COURSE SCHEDULE: Registration is at 8:00 a.m. on the first day. The program begins at 8:30 a.m. and concludes at 4:30 p.m. each day.

CANCELLATION POLICY: Cancellation and full refund will be allowed if written cancellation is received in our office at least six business days prior to the course start date. Registrants who do not attend the course or do not cancel more than six business days in advance are responsible for the full registration fee; you may transfer to a later date provided the course fee has been paid in full. Substitutions may be made at any time. If Global Knowledge must cancel a course for any reason, liability is limited to the registration fee only.

GLOBAL KNOWLEDGE: Global Knowledge programs are developed and presented by industry professionals with "real-world" experience. Designed to help professionals meet today's interconnectivity and interoperability challenges, most of our programs feature hands-on labs that incorporate state-of-the-art communication components and equipment.

ON-SITE TEAM TRAINING: Bring Global Knowledge's powerful training programs to your company. At Global Knowledge, we will custom design courses to meet your specific network requirements. Call 1 (919) 461-8686 for more information.

YOUR GUARANTEE: Global Knowledge believes its courses offer the best possible training in this field. If during the first day you are not satisfied and wish to withdraw from the course, simply notify the instructor, return all course materials, and receive a 100% refund.

In the US:

CALL: 1 (888) 762-4442

FAX: 1 (919) 469-7070

VISIT OUR WEBSITE:

www.globalknowledge.com

MAIL CHECK AND THIS FORM TO:

Global Knowledge

Suite 200

114 Edinburgh South

P.O. Box 1187

Cary, NC 27512

In Canada:

CALL: 1 (800) 465-2226

FAX: 1 (613) 567-3899

VISIT OUR WEBSITE:

www.globalknowledge.com.ca

MAIL CHECK AND THIS FORM TO:

Global Knowledge

Suite 1601

393 University Ave.

Toronto, ON M5G 1E6

REGISTRATION INFORMATION:

Course title _____

Course location _____ Course date _____

Name/title _____ Company _____

Name/title _____ Company _____

Name/title _____ Company _____

Address _____ Telephone _____ Fax _____

City _____ State/Province _____ Zip/Postal Code _____

Credit card _____ Card # _____ Expiration date _____

Signature _____

LICENSE AGREEMENT

THIS PRODUCT (THE "PRODUCT") CONTAINS PROPRIETARY SOFTWARE, DATA AND INFORMATION (INCLUDING DOCUMENTATION) OWNED BY THE McGRAW-HILL COMPANIES, INC. ("McGRAW-HILL") AND ITS LICENSORS. YOUR RIGHT TO USE THE PRODUCT IS GOVERNED BY THE TERMS AND CONDITIONS OF THIS AGREEMENT.

LICENSE: Throughout this License Agreement, "you" shall mean either the individual or the entity whose agent opens this package. You are granted a non-exclusive and non-transferable license to use the Product subject to the following terms:

(i) If you have licensed a single user version of the Product, the Product may only be used on a single computer (i.e., a single CPU). If you licensed and paid the fee applicable to a local area network or wide area network version of the Product, you are subject to the terms of the following subparagraph (ii).

(ii) If you have licensed a local area network version, you may use the Product on unlimited workstations located in one single building selected by you that is served by such local area network. If you have licensed a wide area network version, you may use the Product on unlimited workstations located in multiple buildings on the same site selected by you that is served by such wide area network; provided, however, that any building will not be considered located in the same site if it is more than five (5) miles away from any building included in such site. In addition, you may only use a local area or wide area network version of the Product on one single server. If you wish to use the Product on more than one server, you must obtain written authorization from McGraw-Hill and pay additional fees.

(iii) You may make one copy of the Product for back-up purposes only and you must maintain an accurate record as to the location of the back-up at all times.

COPYRIGHT; RESTRICTIONS ON USE AND TRANSFER: All rights (including copyright) in and to the Product are owned by McGraw-Hill and its licensors. You are the owner of the enclosed disc on which the Product is recorded. You may not use, copy, decompile, disassemble, reverse engineer, modify, reproduce, create derivative works, transmit, distribute, sublicense, store in a database or retrieval system of any kind, rent or transfer the Product, or any portion thereof, in any form or by any means (including electronically or otherwise) except as expressly provided for in this License Agreement. You must reproduce the copyright notices, trademark notices, legends and logos of McGraw-Hill and its licensors that appear on the Product on the back-up copy of the Product which you are permitted to make hereunder. All rights in the Product not expressly granted herein are reserved by McGraw-Hill and its licensors.

TERM: This License Agreement is effective until terminated. It will terminate if you fail to comply with any term or condition of this License Agreement. Upon termination, you are obligated to return to McGraw-Hill the Product together with all copies thereof and to purge all copies of the Product included in any and all servers and computer facilities.

DISCLAIMER OF WARRANTY: THE PRODUCT AND THE BACK-UP COPY ARE LICENSED "AS IS." McGRAW-HILL, ITS LICENSORS AND THE AUTHORS MAKE NO WARRANTIES, EXPRESS OR IMPLIED, AS TO THE RESULTS TO BE OBTAINED BY ANY PERSON OR ENTITY FROM USE OF THE PRODUCT, ANY INFORMATION OR DATA INCLUDED THEREIN AND/OR ANY TECHNICAL SUPPORT SERVICES PROVIDED HEREUNDER, IF ANY ("TECHNICAL SUPPORT SERVICES"). McGRAW-HILL, ITS LICENSORS AND THE AUTHORS MAKE NO EXPRESS OR IMPLIED WARRANTIES OF MERCHANTABILITY OR FITNESS FOR A PARTICULAR PURPOSE OR USE WITH RESPECT TO THE PRODUCT. McGRAW-HILL, ITS LICENSORS, AND THE AUTHORS MAKE NO GUARANTEE THAT YOU WILL PASS ANY CERTIFICATION EXAM WHATSOEVER BY USING THIS PRODUCT. NEITHER McGRAW-HILL, ANY OF ITS LICENSORS NOR THE AUTHORS WARRANT THAT THE FUNCTIONS CONTAINED IN THE PRODUCT WILL MEET YOUR REQUIREMENTS OR THAT THE OPERATION OF THE PRODUCT WILL BE UNINTERRUPTED OR ERROR FREE. YOU ASSUME THE ENTIRE RISK WITH RESPECT TO THE QUALITY AND PERFORMANCE OF THE PRODUCT.

LIMITED WARRANTY FOR DISC: To the original licensee only, McGraw-Hill warrants that the enclosed disc on which the Product is recorded is free from defects in materials and workmanship under normal use and service for a period of ninety (90) days from the date of purchase. In the event of a defect in the disc covered by the foregoing warranty, McGraw-Hill will replace the disc.

LIMITATION OF LIABILITY: NEITHER McGRAW-HILL, ITS LICENSORS NOR THE AUTHORS SHALL BE LIABLE FOR ANY INDIRECT, SPECIAL OR CONSEQUENTIAL DAMAGES, SUCH AS BUT NOT LIMITED TO, LOSS OF ANTICIPATED PROFITS OR BENEFITS, RESULTING FROM THE USE OR INABILITY TO USE THE PRODUCT EVEN IF ANY OF THEM HAS BEEN ADVISED OF THE POSSIBILITY OF SUCH DAMAGES. THIS LIMITATION OF LIABILITY SHALL APPLY TO ANY CLAIM OR CAUSE WHATSOEVER WHETHER SUCH CLAIM OR CAUSE ARISES IN CONTRACT, TORT, OR OTHERWISE. Some states do not allow the exclusion or limitation of indirect, special or consequential damages, so the above limitation may not apply to you.

U.S. GOVERNMENT RESTRICTED RIGHTS: Any software included in the Product is provided with restricted rights subject to subparagraphs (c), (1) and (2) of the Commercial Computer Software-Restricted Rights clause at 48 C.F.R. 52.227-19. The terms of this Agreement applicable to the use of the data in the Product are those under which the data are generally made available to the general public by McGraw-Hill. Except as provided herein, no reproduction, use, or disclosure rights are granted with respect to the data included in the Product and no right to modify or create derivative works from any such data is hereby granted.

GENERAL: This License Agreement constitutes the entire agreement between the parties relating to the Product. The terms of any Purchase Order shall have no effect on the terms of this License Agreement. Failure of McGraw-Hill to insist at any time on strict compliance with this License Agreement shall not constitute a waiver of any rights under this License Agreement. This License Agreement shall be construed and governed in accordance with the laws of the State of New York. If any provision of this License Agreement is held to be contrary to law, that provision will be enforced to the maximum extent permissible and the remaining provisions will remain in full force and effect.